Gardens and Gardeners
of the Ancient World

Linda Farrar

WINDgather
PRESS

To the memory of my sister Jeanette

Windgather Press is an imprint of Oxbow Books

Published in the United Kingdom in 2016 by
OXBOW BOOKS
10 Hythe Bridge Street, Oxford OX1 2EW

and in the United States by
OXBOW BOOKS
1950 Lawrence Road, Havertown, PA 19083

Paperback Edition: ISBN 978-1-909686-85-4
Digital Edition: ISBN 978-1-909686-86-1

A CIP record for this book is available from the British Library

Printed in the United Kingdom by Latimer Trend

For a complete list of Windgather titles, please contact:

United Kingdom
Oxbow Books
Telephone (01865) 241249
Fax (01865) 794449
Email: oxbow@oxbowbooks.com
www.oxbowbooks.com

United States of America
Oxbow Books
Telephone (800) 791-9354
Fax (610) 853-9146
Email: queries@casemateacademic.com
www.casemateacademic.com/oxbow

Oxbow Books is part of the Casemate group

Front cover images: *(centre)* Garden fresco, House of the Marine Venus, Pompeii; *(flanking)* detail
of fresco with garden plants, House of the Golden Bracelet, Pompeii; *(bottom)* fragment of a
tomb-painting in Nebamun's estate garden © The Trustees of the British Museum.

Back cover images (top to bottom): detail of a Persian gardener using a long handled spade,
Shahnama, *c.* AD 1420; Byzantine gardener grafting from the *Homilies* of Gregory Nazianzos;
garden plan (drawing of a miniature fresco), Auditorium of Maecenas, Rome (Daremberg and
Saglio 1900, 3, 288).

Contents

List of Illustrations   vi
Picture Credits   x
Acknowledgements   xi
Time-Chart   xii
Preface   xiii

1. Egyptian Gardens   1
2. Gardens of Ancient Mesopotamia and the Near East   36
3. Gardens of the Greek Bronze Age: Minoan and Mycenaean
   Cultures   71
4. Greek Gardens and Groves of the Archaic, Classical
   and Hellenistic Periods   88
5. Etruscan Gardens   128
6. Roman Gardens   138
7. Byzantine Gardens   185
8. Islamic and Persian Gardens   211
9. Medieval Gardens   244
10. Conclusions   280

Select Bibliography   289

List of Illustrations

1. Pomegranate tree, mosaic detail, Umm Al-Rasas, Jordan   xv
2. Sacro-Idyllic scene   xvii
3. The Egyptian fertility god Min seen in his temple   3
4. Detail of Osiris in white mummy wrappings   3
5. Barley seeds were sown in wooden or ceramic Osiris Beds   3
6. Circular tree/plant pits for a sacred grove beside the pyramid of Pharaoh Sneferu, Dahshur   6
7. Reconstruction of three funerary temples at Deir el-Bahari   7
8. Relief depicting the transport of incense trees from Punt   7
9. 'The Botanical Garden', Karnak Temple   9
10. Hathor emerging from the side of a mountain through papyrus   9
11. Middle Kingdom relief depicting water-carriers and gardeners   12
12. Gardeners pick cucumber-like melons; the lettuce symbol of the fertility god Min   12
13. Detail of a vintage scene, a process undertaken in many gardens   13
14. Figurative hieroglyphs   13
15. Wooden model of a part of a house and garden   17
16. A flower filled garden around a well stocked fish pool at Amarna   18
17. Plan of the house and garden of Meryre, High Priest of Amarna   19
18. Sycomore fig tree with tree goddess dispensing nourishment for eternity   20
19. Plan of Sennefer's garden. Tomb of Sennefer, Thebes   21
20. Doum palm tree (*Hephaene thebaica*). Silsila, Upper Egypt   22
21. Argun palm tree (*Medemia argun*). Tomb of Pasedu, Deir el-Medinet   22
22. Visitors arrive through the garden. Tomb of Neferhotep, Thebes   23
23. Flame coloured flowers of Pomegranate (*Punica granatum*), Cyprus   23
24. Ipuy's house and garden. Tomb of Ipuy, Thebes   24
25. Carob tree represented in the Tomb of Menena, Thebes   25
26. Nebamun's fruitful garden, Tomb of Nebamun, Thebes   26
27. Irrigation channels provide water for a row of trees and flowers next to a crop of wheat   27
28. Details of flowers painted in the Tomb of Ramesses III, Thebes   28
29. Nakht, the court florist, with one of his finest bouquets   28
30. The River Euphrates and the Mesopotamian Plain, seen from Syria   36
31. Map of Mesopotamia and the Levant   37

32.   Seal stone depicting divinities and a snake on either side of a sacred tree   38

33.   Seal stone from Mari   39

34.   Ninhursag (Ki) the Sumerian goddess of vegetation and fecundity   40

35.   Detail of the goddess Inanna and her symbolic standard of reeds   41

36.   Detail from a large fresco from Mari   43

37.   Akkadian gardeners tending trees and irrigating the plants in the garden   45

38.   Impression from a seal stone depicting women in a garden picking dates   46

39.   An Assyrian minor deity is seen fertilising a sacred date palm tree   49

40.   Sargon's garden at Khorsabad, with a *bitanu* pavilion and boating lake   51

41.   Sennacherib's garden at Nineveh   52

42.   Assurbanipal and his queen quaffing wine and feasting in their garden   53

43.   Reconstruction of the famous Hanging Gardens of Babylon   57

44.   A reconstruction of the large formal gardens at Cyrus's palace   61

45.   Relief at Persepolis representing cypress trees   62

46.   A Persian style *paradeisos* game park depicted in a fresco at Pompeii   65

47.   The great Mother goddess sitting under a tree, holding poppies   72

48.   Impressions from seal rings with scenes of a tree cult   73

49.   A selection of flower motifs on Minoan pottery   74

50.   Drawing of lilies in a slender banded vase from Akrotiri/Thera, Santorini   75

51.   Mycenaen goblet with a motif depicting a plant growing in a container   75

52.   Reconstruction showing the lily frescoes in Room 7 at Amnisos, Crete   76

53.   Sand lilies on the Island of Santorini   77

54.   Fresco fragment showing dianthus-like flowers   77

55.   Reconstruction of flower garlands from a Minoan fresco   78

56.   Minoan fresco depicting a garden landscape with tame monkeys   79

57.   Circular enclosure with two trees, Room 5 of the West House, Thera   80

58.   Reconstruction suggesting a rock garden for crocus and other plants   81

59.   Details of men from *Keftiu* from an Ancient Egyptian fresco   84

60.   Hercules in the Gardens of the Hesperides   90

61.   An olive tree sacred to the goddess Athena on the Acropolis, Athens   91

62.   Detail showing Dionysus from a Greek red-figure vase   92

63.   Narcissus hopelessly gazing at his own image   94

64.   Apollo pursuing Daphne   95

65.   Flowers depicted on 5th–4th century BC Greek coinage   96

66.   Rose flower depicted on the reverse of a coin from Rhodes   97

67.   Landscaped gardens such as at Stourhead were inspired by the Classical world   101

68.   Roman marble relief depicting a lady making a sacrifice in front of a cave sacred to Pan   102

69.   The Temple of Hephaestus in Athens: two rows of tree pits with plant pots in each   103

70. Myrtles and pomegranates have been replanted in the pits   104

71. Roman mosaic illustrating Plato discussing in his Akademy grove   106

72. Red-figure vase with girls picking fruit   107

73. Eros offering a bowl of seedlings to his mother Aphrodite   108

74. Adonis flowers (*Adonis annua*) in northern Cyprus   109

75. Plan of the Palace at Aigai, northern Greece   111

76. Plan of the Hellenistic palace at Aï Khanoum   113

77. Palace of Hyrcanus at Araq el Amir, Jordan   114

78. Leopard fountain at the Palace of Hyrcanus at Araq el Amir, Jordan   115

79. Bust of Theophrastus, Greek philosopher   121

80. Dioscorides examining a mandrake plant   122

81. Garden scenes and stylised plants engraved on Etruscan bronze mirrors   132

82. Detail of a stylised plant, possibly an arum   133

83. Detail from an Etruscan mirror depicting crown grafting on a tree   135

84. Venus accompanied by cupids and her sacred flowers roses   140

85. Detail of a sacrifice before an altar and statue of a goddess   144

86. Plan showing three different forms of a Roman house with garden   147

87. Reconstruction of the peristyle garden at the House of the Vettii   148

88. Map of central Rome showing several public portico gardens   150

89. Two miniature frescoes depicting trellis fences forming
     'garden rooms'   152–153

90. Simple reed fences line a garden path at the House of the Chaste Lovers   156

91. Outdoor dining couches   157

92. The remnants of a *biclinium* al fresco dining area and shrine   157

93. Terminal busts of a janiform herm   159

94. An *oscillum* which mimics the form of a *pelta* shield   159

95. A Roman sundial   159

96. Terracotta amphorae were used to provide fish refuges at the House
     of the Triconch Hall   160

97. Typology of Roman pools   160

98. Restored garden with a gutter water-basin running around three sides   161

99. A water garden, House of the Water Jets   161

100. Three intercommunicating pools with central fountain in the garden
     of the Villa at Piazza Armerina   161

101. A freestanding water-stair fountain   163

102. Mosaic and shell covered shrine to a water nymph, Pompeii   163

103. A sea cave that was converted into a dining area for the Emperor Tiberius 164

104. An *arboritor* grafting trees in a mosaic of the calendar year   169

105. Sinuous lines of the topiary hedge bordering a path at Fishbourne
     Roman Palace   169

106. The verdant frescos from Livia's Garden Room at Primaporta   172

107. Reconstruction of a gardener's bench with facsimile Roman flowerpots   173
108. The sweet rocket or dame's violet (*Hesperis matronalis*)   173
109. Hadrian's luxurious dining area beside a vast pool   175
110. Miniature fresco of climbing plants   176
111. Garden Plans   177
112. St Phocas, the market gardener from Sinope, northern Turkey   186
113. Early Christian Church with *atrium* garden   188
114. Fresco of Jonah reclining under a gourd tree   191
115. Detail from a mosaic depicting a Paradise filled with trees and animals   192
116. Mosaic showing white marble walls in a garden setting with a tree, and arching foliage   193
117. Pinecone fountain in a marble cantharus bowl   193
118. Mosaic showing Isaac blessing his son Jacob in his garden   194
119. Rebecca at the well   195
120. A deputation of elders meet Caiaphas in his ornamental garden   196
121. House and garden of Egdon, king of Moab   197
122. Gregory's garden   197
123. Christ and Apostles reclining on a *stibadium* dining couch   200
124. *Gladiolus byzantinus*, Crete   200
125. The Garden of St Anne, mother of Mary   202
126. A two-tiered shallow, rectangular, box-like fountain   203
127. Aspects of agriculture and horticultural husbandry in the *Homilies of Gregory Nazianzos*   206
128. Horticultural workers using bident forks and pruning hooks   207
129. Paradise as a garden   212
130. Abbasid Palace beside the River Tigris, Samarra   214
131. Detail of a Persian gardener using a long handled spade with foot rest   216
132. Plan of an Islamic house with courtyard gardens at Valencia   217
133. Umayyad palace at Madinat al-Zahra, near Cordoba   218
134. A woman looks out over her garden   219
135. Walkways surround an elongated pool flanked by sunken garden beds   223
136. Reflecting pool, Court of the Myrtles, Alhambra, Grenada   223
137. Reconstruction of the layout of a Timurid garden of the 15th century   231
138. A prince seated in his garden   233
139. A Timurid walled garden   234
140. Part of the plan of the monastic gardens at St Gall, *c.*AD 820   247
141. The Physic garden at St Gall   248
142. Eighteen plant beds in the vegetable garden at St Gall   248
143. Recreated rustic garden at the Weald and Downland Open Air Museum   250
144. Details of a *hortus conclusus* enclosed by a lattice fence   253
145. Detail showing a walled *hortus conclusus* of a manor or dower house   256

146. Maugis and La belle Oriande in a scene of courtly love in a garden   258
147. Violets growing in the *bas de page* scene   259
148. A cartwheel frame used to support plants in a garden with raised beds   260
149. Lady holding a finger pot to water choice plants   260
150. A Rhenish painting depicting *The Garden of Paradise*   262
151. Manuscript border filled with realistic flowers   263
152. Detail of a castellated *hortus conclusus* in *Love's Game of Chess*   268
153. Woodcut from the *Roman de la Rose*   269
154. Illustration from the *Roman de la Rose*   270
155. Garden fresco, House of the Marine Venus   281
156. Fresco detail with garden plants, House of the Golden Bracelet   282
157. Recreated medieval garden at Tretower Court, Wales   286

Picture credits

American School of Classical Studies at Athens: Agora Excavations: 69
Ashmolean Museum, University of Oxford: 66
H. Baumann: 53
J.-M. Blas de Roblès (after J.-C. Golvin): 113
Bridgeman Art Library: 27, 106, 146, 150
British Library: 139, 147, 154
British School at Athens (M. Cameron): 52
D. Bruff: 70
G. Carmichael: 3–5, 7–8, 10, 13, 15, 18, 21, 24–25, 32–34, 36–37, 39–43, 51, 54, 57, 59–60, 62, 64, 68, 72, 79, 114, 118–122, 125–128, 134, 138, 144–145, 149, 152
J. Chisnall: 9
Daremberg and Saglio: 73, 89, 110
Evans: 47, 48
G. Farrar: 136
J. Farrar: 124
W. Gell: 2
M. L. Gothein: 16, 19, 22, 38
R. T. Gunther: 80
J. Homan: 81a and b
L. Manniche: 29
G. Morley: 100
M. Shaw: 58
B. Smith: 74
D. Stronach: 44
M. Subtelny and W. Moskaliuk: 137
Trustees of the British Museum: 26
B. Yare: 20

Acknowledgements

There were many people who gave help and I would like to thank them all.

I would especially like to thank my mentor Dr Stanley Ireland, Warwick University Dept of Classics and Ancient History, and the Open Studies Dept; Rev. Prof. Martin Henig for his comments after reviewing the book. Prof. David Stronach for looking at an early draft of Chapter 2 and for comments and helpful suggestions connected with the ancient gardens of Mesopotamia and Iran. Also Prof. Maureen Carroll, Prof. Anne Chapin, Prof. Antony R. Littlewood, Prof. D. Fairchild Ruggles and Dr Joyce Tyldesley for their helpful comments on individual chapters; Gillian Carmichael for producing a number of specially commissioned drawings and Gillian White for giving me that final spur to complete the Medieval chapter. And most of all my husband Jim for his encouragement over the years. I would also like to thank all the individuals, authors and institutions who have given aid or allowed texts and photographs to be reproduced here, including The American School of Classical Studies at Athens, Bridgeman Art Library, The British Library, The British Museum, The British School at Athens, Harvard University for their permission to quote extracts from Pliny's letter, Penguin Books for permission to print Oleg Grabar's translation of Ibn Luyūn's text, Jean-Marie Blas de Roblès, Dr Gillian Brand, Don Bruff, Jeanette Chisnall, Judy Cottrell, Dr Stephanie Dalley, Rev. Geoffrey Farrar, Juanita Homan, Jan Jordan, Prof. Antony Littlewood, Dr Lise Manniche, Prof. Maria Mavroudi, Margaret Morley, Prof. Maria Shaw, Brenda Smith, Prof. David Stronach. Prof. Maria Subtelny, Angela Torpey, Brian Yare, the librarians at Stratford library, and of course my publishers.

Every effort has been made to trace copyright holders and we apologize in advance for any unintentional omissions or errors, these will be rectified in future editions if notification is sent to the publisher.

Simplified Time-Chart

Dates are approximate (rulers' names are in brackets)

TIME	AEGEAN	MESOPOTAMIA/ ASIA MINOR	EGYPT
3,000	Troy I	SUMERIAN CITIES of Ur, Uruk, Susa	EARLY DYNASTIC PERIOD
2,500	" EARLY MINOAN	"	1st Dynasty / OLD KINGDOM
2,000	" MIDDLE MINOAN	" & Assur, Nineveh, Ebla, Mari (Sargon)	MIDDLE KINGDOM
1,900	" "	" " & Ugarit / OLD ASSYRIAN KINGDOM	" (Mentuhotep II)
1,800	" "	" OLD BABYLONIAN PERIOD	"
1,700	" "	" (Hammurabi) "	" 12th Dynasty
1,600	" " MYCENEANS	" " " "	INVASION OF THE HYKSOS
1,500	" " " "	" " Ugarit	NEW KINGDOM
1,400	" LATE MINOAN "	" " " MIDDLE ASSYRIAN	" 18th Dynasty (Hatshepsut)
1,300	" " " "	" " " EMPIRE	" (Akhenaten)
			(Tutankhamun)
1,200	INVASION OF THE SEA PEOPLES	"	INVASION OF THE SEA PEOPLES
			19th Dynasty
1,000	GREEK DARK AGES	" " (Tiglathpileser I)	THIRD INTERMEDIATE PERIOD
900	"	(Solomon) "	" 21st Dynasty
800	"	" (Assurnasipal II)	" 22nd Dynasty
700	ARCHAIC GREECE	" (Sargon II) (Sennacherib)	LATE PERIOD
			25th Dynasty
600	"	NEO-BABYLONIAN " (Assurbanipal) PERIOD (Nebuchadnezzar)	"
500	CLASSICAL GREECE	PERSIAN EMPIRE	PERSIAN PERIOD 27th Dynasty
400	"	"	"
300	ALEXANDER THE GREAT FOLLOWED BY THE HELLENISTIC PERIOD (Seleucus)		(Ptolemy)
200	"	" "	" "
100	ROMAN EMPIRE	ROMAN EMPIRE PARTHIANS	ROMAN EMPIRE "
0	"	IN SYRIA &	" "
AD 100	"	PALESTINE "	" "
AD 200	"	" "	" "
AD 300	"	" SASSANIANS	" "
AD 400	"	" "	" "
AD 500	BYZANTINE EMPIRE	"	BYZANTINE EMPIRE
AD 600	"	ARAB INVASIONS	ARAB INVASIONS

L.Farrar 1999

Preface

....

The history of gardens embraces many aspects of former ancient societies. We see how gardens related to houses and other buildings, how they were used for leisure and as status symbols. It highlights the skills needed by gardeners for landscaping and installing water features, and the use of a gradually increasing range of plants available. A study of gardens involves the art and architecture of the different periods and ancient societies links to religion. The myths and the literature of each period gives a valuable insight into the way people in the past thought and used their gardens. We understand how people enjoyed the fresh air and plants growing in their gardens, how they used art and architecture to enhance their garden spaces.

From the earliest of times people have sought to grow and nurture plants in a garden area. However, there are variations between a garden cultivated solely to provide produce, and one which is both productive and decorative, and finally a purely ornamental garden. The latter will be the main focus of this book. This book will concentrate on evidence for gardens of the early cultures and periods of the ancient world. Each period will be examined in turn, from the beginning of civilisation right up to the fall of Byzantium in AD 1453. In general books on garden history cover all periods up to the present, often placing all ancient gardens in one chapter at the beginning. But there is so much of interest to be found in these early centuries/millennia. Each period appears quite distinctive yet there are at times cross cultural links between them. In the process of gardening people may encounter common problems, and it can be interesting to discover how they develop comparable solutions to similar challenges, an example of this is how garden tools from any culture are easily recognisable because they have evolved to serve a common purpose.

Early civilisations were based on agriculture and lived in close contact with nature and the rhythms of the seasons. Both agriculture, and horticulture, were undertaken to ensure a family or community was self-sufficient. Agriculture developed into the large-scale cultivation of crops in fields, as opposed to horticulture which came to be practised in enclosed areas where special attention and care could be devoted to vegetables and the flowering plants growing there. Many vegetables and flowers require frequent watering and their needs meant that often specialised care was required to tend them. The gardener's role was to provide food for the table but also in some cases to enhance the appearance of garden areas. Gardening and horticulture is a form of improvement on nature, a desire to nurture selected plants in specially cared for and well watered areas. Gardeners the world over improve their land/garden, and hope for a fertile and fruitful crop (of fruit, vegetables and flowers). Previous cultures and civilisations learnt by trial and error and in many cases they passed on the knowledge gained. When difficulties arose, people of each civilisation would also solicit aid from various deities or a god, those that were responsible for aspects of agri-horticulture and fertility. On the surface the deities of each culture appear to be different but many served a similar need. We have to remember that the people of the past were more religious and superstitious than today.

But what is a garden? In the past the concept of a garden was perhaps different to ours, due in part to the particular characteristics of individual societies. Over the centuries there were many forms of a garden and of necessity these changed over time. A garden, though, is essentially cultivated land that is used at least partly as an amenity, whether private or public. Gardens could be areas nurtured with care to provide vegetables and salad crops vital for self-sufficiency. In times of plenty such areas would form market gardens. Some cultures maintained groves that were seen as gardens. Yet others created expansive tree filled areas stocked with game, and these hunting parks were again viewed as a form of large garden. At times gardens were even created around funerary monuments. But, to many societies, a garden was a walled enclosure that could contain either a variety of trees or a combination of trees and flowers. It is when people have time, or workmen to do the work for them, that owners could aim to make their gardens aesthetically pleasing. When time and space allows, a place for relaxation can be made in the garden, be it a pavilion or an al fresco dining area, then the garden becomes an extension of the home. The garden can then be ornamented with specimen plants and sculptural objects. In many societies houses faced inwards around an open court that served as a light-well for surrounding rooms; these areas too were often turned into a garden inside the house. These gardens were then the lungs of the house and over time became areas that could be quite decorative. On large estates space could be made for extensive gardens around the dwelling. When carefully tended, all gardens can enhance the setting and surroundings of buildings. At best a garden is a place where people aim to capture the beauty of nature in a re-creation of their own form of paradise.

At certain locations evidence of ancient gardening and garden art has survived the intervening centuries. Sources are wide ranging, in each period examples of contemporary illustrations of gardens were used such as fresco paintings, sculptural reliefs, mosaics, and manuscript paintings where possible. These may depict stylised versions of contemporary gardens but they allow us to visualise how the people concerned saw their gardens. Sometimes elements within the garden scene are given prominence and these can indicate fashions in garden art. Illustrations of ancient gardens can be compared with descriptions surviving from ancient literary sources and inscriptions, be it a tale of a mythical garden (that sometimes preserves elements of contemporary or earlier gardens) or an

FIGURE I. Pomegranate tree, mosaic detail. Umm Al-Rasas, Jordan, 6th century AD.

actual garden. There is a rich selection of legends and myths relating to gardens and their plants, and because these add so much colour to our understanding of the cultures concerned several have been included in this book.

Ancient authors sometimes make a brief comment (or occasionally a long description) of a particular garden seen by them. In some cases people actually described their own garden, and the details given are enlightening. Also, we are fortunate that several ancient agri-horticultural manuals have survived and together with the herbals they can give an understanding of the plants grown during various periods and of their culture. Such evidence for gardens can be corroborated through archaeological investigations.

Garden archaeology is a relatively new discipline, one that can enhance an interpretation of the environment, and past societies. It is now possible to recover a surprising range of detailed information on early gardens. However, in the past archaeological projects concentrated on uncovering buildings and buried sculpture, and garden areas were generally overlooked. This was mainly because gardens and courtyards were considered to be just an empty space, as any likely features were deemed to be too ephemeral and unlikely to leave discoverable traces, but this is not always the case. On some sites old pathways though the garden can be revealed, and hard landscaping elements can be discovered such as evidence of statue bases or garden shrines and pavilions. The line of a garden wall can become apparent and post holes can provide evidence for fences or trellising. In many cases garden features are only preserved up to a low height, or foundation level, but there are exceptions such as if a garden pavilion was preserved because it was later reused for another purpose. At places like Pompeii however, the volcanic ash covered buildings and gardens and have enabled an in depth study of garden archaeology.

Garden archaeology was pioneered at Fishbourne in southern Britain by Barry Cunliffe and at Pompeii by Wilhelmina Jashemski. With today's modern scientific techniques garden archaeologists are now able to uncover the location of a long buried garden pool, the direction of its water source and if there were any fountains there. On occasion the outline of plant beds can be defined, and depending on soil conditions, plant remains can also be recovered. Items like charred seeds, macrofossils (bits of bark or stem) and pollen can be extracted and examined leading to the identification of a number of plants that were grown in gardens. In addition, in some places, the outline of tree roots can be detected, mainly those of large trees. At Pompeii, however, a greater accuracy was possible. The volcanic eruption of Mount Vesuvius caused the city to be completely covered by volcanic debris, and once the ash covering the houses and gardens had been removed from areas under excavation the original ground surface of gardens were revealed. Garden archaeologists then cleared out the volcanic debris from voids underground left behind after the plant's roots had decayed. Liquid plaster was poured into the cleared spaces, and when the plaster had hardened the soil was cleared away and the shape of the plant root could then be studied and a comparison made with modern equivalents to identify the species of tree or bush.

Modern garden archaeological principles are used to examine desiccated plant material (this is possible in the dry climate of Egypt, for instance). On waterlogged sites (e.g. in pits) the anaerobic conditions stop plant decay and preserve plant material and seeds. Once the ancient layers of garden soil has been taken away, however, evidence for plant material is greatly lessened, but in some cases not all is lost. In some cases traces of ancient flora can be recovered from overlooked pits, or other sealed deposits. Recent developments have been to explore if flora can be retrieved from oily residues in discarded ancient pottery, and from plaster remaining on water tanks, with exciting results (revealed in Chapters 2 and 3).

In different parts of the world local climatic conditions affect natural flora and fauna and these conditions were one of the main influences on the development of gardens and gardening in different societies. There are of course obvious differences between the hot lands and climate in the Egyptian desert and Nile Valley where Pharonic cultures developed, compared to the relatively lush countryside around Vesuvius in Italy cultivated by the Romans. So the plants available for cultivation of necessity differ from period to period. Some societies sought new species and once established this enlarged the flora of their country.

For each chapter I have provided a list of garden worthy plants that were known during that particular period (except for the Byzantine, which would

FIGURE 2. Sacro-Idyllic
scene. Etching by W.
Gell (*Pompeiana* vol. 2,
1835, opp. 159).

be too similar to that of the Romans). Information on the flora of each region
and period was gleaned from plants named in ancient literature discussing
gardens, and by consulting herbal books. Some cultures also produced
agricultural manuals that contained chapters on horticulture and these were a
mine of information on plants used in the relevant periods. In each table of
garden plants there is a list of the common names, and their botanical name.
For the Roman period I have also provided a list of the ancient name for each
one as it is interesting to see the evolution of our modern Latin botanical
nomenclature. Extra columns show the nature of the source material for each
plant, whether a particular one was discovered in contemporary literature,
art, or by archaeological means. Where there was a wide plant distribution
geographically between East and West, or in time (*e.g.* Classical Greece and
Hellenistic Greece) then I have provided columns to distinguish these. Sadly
little archaeology has been possible in closed societies and war zones, therefore
there is little archaeological evidence available on paleo-botany for the eastern
sites and therefore the relevant column for archaeology has been omitted for
the Islamic plant list.

As previously mentioned the gardens studied here are those from the
beginning of civilisation right up to the fall of Byzantium in AD 1453, which
saw the end of Roman/Byzantine influence in the east. Byzantium was seen to
have influenced early Islamic gardens hence their inclusion, and therefore as a
balance it was thought necessary to review evidence for corresponding gardens
of the medieval period in the west. For both of these periods, however, it was
necessary to extend the time scale to the end of the fifteenth century so that
evidence for the Islamic gardens of the Timurid dynasty in Persia could be
considered. Likewise the Middle Ages could be regarded as having ended by
about AD 1500.

One of my challenges was to find out if the Minoans and Etruscan peoples had gardens. For both of these cultures our knowledge is limited to archaeological discoveries, so it was interesting to see what hints could be found. Ancient artefacts can provide surprising results, and fragments of texts that can be deciphered do furnish some clues.

Between different periods and cultures we can notice a variety of spellings for some words. For instance the ancient Greek K is generally turned into a C by the Romans in Latin. Therefore the Greek town of Kyrene in North Africa is the Greek version and Cyrene is the more familiar name for this town. To avoid transliteration in the chapters I have chosen to use the spellings that would be correct for each period, but using our alphabet.

There are also different names for the deities that are common throughout the Graeco-Roman world, and to retain the ambience of each period I have chosen to keep the Greek names with their relevant spellings (such as Herakles) when discussing the Greek period, and when I am mentioning him in the Roman chapter he will be spelt Hercules, which is the more familiar Latin version of his name. It is noticeable that some of the gods and goddesses transmogrify over time and are given different names in different cultures, so we hear of the Greek Aphrodite changing into Turan as known to the Etruscans, or the Roman Venus.

Translations from other languages were sought, but it is perhaps surprising how much some of the spellings vary between different translations, and this is particularly noticeable when researching texts translated from Arabic or Persian. A variety of accents are used, and in some cases none. I have therefore sought to use the current word system if possible.

Having previously published a book on *Ancient Roman Gardens* my research also led to an interest in gardens of other ancient civilisations. I carried out further studies to look for evidence of gardening practices in earlier and later cultures to see if there was an element of continuity. I then gave a series of lectures titled '*How did their Gardens Grow? Gardens of the Ancient World*' and this book is the fruits of all my labours.

CHAPTER ONE

Egyptian Gardens

The climate of Egypt is very hot and dry and in a land with virtually no rain the availability of water is paramount. Most of the country is desert, except for a strip of cultivable land either side of the great River Nile plus the river delta area and a few oases. To the Egyptians their great river – the Nile – appeared to come out of the desert, from an unknown source, so its waters were seen as emanating from the gods. It became a sacred river, that was a blessing because its waters could be used to irrigate the land. Life and agriculture/horticulture developed in Egypt simply as a result of the annual flooding of the Nile. The floodwater would slowly soak into the parched earth, bringing a greater quantity of water onto the land than any man carrying water could ever manage. Also, importantly, the silt (or alluvium) washed ashore by the river was rich in nutrients, and was a very effective natural fertiliser that naturally spread over the land. Besides the annual flooding of the Nile, the Egyptians dug canals from the River Nile so that its vital water could be used for irrigation. To a certain extent the scorching hot sun in Egypt sterilised the top soil from harmful bacteria.[1]

Dating evidence for ancient Egypt is largely based on the reigns of the long lists of Pharaohs. For ease of identification they are grouped into dynasties, starting with Dynasty 0 around 3100 BC, down to the 30th Dynasty in 380–343 BC.[2] A further simplification is to split these into the Old Kingdom (2686–2181 BC), Middle Kingdom (2055–1650 BC), New Kingdom (1550–1069 BC), all these dates are approximate.

Our information about Egyptian gardens comes from archaeological discoveries, ancient texts and from depictions in paintings and carved reliefs on tomb walls. The paintings and carvings often have a religious funerary significance, but many also give details of the life of the deceased. Numerous tombs have scenes of everyday life, which are believed to show real people and objects, with the intention of continuing their existence into eternity. Therefore, the scenes represent that activity continuing for the benefit of the deceased. Most of Egyptian art is rather formalised and somewhat rigid, but the details in their garden scenes are nevertheless very informative. The majority of the tombs appear to belong to the pharaoh, his family, members of his court and other wealthy individuals. In reality however, ancient Egyptian gardens were not confined to the upper classes in palaces and temples, high-ranking officials could also have a garden, and there is also increasing evidence that workmen maintained small gardens and funerary chapels of their own, giving some indication of life at that time from a broad spectrum of society.

There are three main types of gardens in ancient Egypt and these were: sacred gardens, produce gardens and domestic/pleasure gardens. Our earliest evidence relates to aspects of sacred gardens, so those will be examined first. Religion played an important role in the daily life of many Egyptians, and it can also shed light on the meaning behind the choice of some plants that were planted in their gardens.

Fertility cults of Egypt

From a very early date there appears to have been a cult concerned with the fertility of crops/produce, as well as for humans, and in Egypt there are two main deities associated with this aspect: Min and Osiris. Both Min and Osiris are sometimes shown displaying their prominent symbol of fertility (an erect phallus). This is especially the case with Min whose major cult centre for his worship was at Koptos in central Egypt. A large cult statue of Min can be seen in the Ashmolean Museum in Oxford. Images of Min in reliefs and tomb paintings often show him wearing a tall straight crown split in two, and he carries a flail in his hand held aloft. The flail alludes to his role in agriculture/horticulture. In this cult Min was given a special plant, a lettuce, and the one depicted in ancient carvings and frescoes is invariably a tall slender one similar to our 'Cos' type of lettuce. The shape of this lettuce would imitate that of a large phallus. Also, the Egyptians noted that when the stem of a fresh lettuce plant is cut a milky white sap exudes from the plant, and this was seen to be like semen from the god Min. So this plant became a symbol/emblem of the god himself, and as such it is also found depicted next to scenes depicting people gardening. An example can be seen in a tomb at El-Bersheh. In these scenes the symbolic lettuce has three giant leaves. Min's worship was most active in the Old and Middle Kingdom. In the late Middle Kingdom Min appears to merge with Amun, the creator god who became Egypt's principal god in the New Kingdom. Due to syncretism Amun also merged with Re and became known as Amun-Re, and as such he embodied the sun, that all powerful source of light and heat.

Osiris was one of the most important deities of Egypt, and because of the story of his untimely death he takes on associations with death and resurrection, but he also had an important role in assuring fertility. In legend Osiris was the son of Nut. Nut was variously a sky/nature goddess connected to regeneration rituals. He is usually depicted as a mummy. A good representation can be seen in the 18th Dynasty tomb frescoes of Tuthmosis IV, at Thebes. Here Osiris is swathed like a mummy in white wrappings and two other funerary deities are close by: one is Hathor (she is also connected to aspects of fertility and sustenance, see below). The legend, according to the full version attributed to Plutarch, says that Osiris was killed by his jealous brother Seth, who tricked him into stepping into a coffin-like box, which Seth then threw into the Nile. It washed ashore at Byblos in Phoenicia (modern Lebanon). After much searching

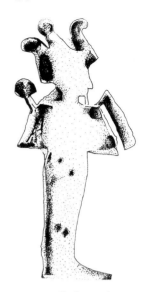

FIGURE 3. The Egyptian fertility god Min seen in his temple.

FIGURE 4. Detail of Osiris in white mummy wrappings, from the Tomb of Thutmosis IV, Thebes, 18th Dynasty.

FIGURE 5. Barley seeds were sown in wooden or ceramic Osiris Beds in a ritual of regeneration and fertility in tombs, ceramic version now in Hildesheim.

his wife Isis eventually found it, and took the box to the marshy area around the Egyptian Delta. However, when she was otherwise preoccupied, Seth stealthily came and cut up Osiris's remains into numerous parts and scattered them throughout Egypt. Isis dutifully searched everywhere for his remains, and buried each part where she found them (there were variously 14–42 parts, according to different sources). His phallus was never found though, because Seth had thrown it into the Nile and it was promptly eaten by carp. This legend indicates why the Nile River and its waters were considered so holy; the water of the Nile was seen as the fertilising semen emanating from the severed phallus of Osiris. To the Egyptians Nile water was literally the waters of life emanating from the god Osiris. His major shrine was at Abydos (in central Egypt) where there was an annual festival around his funerary tomb and garden. Sadly little remains of this garden, however in art his tomb is usually depicted as a mound with tall slender trees on top. In Egypt wild tamarisk trees tend to grow on a mound, so inevitably these trees/bushes became sacred to the god Osiris.

Another notable feature of his cult are the special artefacts known as Osiris beds, sometimes called a 'Corn Osiris', these were often placed in Egyptian tombs. Several wooden Osiris beds have been found in tombs. At a later date they also made little ceramic versions. In both of these, the god's effigy had been hollowed out of the receptacle. This depression was filled with silt from the River Nile, and then planted with seeds of barley, it was then sprinkled with holy Nile water to make the seeds germinate. This ritual symbolised the rebirth of vegetation, which was so linked to the god Osiris.³ To give an indication of the variation in size of these Osiris beds, one found in Tutankhamun's tomb was 202 cm long × 88 cm wide, whereas a terracotta version (now in Hildesheim, another can be seen in the Ashmolean Museum Oxford) is just 24 × 10 cm.⁴

Another important deity was the infant falcon god Horus, son of Osiris and Isis. Horus was a sky god therefore he was often depicted with a falcon's head or fully bird-like. He became associated with kingship. Legends say that after birth he was hidden amongst stands of papyrus in the Delta, so naturally these plants became associated with him. Re the sun god is believed to have been born from a lotus-flower. Egyptians believed that several gods were linked to particular plants, and this was reflected in ceremonies throughout the country. Therefore both papyrus and lotus plants were included into garden contexts so the appropriate rituals could be performed; these took place in sacred and domestic gardens.

Another deity associated with papyrus was the Goddess Hathor, who was often shown with the head or body of a cow. Every day she was believed to emerge from the side of the Western Mountain coming through papyrus plants. There is a fine painting on the Papyrus of Ani (in the British Museum) depicting her in this sacred role. Hathor was linked to the role of royal mother, and at times was likened to a cow suckling its young. Hathor was the daughter of Re and wife of Horus, so it is understandable that she would also be worshipped beside the papyrus beds of garden lakes. Hathor was thought of as a protector and was sometimes referred to as the 'Lady of the West' because the sun set in the west. Horus was correspondingly known as the 'God of the East' and presided over the daily birth of the sun. The sycomore fig tree was considered sacred to Hathor in her role of nourishing the departed, and interestingly Hathor was often also titled 'Lady of the Sycomore'. Both Nut and Hathor have this role and are occasionally depicted in female form as a goddess living in the tree, she became the tree, her lower limbs partly merging with the tree. From a tall slender vase she pours the water of life and gives food to the occupant of the tomb; this stresses the importance of this tree to Egypt. As the sycomore fig was one of the few trees that are considered indigenous to the country it had almost a sacred quality, as did the tamarisk. Both the leaves and fruit of the sycomore were used in herbal medicines.

Sacred gardens

Gardens or groves were often placed next to funerary monuments (mortuary temples, shrines and even some of the pyramids) so that rituals could be performed for the deceased and for their enjoyment in the next life. The ever present idea that their god Osiris had been restored from death to life was so strong that Egyptian tombs became almost a version of Osiris' own tomb. Osiris' tomb and temple at Abydos had been on an island, and around his tomb mound archaeologists found six huge brick lined plant pits that once contained conifers and tamarisk trees.[5] So part of a funerary garden would need to contain a pool or lake of water to replicate the water surrounding the god's last abode and a number of trees at least.

Religious temples were provided with gardens outside and inside the temple complex where sacred rituals could be enacted. Within the walled enclosure of the temple at Karnak there was a large area occupied by a sacred lake. The open area around it would undoubtedly have been planted as a temple garden, and the lake would have provided water for plants nearby. We can also assume this would be the case in the nearby temple of Mut, where there is an even larger enclosure with a sacred lake. Mut was the consort of Amun, hence the closeness of these two temples. Temple lakes were also used for purification ceremonies and offerings, but the lake also acted as a venue to re-enact certain legends: such as the myth of the solar sun which entailed a ritual of greeting the birth of the sun god from a lotus-flower, or of Horus from papyrus. Another ceremony that took place on the lake involved rowing a special boat across the lake.[6] The boat containing a statue of the god, was believed to imitate the sun's passage across the sky. The sun-barque would sail over what was seen as both the cosmos and a substitute of their primeval waters from which all life emerged. Because of these rituals we can assume that these lakes were all stocked with beds of papyrus and lotus so that these ceremonies could take place in a suitable setting. Temple gardens would also have contained flower beds to supply vegetables, such as lettuce for Min, as well as for flowers necessary for floral bouquets that were regularly given to images of the deities. In the Papyrus of Ani a pile of floral bouquets were given to honour the goddess Hathor. Animals and birds were also kept in pens/cages or aviaries in part of the gardens, and in some places they were bred there or nearby.[7] Some were undoubtedly destined to be offerings to a god.

In several cases we can assume that a special tree was planted in sacred gardens to represent the *ished* tree, that was regularly illustrated on temple and royal tomb walls. It was believed that the gods, either Thoth (the god of truth) or more often Seshat (the goddess of writing), wrote the names of the pharaoh on its leaves at coronations and jubilee festivals, being designed to ensure the pharaoh's memory. This magical *ished* tree is sometimes likened to the beautiful persea tree (*Mimusops laurifolius*) which is a large dense leaved evergreen fruit tree that has yellow oblong shaped fruits that are about 4 cm long.[8]

Archaeological evidence for sacred gardens

Perhaps the earliest known sacred garden are those associated with funerary/ mortuary temples, such as at Dahshur, next to the so-called 'Red' pyramid of Sneferu, which belongs to the first Pharaoh of the 4th Dynasty in the Old Kingdom (*c*.2613–2589 BC). This really highlights how early this form of garden is. On the north side of the pyramid at Dahshur, archaeologists discovered a series of hollows in rows indicating pits that had been dug to plant trees, they

FIGURE 6. Circular tree/ plant pits for a sacred grove beside the pyramid of the 4th Dynasty Pharaoh Sneferu, Dahshur, *c*.2613–2589 BC.

can be interpreted as making a sacred grove on at least one side of Sneferu's pyramid.[9] The size of the brick edged planting pits indicated at least two different sizes of trees had been planted in this grove, although sadly no remains survived in the tree pits to identify which species had been planted there.[10] The site at Dahshur is outside the cultivation zone, and is surrounded by desert, so to give the trees the best chance of survival the pits had been dug out of the sand and re-filled with good soil. From then on these trees would have needed to be laboriously watered by hand.

Archaeological excavations have also revealed evidence of tree planting around several royal funerary temples. In the forecourt of the funerary temple of Mentuhotep II (of the 11th Dynasty in the Middle Kingdom *c*.2055–2004 BC) at Deir el-Bahari they found regular rows of tree pits, which would have made a substantial sacred grove to adorn his temple. Fortunately the dry nature of the soil in Egypt has ensured good preservation of plant remains, and the remains found within these pits have indicated that tamarisk and sycomore trees were once grown there. Fifty-five tamarisks root stumps (of *Tamarisk aphylla*) were actually discovered in pits 10 m deep; the tamarisks had been planted in rows on either side of an avenue of sycomore trees leading up to the funerary temple, and there were two flowers beds each about 2 × 7 m.[11] The sycomore is not the maple-like sycamore tree we are familiar with, but a type of fig tree, which has oval shaped leaves (*Ficus sycomorus* is its modern botanical name, as opposed to *Ficus carica*, the true fig). We will hear more of them later. The funerary garden was not complete without a number of statues of the king placed along the tree lined approach of his tomb.

At the cliff site at Deir el-Bahari there were three royal funerary temples and tombs built cheek-by-jowl next to each other by terracing and excavating into

FIGURE 7 *(above).* Reconstruction of three funerary temples at Deir el-Bahari, showing the position and alignment of tree pits and T shaped pools in their associated sacred gardens, from left to right: Temples of Mentuhotep, Tuthmosis III, Hatshepsut.

FIGURE 8 *(right).* Relief depicting the transport of incense trees from Punt, temple of Hatshepsut, Deir el-Bahari.

the cliff: Mentuhotep's is the earliest one (in the reconstruction drawing it is on the left). Later two pharaohs of the New Kingdom Period built their tombs nearby, Hatshepsut's is on the right (1473–1458 BC), and the central one belonged to Tuthmosis III (1479–1425 BC). Hatshepsut was recorded as sending out an expedition to the land of Punt (thought to be Somalia, Ethiopia or Yemen). This was partly to collect incense/myrrh trees for her father's temple. The events of this expedition are carved onto the walls of her temple, and in one of the reliefs we can see men carrying the said trees on a pole on their shoulders. For many years these trees were believed to have been planted in front of Hatshepsut's temple but no remains of myrrh trees have come to light from tree pits discovered in her funerary garden and many pits are now believed to be of later date. But, in the reliefs there are also scenes showing incense trees growing in large pots and these could imply that they had been placed in the garden area to create an incense grove after all. There were however two original tree pits flanking the entry into the enclosed garden which were found to contain preserved root fragments (macrofossils) belonging to the beautiful persea tree.[12] Showing that a variety of trees were judged as desirable for such a setting. On the lower garden terrace there were two large ritual pools, each shaped like a letter T. In the silt of these pools archaeologists discovered fragments of papyrus, indicating that that the rituals of Hathor emerging through papyrus could have been enacted there.

Evidence of tree pits showed that Tuthmosis III's temple also had an avenue of trees leading up to his temple. The pits here were spaced at 6 m intervals and were again very deep (10 m)[13] and were found to be filled with rich black soil, brought in specially to sustain the growth of these trees. Fragments of roots and tree stumps were found there. Around each tree the ancient gardeners had built a low brick wall to protect it from encroaching sand. When watering the trees, the wall would help to contain the water and stop the precious liquid from being wasted. Every drop would be needed for those thirsty tree roots.

Excavators have also found garden areas within the Ramesseum, the funerary temple of Ramesses II (1279–1213 BC) at Thebes. A representation of the garden featured in the tomb of Nedjemger (Theban Tomb 138) who was its head gardener; this sacred garden comprised a T-shaped pool/canal and an orchard or grove.[14] Sadly there are no remains of this garden today. However, at Medinet Habu Ramesses III (1184–1153 BC) constructed another magnificent funerary temple complex which he called his temple of 'Millions of Years'. The huge temple complex itself was surrounded by high walls, as were many temple gardens. Between the entrance gate and the first pylon archaeologists discovered a pool and evidence for a row of trees, then beyond the first pylon gateway and the temple itself, there had been a grove of at least thirteen trees grown in pits protected with low walls. The trees had been planted in three rows 3.50 m apart.[15] A further enclosure was furnished with a T-shaped pool and a well 5 m deep. No plant remains are recorded but we know that gardens once flourished here as Ramesses himself informs us that the temple was:

> surrounded with gardens and arbour areas filled with fruit and flowers for the two serpent goddesses. I built their dwellings with windows, and dug a lake before them supplied with lotus flowers ... I dug a lake before the Temple of Millions of Years, supplied with lotus flowers, flooded with Nun, planted with trees and vegetation like the Delta.[16]

FIGURE 9. 'The Botanical Garden' detailing plants brought to Egypt after the campaigns of Tuthmosis III, Karnak Temple (photo: © J. Chisnall).

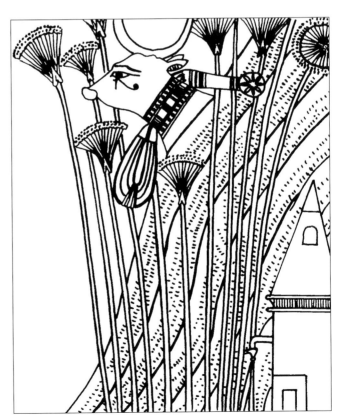

FIGURE 10. Hathor emerging from the side of a mountain through papyrus.

Nun was the primeval waters from which the primeval mound of earth emerged, therefore in Egyptian gardens the concept of a lake with an island originated as a recreation of this early creation myth. The mention of 'Delta' like vegetation probably implies papyrus beds growing at the edge of the lakes mentioned. Apart from the lotus/waterlilies, garden plants are again just mentioned collectively but the species known at that date will be discussed later.

At Amarna, the royal city built by Pharaoh Akhenaten (1352–1336 BC) in Middle Egypt, archaeologists have uncovered two important sacred enclosures, that were in effect walled parks lying side by side, located to the south of the main city. Of the twinned parks called the Maru-Aten, the northernmost is significantly larger and appears to have been associated with royal women. The gardens were designed to make a fitting place on earth for Aknenaten's monotheistic god, the sun who was now called the Aten, he replaced Amun during this heretical period. Both of these gardens have lakes within them, and some buildings around their periphery, but the centre of the northern sacred garden was occupied by a vast sacred lake that was orientated east–west. On the west side of this lake there was a jetty, to enable the royal family and temple priests to sail across the lake to re-enact the ritual of the sun's passage across the sky and over the sacred waters. The lake was roughly rectangular in shape with rounded corners and was about 120 m long by 60 m and 1 m deep.[17] On the opposite side of the lake (to the east) there was a small temple. Some of its columns were decorated with painted waterlilies, leaves and bunches of grapes. Beside the lake archaeologists noted traces of cultivation plots.

Immediately to the north of the small temple within the Maru-Aten Akhenaten constructed a moat surrounding an artificial rectangular island with a small open sided pavilion in the middle. Some paintings on the outside of the shrine featured palm and acacia trees and lakeside plants such as waterlilies, papyrus and reeds, while in the interior several wall tiles were found to be decorated with flowering plants.[18] This pavilion also had columns with lotus-flowers in relief and palm leaf/papyrus capitals, it was indeed a highly ornamental garden-like pavilion. A bridge gave access to this sacred island and to the rear of the shrine another bridge led to an area of cultivation strips which are believed to form ten rows of flowerbeds. A path through these beds led to an elongated enclosure with a series of 11 interlocking T-shaped offering pools, each 6 m long. Interestingly the floors around these pools were of painted plaster, depicting a variety of beautifully painted flowers and plants, as if they were in rectangular plant beds on either side of the pools. These colourful floor frescoes featured clumps of reeds, papyrus, cornflowers and poppies (several are now on display in Cairo's Archaeological Museum). One section of the painted floor resembled a basket full of flowers and on the low walls surrounding the pools there were scenes with vines and pomegranates. These plants and flowers are representative of the many that would have been needed to make bouquets and offerings to the god, and part of the relief carvings in this Maru Aten shows priests bearing bouquet offerings. A Maru means a sacred place, and this delightful example provided a suitable residence on earth for Aknenaten's supreme god where the divine sun would shine onto the pharaoh imbuing him with divine power. A poem dedicated to the Aten shows the depth of Egyptian sentiment for flowers, one part says: 'By the sight of your rays all flowers exist, what lives and sprouts from the soil grows when you shine ...'[19]

While excavating areas within the Workmen's village at Amarna a number of the workmen's funerary chapels were brought to light. It was exciting to learn that two of these were found to have a little funerary garden associated with the chapel. These examples show that in ancient Egypt gardens were tended by a wide section of the population. Chapel 528 had a T-shaped pool of about 5 m in length and small garden plots edged with stones and or mortar.[20] The forecourt to Chapel 531 however had a central path with garden plots on either side, both were again edged with stones. A tree pit was located nearby. Due to the dry conditions in Egypt it has been possible to conduct botanical analyses of the soil deposits in the Workmen's village and within the garden plots macrofossils were found of coriander and celery, seeds of black cumin, juniper, beet, possibly basil, and capsules of what appears to be white mustard or radish.[21] Also, there were flower heads, leaves and seeds of species that would have provided material for making floral tributes such as a species of aster and withania nightshade. The remains of Christ's thorn, acacia and tamarisk are believed to represent shade trees grown in these gardens.

Produce gardens and gardeners

Several temple and tomb reliefs depict agriculture and horticultural occupations. The earliest found in a private tomb were those in the Tomb of Mereruka at Saqqara. Mereruka lived during the Old Kingdom 6th Dynasty, so produce gardening can be dated to *c.*2330 BC at least. The relief shows gardeners carrying water-pots suspended on a yoke, they irrigate what appears to be a grid of square plant beds. Behind them larger than life representations of plants serve to indicate the produce growing there. In the dry climate of Egypt a water-carrier's work was continual and very hard to bear, and his sorry plight is highlighted by a rather melancholy ancient Egyptian text that makes a satire on the different trades in Egypt; it implies that the water-carrier's lot was the hardest of all to bear.

> The water-carrier carries his shoulder-yoke. Each of his shoulders is burdened with age. A swelling grows on his neck, and it festers ... He spends the morning in watering leeks and the evening [with] corianders, after he has spent the midday in the palm grove ... So it happens that he sinks down [at last] and dies because of his hardship, more than any [other] profession.[22]

A series of Middle Kingdom reliefs from tombs in Beni-Hasan and El-Bersheh (in Middle Egypt) show more of these square grid-like vegetable beds. Archaeologists have found the same pattern of plant beds, and in places a similar system is still used for ease of irrigation. In Egypt plants relied solely on the

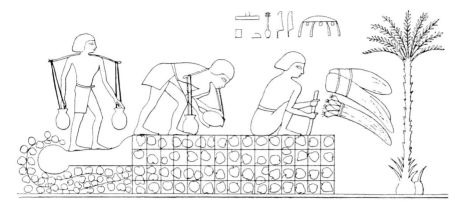

FIGURE 11. Middle Kingdom relief depicting water-carriers irrigating a grid-like plant bed, and gardeners toiling in vegetable gardens. The over-large symbolic representation of a bunch of onions and two cos-type lettuces indicates what was planted there, Beni-Hasan (after Gothein 1966, 1, 8).

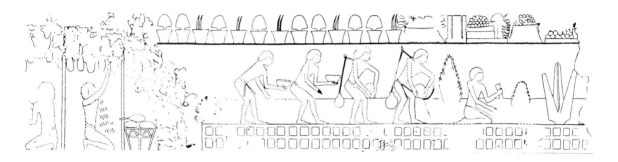

FIGURE 12 *(above)*. On the left, gardeners pick cucumber-like melons. On the far right the huge lettuce symbol of the fertility god Min ensures a good crop. A row of potted plants and baskets of fruit show how productive is the garden, El-Bersheh, Middle Kingdom (after Gothein 1966, 1, 9).

water that was brought to them, there was no rain, so in such places narrow straight paths enabled gardeners to walk between a series of grids, and from there they could lean across to water or weed the beds. In the ancient relief in the Tomb of Khnumhotep at Beni-Hasan two gardeners (again water carriers) approach the square vegetable beds and water the plants, while on the right a gardener bends down to tend the bed. To the right of this gardener there is a representation of the vegetables they are producing: a large bunch of onions and two tall cos type lettuces.

In a similar horticultural scene, from a tomb at El-Bersheh, we see gardeners picking cucumber-like vegetables grown on a trellis frame, these are however a species of melon grown at that time called *cucumis melo chate*.[23] To the right of this image gardeners sow seed and water the square plant beds. On the right another gardener kneels down to weed. To the far right is a different depiction of a huge cos lettuce, it is stylised and has three large leaves, this image is the sacred sign/symbol of the fertility god Min. The owner undoubtedly was hoping that the god would help his crop, and part of it would have been dedicated to the god as a ritual offering. Along the top of this scene there are baskets of picked fruit next to a row of potted plants perhaps being special pot herbs or young plants ready to plant out.

The most frequently mentioned garden vegetables and those that are depicted in reliefs and frescoes are: lettuce (*Lactuca sativa*), cucumber-like melons

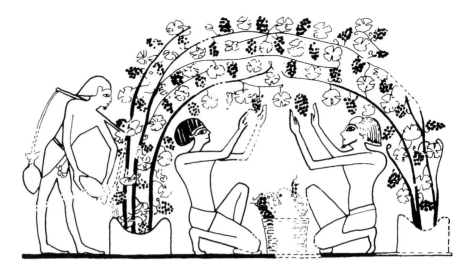

FIGURE 13. Detail of a vintage scene, a process undertaken in many gardens. The vine roots are protected by a *meru* container, Tomb of Kaemwaset, Thebes, 19th–20th Dynasty.

FIGURE 14 *(above)*. Figurative hieroglyphs, from left to right: a pool, lotus, papyrus, plants, tree, a vineyard.

(*Cucumis melo chate*), watermelon (*Citrullus lanatus*), celery (*Apium graveolens*), onions (*Allium cepa*), garlic (*Allium sativum*) and leeks, however the leeks were not the European species but the kurrat variety (*Allium kurrat*).[24] Tuberless radishes (*Raphanus niger* or *R.sativus var.aegyptiacus*), and the herb coriander (*Coriandrum sativum*) were also frequently mentioned in garden contexts, although we cannot identify them in garden scenes.

Vines were introduced into the country at an early date, and scenes of the vine harvest are found. In a Middle Kingdom tomb relief from Beni-Hasan gardeners are shown picking grapes from vines trained to grow in the form of a semicircular bower. To the left a man carries away two baskets full, suspended from a shoulder yoke. A similar scene is reproduced in one of the New Kingdom frescoes in the Tomb of Khaemwaset, at Thebes (TT261). Here the gardeners kneel down to pick grapes from vines growing over a bower. Part of the painting (now damaged) shows a basket between them for their picked fruit. A water carrier gives the thirsty vine tree a perpetual drink, he pours the water directly into the trough-shaped plant container that served to protect the vine's roots and the raised sides make watering the plant easier. This was a *meru* container.[25] Nearby there were additional scenes showing various stages of bringing in the vine harvest, and processing it. Workers tread the gathered grapes, and finally there is the bottling of the wine. Such time honoured scenes would have been performed in many large Egyptian gardens. Interestingly, the figurative hieroglyph for a vineyard resembles the way Egyptian vines were trained to grow in the form of a bower, two forked poles hold up the arching vine stems. Several hieroglyphs are recognisable symbols that alert us to the mention of a tree, flowers or plants in general, papyrus, lotus (growing in a pool), and any form of pool – in this case shown as a traditional rectangular shaped one with wavy lines to represent water.

The ancient Egyptian term for a gardener was *khenty-esh* this seems to have come into use during the New Kingdom; before that the term applied to an attendant or a land planter.[26] During the New Kingdom we hear of the title 'Overseer of the Garden' (*imy-r Khenty-esh*), such as Nedjemger who presided over the Gardens of the Ramesseum.[27] There was also a 'Gardener of the Divine Offerings of Amun' and Nakht was such a fortunate person. He would ensure the well-being of all growing plants within the temple gardens and arrange for the collection of vegetables, fruits and flowers that would comprise the god's offerings. There are even recorded incidences where the post of a temple gardener had passed down the generations from father, son, then to grandson, as seen in inscriptions in the 18th Dynasty Tomb of Nakht the Gardener (Theban Tomb 161).[28] Nakht also had the honour of a second title 'Bearer of the Floral Offerings to Amun', for details of these bouquets see below. One section of Nakht's tomb wall paintings actually depicts him overseeing his workforce of gardeners watering the grid-like garden plots.[29]

Water was drawn up by hand, by lowering a water pot into a well, pool, or water channel. Also, in Egypt agri/horticulturalists made good use of a *shaduf*. This devise was a great help to gardeners, in time and energy. A stout pillar was placed at the water's edge, and a large pole or tree branch was pivoted on top. A water pot or canvas container was roped to one end of the pole so that it could be lowered into the water. Because the pole was counterweighted at the other end the filled water container could be raised almost effortlessly, then the water could be emptied into the water-carrier's pots. A *shaduf* is shown in several tomb paintings. In the tomb fresco of Ipuy's garden (TT217, of the 19th Dynasty) four *shadufs* can be seen in action. Apparently the waterwheel was not known or used during Pharonic times, they are believed to have been introduced at a later date possibly during the Ptolemaic period.

Beside tending the trees, vegetables and flowers, Egyptian gardeners would have had to ensure that birds and baboons would not come into the garden to eat the carefully cultivated vegetation or the fruits on the trees. Some gardeners were provided with sticks to scare the predators away, as seen in the Middle Kingdom Tomb of Bakt at Beni Hasan.

An inscription on a 22nd Dynasty stele discovered at Abydos mentions the purchase of an estate and land at Abydos providing details of prices paid for each item – including a garden and its workstaff.[30] This inscription gives a good comparison between the various ranks of staff employed there and of their worth. Two parcels of land were bought (each measuring 50 *stat*) costing 10 *deben* of silver money. A *deben* and *kidet* (or *kit/kite*) were units of silver weights. A modern equivalent could be lbs and ounces, 10 *kidet/kit* = 1 *deben*.[31] The garden at Abydos cost 2 *deben* of silver, its gardener Harmose son of Penmer was priced in *kidets*. Unfortunately the inscription is damaged at this point, but the gardener appears to have been priced in double figures of *kidets*. His watercarrier (sadly his name is missing) cost six *kidets* of silver. In comparison two named maidservants were priced at 5 *kidets* each, and workers in the spice-kitchen and harvest labourers were 1 *kidet* each.

Orchards

Orchards are also depicted in tomb reliefs and are mentioned in texts. The earliest description of what could be an orchard is that of Meten, a general and high official living *c.*2600 BC during the 3rd/4th Dynasty. He planted numerous trees, including palms, figs and vines.[32] We hear that Ramesses III (*c.*1184–1153 BC) created an orchard of 200 persea trees at Heliopolis for a new temple of Amun.[33] Whereas a large variety of trees are mentioned by Ineni, the architect and royal gardener to Tuthmosis I of the 18th Dynasty (*c.*1504–1492). He mentions in his tomb (TT81) that he once had 540 trees in what must have been a large garden or orchard in which he hoped to enjoy in perpetuity. He names 20 different species of tree but only fifteen can be identified with reasonable certainty, they comprised: 170 date palms (*Phoenix dactylifera*), 120 doum palms (*Hyphaene thebaica*), 73 sycomore fig trees (*Ficus sycomorus*), 31 persea (*Mimusops laurifolia*), 16 carob trees (*Ceratonia siliqua*), 12 grape vines (*Vitis vinifera*), 10 tamarisk trees (*Tamarix nilotica/T.aphylla*), 8 willow trees (*Salix subserrata*), 5 fig trees (*Ficus carica*), 5 pomegranate trees (*Punica granatum*), 5 Christ's thorn trees (*Ziziphus spina-Christi*), 5 *twn* trees (possibly a form of acacia), 2 moringa trees (*Moringa peregrina*), 2 myrtles (*Myrtus communis*), 1 argun palm (*Medemia argun*), and 5 unidentified species of tree.[34] In Egypt fruit bearing trees tended to be planted in rows so that an irrigation channel could be dug alongside, alternatively the trees were planted in a series of plant pits but there was still a tendency to plant these in rows. Again these were all laboriously watered by hand. The orchard had to be planted in the dry zone because if it was planted in an area which periodically flooded, the tree trunks would rot after several months under water.

Inside a small room in the great temple complex of Amun at Karnak there is a surprising series of relief carvings of trees and other plants, which has led to this room being called 'The Botanical Garden' (see Fig. 9 above). The rows of carvings actually record the plants that were considered notable on Tuthmosis III's campaigns in the Levant (*c.*1479 BC); they were conquests albeit botanical ones, and were considered worthwhile to introduce into Egypt. A special orchard or garden would have been provided at Karnak for these trophies. Unfortunately the plants were not labelled, and the style of the carvings is rather stylistic and not drawn to scale therefore it is very difficult to identify the species represented. A few are however recognisable such as: pomegranate, palm and fig trees, vine, lotus, melon, lettuce, myrtle, asphodel, iris and a daisy-like flower.[35] Sadly in the extremely dry climate of Egypt several of the trophy plants would not have survived long without continual care.

Domestic pleasure gardens

Inscriptions in private tombs, for example that of Meten (*c.*2600 BC), suggest that from an early date Egypt's elite could possess their own enclosed garden that would surround their private villa. He informs us that his estate was walled and enclosed a square of about 105 m on each side, filled with trees, arbours and pools for water fowl, he also had a vineyard nearby.[36] Sadly no garden of this early period has survived but from later representations of gardens (whether real or imagined) it is clear that a water source was thought desirable in a garden and a well or pool became a central feature. Pools were usually rectangular or T-shaped. Trees and flowering plants were often planted in beds near the pool because the plants could then be irrigated using water drawn from the pool. This is shown to good effect in one of the remarkable wooden models found in the Tomb of Meketre (TT280) who was a chancellor to Mentuhotep II of the 11th Dynasty (*c.*2055–2004 BC). These models represented boats, houses, or craftsmen at work, all with the intention that the activities represented within them could continue in eternity for the benefit of the deceased in their next life. Two of the models represented a house and garden. The whole was surrounded by a high wall. The house is simply represented by just its columned portico, opening onto the view of a deep pool surrounded by seven trees, believed to be of sycamore figs.

Gardens tended to be located on the north side of buildings, presumably so an open portico on that side would allow any cool breeze from the north to temper the heat inside. The building would also create some welcoming shade in nearby garden areas for part of the day. Trees were also valuable for the shade they gave in a garden, other plants could be grown below their dappled canopy, and an area of seating could be quite welcoming if you wanted to sit out and enjoy the fresh air outside.

Depictions of gardens

Most of our evidence for Egyptian gardens is revealed in the details shown in contemporary tomb paintings and reliefs. Many garden scenes in frescoes date to the New Kingdom, and in particular to the 18th Dynasty (1550–1295 BC) which saw a flowering of artistic skill. The classic elements depicted in these garden scenes are a rectangular or square pool surrounded by plants. Less frequently we see a T-shaped pool,[37] but there does not seem to be any desire to install a pool of a different shape. A rectangular pool was practical, and also would have been easier to construct than one of a more irregular form. The frescoes vary in content, however, for instance in the 18th Dynasty Tomb of

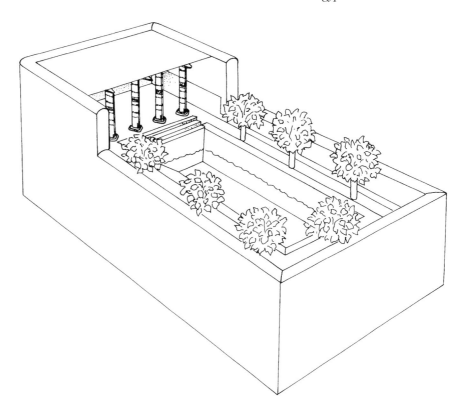

FIGURE 15. Wooden
model of a part of a
house and garden, placed
in the Tomb of Meketre,
11th Dynasty of the
Middle Kingdom Period.
Seven trees surround a
deep pool in the garden.

Minnakht (TT87), and the Tomb of Rekhmire (TT100, both at Thebes), a boat
sails across a lotus filled rectangular pool. The boat is believed to represent a
festival or funerary ritual. In the former we see various trees: date palms and
sycomore figs, and also covered areas where storage jars are kept cool and fresh
by hanging foliage from the rafters, they are shown dangling between each large
pot. This may show a method for keeping flies off the produce stored there. In
the Tomb of Sebekhotep, at Thebes (TT63), he and his wife drink from their
centrally placed lotus pool, while fish swim about. This would be a re-enactment
of them taking the sacred water of life to sustain them in the next world. To
reinforce this concept on either side a sycomore tree goddess presents food and
liquids for sustenance throughout eternity. Two rows of trees surround the pool,
all shown laden with fruit.

Garden scenes are often painted as if from a bird's eye view, but with the
plants drawn in profile, so that the scene is reminiscent of a plan. No perspective
is shown. Some artists however chose to include a scene depicting a profile view
of the owner's house and garden, as in the Tomb of Ineni (TT81). In the Tomb
of Neferhotep at Thebes (TT49) we see a lively scene depicting visitors arriving
at a villa in Thebes. They proceed through the gateway on the left; the house and
welcoming party are on the right. Some guests walk through the gardens. There
is a fine vine covered pergola above, with lotus-like columns. The trees below
are pomegranates, that can be clearly identified by the characteristic remnants

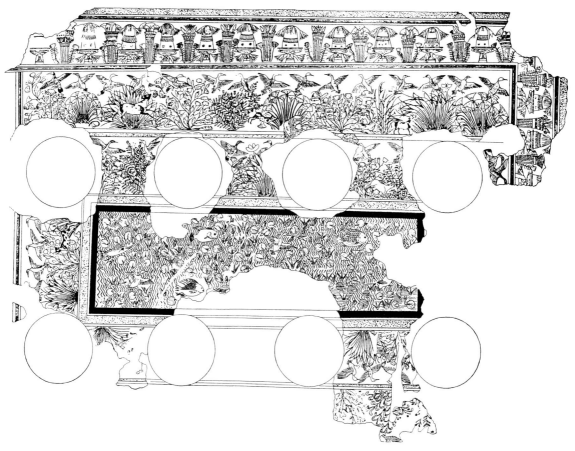

of its flower protruding out. Pomegranates were an introduced fruit tree highly valued for its flame coloured flowers, as well as for its sweet juicy fruit.

There were also wonderfully painted plaster floors with garden scenes, and several have been discovered in the great palace at Amarna (dated *c.*1350 BC). The newly built city was abandoned after the death of the heretical pharaoh Akhenaten after only 25–30 years therefore the site preserves valuable evidence of this particular period. The floor paintings give a marvellous indication of the possible appearance of a royal Egyptian palace garden. Although they were painted inside buildings they were meant to represent gardens outside. The scenes (painted as seen from above) are fragmentary. In the 'Main Room', which is the most damaged, the floor appears to show four rectangular fishponds; while in Room F the 'garden' features a pair of elongated rectangular fishponds. However, in the better preserved 'garden' within Room E the centre is occupied by a single large rectangular fishpond; this floor painting measures 15.6 × 6.5 m.[38] All fishponds in the three rooms were outlined with a dark border and there is a path around each pool. Blue wavy lines reflect water in the pond and all are shown teeming with fish, ducks and lotus plants. Flowerbeds and reeds surround these ponds. In room E a second row of plants decorated the two long

FIGURE 16. A flower filled garden around a well stocked fish pool painted on the floor of Room E in Akhenaten's Palace at Amarna, 18th Dynasty. The blank circles mark the position of columns.

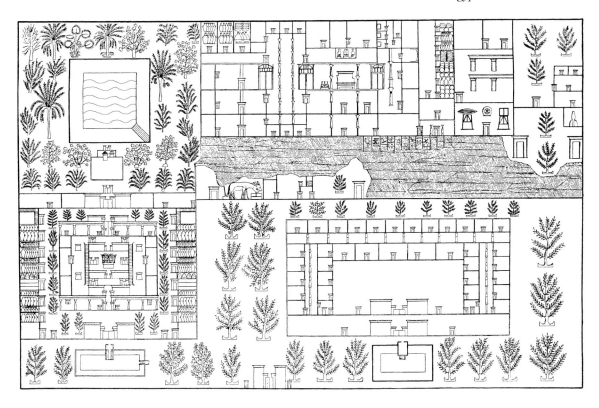

FIGURE 17. Plan of the house and garden of Meryre, High Priest of Amarna, Tomb of Meryre, 18th Dynasty (after Gothein 1966, 1, 13).

sides. Wildfowl fly above the foliage, and deer bound through the clumps of plants, bringing life to these delightful scenes. These 'gardens' all show abundant healthy plant growth, and this concept is reinforced by an outer painted border composed of facsimiles of offerings and bouquets.

Fortunately some of the officials of Amarna have also left tomb wall paintings that depict what may have been their own home and garden in life, helping us to visualise how they would have appeared in reality. A good example is that of Meryre, the High Priest of Amarna. In this fresco, which resembles a plan, his large residence is surrounded by a rectangular wall; the entrance gate is shown at the bottom. Large trees shade the first enclosure on entering the property, the trees may be sycomore figs. Each tree has a low retaining wall of dried mud, which is shown in cross-section; these would be the *meru* receptacles/ containers which were made of brick/mud. Immediately in front of the house and storeroom block there is a large rectangular fishpond, with a means of access placed in line with both entrance gateways. Large areas are reserved as living quarters, for Meryre himself and his staff which included his gardeners. The central route through the numerous storerooms (on the left) led to a large decorative garden (top left in the fresco drawing). This was designed with a large deep square shaped pool, slightly off centre in the garden. Between the garden gateway and the pool Meryre had installed a garden pavilion/kiosk so he and his family could relax and enjoy his garden, in the shade, and benefit

FIGURE 18. Sycomore fig tree with tree goddess dispensing nourishment for eternity, Thebes (after Rosellini *Monumentii*, Pisa, 1832–44).

from cleaner air emanating from aromatic foliage and flowers in the garden. A variety of trees and bushes were grown here, of these we can identify palms, figs, and tamarisk.

The pool in Merye's garden had a flight of steps located on the bottom right corner, to enable gardeners to draw water from it. Several garden representations show deep pools and it appears that this was specifically done to enable groundwater to seep into the pool, especially after the annual floods. When the surrounding water-table fell the water in the pool would also fall so the steps would enable the water-carriers to reach the shrinking water level later in the year. There was no piped water supply so garden pools were filled in this way or by slaves laboriously transporting water from the Nile to the pool by hand.

The most extensive plan of an Egyptian garden was painted on the walls of Sennefer's tomb at Thebes (TT96, *c*.1427–1400 BC). One of Sennefer duties was to be the overseer of the Gardens of Amun, therefore as you would expect his gardens would be special. The walled garden is shown fronting onto the river or canal, and has a tree lined aspect. The shape of the large trees on the river front indicate two different varieties are represented here, probably the sycomore and persea which are often similarly drawn. One has a rounded appearance whereas the other has a relatively more pointed shape, the latter would be the persea (*Mimusops laurifolia*). As you entered through the large red door of the gateway (here all doors are painted red) you would immediately notice that the layout of the garden is formal and almost symmetrical. The centre of the garden is completely occupied by thriving grapevines supported on wooden

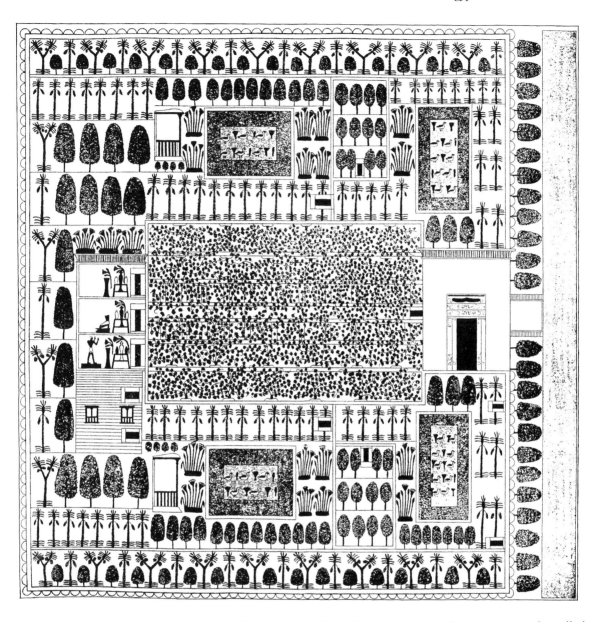

FIGURE 19. Plan of Sennefer's garden. The centre is covered by grapevines, and on either side are separately walled fruit orchards, and four fish pools surrounded by papyrus beds and trees: sycomore, date and doum palms, Tomb of Sennefer, Thebes, 18th Dynasty.

pergolas. On either side a smaller red doorway opened into a separately walled section of the garden which comprised a rectangular pool surrounded by more sycomore trees, date palms and special beds growing papyrus flowers. Then, inside these gardens were other walled enclosures protecting twelve pale green trees with dots – these would be tender fruit trees. To the north and south the garden is edged with a border of alternating palms and green trees.

Two different species of palms are shown in the border of Sennefer's garden. One is the familiar date palm (*Phoenix dactylifera*) which is ubiquitous in Egypt and the Middle East. The second is the doum or dom palm (*Hyphaene*

thebaica) – both spellings are current. The doum palm has a more rounded pattern of palm fronds and has a distinctive bi-forked trunk. Sadly now it only grows wild in Upper Egypt and in desert oases and is relatively rare elsewhere.[39] It was though once a very popular tree. Ineni, a military chief living in the 18th Dynasty at Thebes, mentioned that he had no less than 120 doum palms in his garden, and Ramesses III is recorded as having planted doum palms in Heliopolis. It was prized for its fruits, as well as for its graceful appearance, but later it was found to be more useful in the building trade and this decimated its range. However, there is a third species of palm known in ancient Egypt: a fan palm called the argun (its botanical name is *Medemia argun*). It is like the doum palm, but its trunk is unbranched, I believe that it is represented in a fresco in the 20th Dynasty Tomb of Pashedu at Deir el-Medine (TT3). The fruit of the argun palm is edible, but is rather stringy. It is now quite rare in Egypt, but apparently it was also a popular garden tree in ancient times. Ineni had ensured that at least one of these palm trees was in his garden. In the fresco Pashedu is shown bowing down behind the argun tree and is about to drink the water of life, from a clear blue pool painted below. It can be noted that the fruits of all three forms of palm trees were often placed in tombs. In some museums (such as the archaeological museum in Florence) there is a well preserved basket full of doum fruit, they are about the size of an apple. In the Ashmolean Museum

FIGURE 20 *(left)*. Doum palm tree (*Hephaene thebaica*), Silsila, Upper Egypt (photo: © 2012 Brian Yare)

FIGURE 21 *(right)*. Argun palm tree (*Medemia argun*), Tomb of Pasedu, Deir el-Medinet, 20th Dynasty.

FIGURE 22 *(above)*. Visitors arrive through the garden. At the top grapevines grow under a pergola; in the row below there is a fruit laden pomegranate tree, Tomb of Neferhotep, Thebes, 18th Dynasty.

FIGURE 23 *(right)*. Flame coloured flowers of Pomegranate (*Punica granatum*), Cyprus.

in Oxford you can compare the shape and size of a desiccated doum palm fruit with a sycomore fig and grape pips that had been discovered well preserved in the dry conditions of ancient Egyptian tombs.

In Egyptian art the trees and flowers are formalised, and it is sometimes difficult to identify them. However, in the Tomb of Pashedu (TT3 at Deir el-Medinet), one of his frescoed walls has a good representation of one of the most important trees in Egypt, the evergreen sycomore fig tree (*Ficus sycomorus*) as opposed to *Ficus carica* the more familiar fig. The leaves are smaller and oval shaped rather than the large tri-lobed ones of the true fig; the fruit of the

sycomore is more rounded in shape. There was an added benefit in that they produce fruit all year round, therefore sycomore trees were often planted near houses, and understandably this species of fig was also an important food for the poor. They are sweet to eat, but before picking them off the tree you needed to make a cut downwards on each one. The sycomore fig is normally sterile in Egypt (it originated further south) but a parasitic wasp tended to burrow into the fruits. This was not such a danger as one might think because the wasps complete the necessary fertilisation of the fig, and notching/cutting the figs would allow the wasps to get out.[40] In wall paintings you can often see some of the fruits on the trees have the characteristic slit marks (downwards) on the fruit. Also, in this particular tomb fresco the tree has a female figure inside it; she is the sycomore tree goddess.

Three other tree species are sometimes depicted in tomb paintings: the acacia, carob and olive. A good example of how the Egyptians depicted carobs is seen in the Tomb of Menena at Thebes (TT69). The fruits are a knobbly elongated pod and are shown like inverted candles on the tree. A seated woman below has gathered some of the fruits into a bowl. She had a young child strapped to her in a sling so that she could work while her child suckled. The pods of the carob (*Ceratonia siliqua*) are rich in protein, starch and sugar; they are flavourful, and even today are used for animal fodder. It was also a useful plant because it is drought resistant. Ineni, recorded that he had 16 carob trees in what must have been a large garden (or his imagined garden that he could enjoy through eternity). Sadly the fresco of Ineni's garden is rather fragmentary, there is a small rectangular pool and five rows of trees but the individual traits of these trees are not sufficiently clear to tell which are the trees mentioned in his orchard garden. However, Ineni must have been proud of them to want them recorded in such detail.

In comparison several trees were drawn with care in the wonderful 19th Dynasty fresco of the decorative garden of Ipuy at Thebes (TT217). Gardeners (one accompanied by his pet dog) raise a *shaduf* from the pools to irrigate the trees and flowers in his garden. To the right of the building behind the white

FIGURE 24. Ipuy's house and garden. A gardener uses a *shaduf* to water the garden. The garden is stocked with a fruiting pomegranate and Sycomore fig, a heavily pruned willow, blue cornflowers and yellow mandrakes, papyrus and white waterlilies/lotus, Tomb of Ipuy, Thebes, 19th Dynasty.

FIGURE 25. Carob tree represented in the Tomb of Menena, Thebes, 18th Dynasty.

pillar of the *shaduf* is a flowering pomegranate tree, its distinctive flame coloured flowers stand out. Directly in front of the pillar there are wispy green leaves and stems sprouting up from a heavily pruned willow. There is another pomegranate tree on the far left, then nearby is a persea tree with its small yellow fruits, and a thickly girthed sycomore fig also laden with fruit. Between the trees are a range of flowers, blue flowered cornflowers, red poppies and mandrakes, while in the black lined pools below there are a number of white waterlilies. Close to the building are tall stems of papyrus flowers.

A greater selection of flowers and trees are included in the 18th Dynasty Tomb of Nebamun. The sycomore goddess is present dispensing fruit and drink in the top right hand corner. Here the large trees are treated differently: five carry large yellow fruit bunched in threes, which could identify sycomores; whereas four trees with darker branches and small fruit could represent persea. A wide branched tree in the bottom left corner would be our more familiar fig tree. Many garden frescoes depict trees but relatively few include flowers, other than lotus, however in this fresco (as in the palace scenes at Amarna) there is a flower border surrounding the rectangular pool filled with white waterlilies/lotus, fish and ducks. The flowers form a continuous band, each flower is shown as a many headed clump, but because they were painted onto a dark grey background they are difficult to identify properly. Flowers are coloured blue, red and white (daisy-like).

Flowers and trees are portrayed with greater clarity in the Tomb of Sennedjem at Thebes (TT1). The scene is predominantly depicting a cultivated field and irrigation channels. On the third row there is a large willow tree, then below that a row depicting three alternating species of trees (the two main types of palm and a narrow leaved tree, possibly a persea). On the lower register there is a long bed of flowers, they are stylised but identifiable. From left to right they are: mandrakes, identified by their distinctive shaped yellow fruits and strap-like leaves; blue flowered cornflowers, large headed red poppies. These are the most common flowers depicted in Egyptian wall paintings. Less frequently we see the pink flowers of mallow, the white daisy-like flowers of chamomile, a yellow flowered mayweed/chrysanthemum and a plantain-like plant which is thought to be cyperus grass (*cyperus esculentus*) a popular plant with small edible roots known as tiger nuts.

Some flowers have a special significance, beyond their decorative elements. An indication of the special place that the blue lotus held in Egypt is that it became the symbol of Upper Egypt. The flowering heads of papyrus became the sacred plant and symbol of Lower Egypt. In the charming ivory panel of

King Tutankhamun and his wife Ankhsenamun, we see the king and queen sniffing the beautifully scented flowers of blue lotus. Scented flowers were especially admired and you often see images of people holding a choice flower to their nose. Below the royal couple there is a narrow scene showing serving girls picking mandrake fruits, but these are extremely large, much larger than in reality, mainly because they wanted to emphasise that these plants were a highly prized commodity. The mandrake is decorative, but it also holds a special place as a medicine and as a narcotic drug.

Floral bouquets

Flowers were used to make floral bouquets, and these are often depicted in tomb paintings. On occasion fruit, such as pomegranates are added to them. Many painted bouquets are quite elaborate and seem to have been fixed into a long

FIGURE 26. Nebamun's fruitful garden, with ducks swimming amongst white lotus in a well stocked fishpond. The pool is surrounded by a border of flowers and trees: Date palms, Persea, sycomore and true fig trees. Restored colours, Tomb of Nebamun, Thebes, 18th Dynasty (© The Trustees of the British Museum. All rights reserved).

slender container, which could be placed into a special holder, or be wedged into the ground to be free standing. Some frescoes capture the moment of making the floral tribute and we see men in the act of adding extra blooms to enhance the effect of their bouquet. Understandably the long stemmed sweet scented blue lotus was a favourite ingredient for these bouquets. Sometimes just a single bloom and two buds of long stemmed lotus are depicted, with their three stems looped together, then placed on to a pile of offerings to the gods or tomb owners. Huge quantities of floral bouquets are recorded as gifts in religious rituals. For instance, Ramesses III offered 1,975,800 bouquets for the god Amun at the god's sacred Temple (in a 3-year period) and 21,000 were given to honour the god Ptah in the same period.[41] This highlights the importance of flowers in this period. Huge quantities of flowers were grown in sacred temple gardens for this. Market gardens would have also catered for the floral requests of the wealthy at court. The most wonderful bouquets are found in the frescoes of the Tomb of Nakht (TT161) who was a court florist, living in the 18th Dynasty at Thebes. Some of his bouquets were huge and multi-tiered, with extra bouquets added for good measure.[42] Actual bouquets have been found in tombs, where the dry airless conditions inside has meant that they have survived, but they are very fragile; they crumble to dust very easily. Flower and foliage were used in bouquets and one of the most frequent arrangements found in the tombs is one where a base of persea leaves was used, to which other flowers/plants were added. Two large bouquets with persea were found in Tutankhamun's tomb.[43]

FIGURE 27. Irrigation channels provide water for a row of trees and flowers next to a crop of wheat. Three different flowers are represented here, from left to right: yellow mandrake, blue cornflower, and red poppies, Tomb of Sennedjem, Thebes. New Kingdom, Dynasty XIX (De Agostini Picture Library. G. Sioen. The Bridgeman Art Library).

FIGURE 28. Details of flowers painted in the Tomb of Ramesses III, Thebes, 20th Dynasty (after J. G. Wilkinson, *The Ancient Egyptians*, London, 1854, 365).

FIGURE 29. Nakht, the court florist, with one of his finest bouquets, Tomb of Nakht, Thebes, 18th dynasty.

Flowers grown for floral collars

Floral collars were also made from garden plants, and several are depicted in wall paintings. They were multicoloured and were made of numerous flower petals and leaves, which had to be sewn onto strings and then stitched together. Unbelievably some of these highly ephemeral collars have also survived the millennia in Egypt's tombs. The one that had been placed around the neck of Tutankhamun's image on the innermost coffin was particularly well preserved. The range of flowers used in the actual bouquets and wreaths that had been left in the tombs extends the list of known species at that time: Hollyhock (*Alcea ficifolia*), white mayweed/camomile (*anthemis pseudoctula*), blue cornflower (*Centaurea depressa*), golden mayweed (*Chrysanthemum cororonarium*), convolvulus (*Convolvulus arvensis*), cordia with a plum-like flower (*Cordia gharaf and myxa*), pink morning glory (*Cressa cretica*), delphinium (*Delphinium orientale*), jasmine (*Jasminium sambac* or *J. grandiflorum*), lettuce – the cos type (*Lactuca sativa*), Madonna lily (*Lilium candidum*), sweet clover (*Melilotus indica*), mint (*Mentha sativa*), persea (*Mimusops laurifolia*), waterlily (*Nymphaea*), olive (*Olea europea*), poppy (*Papaver rhoeas* and *P. somniferum*), pomegranate (*Punica granatum*) and wild celery (*Apium graveolens*).[44] There are perhaps some surprises here, we might think it strange to include convolulus, as it is such a pernicious weed, but we should admit that it does have a nice flower.

Flowers were also used for making perfumes and one of Egypt's favourites was made from the lily. This would be *Lilium candidum* the Madonna lily. Lilies are rarely depicted in Egyptian art, however one Late Period tomb relief of the 26th Dynasty shows women carefully gathering the blooms of lilies in what must be a large special bed solely devoted to its culture. They may well have been grown commercially for the bulk that would be needed in perfumery. The rose and narcissus were late introductions into Egypt, under the Ptolemaic Rulers, and as such are out of our scope of this chapter as we are more concerned about plants of the Pharonic times.

There may have been a limited variety of trees and plants grown in Egyptian gardens, but they obviously used them in the best way they could. Many seem to have been placed around the margins of a rectangular pool, which was for practical reasons: you then did not have so far to go to water the plants. An interesting text in the Tomb of Rekhmire (TT100) sums up how much the Egyptians valued their garden flowers. Rekhmire invited guests at his own funerary banquet to take the scented flowers which he had brought for them, from the pick of the plants which were in his own gardens.[45] Flowers decorated tables and persons. One of the abiding characteristics of the Egyptians, that highlights just how much they loved their gardens, is that so many Egyptians included a prayer in their tombs so that after death they might be able to return and sit in the shade of their garden and eat the fruit of the trees that they had planted, and be nourished forever by the tree goddess within their garden.

Evidence from archaeology for gardens in Egypt

Few actual gardens have been excavated in Egypt, as modern settlements overly ancient ones. However at the abandoned ancient city of Amarna this is not the case, therefore archaeological work has continued to be undertaken. Beside the Maru-Aten and the painted garden floors of the Great Palace (mentioned above) archaeologists have recently been re-examining the area of the North Palace. In the main inner court they discovered evidence of tree planting, with a row of tree pits on the north side of a large depression that appears to have been a deep open well or pool. Also the slightly sunken area in the open centre of the rectangular Garden Court within the North Palace was found to have been subdivided into a grid of cubit-sized plots with mud ridges (as seen in the reliefs of produce gardens).[46] We can imagine these plant beds filled with pleasant flowers and other plants, perhaps to echo the painted walls of the surrounding chambers especially in the 'Green Room' that still bore traces of frescoes with palm trees and lush vegetation above a narrow elongated lotus filled pool that formed a frieze across the full width of the room.

These luxuries can be compared with the small garden plots tended by workers and their families in the Workmen's village at Amarna. Garden areas were small comprising several plant beds filled with alluvial soil brought up from the Nile floodplain. Preliminary work analysing the species of plants that were grown in these beds suggest the following: a variety of herbs, vegetables such as onion, garlic, a variety of *cucumis*, pomegranate, grape, watermelon, fig, olive, almond and date.[47]

Palaeobotanical investigations have recently taken place at Amarna, Saqqara and in the Fayum to find the ancient flora of the region. Unfortunately the soil within the Delta area is too moist to allow such a good state of preservation as is found in the dry zones. Data were collected from all the archaeological sites (and from earlier digs) that mentioned the survival of seeds, pollen and macrofossils (remnants of twigs, branches, tree stumps, fruit, pods, flowers, leaves *etc.*) and was complimented by the quantities of desiccated fruits and floral tributes found in tombs. The information thus gathered was the basis for the *Codex of Ancient Egyptian Plant Remains* compiled by Vartavan and Amorós.

From all the sources pertaining to sacred and domestic gardens mentioned in this chapter I have compiled a list of the species of trees and plants that could have grown within an Egyptian garden. I have included columns listing whether there exists a contemporary illustration of that plant, whether it was mentioned in Egyptian literature (such as in poems, inscriptions or medicinal texts), and if botanical remains were found of that plant species.

Evidence gleaned from excavations and illustrations reveals that over the centuries the form of an Ancient Egyptian garden sees little change. In Egyptian art there is a more fluid style during the Amarna Period, but as far as can be seen the art of gardening during that brief interlude retains the traditional pattern of before.

Ancient texts concerning Egyptian gardens

Literature of this period was primarily discovered within tombs, being either hieroglyphic script written on interior tomb walls and on papyrus, or in hieratic script. Texts are varied, a great number of medical texts have survived, and these indirectly give valuable information on the plants grown in Egypt. The Egyptian pharmacopoeia from the time of Imhotep (the great architect and physician of *c.*2700 BC) contained about 300 herbal remedies. In later years the number rose to 700 or so remedies. These have been studied recently and the *Egyptian Herbal* written by Lise Manniche explains the use of 94 species of plants and trees used for medicines, cooking, cosmetics and perfumery, making it a good informative resource.

Some inscriptions mention gardens created by the deceased, but again few describe gardens sufficiently by giving details and layout of planting schemes, but the texts do help to give an understanding of the times, the character of their gardens, and their place in society. Some of these texts also give hints as to the plants you are likely to find in an Egyptian garden. There are also several love poems that have a setting in the garden where trees or an arbour could make an ideal trysting place.

One popular epic, which was set in the period *c.*1960 BC tells of the adventures of Sinuhe. He was an Egyptian official who went into exile. However, after several adventures he contemplated his life and grew homesick. Luckily he was allowed to return. Towards the end of this epic we learn that after his return he was provided with the customary facilities of court officials:

> I was allotted the house of a nobleman ... and its garden and its groves of trees were replanted with plants and trees ... And the site of a stone pyramid among the pyramids was marked out for me ... I acquired land round it. I made a lake for the performance of funerary ceremonies, and the land about it contained gardens, and groves of trees ...[48]

This text supports the concept of how court officials possessed both a domestic garden and a funerary garden, it was expected of them.

The so-called letter of Panbesa describes the city of Piramesse (in the Delta area) that was transformed into a royal residence and court by Ramesses II, thereby giving rare information on garden areas within a city in Lower Egypt:

> Its canals are rich in fish, its lakes swarm with birds, its meadows are green with vegetables, there is no end of the lentils; melons with a taste like honey grow in the irrigated fields ... Onions and sesame are in the enclosures and the apple-tree blooms. The vine, the almond tree and the fig-tree grow in the gardens ... Fruits from the nurseries, flowers from the gardens, birds from the ponds, were dedicated to him [Ramesses] ...[49]

Interestingly we hear that there was a considerable number of people who would have had access to gardens, not just the owners, but the gardener's family as well, as is revealed in this delightful Egyptian love poem. On this occasion a tree is made to speak and invites the gardener's daughter under its shade.

Mekhmekh-flowers, my heart inclines towards you,
I shall do for you what it seeks, when I am in your arms …
I am your best girl: I belong to you like an acre of land
which I have planted with flowers and every sweet-smelling grass.
Pleasant is the channel through it which your hand dug out
for refreshing ourselves with the breeze.
A happy place for walking with your hand in my hand …
Hearing your voice is pomegranate wine, for I live to hear it …
The little sycomore, which she planted with her hand, sends forth its words
     to speak.
The flowers [of its stalks] [are like] an inundation of honey;
beautiful it is, and its branches shine more verdant [than the grass].
It is laden with the ripeness of notched figs, redder than carnelian,
like turquoise its leaves, like grass its bark.
Ita wood is like the colour of green feldspar, its sap like the *besbes* opiate;
it brings near whoever is not under it, for its shade cools the breeze.
It sends a message by the hand of a girl, the gardener's daughter;
it makes her hurry to the lady love: come spend a minute among the maidens.
The country celebrates its day.
Below me is an arbour and a hideaway;
my gardeners are joyful like children at the sight of you …
Come spend the day happily, tomorrow and the day after tomorrow, for
     three days,
     seated in my shade …[50]

It sounds very welcoming there. The tree later says that she is discreet and will not say what she has seen! Sometimes as above the narrator likens his beloved's features to garden plants, another example is as follows:

Come through the garden, Love, to me.
My love is like each flower that blows;
Tall and straight as a young palm-tree,
And in each cheek a sweet blush-rose.[51]

A later tomb inscription (*c.*1400 BC) expresses well the sentiments of those times, the owner wished that he would be able to enjoy these ideals:

[so that] Each day I may walk unceasingly on the banks of my water,
That my soul may repose on the branches of the trees which I planted,
That I may refresh myself under the shadow of my sycomore.[52]

Garden Plants of Ancient Egypt

Common Name	Botanical Name	Tomb Fresco/ relief	Literature	Botanical Remains
Acacia	*Acacia nilotica*	x	x	x
Argun palm	*Medemia argun*	x	x	x
Beet	*Beta vulgaris*			x
Camomile (white mayweed)	*Anthemis pseudoctula*	x		x
Carob	*Ceratonia siliqua*	x	x	x
Carrot	*Daucus carota*			x
Castor-oil plant	*Ricinus communis*		x	x
Celery	*Apium graveolens*		x	x
Chrysanthemum (golden mayweed)	*Chrysanthemum coronarium*	x		x
Cornflower	*Centaurea depressa*	x		x
Convolvulus	*Convolvulus arvensis*			x
Coriander	*Coriandrum sativum*		x	x
Cordia (Egyptian plum/sebesten)	*Cordia gharaf, C.myxa, C.sinensis*			x
Cyperus grass (tiger nuts)	*Cyperus esculentus*	x	x	x
Delphinium	*Delphinium orientale*			x
Date palm	*Phoenix dactylifera*	x	x	x
Doum/dom palm	*Hyphaene thebaica*	x	x	x
Fig	*Ficus carica*	x	x	x
Garlic	*Allium sativum*		x	x
Grape Vine	*Vitis vinifera*	x	x	x
Jasmine	*Jasminum sambac*			x
Leek	*Allium kurrat*			x
Lettuce (Cos)	*Lactuca sativa*	x	x	x
Madonna lily	*Lilium candidum*	x		x
Mallow/Hollyhock	*Malva alcea/Althaea ficifolia*	x		x
Mandrake	*Mandragora officinarum*	x		x
Melilot (Sweet clover)	*Melilotus indica*			x
Melon	*Cucumis melo chate*	x		x
Mint	*Mentha sativa*			x
Moringa	*Moringa pterygosperma*		x	x
Morning glory, pink	*Cressa cretica*			x
Mustard (white)	*Sinapis alba*			x
Myrtle	*Myrtus communis*		x	x
Narcissus	*Narcissus tazetta*			x
Olive	*Olea europaea*	x	x	x
Onion	*Allium cepa*	x	x	x
Papyrus	*Cyperus papyrus*	x	x	x
Persea	*Mimusops laurifolia*	x	x	x
Poppy	*Papaver rhoeas & P.somniferum*	x	x	x
Pomegranate	*Punica granatum*	x	x	x

Common Name	Botanical Name	Tomb Fresco/ relief	Literature	Botanical Remains
Radish	*Raphanus niger* (or *R.staivus* var.*aegyptiacus*)			x
Safflower	*Carthamus tinctorius*		x	x
Sycomore fig	*Ficus sycomorus*	x	x	x
Tamarisk	*Tamarix nilotica, T.aphylla*	x	x	x
Waterlily (white lotus)	*Nymphaea lotus*	x		x
Waterlily (blue lotus)	*Nymphaea caerulea*	x	x	x
Watermelon	*Citrullus lanatus* & *C.colocynthoïdes*	x	x	x
Willow	*Salix subserrata*	x	x	x
Withania nightshade	*Withania somnifera*			x
Wormwood	*Artemisia absinthium, a.judaica*		x	x
Ziziphus (Christ's thorn)	*Ziziphus spina-Christi*		x	x

Notes

1. From personal communication with Dr Joyce Tyldesley.
2. I have used the dates in Shaw, I. and Nicholson, P. *British Museum Dictionary of Ancient Egypt*, London, 1995, 310–311. I have not included the Persian, Ptolemaic or Roman periods as they will be dealt with in later chapters.
3. It is mentioned in the Coffin Texts, Spell 269 (Wilkinson 1998, 117).
4. Respectively: Hepper 1990, 54; Schulz, R. and Seidel, M. (eds) *Egypt, the World of the Pharaohs*, Könemann, Cologne, 1998, 379, fig. 86.
5. Wilkinson 1994, 3.
6. Wilkinson 1998, 127–8.
7. Wilkinson 1994, 5.
8. Manniche 1999, 121.
9. Stadelmann, R. 'Pyramiden und Nekropole des Snofre in Dahscher, Dritter Vorbericht über die Grabungen des Deutschen Archäologishchen Instituts in Dahschur'. *Mitteilungen der Deutschen Archäologischen Instituts, Abteilung Kairo* 49, 1993, 261.
10. Wilkinson 1998, 68.
11. Wilkinson 1998, 69.
12. Wilkinson 1998, 76–77. Keimer, L. *Die Gartenpflanzen im Ägypten* 1, Berlin, 1924.
13. Winlock, H. *Excavations at Deir el-Bahari*, New York, 1942, 6, fig. 1, pl. 68.
14. Wilkinson 1998, 89.
15. Hölscher, U. *The Excavation of Medinet Habu*, 4, Chicago, 1951, 19.
16. After Breasted, J. H. *Ancient Records of Egypt* 4, Chicago, 1906, 194–189; Wilkinson 1998, 93.
17. Wilkinson 1998, 149.
18. Wilkinson 1998, 150–151.
19. Lichtheim, M. *Literature: A Book of Readings: New Kingdom*, vol. 2, Berkeley, 1973, 92.
20. Kemp, B. J. 'Report on the 1984 Excavations Chapel Group 528–31'. *Amarna Reports* 2, London 1985, 45.
21. Stevens and Clapham 2014, 160–161; see also Renfrew, J. M., 'Preliminary Report on the Botanical Remains'. *Amarna Reports* 2, London, 1985, 175–190.

22. Simpson, W. K. *The Literature of Ancient Egypt*, Yale, 1973, verse 12.

23. Brewer *et al.* 1994, 65.

24. Brewer *et al.* 1994, 65–75.

25. Private communication with Angela Torpey.

26. El-Maenshawy 2012, 58.

27. Wilkinson 1998, 89.

28. El-Maenshawy 2012, 59–60.

29. Manniche 1999, 16; Wilkinson 1998, 136; British Library (Hay MSS 29822,96).

30. Breasted, J. H. *Ancient Records of Egypt* 4, Chicago, 1906, 682; Brugsch-Bey, H. *History of Egypt Under the Pharaohs*, 2, trans. P. Smith, London, 1881, 210–211.

31. Schulz, R. and Seidel, M. (eds) *Egypt, the World of the Pharaohs*, Könemann, Cologne, 1998, 513 and 516. The exact value today is unknown as the value of silver fluctuates.

32. Gothein 1966, 8; Bellinger 2008, 14; Wilkinson 1998, 25.

33. Gaballa, G. A. 'Three documents from the reign of Ramesses III,' *Journal of Egyptian Archaeology* 59, 1973, 113.

34. Bellinger 2008, 18; Bigelow 2000, 10; Manniche 1999, 10.

35. Wilkinson (1998, 138) identifies other plants in the reliefs of the 'Botanical Garden'.

36. Gothein 1966, 8.

37. As in the Theban Tombs of Tjanefer and Neferhotep.

38. Weatherhead, F. 'Painted pavements in the Great Palace at Amarna', *Journal of Egyptian Archaeology* 78, 1992, 179–194.

39. Brewer *et al.* 1994, 50.

40. Brewer *et al.* 1994, 54.

41. Manniche 1999, 24.

42. Manniche 1999, 22.

43. Manniche 1999, 122.

44. Wilkinson 1998, 40.

45. Wilkinson 1998, 105.

46. Amarna Project, the North Palace, Online.

47. Northseatle.edu. Amarna workers village. p. 6; fig. 3.

48. Wallis Budge, E. *The Literature of the Ancient Egyptians*, London, 1914, 168.

49. Brugsch-Bey, H. *History of Egypt Under the Pharaohs*, 2. trans. P. Smith, London, 1881, 101.

50. Simpson, W. K. *The Literature of Ancient Egypt*, Yale, 1973, verses 17–34.

51. Murray, M. A. *The Splendour that was Egypt*, London, 1977, 210.

52. Gothein 1966, 20.

CHAPTER TWO

Gardens of Ancient Mesopotamia and the Near East

In some ways Mesopotamia has features similar to Egypt, but instead of one great river it has two: the Tigris and the Euphrates that are the life blood of their heartland. The word Mesopotamia is Greek, *meso* means between and *potami* can be translated as rivers, it is therefore 'the land between the rivers'. These two important rivers flow out of the mountains in Turkey then through a relatively flat plain, making irrigation from the rivers practicable. As with Egypt it was in these irrigated areas that settlements could grow on an organised basis and how some of the earliest great civilisations of humankind were able to develop. Outside the river valleys and irrigated areas most of the country is desert with extremely hot dry summers.

The region encompassed in this chapter is however wider than the land between the two rivers, it will include the land lying to the east up to the Zagros mountains that border with Persia, in the north the mass of the Taurus mountains forms a natural boundary, and on the west is the Mediterranean Sea. The territory therefore comprises the modern countries of Lebanon, Israel, Syria, Iraq and part of south-east Turkey. The land beside the Mediterranean Sea is fertile and well watered by rivers flowing from the two mountain chains of the Lebanon and Anti Lebanon mountains. However these mountains tend to

FIGURE 30. The River Euphrates and the Mesopotamian Plain, seen from Syria.

cut off most of the rain-bearing westerly winds and tends to leave the territory east of these mountains rather parched and dry. This creates in effect two distinct climatic zones and the phrase 'the fertile crescent' is sometimes used with justification to describe a great arc that included those areas that had a good water supply for irrigation. This fertile region extended across the lower slopes of the mountains to the west and north and the great river valleys where agriculture and horticulture was possible.

The timescale of ancient cultures in ancient Mesopotamia and the Levant is huge; it goes back to the dawn of civilisation, where people first settled into city communities. Unlike Egypt these lands saw a succession of different ruling powers therefore garden art sees more change over the centuries. The first major power in the area was the Sumerians (dating from the late 4th millennium BC) who lived in several cities in the south (Ur, Uruk, Lagash and Nippur *etc.*) and Mari on the middle Euphrates. After time the Sumerian cities were taken by the Akkadians under Sargon of Akkad (*c.*2334–2154 BC) some cities continued under their new overlords. Two great powers emerged: the Babylonians based at Babylon on the Euphrates in the southern part of Mesopotamia, and the Assyrians based at Nineveh on the Tigris in northern Mesopotamia. As the former's power waned, the latter rose, and the process repeated over the centuries, with conquests and expansion. Then in the mid-6th century BC the Persians came into the ascendancy, their empire lasted from 550 to 330 BC. At times the whole of the fertile crescent was dominated by powerful states/cultures based in Mesopotamia.

FIGURE 31. Map of Mesopotamia and the Levant, showing important cities, and the approximate area of the Fertile Crescent.

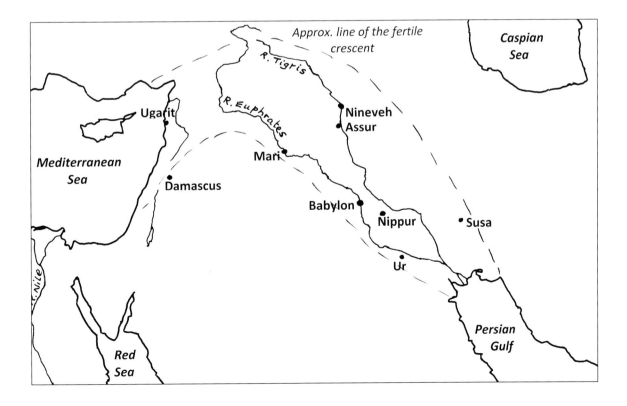

FIGURE 32. Seal stone depicting divinities and a snake on either side of a sacred tree; Known as 'The Temptation Seal' because of its likeness to the Biblical story of the Garden of Eden, 3rd millennium BC, British Museum.

Despite the problems besetting this region, some of the earliest artefacts do show an admiration for nature. The most beautiful example being the headdress from Ur with a band of pendant golden leaves and three nodding golden flowers on top, which is dated to the 3rd millennium BC. A great number of personal items such as stone seals used to prove ownership have been discovered by archaeology. The seals both in a stamp or cylinder form were intricately carved and many of them portrayed scenes with plants, trees and deities providing glimpses of aspects of ritual and horticulture. Evidence for gardening in this period is also found in contemporary texts written in a cuneiform script, which help to enlighten us on life in this part of the world.

Nature/fertility cults of Mesopotamia

In some cases the earliest deity did not have a human form but could be represented by just a simple pillar. In an area where life was hard won, and dependent on the providence of nature and the availability of water, it is understandable that the ancients sought to placate a deity that would relate to aspects of nature around them. Therefore through time a specific god associated with fertility came into being. As in the case of the Sycomore Goddess of Egypt, we find a Mesopotamian deity that was seen to be living in a tree – as part of the tree, and this tree therefore came to be known as 'The Tree of Life'. Ningizzida was the Sumerian equivalent the 'Lord of the Tree of Life'.[1] The tree most often represented in this way is the date palm. Dates are rich in proteins and carbohydrates and are a useful source of iron so they were a staple food in antiquity, they also stored well. So it is not surprising that this tree held such an important role in daily life and religious rituals.

Several seal stones depict worship beside a tree, a sacred tree; a good example is the so-called 'Temptation Seal' dated to the 3rd millennium BC (now in the British Museum). This carved seal depicts a male and female divinity with a rather stylised tree in the centre. The snake on either side has led many people to compare it with the Biblical story of the Garden of Eden, and shows that

FIGURE 33. Seal stone from Mari. Rivers flow from the central mountain to nourish a water deity (on the right) a tree god (on the left) and 'Ninurta of the Hoe' an agricultural/horticultural deity (far left), 2250 BC, Damascus Museum.

our concept is in fact very old. Interestingly, Sumerian texts mention a place called *Edin* or Eden, this word meant a cultivated place/plain.

Ancient cultures in this region also believed in the sacredness of water, which was so important to nourish plants and crops, leading to the belief in the 'water of life'. A seal stone from Mari (of 2250 BC, now in Damascus Museum) features and emphasises this age-old importance of water. There is a mountain deity in the centre; water issues from sources at either side of the mountain beneath it. This is a fair representation of reality, for springs often arise from the base of hills. In fact the two streams could represent the two great rivers of Mesopotamia: the Euphrates and the Tigris. To the right of the mountain, one stream flows to a water goddess holding a vase. Often water deities are shown pouring their water to symbolize the source of a spring or river; in this instance she just holds the vase ready. The second stream flowing to the left nourishes a tree deity, and on the far left another god represents the land receiving nourishment so that it can be tilled and hoed. Because this land deity has what looks like an agricultural/horticultural tool in his hand he could be equated with a gardener. This deity could be 'Ninurta of the Hoe', who was primarily a war god but was also concerned with horticultural/agricultural activities. In the Sumerian texts Ninurta is credited with giving advice on aspects of farming throughout the year. In cosmology he was linked to the planet Saturn.

Ninhursag (earlier known as Ki) was the Sumerian goddess of vegetation and fecundity; she was also looked upon as a mother goddess. In some ways she was linked to her son Ninurta, who later called her 'Lady of the Mountains'. This title mirrors the appellation sometimes given to the Egyptian goddess Hathor, and could signify intercultural links between Mesopotamia to Egypt. Ninhursag is found carved on a basalt relief from Lagash (now in Berlin). She wears a leafy crown on her head. Her shoulders are covered with sprouting branches and her hair flows out behind her. Ninhursag holds the branch of fertility in her hand. Another relief in limestone, from Girsu (now in the Louvre) shows Ninhursag with a naked acolyte who pours a libation onto a plant within an elongated vase or plant pot. This act is a clear sign of the goddess's association with plants. Temples were dedicated to her in a number of cities, such as at Girsu, Mari and Kish. She had a special connection with the latter, because she was also sometimes noted as 'She of Kish'. In legend Ninhursag and Enki bore many children and among their offspring was Ninsar (Lady of Greenery) whose granddaughter was Uttu, a goddess of plants.

Several cities and cultures have different names for their own gods/goddesses, and over time these merge. We also hear of another Sumerian fertility/love goddess named Innana, she was often represented in art by a symbolic reed-like standard with a ring top.

Over time the Sumerian 'Ninurta of the Hoe' becomes or equates with the all powerful Babylonian god Marduk. In the Babylonian Creation Myth (dated to the 12th century BC) Marduk is honoured with 50 titles, being the names of other gods who became subordinate to him. Of these three have relevance here: Asaru, Gugal and Hegal. Asaru was a god who 'cultivates the sown, conducts water by small channels for seed-time, for shooting green and harvest grain.'[2] Gugal was said to be 'in the orchards of the gods [where] he watches the canals, he fills the store-room with sesame, emer, abundant grain.'[3] Hegal was once responsible for providing rain: 'into the world he sends sweet rain and greenness.' Likewise the important Sumerian goddess Innana later becomes/merges with the Akkadian goddess Ishtar, who eventually evolves into Astarte. Ishtar had a dual aspect of goddess of love and war, and is often depicted in battledress carrying a bow and quiver of arrows. She is regularly shown next to or standing on top of a lion, which became her sacred animal. Ishtar was usually associated with the morning star Venus and therefore a star is often placed beside her image.

Early Mesopotamian writing was made up of pictograms, based on simplified representations of real objects. The pictogram symbol used for an orchard was a rectangular box surmounted by two twig-like trees, a canal was shown as two wiggly parallel lines, a vine leaf resembled an arrow, a date palm looked like a tufted stick, and the symbol for a spade was easily recognisable. The spade was later used to represent the Babylonian supreme god Marduk. Later the pictograms evolved into the wedge-like script we know as cuneiform, which was written on clay tablets discovered in the archives of the ancient cities.

FIGURE 34. Ninhursag (Ki) the Sumerian goddess of vegetation and fecundity. She wears a leafy crown, branches sprout from her shoulders, and she holds the branch of fertility in her hand (a frond full of ripe dates), relief from Lagash, now in Berlin.

Temple gardens

Gardens or groves were provided around some temples, to complement the building and to provide space for rituals to take place. Also as in Egypt the sacred garden could furnish additional materials for offerings. One Early Babylonian text says: 'I planted a pure orchard for the goddess and established fruit deliveries as regular offerings.'[4] The only indication of which trees or plants were planted in such gardens is from an early Assyrian text (*c.*1814–1782 BC) that suggested juniper trees could be planted in the new proposed temple garden for the god Addu.[5] But, at Uruk a temple that had been constructed in honour of Innana (*c.*1400 BC) had decorative brick walls with relief images of water deities, centaur-like creatures and palm trees, the latter may have been representative of the trees that would have surrounded the temple. There are references to sacred gardens in the Bible however the Israelites scorned those who made sacrifices on altars in sacred groves/gardens.[6]

The earliest gardens, mentioned in literary sources

The earliest Sumerian text concerning the very beginnings of garden culture dates back to a myth about the goddess Innana and is known as the 'The Gardener's Mortal Sin' this is dated to the 4th–3rd millennium BC. This myth hints at the initial impetus in gardening when a man called Shukallituda discovered that by planting a shade-giving tree other plants were able to grow below in its shade (otherwise they suffered under the relentless rays of the sun); shade gardening is still practised today.

FIGURE 35. Detail of the goddess Inanna and her symbolic standard of reeds, from the Warka vase, *c.*3500 BC.

> In the garden, in five to ten unapproachable places,
> In those places he planted one tree as a protecting cover,
> The tree's protecting cover – the *sarbatu*-tree of wide shade –
> Its shade below, dawn, noon, and dusk, did not turn away.
> One day my queen, after crossing heaven, crossing earth,
> Inana, … after crossing Elam and Shubur, After crossing …
> The hierodule (Inanna) in her weariness approached [the garden], fell fast asleep,
> Shukallituda saw her from the edge of his garden, …
> Copulated with her, kissed her, Returned to the edge of his garden.[7]

When she awoke she was very angry and she tried to find who had defiled her; as a result three plagues were put on the land. 'All the groves and gardens of the land she sated with blood.' This last statement does indicate there must have been other gardens/groves in the region.

The early texts give just the briefest of information on where gardens might have flourished. The famous *Epic of Gilgamesh* (the earliest epic of mankind) was already ancient when it was finally written down in the 2nd millennium BC. It had been passed down orally until written on clay tablets in cuneiform script. In the tale we hear of an enclosed sacred wood around a 'cedar mount, the dwelling of the gods, the sanctuary of the Irini.' Another passage says: 'Then thou lovedst Ishullanu, thy father's gardener, who baskets of dates ever did bring to thee, and daily did brighten thy table …'[8]

This text shows that there were cultivated date palm groves which were evidently regarded as a form of garden. At this date gardens were really fruit and vegetable plots, the general population was more concerned with growing sufficient to eat.

During the reign of King Sargon the Great, the founder of the Akkadian Dynasty (2340–2284 BC), gardens and date groves were given a special status. Sargon was of humble origins, his mother was a priestess, but like the Biblical Moses, Sargon had been cast into the river soon after birth and was found by a gardener. His 'Birth Legend' says:

> The river bore me up and carried me to Akiki, the drawer of water.
> Akki, the drawer of water, [took me] as his son (and) reared me.
> Akki, the drawer of water, appointed me as his gardener.
> While I was a gardener, Ishtar granted me (her) love, …[9]

King Sargon was noted for his skills as a gardener, and even though he eventually became king he was known to work in the garden himself.

In the early 18th century BC the great Babylonian King Hammurabi established a detailed law system that has come to be known as the 'Code of Hammurabi'. Some of the laws in this code (59–66) cover the rights of a landowner, and those of a gardener to whom garden land is leased. This is what two of the clauses stipulate:

> 60: If, when a seignior gave a field to a gardener to set out an orchard, the gardener set out the orchard, he shall develop the orchard for four years; in the fifth year the owner of the orchard and the gardener shall divide equally, with the owner of the orchard receiving his preferential share.

> 64: If a seignior gave his orchard to a gardener to pollinate, the gardener shall give to the owner of the orchard two-thirds of the produce of the orchard as rent of the orchard as long as the orchard is held, with himself taking one-third.[10]

The terms used in this text still indicate that in law a garden was usually an orchard, potager or vegetable growing area, or a palm grove and not really an ornamental garden.

The earliest evidence for a decorative garden was found at Mari, on the middle Euphrates. Evidence here, takes garden culture back to the 19th century BC, although the city itself was founded in the 3rd millennium BC. Excavations at Mari have suggested that plants/trees were grown in some of the palace courtyards; one has been called the palm court after a text mentioning this name and also by the finds discovered there. At Mari a cache of cuneiform writing tablets from the city's royal archives have produced several interesting insights into daily life from *c.*1810–1760 BC. One of the

FIGURE 36. Detail from a large fresco from Mari, depicting on the left two scenes where King Zimri-Lim appears before the goddess Ishtar, with two water deities below. On the right there are two tall trees: a date palm and perhaps a tamarix (as featured in a popular tale), 19th century BC, now in the Louvre.

texts from Mari pertains to the important annual offerings to Ishtar 'in the garden of the king'. Apparently, 420 litres of sweet *alappanum*-beer, was served to the king and his men on this occasion 'in the garden of the king'.[11] In this ceremony the king would renew his vows and be reinvested with the insignia of kingship by the gods. A fresco discovered inside the palace is believed to commemorate this official occasion. The fresco has three parts, on the right is a garden scene and on the left are two rows of figures. In the upper scene King Zimrilim stands before the goddess Ishtar (standing on the back of a lion). Below two female water deities each proffer with both hands a plant growing out of a vase. Streams of water teeming with fish, flow through the goddesses clothes, they water the plants and continue to irrigate the land. The scene is there to show the desired continuity and fruitfulness of irrigated lands and gardens. This image of a water goddess holding a water pot is replicated in one of the most spectacular archaeological finds at Mari: a beautiful statue in white marble. Rivulets with fish were carved down both sides of her clothing, and the vase held close actually functioned as a fountain. A tank of water was located behind the statue and servants could top up the water level to keep the fountain working. Such items were usually placed in important locations, such as a throne room, or a garden setting.

The section of this fresco depicting a garden scene comprised two tall trees with a bird alighting on a branch. One of the trees is clearly a date palm, the other is rather schematic but its identity can be assumed to be a tamarisk. I say this because these two trees feature in a popular Mesopotamian story, which is a tale of one-upmanship.

> The king plants a date-palm in his palace and fills up the space beside her with a tamarisk. Meals are enjoyed in the shade of the tamarisk, skilled men gather in the shade of the date-palm, the drum is beaten, men give praise, and the king rejoices in his palace.
>
> The two trees, brother and sister, are quite different; the tamarisk and the palm-tree compete with each other. They argue and quarrel together. The tamarisk says: 'I am much bigger!' And the date-palm argues back, saying: 'I am much better than you! You, O tamarisk, are a useless tree. What good are your branches? There's no such thing as a tamarisk fruit! Now, my fruits grace the king's table; the king himself eats them, and people say nice things about me. I make a surplus for the gardener, and he gives it to the queen; she, being a mother, nourishes her child upon the gifts of my strength, and the adults eat them too. My fruits are always in the presence of royalty.'
>
> The tamarisk makes his voice heard; his speech is even more boastful. 'My body is superior to yours! It's much more beautiful than anything of yours. You are like a slavegirl who fetches and carries daily needs for her mistress.' He goes on to point out the king's table, couch, and eating bowl are made from tamarisk wood, that the king's clothes are made using tools of tamarisk wood; likewise the temples of the gods are full of objects made from tamarisk. The date-palm counters by pointing out that her fruits are the central offering in the cult; once they have been taken from the tamarisk dish, the bowl is used to collect up the garbage.[12]

This text highlights just how important both trees were to the economy of the region, and why they might have been chosen to appear in the fresco of the king's garden. Texts from Mari give details of the large quantities of food prepared for feasts in the city. Huge quantities of dates and pistachios were used for making *mersum*-cake, for instance. Kitchen deliveries were also made of apples, medlars, figs, pears, onions, garlic, coriander, cumin, saffron and mint; these indicate the variety of fruit, vegetables and spices, most of which must have been grown locally.[13]

A later governor of the district around Mari, named Shamashreshusur (8th century BC), recorded that he had 'planted palm trees in the courtyard of the palace in the town of Ribasharru.'[14] He also planted palm trees in another palace courtyard and in a shrine. He claims that he introduced [re-introduced] beekeeping, he says that he 'made them settle in the orchards of the town.'[15] He taught the gardeners how to tend them and collect the honey and wax.

A library of cuneiform texts was also discovered at Ugarit situated close to the Mediterranean Sea in north-west Syria. This ancient maritime city thrived from 1500–1200 BC. Researchers deciphering the texts have discovered that several mentioned trees and plants; some may have been traded and therefore reveal information on the economy of the city, but the plants also give a valuable snapshot of the botanical flora of this more westerly region of the Levant, as opposed to that of Mesopotamia. The citizens of Ugarit traded with the Canaanites for cedar and even ebony. Oak and ash are mentioned, but of the garden worthy trees the following can be identified: date palm, olive, zizyphus, terebinth, cypress, juniper, strawberry tree, pine tree, almond, tamarisk, plane, box, mulberry, pomegranate, wormwood, others are worded simply as just an aromatic tree. We also hear of 'the perfumes of seven tamarisks' and of a 'Farmstead of the Junipers.'[16] Of the possible garden flowers and herbs the following were mentioned in the Ugaritic texts: anemone, artemisia, black cumin, broom, buttercup, cane, caper-bush, clover, coriander, cress, fennel, garlic, hound's tongue, lentil, madder, marsh plant, mint, onion, primrose, ranunculus, rocket, sage, sesame, soapwort, spice plant, vetch.[17] Sadly some of the words in the texts refer to just a medicinal plant, a fragrant plant or an aromatic bush, without specifying the species concerned. There were remedies for ailments of horses, for instance to cure a horse from snakebite a concoction including juniper berries and hound's tongue was given. For someone who had fallen down drunk their hangover would have been cured by applying a poultice on their foreheads containing colocynth, olive oil and 'hair-of-a-dog', the latter (*sr klb*) once more was the useful herb hound's tongue.[18] One of the medicinal claims of *Cynoglossum* is to soothe the digestive organs.[19]

Depictions of early gardens on seal stones

Gardens or garden elements are actually depicted on a number of seal stones. One scene dating to the Akkadian Period that was carved on a shell seal stone (*c.*2470–2285 BC, now in the Louvre) features men working in a garden. As shell is a soft material it has worn badly but the details can still be made out. The scene is framed by two wide branching trees with blobs for leaves. A tall gardener tends a palm tree in the centre, while below another gardener bends down to water the trees and plants. On the right a man pulls the rope of a shaduf, its counterweight is partly raised.

FIGURE 37. Akkadian shell seal stone featuring gardeners tending trees while others carry pots to irrigate the plants in the garden, *c.*2470–2285 BC, now in the Louvre.

FIGURE 38. Impression from a seal stone depicting women in a garden picking dates.

A fragmentary seal stone from Susa shows that women may have worked in the groves too as they appear to be picking fruit. However in this case the trees are a similar height so the trees may be dwarf palms or fruit trees.[20] A third cylinder shaped seal stone made of jasper shows three women and two birds in a garden,[21] the women collect dates from the large central tree. Below its canopy are three different varieties of tree, one may be a dwarf palm but the other two are sadly unidentifiable.

Archaeological evidence for early gardens

Remains of Kurrat leeks have been found in Early Bronze Age levels at Jericho,[22] as these require regular watering it would suggest vegetable beds were provided nearby. Also at Jericho there was evidence for grape cultivation. In Deuteronomy (34.3) the city was dubbed the City of Palms which indicates the staple food here and the economy of the valley.

Apart from the Palm court at Mari (mentioned above) there is archaeological evidence for decorative gardens at Ugarit, on the north Syrian coast. This maritime city thrived, in part, from 1500–1200 BC. Within this large well-appointed palace the throne room was furnished with a fountain, and a nearby open court was fitted with a large stone-lined ornamental pool, the oldest known to date.[23] From there, a corridor led out to a rectangular garden that is today a riot of colour filled with wild flowers. When looking at the thick lush growth it is evident that the garden soil is still fertile as the flowers are thriving so well. The garden was partly enclosed by a low wall, with access through a series of pillars, the bases still survive. A large room opened onto this porticoed verdant garden, but we can only imagine what was once planted there. The palace was excavated before garden archaeology was practised therefore no botanical remains were recorded, but the excavators noted that as no remains of buildings were found below the garden soil this area must be counted as being a true garden.

Of the artefacts discovered from Ugarit a well preserved bronze tripod was found to have numerous little pomegranate fruit pendants dangling around its circular rim. It provides evidence that these tasty fruits were appreciated in this city. The tripod is now in the Louvre.

Gardens and plants mentioned in Bible sources

The Old Testament Bible can be used as a document relevant to the history of part of the Levant and within its many pages are a number of references to plants. Many of these refer to wild species, but the scriptures do mention some that could be counted as garden worthy varieties.[24]

Few passages actually recount details about actual gardens but the most famous of them all is the Garden of Eden, a garden in the East where:

> all kinds of trees grow out of the ground – trees that were pleasing to the eye and good for food. In the middle of the garden were the tree of life and the tree of the knowledge of good and evil. A river watering the garden flowed from Eden; from there it was separated into four headwaters...[25]

Only two of the trees can be specified in this orchard that was Eden, traditionally there was the forbidden apple that the snake tempted Eve to eat and a fig tree that clothed Adam and Eve's nakedness. This age old story (with Sumerian antecedents) would be referred to time and again through the centuries in Jewish, Christian and Muslim communities.

We know that King Solomon's palace in Jerusalem was located near the city walls and it was believed to have had a garden. One passage in the Bible mentions a concealed gateway in the garden that was used at times to escape when under siege (2 Kings 25.4), but the garden itself is not described. Later in *Ecclesiastes* King Solomon boasts 'I undertook great projects: I built houses for myself and planted vineyards. I made gardens and parks and planted all kinds of fruit in them. I made reservoirs to water groves of flourishing trees'.[26] He was known to love the peacefulness of a garden, and in Solomon's *Song of Songs* he uses similes to reveal how his beloved could be likened to the many plants growing within his beautiful gardens. In doing so he reveals the most prized plant species of that time:

> You are a garden locked up, my sister, my bride; you are a spring enclosed, a sealed fountain. Your plants are an orchard of pomegranates with choice fruits, with henna and nard, nard and saffron, calamus and cinnamon, with every kind of incense tree, with myrrh and aloes and all the finest spices. You are a garden fountain, a well of flowing water streaming down from Lebanon. Awake, north wind, and come, south wind! Blow on my garden, that its fragrance may spread abroad.[27]

In another passage the narrator says 'My lover has gone down to his garden, to the beds of spices, to browse in the gardens and to gather lilies.'[28] He hints at orchards when he recounts that 'I went down to the grove of nuts to look at the new growth in the valley, to see if the vines had budded or the pomegranates were in bloom.'[29] Other garden plants mentioned in the Song of Solomon include the rose of Sharon, the lily of the valleys, apple trees, palms and mandrakes. Some of the plants named in the King James Bible differ from later translations (such as the New International Version used here) as translators seek to clarify the meaning of passages. However both versions list crocus flowers which features in Isaiah (35.1); myrtle, caraway and cummin;[30] and hyssop 'that grows out of the walls;'[31] the sycomore fig;[32] tamarisk;[33] vines, figs and olives;[34] a broom tree under which Elijah fell asleep;[35] the flowers of the field;[36] bitter herbs (meaning wormwood);[37] and Aaron's staff that sprouted into an almond tree;[38] also the spices, myrrh and balm from Gilead.[39] A notable change in the newer translation is Jonah's gourd tree which is now a vine.

Jonathan's parable (Judges 9.8–14) concerns a group of trees that ask three named trees in turn if they would be their king. Each tree replies, in a similar fashion to the Mesopotamian tale of rivalry between the date palm and tamarisk (mentioned above). The first was the olive who answered 'Should I give up my oil, by which both gods and men are honoured, to hold sway over the trees?' The fig responded thus: 'Should I give up my fruit, so good and sweet ...' The vine also declined 'Should I give up my wine, which cheers both gods and men ...'[40] The emphasis on these three trees, the olive, fig and vine is primarily for their association with religion and ritual libations but they were also of vital importance to the region, and would have been nurtured in cultivated areas and gardens.

In 1 Kings.21 we hear that King Ahab coveted Naboth's vineyard as it was close to his palace. Ahab thought to convert it into a vegetable garden, but Naboth famously refused. Another vineyard and a lodge within a cucumber/melon garden is mentioned in Isaiah (1.8). In this period vegetable gardens, like palm groves, tended to be located outside of the city but close to a water source.

Leviticus (23.39–40) details preparations for the Jewish Feast of the Tabernacles celebrated annually on the fifteenth day of the seventh month. This important week-long festival celebrates the arrival of the Jews into the Promised Land, and as part of the celebrations traditional plant offerings are ritually made. One is a bundle of twigs being representative of the four species found by the Israelites, these are the *lulav* (a palm branch), *hadas* (myrtle), *arava* (willow) and *etrog* (citron), which all still hold great significance for Jewish people. There was also a basket symbolically containing the seven First Fruits which included pomegranates, figs, dates, grapes in the form of wine, olives in the form of olive oil, wheat and barley. The distinctive Menorah candlestick used by all Jewish people is believed to have developed from the pattern of branches seen growing on a sage bush.

FIGURE 39. An Assyrian minor deity is seen fertilising a much stylised sacred date palm tree, with bucket and pollinating tool in hand.

Evidence for Assyrian gardens

Assyrian deities

The Assyrians worshipped many different gods including the goddess Ishtar and a creator-god named Ashur. They also venerated a form of the 'tree of life', and several stone carved reliefs display the Assyrian version of this theme. The tree is usually very stylised, but again is meant to represent a palm tree. Many of these also depict a god in the act of fertilising the tree, reflecting practices still current. Date palm trees are able to cross pollinate, but to ensure large quantities of dates it was found necessary to climb each tree to fertilise each flower by hand (as seen in the earlier fragmentary fresco from Mari). In Assyria the gods are regularly shown with a bucket and pollinator tool in their hands.

Temple gardens

As mentioned above, some temples were provided with a sacred grove or garden. We even hear how the conquering Assyrian king Assurbanipal rased the city of Susa and destroyed the city's temple and entered an Elamite 'secret grove' of their goddess.[41]

Archaeologists have discovered evidence for the extensive introduction of trees both in the court of the New Year Festival Temple located a little to the north of Assur as well as in the immediate surroundings of this important sacred structure. The complex is dated to the reign of Sennacherib (704–681 BC). The trees, more than 2000 in number, were planted in regular rows of rock-cut circular pits each 1.5 m deep, but sadly no remains survived to identify which species were planted there.[42] Rock-cut water conduits were also introduced throughout the planted areas in order to irrigate the trees. Temple gardens were seen as beautiful havens, to glorify the gods and give them a pleasing ambience in which to stroll. They also made excellent trysting places, as this Mesopotamian text reveals.

> The shade of the cedar … is the king's shelter.
> The shade of the cypress is for nobles.
> The shade of the juniper is shelter for my Nabu and for my games!
> For what, O what, are you dressed up, my Tashmetu?
> So that I may go into the garden with you, my Nabu,
> let me go into the garden, into the garden to my lord.
> Let me go alone into the beautiful garden …
> May my ears hear the song of your birds …
> Let my Tashmetu come with me into the garden.[43]

Inscriptional evidence for Assyrian gardens

Few ancient illustrations actually depict gardens, but we know that gardens existed, the texts confirm this. Trees were so highly prized that they were sometimes listed as plunder or tribute after a battle. As far back as *c.*1000 BC King Tiglathpileser I recorded his achievements for posterity in inscriptions carved on stone stelae, as well as on clay tablets.

> I took cedar, box-tree, and Kanish oak from the lands over which I had gained dominion – such trees as none among previous kings, my forefathers, had ever planted – and I planted [them] in the orchards of my land. I took rare orchard fruit which is not found in my land and filled the orchards of Assyria.[44]

This dissemination of plant species continued under Assurnasirpal II who, in the 9th century BC, used them in his newly created garden at Nimrud. An inscription recording his achievements gives an insight into the type and range of plants used in royal Assyrian gardens at that time.

> I dug out a canal from the Upper Zab, cutting through a mountain peak, and called it Abundance Canal. I watered the meadows of the Tigris and planted orchards with all kinds of fruit trees in the vicinity. I planted seeds and plants that I had found in the countries through which I had marched and in the highlands which I had crossed: pines of different kinds, cypresses and junipers of different kinds, almonds, dates, ebony, rosewood, olive, oak, tamarisk, walnut, terebinth and ash, fir, pomegranate, pear, quince, fig, grapevine …
>
> The canal-water gushes from above into the gardens; fragrance pervades the walkways, streams of water as numerous as the stars of heaven flow in the pleasure garden … Like a squirrel I pick fruit in the garden of delights.[45]

A tribute list describing the quantity of fruit trees sent to Sargon II in the 8th century BC shows a continuing interest in arboriculture/horticulture.

> I have levied upon the people of Nemad-Istar the supply of 2,350 loads of apple trees, and 450 loads of medlar trees. [The people of Suhu province] are collecting saplings of almond, quince and plum trees, and they are transporting them to Dur-Sharrukin. The people of Suhu are also bringing saplings from the land of Laqe: 1,000 loads of apple trees …[46]

Sargon (in 714 BC) also makes some comments on the town of Ulhu in Urartu, and we realise that many other towns were provided with gardens: 'the gardens which were the pleasant feature of the city, loaded with fruit and bunches of grapes …'[47] Often land was provided outside the town beside the river for the creation of private individual gardens, mainly as an orchard or potager-style vegetable garden, as seen in a relief showing the Elamite town of Madahtu. This town was enclosed by walls. The river, swimming with fish, made a loop right round the town. Two kinds of trees are shown (palms and fruit trees) they highlight the location of the extramural gardens, and the proximity of these gardens to the river indicates that the river was their source of water for irrigation.

Reliefs depicting elements of an Assyrian garden

There are a series of ancient stone reliefs from Nineveh, the Assyrian capital (just outside Mosul in northern Iraq) which mainly record the military campaigns of their kings, but fortunately some also depict landscape and garden themes. A relief now in the Louvre, shows an almost life-size Assyrian man holding a bunch of poppies in one hand, but stands with his other hand raised as if to salute the tree directly in front. This was a flowering fruit tree of some kind, the blooms resemble lily-like flowers, but it is possible that it was meant to represent an idealised fruit tree.

Another relief is believed to represent the famous garden created by Sargon II (722–705 BC). He established a new capital at Khorsabad (12 km north-east of Mosul in northern Iraq). In the important central position of this garden scene there appears to be a garden pavilion beside a boating lake. Texts mention how Sargon II introduced a new portico-style palace 'In the manner of the Hittites', so this could well commemorate his particular achievement as well as

FIGURE 40. Sargon's garden at Khorsabad, with a *bitanu* pavilion and boating lake.

the beautiful garden he created. To the right of the lake and building, there is a tree covered hill frequented by birds, and on the summit of this hillock stands an altar located in the traditional position on a 'high place'.

Sargon's son Sennacherib (dated 704–681 BC) returned to Nineveh and built his own new palace and gardens there. He constructed an aqueduct to bring water to his spacious capital with its many gardens; remains of the aqueduct have been found at Jerwan. A detailed commemorative relief was made by his grandson Assurbanipal commemorating the great achievements of Sennacherib (it is now in the British Museum). The relief includes, in the top right hand corner, an image of Sennacherib's great engineering feat – the new aqueduct bringing an abundant supply of water to Nineveh. The water channel was carried on an arched support. Fish swim in the water that flowed towards the columned frontage of a pavilion, and then diverts into several channels to irrigate the whole garden below. Sennacherib himself may be represented on a freestanding stone stela that stands beside the pavilion, so his figure would seem to look over his garden. There are tall trees beside the aqueduct channel and along the slope of the hill, but otherwise there are only three different varieties of tree here. The oval-shaped trees may represent pine trees, while the more wide spreading trees could be fruit trees. Small bushes are shown growing below the canopy of the trees.

FIGURE 41. Sennacherib's garden at Nineveh, depicted in a relief from Assurbanipal's palace. An aqueduct (top right) brings water to irrigate the arboretum style garden, mid-7th century BC, British Museum.

A straight path led up the hill to the palace, an altar is sited close to the palace almost blocking the path. We can compare this idyllic scene with Sennacherib's own description of his garden:

> [The royal gardens contained aromatic trees and fruit trees] such as grow in the mountains and in Babylonia… all the aromatics of Syria (Hatti)… every type of wild vine and exotic fruit tree, aromatics and olive trees, on the (newly) broken land which is beside the game park…(*ambassi*).[48]

Water channels are also mentioned, but the bulk of the description is quite different to what we see in the image. He describes how he made a marsh with cane-brakes which he stocked with wildfowl and animals, but this is not represented in the surviving section of the garden relief, and the text implies that a large part of Sennacherib's garden must have been a game park, set apart from his arboretum, rather than the ornamental garden we have just seen. A second relief shows a clearer representation of the variety of trees that are likely to have been cultivated in his garden. From left to right we can make out: a heavily laden grapevine, a pine tree, fig tree, another pine tree and a pomegranate tree. At the bottom of the rocky hillock there is a small date palm and another pomegranate.

The creation of a garden was evidently regarded as a statement of power, somewhere to display your trophies, botanical, faunal or otherwise. Royal gardens were places to hunt in yet there were quieter areas in gardens where they could entertain out of doors. The latter is illustrated in a revealing relief (*c.*650 BC) from Nineveh. It shows Assurbanipal and his queen quaffing wine and feasting in their garden. They are attended by numerous servants and musicians. Vines provide shade for the diners; the vine arbour is created by twining the vine stems around the trunk of a nearby tree. This method of growing vines using a supporting tree was often used in this region. This idyllic scene is set in an arboretum composed of alternating date palms and pine trees, but this is marred by reminders of the warlike nature of the Assyrians. Trophies such as an enemy's decapitated head were hung onto branches in the trees nearby!

FIGURE 42. Assurbanipal and his queen quaffing wine and feasting in their garden, attended to by numerous servants and musicians. They are shaded from the hot sun by vines twining up two pine trees, mid-7th century BC, British Museum.

Names of gardens and gardeners

From the cuneiform tablets we know that there were at least two Assyrian names for a garden, which were in fact an adoption of a Sumerian word. The first was *kiri* or *kirû*, (dating back to *c.*1200 BC) this was mainly used when mentioning an arboretum or botanical form of garden; while the *kirimahu* was a term used when referring to an ornamental or pleasure garden; this was first used by Sargon II.[49] In the annals of King Sennacherib we hear that he created a fine *kirimahu* beside his palace at Nineveh. A game park was known as an *ambassi*. The garden pavilions or kiosks seen in the relief carvings were called a *bitanu*,[50] a name which might relate to the *bit hilani* of the Neo Hittites who lived in the area of Northern Syria/South-East Turkey. Sargon mentions this word when recording for posterity his building achievements at Khorsabad, he says: 'a portico patterned after a Hittite palace, which they call a *bit hilâni* in the Amorite tongue.'[51] This appellation is also confirmed in inscriptions referring to King Esarhaddon's building works at Nineveh (*c.*680–669 BC) where one part was called a *bitanu* and the garden (the *kirimahu*) was planted around it and the palace.[52]

Gardeners (male and female) are mentioned in some of the Assyrian texts; the Assyrian word for a gardener was *nukaribbu*, a female gardener was called a *nukaribbatu*.[53] We hear of a Judean gardener held in Babylon by Nebuchadnezzar II who was given palace rations, this must have been because he had particular skills.[54] Large numbers of gardeners were needed in the fields and in palm groves and some of these would have been slaves, but the profession of gardener is attested in all periods. Records show that most were not slaves but were employed and were paid for their work, which was often specified.

A vegetable/medicinal garden

Plant remains were noted in excavations at Nimrud these included evidence for dates, figs, grapes, hazelnuts, olive and pomegranates, but the only vegetables that could be identified came from two seeds of cucumber.[55]

However details of an actual vegetable garden have survived in a late 8th century BC Babylonian cuneiform tablet describing the contents of the garden of the Babylonian King Merodarch Baladan (British Museum, Tablet No. 46226). Sixty-seven plants were listed and appear in two columns that are subdivided into groups (with 3–7 plants listed in each group), these groups perhaps represented individual plant beds. A special sign was added at the end of most of the plant names which informed that the plant was either strong-smelling or aromatic.[56] Sadly, only 26 plant names have been identified with certainty and these are ones you would find in a vegetable or medicinal garden rather than in a pleasure garden. The list probably forms a record of what was actually in the king's kitchen garden. The identifiable plants were: leeks, onion, garlic, lettuce, radish, cucumber, gherkin, cardamom, caraway, dill, thyme, oregano, fennel, coriander, cumin, fenugreek, rue, colocynth, sagapenum and lucerne.[57] The plants were identified by comparing them against Aramaic/Syriac plant names, many of these were studied by Thompson and others *c.*1902–1924.

An Assyrian Herbal

Thompson applied all his extensive linguistic skills to the 660 tablets of Assyrian Medical texts (some dating as far back as the 19th century BC). The majority of the texts were found at Nineveh, but others were discovered in excavations at Assur, Babylon, Borsippa, Nippur, Ur and Uruk. The cuneiform clay tablets give a great deal of information on drugs obtained from herbs and other plants. So, in Assyria and Babylonia there would also have been gardens not only laid out into herb and vegetable beds, but also ones to provide medicinal supplies. A physician was called an *asu*, and an exorcist cum healer using magic spells was an *ashipu*.[58] To most Assyrians the art of healing was mysterious and because they were so superstitious the two practitioners often worked together. Over 250 plants have been identified by Thompson in the Assyrian Herbal. Several of the species listed also have an ornamental value. The *kasû* (the rose) was mentioned 181 times in the medical texts; it is thought to have originated in Persia, and was perhaps a rarity in Mesopotamia, apart from garden contexts.[59] Often its scent is mentioned and in many cases it was used in the form of rose water. Another ancient contender for the rose is the *amurdinnu*, and this name is thought to have survived into the Arabic word for rose (*ward*). It is possible that two species of rose were cultivated – one being the briar rose or *rosa phoenicia*.

There are 106 occurrences of the word for tamarisk (*binu*) which was mostly applied externally to reduce swellings. Citrus appears ten times, presumably this was the citron which is the oldest form of this fruit family, and a lemon-like pip was actually found at Nippur. Apparently the name given to this fruit was Sumerian and has been translated as 'Juice of Might' which is a testimony to its usefulness.[60] The laurel (our bay) was used to fumigate the ears, eyes and temples. It could also be drunk and used as a stomachic! The mandrake appears here too, and was called *namtar.ira*, and this was used for toothache and for jaundice. The apricot was well known, there was even a Sumerian word for it (*ma gunu.kur.ra*), in Assyrian it was *armânu*, which later became armeniaca in Latin.[61] The name is often considered to reflect the region of the fruit's origin being Armenia.

The Hanging Gardens of Babylon

We could say that the Hanging Gardens of Babylon were the culmination of garden art in ancient Mesopotamia; they were thought to be so spectacular that they were later included in the famous list of 'The Wonders of the Ancient World'. The legend that surrounds these gardens says that they were built by King Nebuchadnezzar in the 6th century BC. He had them built on tiered terraces, supposedly because his wife was homesick for the forests and mountains of her native Media (an area of modern Iran). The surviving texts describing these beautiful gardens mostly dwell on the construction of the substructures and its water supply and do not give a full picture of their overall appearance. People have therefore automatically visualised the gardens as looking like a mountain or the ziggurat of Babylon (a step-like structure with a temple on top). No contemporary illustration or text about these gardens has survived.

Numerous romantic artistic interpretations have been attempted over the years based on surviving texts, although these are of a later date – mostly Greek and Roman. As the site of the gardens has not been conclusively identified there has been some controversy as to their location. Archaeologists have had considerable difficulties, partly because the modern city has encroached and because most buildings in this region were made with dried mud brick, which has largely crumbled away. Ancient records mention the use of stone in parts of the supporting structure of the gardens. The gardens were also noted as being close to the River. A possible area with extremely thick foundations was discovered but that is now discounted as it is thought to have been used as storerooms. Some people have suggested that the tall many tiered ziggurat temple of the god Marduk had plants growing on its terraces and may have been the hanging gardens. The Terraced gardens would need considerable foundations and therefore the most likely site lies to the north of the massive 'Western Outwork' near the Northern Palace where there is perhaps such a site that would allow a series of terraces stepping down to a large courtyard below.[62] The effect would appear to resemble one or two slopes of a hillside, and that at least would reflect the description given by Diodorus Siculus in the 1st century BC (see below).

Some scholars (such as S. Dalley) have suggested that these famous gardens were not in Babylon at all, but were a remembrance of the beautiful gardens built by Sennacherib at Nineveh. However, Nineveh fell to the Medes and Babylonians in 612 BC and the city was thoroughly sacked. So the Graeco-Roman historians writing after the conquests of Alexander the Great in the 4th century BC (300 years later) were not likely to be aware of gardens at Nineveh. Alexander did not actually go near Nineveh, which was abandoned at that time. He eventually chose Babylon as his main residence and he would probably have made the city his capital if he had lived longer. The Graeco-Roman ancient sources utilised earlier accounts that had been made by men who accompanied Alexander throughout his conquests, such as the philosopher and historian Onesicritus. Also, the important commentator Berossus, a Persian historian (4th–3rd century BC) was used as a source by the Jewish writer Josepheus and others; Berossus was a scholar and had been a priest of Marduk in Babylon. Therefore we can imagine that Berossus would have been well placed to describe the gardens correctly, and interestingly both he and Josepheus mention that the gardens were built by Nebuchadnezzar not Sennacherib, which implies they were located at Babylon not Nineveh.

One thing that is certain is that they would be close to the river to provide a regular water supply to adequately irrigate all the plants. This is how the Greek geographer Strabo records it in the 1st century BC:

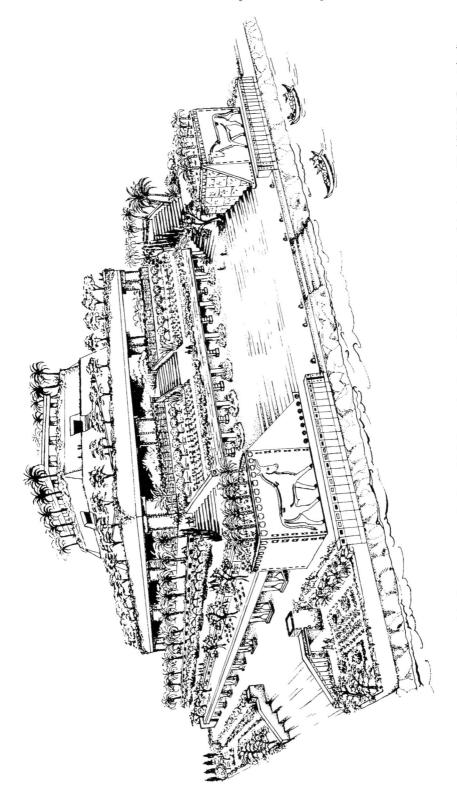

FIGURE 43. Reconstruction of the famous Hanging Gardens of Babylon, said to be one of the 'Seven Wonders of the Ancient World' (© G. Carmichael).

The ascent to the uppermost terrace-roofs is made by a stairway; and alongside these stairs there were screws [waterscrew pumps], through which the water was continually conducted up into the garden from the Euphrates by those appointed for this purpose. For the river, a stadium in width, flows through the middle of the city; and the garden is on the bank of the river.[63]

Quintus Curtius writing in the 1st century AD explained that the gardens were:

as high as the top of the walls and owe their charm to the shade of many trees. The columns supporting the whole edifice are built of rock, and on top of them is a flat surface of squared stones strong enough to bear the deep layer of earth placed upon it and the water used for irrigating it. So stout are the trees the structure supports that their trunks are eight cubits thick and their height as much as fifty feet; they bear fruit as abundantly, as if they were growing in their natural environment.[64]

Philo of Byzantium was an engineer working around 250 BC; from his description of the gardens we would easily believe that he had been to this city, seen the gardens and studied the structure himself. The base and foundations needed to be strong enough to carry the weight of moist soil and trees. Apparently palm trunks were used for beams as this wood tended not to rot as easily as others, and it would have been locally grown. Philo details the provision of water to various levels, which appears to be partly by using a waterscrew. He also mentions that these gardens were well stocked:

This structure supports an extensive and deep mass of earth, in which are planted broad-leaved trees of the sort that are commonly found in gardens, a wide variety of flowers of all species and, in brief, everything that is most agreeable to the eye and conducive to the enjoyment of pleasure. The whole area is ploughed in the same way as solid ground, and is just as suitable as other soil for grafting and propagation. Thus it happens that a ploughed field lies above the heads of those who walk between the columns below ... and its most striking feature is that the labour of cultivation is suspended above the heads of the spectators.[65]

Diodorus Siculus writing in the 1st century BC gives more indications of the shape of the structure supporting the gardens, his is the fullest description:

since the approach to the garden sloped like a hillside and the several parts of the structure rose from one another tier on tier, the appearance of the whole resembled that of a theatre. When the ascending terraces had been built, there had been constructed beneath them galleries which carried the entire weight of the planted garden and rose little by little one above the other along the approach; and the uppermost gallery, which was fifty cubits high, bore the highest surface of the park, which was made level with the circuit wall of the battlements of the city. Furthermore the walls, which had been constructed at great expense, were twenty-two feet thick, while the passageway between each two walls was ten feet wide... [*he gives details of its construction... the terraces were*] thickly planted with trees of every kind that, by their great size or any other charm, could give pleasure to the beholder. And since the galleries, each projecting beyond another, all received the light, they contained many royal lodges of every description; and there was one gallery which contained openings leading from the topmost surface and machines for supplying the gardens with water, the machines raising the water in great abundance from the river, although no one outside could see it being done.[66]

Travellers' tales, ancient or modern, do not lose in the telling, but it must be significant that the structure chosen as one of the Wonders of the World was not the huge walls, palaces or ziggurats of Babylon, but its garden.

The Mesopotamian cultures understood the use of shade planting, artificial pollination, large scale irrigation, and the use of land as an amenity. Evidence seems to suggest that Mesopotamian gardens were mostly to be found in association with royal palaces. However gardens were also planted around important temples and public gardens were planted next to rivers. There appears to be four main forms of garden used by these cultures: a combined orchard/produce garden, an arboretum, a game park and a pleasure garden. Trees were highly valued and many were brought from distant lands to enrich the gardens of Assyria. However, there is little emphasis on the cultivation of flowers other than of herbs. Few flowers are depicted in reliefs or elsewhere, the majority of plant images are of trees, but one of the most clearly defined images of a flower is seen in a relief of a lily from Nineveh dating to the reign of Assurbanipal. In this scene lilies and a daisy-like flower are shown beside a pair of lions! Flowers may have been planted in selected areas of pleasure gardens, aromatics are often mentioned, and occasionally a flower of some kind is shown in the hand of an individual (*i.e.* in the hands of Assurbanipal and his queen reclining in their garden) but individual flowers may have seemed less important than trees.

However, a testimony to the horticultural legacy of Mesopotamian cultures is that a number of their plant names have survived into modern times, by evolving through the Greek, Roman and Arabic languages. Among those studied by Thompson in his *Assyrian Herbal* are: Apricot, Crataegus azarolus, Asafoetida, Saffron, Liquidamber, Colocynth, Carob, Cardamon, Cummin, Tumeric, Cherry, Silphium, Phaseolus, Myrrh, Mulberry, Mandrake, Almond, Poppy, Styrax, Sesame and Cypress.[67]

Examples of the Evolution of Plant Names

Sumerian/Assyrian	Greek/Latin	Modern Name
Armânu	Armeniaca	Apricot
Arzallu	[Azarolus]	Crataegus azarolus
As	[Asa]	Asafoetida
Kamunu	Cuminum	Cumin
Kurkanû	Curcuma	Turmeric
Lasirbitu	Laserpicium	Silphium
Murru	Murra	Myrrh
Namtar Ira	Mandragoras	Mandrake
Nušḫu	Nux amara	Nut/Almond
Pa.pa	Papaver	Poppy
Šamaššammu	Sesamum	Sesame
Ṣarbatu	Stobrus/Styrax	Storax

Because the region encompassed in this chapter is so large I have used two columns in the list of garden plants of this period. One column highlights plants that were growing in the western part, the Levant (such as those from Ugarit and the Bible lands). The next column lists plants from the eastern section known as Mesopotamia (this includes Mari, Sumer, Assyria and Babylonia). The two columns will then reflect the climatic difference that would affect the choice of plants, and also the different cultures.

Achaemenid Persian gardens

Under the leadership of Cyrus the Great, the Achaemenid Persians of the mid-6th century BC conquered the Medes in *c.*550 BC and then the Babylonians in 539 BC. (Earlier, the joint forces of the Medes and the Babylonians had sacked Nineveh, the last capital of Assyria in 612 BC). The Persians consolidated their many gains and expanded their empire until it encompassed modern Turkey, Syria, Lebanon, Egypt, Iraq, Iran, and parts of the Indian subcontinent and central Asia. The empire lasted from 550–330 BC.

Archaeological discoveries of Achaemenid gardens

Circa 546 BC Cyrus the Great founded a number of palatial buildings in an idyllic garden setting at Pasargadae (in south-western Iran) from which he ruled his vast Empire. This is the only royal ancient Persian garden that has been thoroughly excavated by archaeologists. The core of the site was situated in what was a vast park. Within this area there were many open sided porticoed pavilions. In such a hot and dry country there was a need to catch any breeze that could be found during the long summer months and deep shaded porticoes were a welcome amenity. The site was situated on a largely level plain that could be irrigated from a nearby river, and archaeologists discovered a series of stone water channels in the gardens. The water channels were 25 cm wide and at about 14 m intervals the channels widened into square basins that were 80 cm in width.[68] The main garden was that sited next to a structure that archaeologists referred to as Palace P. The rectangular-shaped garden measured 230 × 200 m. There was a broad path around the main part of the garden, although it was narrower on the south side. The water channels were laid around the outer perimeter of the garden, then crossed the outer path to irrigate the central, rectangular garden. There is also evidence to suggest that some of the principal water channels and an open line of sight on the long axis of the garden combined to divide the garden into four separate compartments or 'parterres'. Also, since Cyrus took the ancient Mesopotamian title 'king of the Four Quarters' when he conquered Babylon, the plan of the royal garden may have been seen to represent the empire in microcosm. Such a quadripartite garden pattern appears to have lived on in the fourfold design of the Islamic Persian garden: the *chahar bagh* (or *chaharbagh*).

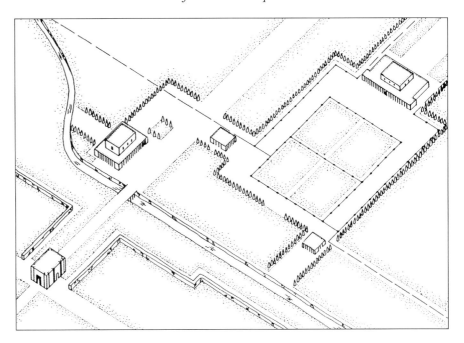

FIGURE 44. A reconstruction of the large formal gardens at Cyrus's palace at Pasargadae. A wide path encircles one section of the garden, and stone-lined water channels combine with an open, longitudinal line of sight to divide the central part into four quarters. (Stronach 1989, fig. 3).

Botanical evidence for plants grown in the garden at Pasargadae is sadly lacking. This is partly due to the fact that the whole area of the garden was subject to deep ploughing for some 15 years before the last major excavations began. However, testimony from the time of Alexander's first visit to the site in 330 BC indicates that there were many trees in the vicinity of Cyrus's tomb. As Arrian, drawing on earlier sources, has indicated the tomb 'was in the royal park at Pasargadae; a grove of various sorts of trees had been planted around it; there were streams of running water and a meadow with lush grass.'[69]

Unlike Pasargadae, where gardens appear to have surrounded the various palaces and pavilions, the elevated terrace of the later Achaemenid capital, Persepolis, was marked by more limited garden spacing. In part of the site, in an area that accommodated the private palace of Darius I (522–486 BC), archaeologists found a stone water channel and a carved basin. Plant pits have also been discovered, and one of the documents found during excavations lists types of trees and seeds that were presumably cultivated in the area. A fountain and water channels found outside the complex could perhaps also indicate the presence of an irrigated landscape park.

Far to the west, the remains of a palace and garden that once belonged to a Persian satrap (or governor) have also come to light at Ramat Rahel near Jerusalem (although there was an earlier Assyrian presence in the same location). This site featured an advanced irrigation system based on the careful collection of rainwater. Attempts to discover botanical evidence from soil samples proved futile, but specialists succeeded in recovering ancient samples of pollen in a plaster coat that had been applied to the ancient pools and water channels at some point in the 5th–4th centuries BC. As the plaster was drying windblown pollen from flowering plants in the vicinity settled on the still damp plaster where it was trapped and was eventually recovered intact. The species represented in this way included: birch trees, cedar of Lebanon, citron, fig, grape vine, myrtle, olive, poplar, Persian walnut, waterlilies and willow.[70] The cedar and citron would have been imported for their aromatic qualities as well as being exotics. The finding of citron/etrog caused great excitement as it plays such a valued role in the Jewish feast of Sukkot (the Feast of the Tabernacles), and this is the first archaeologically attested example discovered in Israel. In addition, the on-going excavations have shown that the garden covered a large area that flanked the palace on three sides.

In the valleys of their upland homeland the Persians could divert water from rivers into canals to irrigate their fields and gardens. In a hot climate this could lead (as it often did in Mesopotamian cultures) to a build up of salinity in the soil. At the same time the Persians also employed an entirely different system of irrigation, especially in the dry internally draining basins of the Iranian Plateau. This latter system involved the use of long underground channels or *qanats*. A *qanat* consists of a gently sloping tunnel that starts at the bottom where water is needed and extends back towards higher ground where the tunnel taps into water-bearing strata. Water is then conducted by gravity flow, where it seeps into the upper end of the tunnel, to an outlet and an irrigation canal at the lower end. Viewed from the air, the most distinctive feature of a *qanat* is the alignment of its ventilation shafts, each of which is surrounded by earth that was removed in the course of its construction and maintenance; with this system fresh cool mountain water could be brought straight to a settlement, garden or field. In addition, such long underground channels reduced the loss of precious water through evaporation. The Achaemenid Persians are thought to have introduced the *qanat* into the western and southern oases of Egypt (under Darius *c.*490 BC)[71] where its employment substantially enlarged the areas that could be cultivated.

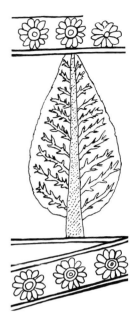

FIGURE 45. Relief at Persepolis representing cypress trees, early 5th century BC.

Depictions of trees and plants in the Achaemenid period

Few plants are depicted in Persian art, but at Persepolis a limited range of plants appear in a series of carved reliefs that survived the fire that destroyed large parts of the site in 330 BC. In, for example, the finely carved reliefs of the east staircase of the Apadana (the great audience Hall) each of the subject peoples from different parts of the empire is separated from the next delegation by a stylised tree. The trees are all depicted in the same way and they could be representative of a cypress with branches, needles and cones. The different registers of the same relief are also separated by horizontal bands that are decorated with rosettes; and some writers have suggested that these 12-petalled rosettes could represent a lotus flower. The king, nobles and other individuals are frequently shown holding a lotus flower/bud in one hand.

The pomegranate is native to Persia and accordingly it was given high status. Its distinctively shaped fruit is frequently seen in Achaemenid art. One example is the small model pomegranates that adorned a pair of gold earrings excavated at Pasargadae in 1963.[72]

Literary evidence for gardens of the Achaemenid Persians

Major Achaemenid gardens also appear to have existed in the vicinity of Sardis, Sidon, and Susa. While Susa was chosen as one of the new capitals of the Achaemenid empire by Darius I (522–486 BC), it was under a later king that the Biblical story of Esther was set there; she was made Queen by Assuerus (who may have been King Artaxerxes). The palace at Susa (Biblical Sushan) is described as having a 'court of the garden of the *bîtan*' where a feast was held. The *bîtan* is a local variant of the word *bitanu* (which as we have seen is used to distinguish a pavilion or porticoed kiosk).[73] Although this garden is mentioned several times there is no indication how it was planted, but there is a reasonable possibility that it would have been filled with shade trees.

Another bible story, of Susanna and the Elders in Daniel (13.15–18) is set during the period of Persian rule. The narrative takes place in a walled orchard garden. We hear of a pool, or water source, within the garden where Susanna goes to wash herself. At this point the elders spy on her! As in earlier cultures Persian gardens could be functional enclosed ones, where palms, fruit trees and vegetables were tended, but other Persian gardens could be more luxurious with the addition of multiple quadrilateral spaces.

The remainder of the literature concerning the gardens of the Persian Empire comes from Graeco-Roman sources, partly as a result of the Macedonian conquest of the Persian Empire by Alexander the Great in 330 BC. Writers were primarily interested in the events of Alexander's campaign against the Persians rather than their surroundings. A history called the *Babyloniaka* written in Greek *c.*280 BC by the Babylonian scholar Berossus might have provided further details of Persian life and perhaps horticulture too, but sadly it has not survived. Fortunately Berossus was on occasion quoted by later writers.

We know that the Persians were fortunate that they had the legacy of plant collection and gardening from the Assyrian and Babylonian cultures before them, and there was a long history of care for trees in this part of the world. Apparently all Persians, including the king, were given training in horticulture and arboriculture. One incident that highlights the care given to a particular fine specimen of a tree is mentioned by the ancient Greek historian Herodotus, he reveals that when King Xerxes was travelling to Sardis 'he came across a plane-tree of such beauty that he was moved to decorate it with golden ornaments and to appoint a guardian for it in perpetuity.'[74] Later, his son King Artaxerxes reveals a similar love for trees. One day he and his army were out on manoeuvres in very cold weather. They became so close to death that he allowed his men to enter one of his own domains 'where there were gardens and parks of great extent and beauty ...'[75] Artaxerxes then told his men to cut trees down to make fires so they could keep themselves alive. The soldiers were loath to touch trees of such size and beauty, so the king had to take an axe himself to force them to save themselves. Such was their fondness for arboriculture that they were loath to cut such fine specimens of trees.

A satrap, who was a governor of a specific area, would have had a luxurious palace complex that would not have been considered furnished without a garden. One source says: 'Now country houses in that part of the world possess ample grounds attractively planted with trees, a special source of pleasure for kings and satraps.'[76] We hear of the gardens of the satrap Tissaphernes of the late 5th century BC. His garden is said to have: 'excelled in beauty, and was remarkable for the salubrity of its streams and freshness of its meadows, which was set off with pavilions royally adorned, and retirements finished in the most elegant taste.'[77]

The ancient Persian word for a garden was *pairidaeza*, which literally means a walled garden (*pairi* = around and *daeza* = wall). The Greeks when trying to pronounce this word called them a *paradeisos* (plural: *paradeisoi*). Later the Romans translated this word into Latin, and it has now come down to us as a paradise. References do indicate the *pairidaeza* lived up to our concept of paradise.

Xenophon, was the first Greek writer (*c.*394 BC) to exclaim with wonder at the 'beauty of the trees' he actually saw growing in Persian *paradeisoi* gardens. He had previously served as a mercenary officer who had fought in a contingent of 10,000 Greek mercenaries for a claimant to the Persian throne. He however did notice things along the way, and after his return to Greece he wrote about the beautiful garden of Cyrus (a later prince, not Cyrus the Great) located near Sardis. Xenophon gives some vital clues on the appearance of the special gardens of Cyrus. He mentions how the trees were well spaced in straight rows and that the fruiting and non-fruiting trees were planted separately. He was also impressed by 'the multitude of sweet scents that clung round them as they walked.'[78] When praised on the gardener's skill in measuring the distance between the trees Cyrus cheerfully said that 'the whole of the measurement and arrangement is my own work, and I did some of the planting myself.' Cyrus confessed that he spent as much time as he could in his gardens, and that wherever he went he would reside in or near a *paradeisos* 'stocked with trees and all other beautiful plants that the soil produces.'[79]

Ancient sources mention a town called *Triparadeisos*, which was a rendezvous for several Hellenistic armies in 321 BC. The name is interesting because it implies that there would have been three paradise gardens there, but sadly no description of the place was given. From the itinerary given in the text of Diodorus Siculus (XVIII, 39) we can locate the town in upper Syria, but even its exact whereabouts is not known today. Strabo places a similarly named town called *Paradeisus* in this vicinity in the land of the Apameans.[80] The two towns could in fact be one and the same, and the land around Apamea is very lush and fertile being close to the River Orontes. A good water supply would have been necessary for three large paradise gardens.

FIGURE 46. A Persian style *paradeisos* game park depicted in a fresco at Pompeii, House of M. L. Fronto.

Sources speak of another form of *paradeisos* which was stocked with game. These special gardens were really a large park or reserve in which wild animals could be hunted. Quintus Curtius Rufus, the Roman author of Alexander's Persian conquests explains what these hunting parks were like:

> In that part of the world there are no better indicators of the wealth of the barbarians [here he means the Persians] than their herds of fine animals enclosed in spacious tracts of wooded grazing-land. They select for this purpose large areas of forest, attractively watered by numerous year-round springs. The woods are encircled by walls and contain lodges which serve as shelters for hunters. Alexander... and his whole army entered one such forest ...[81]

Xenophon (mentioned earlier) returned to Greece, and when he retired, he decided to create his own Persian style *paradeisos* garden on his estate at Scillus near Olympia.[82] This was to be the first park-like private garden in Greece. We learn that he stocked the park with game and hunted all kinds of animals. It was this form of garden rather than a more ornamental garden that he chose to emulate.

The *paradeisos* then could be either a game park, a pleasure garden, a productive vegetable growing area or orchard. By definition all would have been enclosed. A *paradeisos* could also provide a verdant setting for a palace, and it was a place where you could walk or rest. On the whole they were associated with high status living. The overriding characteristic element of ancient Persian gardens is that they were largely composed of orderly rows of trees, and again the species are not usually identified in ancient literature.

The existence of flowers and flowering shrubs in these gardens is implied by the term 'all other beautiful plants'. We hear that chaplets were worn by the Persians at times, and that there were chaplet makers employed in the royal households. Athenaeus mentioned that there were 46 male chaplet weavers in the list of staff of Darius III (336–330 BC) that fell into the hands of Alexander at Damascus.[83] However, our sources are silent on which species of flowers were favoured at this date for making these ephemeral items. It is possible that some of the complicated wreaths mentioned by Athenaeus may have had an origin in this part of the ancient world.

Garden Plants of Ancient Mesopotamia and the Near East

Common name	Botanical Name	Fresco/ Relief	Literature	Levant	Mesopotamia
Almond	*Amygdalus communis*		x	x	x
Aloe	*Aloe vera*		x	x	
Anemone	*Anemone coronaria*		x	x	x
Apple	*Malus sylvestris*		x	x	x
Apricot	*Prunus armenaica*		x		x
Ash	*Fraxinus ornus*		x	x	x
Azarole	*Crataegus azarolus*		x		x
Bay	*Laurus nobilis*		x		x
Box	*Buxus*		x	x	x
Broom	*Cytisus*		x	x	
Caper	*Capparis spinosa*		x	x	
Cardamom	*Elettaria cardamomum*		x		x
Caraway	*Carum carvi*		x	x	x
Carob	*Ceratonia siliqua*		x	x	x
Cedar	*Cedrus libani*		x	x	x
Chamomile	*Anthemis nobilis/ Matricaria Parthenium*		x		x
Cherry	*Prunus avium*		x		x
Citron	*Citrus medica*		x	x	x
Clover	*Trifolium* spp.		x	x	
Colocynth	*Citrullus colocynthis*		x	x	x
Coriander	*Coriandrum sativum*		x	x	x
Cress	*Lepidum sativum*		x	x	
Cucumber	*Cucumis melo*		x	x	x
Cumin	*Cuminum cyminum*		x	x	x
Cypress	*Cupresus sempervirens*		x	x	x
Date palm	*Phoenix dactylifera*	x	x	x	x
Dill	*Anethum graveolens*		x		x
Fennel	*Ferula galbaniflua*		x	x	x
Fenugreek	*Trigonella foenum graecum*		x		x
Fig	*Ficus carica*	x	x	x	x
Fir	*Abies cilicica*	x	x	x	x
Garlic	*Allium sativum*		x		x
Grape Vine	*Vitis vinefera*	x	x	x	x
Hound's tongue	*Cynoglossum creticum*		x	x	x
Juniper	*Juniperus excelsa*		x	x	x
Leek	*Allium kurat/A.porrum*		x	x	x
Lentil	*Lens esculenta*		x	x	
Lettuce	*Lactuca sativa*		x	x	x
Lily	*Lilium candidum*	x	x	x	x
Lotus/waterlily	*Nymphaea lotus*	x		x	
Madder	*Rubia tinctoria*		x	x	
Mandrake	*Mandragora officinarum*		x	x	x

Common name	Botanical Name	Fresco/ Relief	Literature	Levant	Mesopotamia
Marsh plant/mallow	*Althaea officinalis*		x	x	
Medlar	*Mespilus germanicus*		x		x
Mint	*Mentha longifolia*		x	x	x
Mulberry	*Morus nigra*		x	x	
Mustard	*Sinapis arvensis*		x		x
Myrtle	*Myrtus communis*		x	x	x
Oak	*Quercus ithaburensis*		x	x	x
Olive	*Olea europaea*		x	x	x
Onion	*Allium cepa*		x	x	x
Oregano/hyssop	*Origanum syriacum*		x	x	x
Pear	*Pyrus communis*		x		x
Pine	*Pinus pinea*		x	x	x
Plane	*Platanus orientalis*		x	x	x
Plum	*Prunus domestica*		x		x
Pomegranate	*Punica granatum*	x	x	x	x
Poppy	*Papaver somniferum*	x	x		x
Primrose	*Primula vulgaris*		x	x	
Quince	*Cydonia oblonga*		x		x
Radish	*Raphanus sativus*		x	x	x
Ranunculus	*Ranunculus*		x	x	
Rocket	*Eruca sativa*		x	x	x
Rose	*Rosa phoenica?*		x	x	x
Rue	*Ruta chalepensis/ R.graveolens*		x	x	x
Saffron/crocus	*Crocus sativus*		x	x	x
Sage	*Salvia judaica*		x	x	
Sesame	*Sesame*		x	x	x
Soapwort	*Saponaria*		x	x	
Spikenard	*Nardostachys jatamansi*		x	x	
Strawberry tree	*Arbutus unedo*		x	x	
Styrax	*Styrax officinalis*		x	x	x
Sycomore fig	*Ficus sycomorus*		x	x	x
Tamarisk	*Tamarix aphylla*	x	x	x	x
Terebinth	*Pistacia atlantica*		x	x	x
Thyme	*Thymus*		x		x
Vetch	*Vicia sativa*		x	x	
Walnut	*Juglans regia*		x		x
Wormwood	*Artemisia*		x	x	x
Zizyphus	*Zizyphus spina-Christi*		x	x	x

Notes

1. Sandars, N. K. *Poems of Heaven and Hell from Ancient Mesopotamia*, Harmondsworth, 1971, 180.
2. Sandars, 1971, 103.
3. Sandars, 1971, 106.
4. *Oxford Companion to Gardens*, 1986, 369.
5. Carroll 2003, 64. C.f. Margueron, J.-C. 'Die Garten im Vorderen Orient' in Carroll-Spillecke 1992, 61.
6. Isaiah 65.3.
7. trans. S. N. Kramer, *History Begins at Sumer,* London, 1958, 113.
8. trans. E. A. Speiser, *Ancient Near Eastern Texts* (*ANET*), *The Epic of Gilgamesh* Tablet IV, Princeton, 1958, lines 64–66.
9. Speiser, 1958, 119.
10. trans. T. J. Meek. *The Code of Hammurabi, ANET*, 163–164, 166–177 (the sections dealing with a date orchard are similar to the biblical passage in: Lev.19:23–25.
11. Dalley, S. *Mari and Karana*, London, 1984, 134.
12. trans. S. Dalley. Dalley 1993, 1. *The Tale of the Palm-tree and the Tamarisk* dates from 2000 BC.
13. Dalley, S. *Mari and Karana*, London, 1984, 83–84.
14. Dalley, 1984, 202.
15. Dalley, 1984, 203.
16. Watson 2004, 114.
17. Watson 2004,119.
18. Watson 2004, 135.
19. Brockhampton's *Guide to Herbal Remedies,* London, 1996, 76.
20. W. Hinz, *The Lost World of Elam*, London, 1972, 24 and fig. 10.
21. Gothein 1966, fig. 35.
22. Leach 1982, 10.
23. Saadé, G. *Ugarit, Canaanite Metropolis*, trans. C. F. Richardson, Latakia, 1978, 89.
24. Botanical references in the Bible have been studied by M. Zohary, F. N. Hepper and W. James.
25. Genesis 2.8–10 New International Version of the Bible, henceforth (NIV).
26. Ecclesiastes 2.4–6 (NIV).
27. Solomon's *Song of Songs* (4.12–16), NIV.
28. Soloman's *Song of Songs* (6.2), NIV.
29. Soloman's *Song of Songs*, 6.11 (NIV).
30. Also in Isaiah (55.13; 28.25).
31. 1 Kings 4.33 (NIV).
32. 1 Kings 10.27 and Amos 7.14.
33. 1 Samuel 22.6 and 31.13.
34. Deuteronomy 8.8.
35. 1 Kings 19.4.
36. Isaiah 40.6.
37. Lamentations 3.15.
38. Numbers 17.8.
39. Genesis 37.25.
40. All three are translations from the NIV.
41. Hinz 1972, 58.
42. Gothein 1966, 32; Carroll 2003, 64.

43. Dalley 1993, 6.
44. Dalley 1993, 3.
45. Dalley 1993, 4.
46. Dalley 1993, 4.
47. Wiseman 1983, 137.
48. Wiseman 1983, 138.
49. Oppenheim 1965, 331; Wiseman 1983, 137.
50. Wiseman 1983, 137.
51. S. Lloyd, *Early Anatolia*, Harmondsworth, 1956, 165.
52. Oppenheim 1965, 139.
53. Wiseman 1983, 143.
54. Wiseman 1983, 143.
55. Leach 1982, 6.
56. Budge 1927, 49.
57. Leach 1982, 6.
58. Budge 1927, 51.
59. Thompson 1924, 86.
60. Thompson 1924, 182.
61. Thompson 1924, 179.
62. Wiseman 1983, 140; Finkel 1989, 56–57.
63. Strabo, *Geography* XVI, 1, 5. trans. H. L. Jones, London, 1930.
64. Quintus Curtius, V, 1,32–33. trans. J. Yardley, London, 1984.
65. Philo of Byzantium, *Libellus de Septem Orbis Spectaculis*. trans. D. Oates. Cited in Finkel, 1989, 45–46.
66. Diodorus Siculus II, 10,5–10. Trans. C. H. Oldfather. London, 1960.
67. Thompson 1924, 6–7. He lists 32 plant names; some derivations are more obscure that those listed above.
68. Stronach 1994, 6; cf. Stronach D., 1989, 'The Royal Garden at Passargadae: Evolution and Legacy', in De Meyer, L. and Haerinck, E. (eds). *Archaeologia Iranica et Orientalis: Miscellanea in Honorem Louis Vande Berghe* 1, Ghent, 475–502.
69. Arrian, *Anab* 6, 29, 4. trans. A. De Selincourt, London, 1971.
70. American Friends of Tel Aviv University 'Fossilized pollen unlocks secrets of ancient royal garden.' *Science Daily*, sciencedaily.com, accessed 16 Feb. 2012.2; Langgut *et al.* 2013, 115–129.
71. Olmstead 1948, 224.
72. Stronach 1978, pl. 148 and fig. 85. The earrings are now in Tehran Museum.
73. Oppenheim 1965, 328–329. The *bitan* is found in Esther 1.5; 7.7–8.
74. Herodotus, *Histories* 7,31 trans. A. De Sélincourt, Harmondsworth, 1983.
75. Plutarch, *Life of Artaxerxes*, 25, 1–2. trans. J. W. Langhorne, London, 1838, 698–99.
76. Quintus Curtius Rufus, *The History of Alexander* 7, 2, 22. trans. J. Yardley, London, 1984.
77. Plutarch, *Life of Alcibiades*, 24, 5. trans. J. W. Langhorne, London, 1838, 151.
78. Xenophon, *Oeconomecus* 4, 21. trans. E. C. Marchant, London, 1923.
79. Xenophon, *Oeconomecus* 4, 13. trans. E. C. Marchant, London, 1923
80. Strabo, *Geographica*, 16, 2, 19. trans H. L. Jones, London, 2000.
81. Quintus Curtius Rufus, *History of Alexander* 8, 1, 11, trans. J. Yardley, London, 1984.
82. Xenophon, *Anabasis*, 5, 3, 7–11. trans. O. J. Todd, London, 1922.
83. Athenaeus, *Deipnosophistae*, 13, 608. trans. C. B. Gullick, London, 1959.

CHAPTER THREE

Gardens of the Greek Bronze Age:
Minoan and Mycenaean Cultures

In the Bronze Age period there were two main (but linked) cultures in Greece and its islands: the Minoans and Mycenaeans. The Minoans, who had their capital at Knossos on the Island of Crete, were a maritime people and, besides being in control of the whole of Crete, nearby islands were also under their influence. The Minoans traded with surrounding peoples, and Minoan artefacts have been found in Egypt and at several locations in the eastern Mediterranean. A great deal of evidence comes from Palace sites, such as at Knossos on Crete and also the Minoan town of Akrotiri on Thera (the Island of Santorini). This island is thought to be the unfortunate city in the myth of Atlantis which was destroyed by the cataclysmic eruption of a volcano. Practically all the island exploded, rock and ash was flung far and wide. Earthquakes and huge tsunamis did untold damage which contributed to the decline of the Minoan culture. The date of this eruption has been subject to much research and debate but is now generally accepted to have to have happened around 1600 BC.[1] To ease the difficulties of dating, Minoan culture is usually identified by three phases: Early Minoan (EM) 3000–2000 BC, Middle Minoan (MM) 2000–1600 BC, and Late Minoan (LM) 1600–1200 BC. These roughly coincide with the Egyptian Pharonic King Lists (Old, Middle and New Kingdom).

The Mycenaean Civilisation was named after their most important site in Greece, at Mycenae, in the Peloponnese. The Mycenaeans were a more warlike people; they had fortified towns and citadels, but their art and culture was akin to the Minoans. The Mycenaeans are believed to have taken advantage of the destruction of Crete as a result of the volcanic eruption of Santorini, and afterwards Mycenae came into the ascendancy.

Unfortunately the Minoans and Mycenaeans had only a limited system of writing; they had two scripts that we call Linear A and B. Only the latter has been deciphered (by Chadwick and Ventris), but sadly it appears that this script was largely used for inventories of stores in the palaces and no literary texts have been discovered as yet. Recollections of Bronze Age Greece and Crete feature in the *Iliad* and *Odyssey* of Homer, works which although written *c.*750 BC contain many references to their distant past. Groves and gardens are mentioned but,

FIGURE 47. Gold Mycenaean seal ring engraved with a scene depicting the great Mother goddess sitting under a tree, holding poppies. Attendants bring her more flowers, 15th–14th century BC, Athens Museum.

because of the time lapse, they bear more resemblance to features prevalent in the Greek Archaic Period so will be dealt with in the next chapter. Therefore, when searching for evidence of horticulture in Greece and its islands in Minoan and Mycenaean cultures we need to look for other source material, especially at the artefacts they left behind which have been discovered by archaeology. It was found that most garden evidence dates from the Middle and Late Minoan periods.

Sacred trees and a tree goddess

Archaeological evidence shows that the Minoans had a deep love of nature, because we see flowers and trees used frequently as decorative motifs. We can also see that there must have been a veneration of sacred trees. A sketchy sacred tree is shown on both the long panels of the painted chest from Haghia Triada in Crete (LM *c.*1400 BC). On one panel the tree stands next to a shrine. A priest or the deceased stands at the entrance, and worshippers arrive bearing gifts, while on the opposite side a slightly better defined tree appears to be growing inside the shrine or behind it. A fragmentary Theran fresco also shows a tree next to a shrine;[2] the closely spaced leaves indicate that it may have been an olive tree. Sacred trees feature on a number of seal stones from rings found on Crete, and at some Mycenaean sites showing that the cult was quite widespread in the Middle and Late Minoan period.[3] Many seal stones also show a mother goddess and her worshipers next to trees, these may possibly indicate that she was a particular fertility goddess called Eileithyia who is named on several Linear B tablets.[4]

FIGURE 48. Impressions from seal rings with scenes of a tree cult.

A beautiful gold ring found at Mycenae depicts the goddess sitting under a tree, the pattern of leaves indicates that this is possibly a terebinth tree which was considered as having sacred powers. Resin from this tree was seen to have healing abilities and purification properties.[5] On this ring attendants present the goddess with poppies, irises and other flowers, while another attendant tends the tree. The all important sun and moon (to indicate the realms of day and night) are present in the sky above. Another seal stone from Mycenae features a man giving homage to a tree enclosed by a protective surround. Two other seal stones depict three tree branches or plant stems on top of an altar, which is in some ways reminiscent of the three-leaved symbolic depiction of the Egyptian God Min. This could imply a similar need for an agricultural/horticultural fertility deity. A carved crystal stone found in the Idaean Cave Sanctuary (central Crete) shows one attendant using a giant sized conch shell to pour a libation upon the symbolic triple tree branches. Whereas, in the example from Vapheio in Greece, a pair of mythical beasts use flagons to give a libation.

Plants depicted on Minoan ceramic vessels

One of the distinctive features of Middle and Late Minoan ceramic vessels is their use of decorative spirals, rosettes and schematic floral designs showing a variety of plants. Several portray foliage or twigs of shrubs and some display different forms of grass-like stems or reeds, some of which are flowering. The opposite paired pattern of some leaves resemble myrtle or olive. The rosettes could represent a rose-like flower, which may be either a dog rose or a rock rose (perhaps *Cistus creticus* which is still common on the island). Many plants are rather stylised, and not all are identifiable, but those that can be distinguished are: caper, crocus, a daisy-like flower, ivy, lilies, palm trees and vines (more specifically bunches of grapes). The climate in the Bronze Age is generally thought to have been wetter than it is today,[6] so the range of plant species on Crete and the Greek islands could well have been greater in the past. Therefore it is difficult to specify particular flowering plants today. Two examples are the appearance of a distinctive looking flowering plant on a vase from Thera which looks similar to a white helleborine, and a nodding solitary flower that may represent a form of wild fritillary which appears on a jug from Phylakope; these could be plants that are now extinct in Crete or are varieties that have continued to evolve over the centuries.

A bowl from Thera was found to depict 'a remarkably faithful picture of one of the three Cretan species of Tulip, namely *Tulipa cretica*' this plant was accompanied by a form of '*Ranunculus asiaticus*'.[7] The countryside of Crete abounds in wild flowers and herbs and it is no surprise that this great abundance would be reflected in their art. But by far, the most frequent floral subjects are lilies

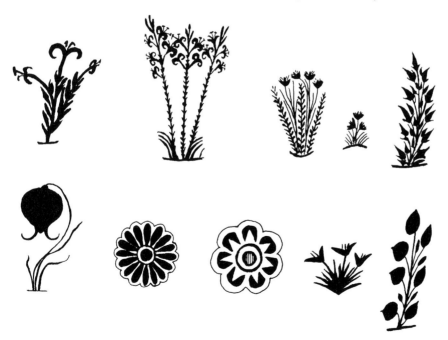

FIGURE 49. A selection of flower motifs on Minoan pottery.

and crocus. These two flowers must have held great significance for the Minoans, and they may even have become sacred, the reasons for this will be discussed later.

Some of the painted jugs and vases are decorated with a single species of plant; often the depiction is bold and vigorous. An example is a vase from Thera which has lily plants springing from a broad band at the base; each lily sprouts three flowers, one facing upwards in the centre and one on either side leaning outwards. They were painted in white on a dark background to make them stand out more clearly. An elegant tall vase from Knossos again depicts lilies but in this case there are four lily flowers at the upper part of each stem with three flower buds yet to open at the top. Strap-like leaves are shown at the base. These differing modes of depiction could indicate two different species of lily.

An interesting range of flowering plants were displayed on one vessel discovered in a LM tomb, at Chamalevri on Crete. The lid was decorated with a horizontal band of stylised lilies, and on the body of the vessel there were groups of papyrus, lilies, crocus and caper, then an unidentifiable herb on its base.

Plant containers

A shallow dish-like plant container features as a small motif picked out in gold on a silver goblet found at Mycenae. Growing out of the container are five stems with closely spaced opposite leaves, and the terminal flower on each stem appears somewhat akin to a daisy or chamomile. On either side of the container there are groups of strap shaped leaves indicating secondary leaves or different plants. Sadly, the plants in question are generalised and their identity can only be guessed at. Another shallow dish can be seen in a fragmentary fresco from Knossos (the Saffron Gatherer) which contains flowering crocus plants. The bowl appears to be ceramic and has looped handles. These small details provide evidence of a form of gardening; for tending plants is the first step to horticulture. This is corroborated by finding some pots with a hole in their base at Knossos and Mallia, which are thought to be flowerpots.

FIGURE 50 *(left)*. Drawing of lilies in a slender banded vase. One of a pair, painted on frescoed window jambs. The next best thing to having real flowers on your window sill, from Akrotiri/Thera, Santorini.

FIGURE 51 *(right)*. Silver goblet from Mycenae with a gold motif depicting a plant growing in a shallow container.

Interestingly, two small Theran frescoes, on either side of a window jamb of a townhouse, were painted with a realistic rendition of tall stems of red coloured lilies in a banded vase. The lilies may have represented cut flowers placed into the vase, but they could equally have been planted in the pot specifically to add a bit of colour and nature in the house, where they could remind the owner of the joys of the countryside or garden.

Plants in Minoan frescoes

The flowers that can be identified in Minoan frescoes are: crocus, lily, iris, rose, dianthus-like flowers (from Hagia Triada), and large yellow and white flowers that appear similar to an oxeye daisy which may be *Chrysanthemum coronarium* var. *discolor* (found in the Unexplored Mansion at Knossos). Of this group of flowers the most frequently painted ones are again the lily and crocus.

There is a hauntingly beautiful fresco (the so-called 'Spring landscape' from Thera) that depicts a very rocky ground from which clumps of red lilies grow, while swallows fly acrobatically above. The fantastic rocky landscape though is not mere imagination as some people believe but resembles an area just one kilometre to the west of the excavations at Thera. The artist's free style had a basis of truth, and he wanted to convey his delight in his own surroundings. The frequent depiction of the Lily is not only because of their elegant beauty, the flowers only last a few weeks, but because they have such a fabulous memorable scent.

Two different species of lily (sometimes identified as iris)[8] were painted on the walls of room 7 at a large villa/palace at Amnisos on Crete (dated to *c.*1600–1500

FIGURE 52
Reconstruction by M. Cameron showing the lily frescoes in Room 7 at Amnisos, Crete, (reproduced with permission of the British School at Athens)

FIGURE 53 *(left)*. Sand lilies on the Island of Santorini.

FIGURE 54 *(right)*. Fresco fragment showing dianthus-like flowers, from Hagia Triada.

BC; see Fig. 50). Here the larger than life size representations of lilies dominate the walls. One wall featured white lilies, set off against a red background; these would be representative of the Madonna Lily (*Lilium candidum*). Another wall showed red flowering lilies which are thought to be *Lilium martagon* the so-called Turk's Cap lily, or possibly *L. chalcedonicum*. The red lilies were interspersed with a non-flowering bush or herb (that may be mint),[9] but both of these appear to have been planted into a wide planter with incurved sides, showing that these beautiful flowering plants had now become cultivated and must have belonged to a garden area.

The Minoan frescoes display a greater range of flora than can be seen on their ceramics. Frescoes from Crete are displayed in the Archaeological Museum at Herakleion. Theran frescoes (from the archaeological site of Akrotiri on the island of Santorini) are displayed in the National Archaeological Museum at Athens. Among the plants illustrated newly discovered fragments from Knossos show sprays of olive.[10] Vines feature in another fresco from Knossos, ivy at Hagia Triada, pine and palm trees at Thera.[11] Several frescoes portray reeds or sedges, which are thought to be either the galingale or *Cyperus esculentus* which is known to have been cultivated for its edible tubers (tiger nuts). It is often shown flowering, so too are fronds and umbels of papyrus. The latter however is not believed to have been a native plant, and may be represented in Minoan art because of its exotic qualities and associations with Egypt where it grows abundantly in the wet areas of the Nile Delta. Papyrus, the paper reed, is thought to feature in the large fresco found in the House of the Ladies at

Thera. These plants are large and their representation matches this, but because these flowers have a series of kidney shaped dots above each flower umbel they could represent anthers on stamens which papyrus do not possess. Therefore, it is now believed that they may in fact represent the smaller native sand lily/sea daffodil *Pancratium maritimum*.[12] Perhaps the artist had not seen a papyrus plant before and based this image on his more familiar native lily. Another important flowering plant of Crete is the iris (*Iris cretica*) its slender leaves and flowers are faithfully rendered in two frescoes from the House of Frescoes at Knossos, where their flowers were painted blue.

Some of the roses depicted in Minoan frescoes show an open flower and therefore there is some ambiguity as to whether it depicts a true rose or the rock rose. However the so-called 'Blue Bird' fresco from Knossos depicts what must be a true rose flower, with its distinctive leaves and buds; this image is the earliest representation of a rose in Europe.[13]

A wonderful fresco from Knossos depicts a series of circular flower garlands in a frieze that may have originally run along the top part of a wall. Every garland had decorative strings tied into a bow at the top, with the remainder of the long strings left to dangle like a pendulum. Each garland is composed of one particular species of flower making them unique. The flower species represented in this instance appear to be of: crocus, lily, myrtle, olive, rose or rock rose, and a dark red flower that could be either an anemone or a red *ranunculus asiaticus*.[14] The care taken in the portrayal of each garland is remarkable and is a sign that the Minoans sought to beautify their houses as well as their person.

Some of the frescoes form a continuous miniature landscape with a little stream running throughout the length of the frieze, as in the 'nilotic scene' in the West House on Thera. The plants may at first glance be thought as wild ones in the countryside, but the plants are often small (such as the dwarf palms) and could imply a managed and well tended landscape. Palms are propagated by transplanting suckers from an adult palm, mostly from a female palm, and the stream nearby would supply the necessary water for these newly planted

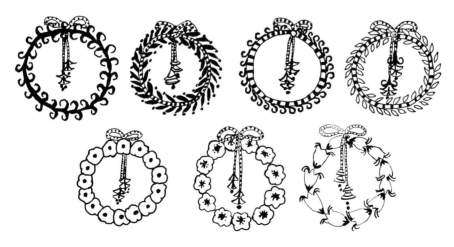

FIGURE 55. *Top row, l to r:* lily, myrtle, ?, olive; *Bottom row, l to r:* anemone/ranunculus, rock rose/dog rose and crocus, Knossos (redrawn from J. Clarke in Morgan, 2005).

FIGURE 56 *(left)*. Detail from a Minoan fresco depicting a garden landscape with tame monkeys. House of the Frescoes, Knossos, (after M. Cameron in Shaw 1993, 669).

saplings. Sometimes monkeys are shown in these frescoes. Monkeys were imported into the Aegean areas as exotic pets, they were not native animals, and therefore they would have only been allowed to roam in controlled areas. This would then suggest that the area was a form of park or landscaped garden.[15] The scenes are captivating, and were freely drawn. Birds and other animals are shown in the foliage of these lively frescoes. In one section a cat chases a duck by a little stream surrounded by sand lilies and young palms.

The second most popular plant was the crocus. Minoans painters had a limited colour palate therefore some of the identifications of plants are not as clear as we would like and we find that most crocus flowers are painted in a maroon red colour which is meant to represent the purple flowers of *Crocus cartwrightianus* or *Crocus sativus* the saffron crocus.[16] Each has two-four prominent bright orange stamens. However, in some cases the crocus-like flowers are painted blue, and these may imply a flower of the campanula family,[17] perhaps *Symphyandra cretica* or *trachelium asperuloides*. Several frescoes found at Knossos and on Thera suggest that the Minoans cultivated and picked saffron from their crocus plants. One fresco of particular note shows the procedure. One wall in Room 3, Xeste 3 at Thera, shows two girls in a crocus filled landscape picking the flowers with their valuable stamens, in their other hand they carry a basket with looped handles. On two other walls a girl carries a filled basket on her shoulder, while another empties the basket into a much larger wicker basket. At this point you can clearly see that

the whole flower was picked, not just the stamens. In the centre of this tableau a large monkey presents a sample of their produce to a giant sized seated mother goddess figure. The regal status of the goddess is highlighted by her greater size and by a royal griffin at her side. The presence of the monkey may seem strange, but at Knossos a fragmentary fresco depicts what some believe to be monkeys picking saffron crocus. It is possible that the Minoans trained monkeys to do this back breaking job. In both frescoes mentioned crocus are shown growing on rocks. In the Theran example they are also shown as a repeat pattern in the background to imply wide spread cultivation.

FIGURE 57. Circular enclosure with two trees (perhaps representative of more) that indicates what could be an orchard. Detail from a Theran fresco of city and seascape scenes, from Room 5 of the West House, 15th century BC.

Depictions of an enclosure garden

In Room 5 of the West House on Thera, within the long frieze depicting city and seascape themes, there is a painted detail that features a circular fenced enclosure surrounding two trees. This enclosure appears to be an orchard, as the two trees could be representative of more. The scene is close to a building/house and nearby (to the right) grazing animals are being tended. Their proximity suggests that the fenced enclosure would keep livestock away from precious trees. This section of the fresco therefore shows aspects of Theran life: animal husbandry and horticulture.

Another 'garden' appears on a gold disc shaped seal from Poros.[18] Here a tree with three distinct branches is shown behind a crenelated wall made of coursed brick or stone. Interestingly a large dog is positioned between the wall and the tree, as if it was guarding the garden. The stepped wall shown here is reminiscent of the plain white wall seen behind white lily plants in the aforementioned fresco of the lilies from Amnisos.

FIGURE 58.
Reconstruction drawing suggesting a rock garden for crocus and other plants, in the Palace at Phaistos, Crete, 15th century BC (M. C. Shaw and G. Bianco in Shaw 1993, fig. 23).

Two thick-girthed large trees feature in a miniature fresco from Knossos that is thought to represent a sacred grove.[19] The tree species cannot be identified but as this grove is close to an entertainment area they may in fact have been planted there as shade trees. A wall (or pathway seen from above) separates this grove from a group of dancers watched by quite a crowd. Another walled grove is suggested on the fragment of a serpentine rhyton drinking vessel from Knossos, again the wall marks the limit between the grove and a recreation area. The tall mature tree has large leaves that are dissected into three, it is believed to represent a fig tree (*Ficus carica*).[20]

The Minoans are believed to have cultivated fruit trees, such as quinces and pears, presumably in orchards. The botanical name for quince (*Cydonia oblongata*) provides a clue because the ancient Greek word for quince is *Kydonia*.[21] The fruit was actually named after a Cretan town Kydonia (modern Khania) which appears on the Minoan Linear B tablets as *Kudonija*. The fertile plain around this town is still a good fruit producing area. Seeds of pear/apple were discovered by archaeologists at Kommos, along with almond, fig, olive and carob that may have grown in cultivated areas near the town.[22] Tablets found at Knossos mention trees of the *Pistachia* family, perhaps indicating that they too grew in Crete at that date.[23]

Archaeological discoveries of gardens

Recent archaeological research has now actually provided evidence that suggests crocus were grown in gardens. At the Palace of Phaistos in central Crete an hitherto unidentified garden area was discovered, where one portion had been turned into a rock garden for crocus plants (see Fig. 56).[24] This garden would have brought their favourite plants close to the home, where they would have extra care, the owner would enjoy the sight of them in flower and still be able to harvest the saffron and extra corms they might make. The mass of crocus would have been a wonderful sight. The rocks were cleared of soil and numerous depressions were noted which could have been sufficient for planting bulbs or corms. The holes were roughly circular and 10–30 cm wide and 6–10 cm deep; some of the holes shelved which would have helped drainage, although the rocks here tend to be porous.[25]

Other palaces may have had garden areas and/or orchards or groves; an orchard has been suggested in an area south-east of the palace at Zakros, and a possible grove may have existed to the south of Hagia Triada (both on Crete). Residential quarters in a palace are often located close to a series of doorways or columns akin to a loggia opening onto garden terraces.[26] Archaeologists found one of these on the north-western edge of the Palace at Mallia, on the northern coast of Crete. The garden here was roughly rectangular with a pillared loggia on one side giving access into the area. However, when it was excavated no paleobotanic record was taken, so we do not know which plants originally grew there. However, Mallia is known as the findspot for a strikingly beautiful gold pendant of a pair of bees. The island is well known for its honey production even today, and Minoan pottery beehives have been discovered. One can make a conjecture that cultivated herbs and plants from this garden were utilised to make honey at Minoan Mallia, as well as the profusion of wildflowers in the Cretan countryside.

The fluctuating climate of Greece and its islands does not favour the preservation of paleobotanical specimens (unlike Egypt where the dry air desiccates remains), and little garden archaeology has taken place. However at Akrotiri, in the areas sealed by the eruption of Santorini some evidence has been unearthed, such as a stump of an oak tree within the ancient settlement.[27] Such a large tree would have provided ample shade below its canopy.

Evidence for vegetable gardening has come to light through recent scientific studies on the residues left behind inside Minoan and Mycenaean ceramic vessels (cooking pots, drinking vessels, storage jars, etc.). Waxes and oils are secreted by some plants and after time in storage, or as a result of cooking, the waxes and oils had been absorbed by the unglazed inner walls of these pots. Valuable evidence can be found on the former contents of individual vessels, which in turn informs on the diet of people in this period. An analysis of these residues shows that some vessels once contained liquids (*e.g.* from drinking cups and jugs and amphorae) whereas some of the cooking pots indicated that a combination of ingredients were being cooked together (or on separate occasions each leaving a trace). We now know that vegetables and sometimes fruit formed ingredients cooked in a form of stew, occasionally with meat. It appears that copious amounts of olive oil was commonly used in Minoan and Mycenaean recipes, and that a wine flavoured with resin was appreciated as far back as Early Minoan Crete.[28] Some residues however can only be identified as 'waxes from fruit and leafy vegetables.'[29] Of these vegetables there are indications that a form of sweet courgette was being consumed at Apodoulou,[30] but identifying multiple ingredients in a specific pot proves very difficult. However, in other cases the researchers can be more specific, and plant residues include almond, fig, grape, olive, pear, and possibly apple, lentils, chick pea, grass pea, and faba bean, the last of which requires constant watering that implies horticulture. These would indicate that the plants to produce these results were growing nearby.

Some of cooking pots were found to have contained resinated wine with the addition of one or more aromatic herbs, showing that at times the Minoans took what may have been a medicinal or ritual brew.[31] The herbs used in these cases were: laurel, lavender and sage, one cooking pot even had wine with rue which would act as a stimulant.[32] The natural sweetener honey has been assumed from traces of beeswax found in a few jars and bowls used for storage. Apparently honey, or a honey mead, was also added to make a fermented beverage comprising wine; such a 'honeyed wine' is mentioned on the Linear B tablets.[33] Honey was even added to a barley beer, and on occasion to make a brew with wine, honey and beer all together![34]

In some cases evidence of flowering plants were found by the analysis of residues, and on one remarkable occasion residues of oil of iris had survived inside a small pot from Armenoi on Crete (LM).[35] This rare find is evidence of the importance of iris in the Minoan period and of the production of perfumery. Oil of Iris is made from the root of the plant and today it is the most expensive ingredient in perfumes. So we can appreciate the importance of this plant to the Minoan economy, both for home use and for export.

Botanical references on Linear B tablets

Sadly there is no Minoan equivalent to the Egyptian/Assyrian herbals. The only clue to the practise of medicine and the culture of medicinal plants is found in a Linear B text mentioning the word *pamako*, which is similar to the Greek word for pharmacy. Chadwick and Ventris found that Linear B words bore some similarities to archaic Greek, and this really helped to decipher the language and script. Few Linear B texts mention flowers though, but there are references to: poppies, roses, saffron (crocus), safflower and hibiscus. The ancient hibiscus is not the shrub we know today but is likely to be a tree mallow or *Althea officinalis* the marsh mallow. The ancient name for iris, which was so prized, has not been identified yet, but it is suspected to be the root called *wi-ri-za* that is always accompanied by an ideogram implying it needed straining – for perfumery.[36] Apart from medicinal and perfumery, garden herbs were also used in Minoan and Mycenaean cooking;

one of the most frequently mentioned herbs in the Linear B tablets was coriander. In palace inventories at Mycenaean Pylos, it was called *Koriadnon* which again is very close to our present word for this herb. Large quantities of coriander were recorded at Pylos, around 576 litres.[37] Other herbs mentioned in the tablets are celery, cress, cumin, fennel, mint/pennyroyal and sesame.[38]

Tablets, and archaeology, have shown that medicinal plants were gathered and prepared in Crete and Mycenae. It is also clear that exports of medicinal and aromatic plants were made to Egypt, although it is uncertain if they were traded or were a form of tribute. This scenario is seen to good effect in an ancient Egyptian fresco, from the Theban Tomb of Rechmire (15th century BC), which records an instant when tribute was brought to Egypt by foreign nations. Included in this documentary fresco is a line of men from *Keftiu* (the Egyptian name for Crete) carrying their distinctive pottery vessels. Some of the wider vases are filled with very stylised flowering plants, four different species are represented here, but sadly they are not named. The produce from *Keftiu* is stacked up at the end of the line while a scribe notes them all down. Iris, lilies and saffron crocus may well have been items sent to Egypt, and because of their great value they would have been treated with extra care, the Cretans perhaps even accorded them sacred qualities, and as we have seen they are frequently depicted in their art. Interestingly there are Egyptian texts referring to special 'Beans from Keftiu', which were evidently imported for medicinal purposes, apparently they were useful to clear out blockages.[39]

Evidence from Minoan pottery and frescoes both point to a deep love of nature. Flowering plants held a special place in their hearts and minds, especially lilies and crocus. The Cretans utilised their abundant wealth of wild and cultivated flowers and herbs. The mountains of Crete are still covered with aromatic herbs, which make it a botanist's paradise. But it is noticeable that the plants depicted in Minoan frescoes are in the main cultivated garden species not wild ones.

Botanical remains/residues are listed in the table of known garden plants for the Greek Bronze Age. Two separate columns indicate if the plant was illustrated and/or was mentioned in Linear B tablets.

FIGURE 59. Details of men from *Keftiu* (the Egyptian name for Crete) taken from an Ancient Egyptian fresco of foreign vassals or traders carrying their respective goods/tribute. This selection highlights Minoans carrying herbs or precious aromatic plants in their distinctive pottery vases, 15th century BC. Tomb of Rechmire, Thebes.

Garden Plants of the Greek Bronze Age

Common Name	Botanical Name	Fresco/ vase	Linear B	Botanical remains/ residues
Almond	*Amygdalus communis*			x
Broad bean	*Vicia faba*			x
Campanula family	*Symphyandra cretica* or *Trachelium asperuloides*	x		
Caper	*Capparis spinosa*	x		
Celery	*Apium graveolens*		x	
Coriander	*Coriandrum sativum*		x	
Cress	*Lepidium sativum*		x	
Crocus	*Crocus cartwrightianus*	x	x	
Crocus (saffron)	*Crocus sativus*	x	x	
Cumin	*Cuminum cyminum*		x	
Cyperus grass (tiger nuts)	*Cyperus esculentus/C. rotundus*	x	x	
Daisy-like	*Matricaria chamomilla*	x		
Date palm	*Phoenix dactylifera*	x	x	
Dianthus (pink)	*Dianthus*	x		
Fennel	*Foeniculum vulgare*		x	
Fig	*Ficus carica*		x	x
Grape Vine	*Vitis vinefera*	x	x	x
Hibiscus/mallow	*Althea officinalis?*		x	
Iris	*Iris cretica*	x		x
Lily	*Lilium candidum*	x		
Lily (Turk's cap)	*Lilium martagon/L.chalcedonicum*	x		
Mint/ pennyroyal	*Mentha*		x	
Nettle tree	*Celtis australis*			x
Olive	*Olea europaea*	x	x	x
Oxeye daisy?	*Chrysanthemum coronarium* var. *discolor*	x		
Papyrus	*Cyperus papyrus*	x		
Pear	*Pyrus communis*			x
Pea (grass pea)	*Lathyrus sativus/L.cicerus*			x
Pine	*Pinus halepensis/P.pinea*	x		x
Poppy	*Papaver somniferum*	x	x	x
Quince	*Cydonia oblongata*		x	
Rock rose	*Cistus creticus*	x		
Rose	*Rosa*	x	x	
Rue	*Ruta*			x
Safflower	*Carthamus tinctorius*		x	
Sage	*Salvia*		x	x
Sea daffodil	*Pancratium*	x		
Sesame	*Sesame*		x	
Terebinth (for its resin)	*Pistacia terebinthus/P. lentiscus*	x	x	x
Tulip	*Tulipa cretica*	x		
Turban buttercup	*Ranunculus asiaticus*	x		

Notes

1. See Manning, S., *A Test of Time and a Test of Time Revisited*, Oxford, 2015, for the latest discussion.

2. On the East Wall of Room 3a, Xeste 3, Akrotiri (Vlachopoulos, A. 'The Wall Paintings from Xeste 3 Building at Akrotiri: Towards an Interpretation of the Iconographic Programme', in Brodie, N. *et al. Horizon: A Colloquim on the Prehistory of the Cyclades*, Cambridge, 2008. fig. 41.10).

3. Evans 1901, 99–204; Krzyszkowska, O. 'Impressions of the natural world: landscape in Aegean glyptic,' in Krzyszkowska, O. (ed.) *Cretan Offerings*, Athens, 2010, 178–184.

4. Castleden, R. *Life in Bronze Age Crete*, London, 1990, 51; Tzedakis and Martlew 2002, 266.

5. Beckmann, S. 'Terebinth in Eastern Mediterranean Bronze Age Crete,' *Athanasia* 2012, 30.

6. Evans cited in Raven 2000, 29.

7. Raven 2000, 29.

8. Morgan 1988, 40; Immerwahr, S. A. *Painting in the Bronze Age*, London, 1990.

9. Beckmann 'Terebinth in Eastern Mediterranean Bronze Age Crete,' *Athanasia* 2012, 39.

10. Morgan 2005, 57–8; 147 and pl.3.2. Also, olive branches have been found in fragments at Pylos.

11. A fresco with vine leaves can be seen at House of Frescoes, Knossos; Ivy in the Cat and Bird fresco, Hagia Triada; ivy is also present in the upper zone of the Boxers and Antelope frescoes, House Beta 1, Akrotiri. A possible branch with pine needles appears in Room 5, Xeste 3, Akrotiri. Several dwarf palms are in the Nilotic Landscape frieze, West House, Akrotiri.

12. Baumann 1993, 176, figs 346–349; Raven 2000, 29.

13. Phillips, R. and Rix, M. *The Quest for the Rose*, London, 1993, 12.

14. Warren, P. 'Flowers for the goddess? New fragments of wall paintings from Knossos', in Morgan 2005, 142–143 (cf. pl. 16 painted by J. Clarke).

15. Morgan 1988, 39; Shaw 1993, 668–669.

16. Shaw 1993, 674.

17. Warren, P. 2005, 143 and 146.

18. Dimopoulu, N, 'A gold discoid from Poros, Herakleion: the guard dog and the garden', in Krzyszkowska, O. (ed.) *Cretan Offerings*, Athens, 2010, 89–100.

19. Morgan 2005, pl.10.2.

20. Morgan 1988, 18.

21. Castleden, R. *Life in Bronze Age Crete*, London, 1990, 46.

22. Shay, C. T. *et al.* 'The modern flora and plant remains from Bronze Age deposits at Kommos,' in Shaw, J. W. and Shaw, M. *Kommos* I, Princeton, 1995, 126 and table 4.12.

23. Castleden, R. *Life in Bronze Age Crete*, London, 1990, 52. Charcoal of lentisc (*Pistacia*) was found at Kommos (Shay, C. T. *et al.* 'The modern flora and plant remains from Bronze Age deposits at Kommos,' in Shaw, J. W. and Shaw, M. *Kommos* I, Princeton, 1995, 126)

24. Shaw 1993, 683–685. Shaw also suggests miniature iris and sweet violet were possible here.

25. Another suggestion is that these holes could have been used for grinding grain, but the rocky slope would be too difficult for this purpose.

26. As mentioned by Graham, J. W. *The Palaces of Crete*, Princeton, 1962, 87, 89, 91 (relating to Mallia); 123, 241. Also cf. Shaw 1993, 680.

27. Rackham, O. 'The flora and vegetation of Thera and Crete before and after the great eruption,' *The Thera Foundation.org*. 4.

28. Tzedakis and Martlew 2002, 142.
29. Tzedakis and Martlew 2002, 96.
30. Tzedakis and Martlew 2002, 85 and 89.
31. Tzedakis and Martlew 2002, 146.
32. Tzedakis and Martlew 2002, 164.
33. Tzedakis and Martlew 2002, 207–208.
34. Tzedakis and Martlew 2002, 166.
35. Tzedakis and Martlew 2002, 54–55.
36. Vlazaki, L. '*Iris cretica* and the Prepaltial workshop of Chamalevri,' in Krzyszkowska, O. (ed.), *Cretan Offerings*, Athens, 2010, 359–366.
37. Castleden, *Life in Bronze Age Crete*, London, 1990, 52.
38. C.f. Shaw 1993, 663; Tzedakis and Martlew 2002, 266.
39. R. Arnott, from a lecture on medicine and herbs in the Aegean Age, held at the Gas Hall, Birmingham, Sept. 2002.

CHAPTER FOUR

Greek Gardens and Groves of the Archaic, Classical and Hellenistic Periods

Mycenaean culture collapsed around 1200 BC at about the same time that other contemporary cultures in the eastern Mediterranean were disrupted. There was a widespread movement of migrating people and internecine wars are also thought a possible contributor to the downfall of Mediterranean societies. The two great epics of Homer relate back to this turbulent time and have echoes from life in the Bronze Age. The epics were essentially oral tales that were finally written down in the 8th century BC, but inevitably over the centuries the epics had been embroidered and therefore contain later elements. However, they provide a link from the Bronze Age right through the so-called Greek Dark Ages and into Archaic Greece. Archaic Greece is generally accepted as extending from the 7th century BC to 480 BC, which is the date of the Greek victory over Persian invaders. After the Greek victory there was a flowering of the arts in what we term the Classical Greek period, which extended to 323 BC; this date marks the death of Alexander the Great and the start of the Hellenistic era.

Homeric gardens

In the second Homeric epic, dealing with the wanderings of Odysseus, there are descriptions of landscapes and even gardens. The first description of note relates to the surrounding area of the cave inhabited by the nymph Calypso:

> right about the hollow cavern, extended a flourishing growth of vine that ripened with grape clusters. Next to it there were four fountains, and each of them ran shining water, each next to each, but turned to run in sundry directions; and round about there were meadows growing soft with parsley/celery and violets, and even a god who came into that place would have admired what he saw, the heart delighted within him.[1]

In many ways this idyllic scene reflects the naturalistic lily/iris filled areas of the Minoan world, and could be a memory passed down in an altered form. But, the details given in the longer descriptions of the gardens of Laertes and Alkinoös appear to be those familiar to the writers of the epic, rather than an earlier memorised one. They are nevertheless a very important source of information on early Greek gardens. One chapter in the Odyssey gives details about the palace and cultivated land (the garden) of Odysseus's father Laertes. Tradition has it that these were on the Island of Ithaca. We hear that when Odysseus searched for his father he saw the familiar stone retaining wall of his father's orchard, and found his father working around a plant. Odysseus spoke to him: '… everything is well cared for, and there is never a plant, neither fig tree nor yet grapevine nor olive nor pear tree nor leek bed uncared for in your garden.'[2]

In another section we hear about the garden of Alkinoös, the king of the mythical Phaiakians. These gardens became famous in antiquity as the ideal garden. A proverbial garden that was fertile, well watered and was abundantly fruitful – so much so that you could guarantee a never-ending supply of produce.

> On the outside of the courtyard and next the doors is his orchard, a great one, four land measures, with a fence driven all around it, and there is the place where his fruit trees are grown tall and flourishing, pear trees and pomegranate trees and apple trees with their shining fruit, and the sweet fig trees and the flourishing olive. Never is the fruit spoiled on these, never does it give out, neither in winter time nor summer, but always the West Wind blowing on the fruits brings some to ripeness while he starts others. Pear matures on pear in that place, apple on apple, grape cluster on grape cluster, fig upon fig. There also he has a vineyard planted that gives abundant produce, some of it a warm area on level ground where the grapes are left to dry in the sun, but elsewhere they are gathering others and trampling out yet others, and in front of these are unripe grapes that have cast off their bloom while others are darkening. And there at the bottom strip of the field are growing orderly rows of greens, all kinds, and these are lush through the seasons; and there two springs distribute water, one through all the garden space, and one on the other side jets out by the courtyard door, and the lofty house, where townspeople come for their water. Such are the glorious gifts of the gods at the house of Alkinoös.[3]

These texts are useful in giving an indication of plants commonly planted in archaic Greek gardens, but it is clear that these texts do not describe a decorative garden as we would know it. Instead they seem to show a combined orchard and vegetable garden, and this practical way of gardening would have continued through the ages on properties in the countryside.

Greek names for a garden

The Greek word for a garden is *Kepos* (κῆπος) plural: *kepoi*. But, throughout the Archaic and Classical Greek periods this term usually referred to an enclosure of cultivated greens, more of a vegetable kitchen garden, or market garden, rather than a decorative garden. On occasion we hear of a *kepouros* (κῆπουρος) which was a garden keeper, this is the closest term we have for a Greek gardener. A garden plot or plant bed was called a *prasiai* (πρασιαί) a term that was already in use during the eighth century by Homer. The ancient Greek word used to specify an orchard was *orchatos* (ὄρχατος).

FIGURE 60. Hercules in the Gardens of the Hesperides, depicted on a Greek red-figure vase painting by the Meidias Painter. A snake guards the famous golden apples in this orchard garden, *c*.410 BC. British Museum, London.

The mythical Garden of the Hesperides

Several Greek myths centre around a garden, or garden plant, perhaps the most famous being the Garden of the Hesperides. These mythical gardens are associated with that great hero Herakles (known as Hercules by the Romans). Herakles was given 12 great Labours to accomplish, and the 11th of these was to collect the apples from this garden. The garden was said to have been far away in the west, on an island or close to the sea, and was tended by three nymphs called the Hesperides. A snake guarded the tree bearing the 'golden apples', Herakles had to kill this snake in order to get to the precious golden fruit. It is now generally believed that these fruit were quinces rather than apples, or alternatively they may have been citrons. This arduous task is immortalised in a Greek red figure vase painted by the Meidias painter. The vase is dated to *c*.410 BC, and is now in the British Museum.

Fertility cults

Every culture seems to have a basic need to pray to a higher being with the hope that they would come to their aid, whether asking for rain or for fertility in growing plants or agricultural crops. The Greeks sought to explain their own world and the lives of their gods and goddesses with a series of stories that became increasingly elaborate and these evolved into Myths. What is so interesting about the Greek myths is that so many of their gods interact with mortals. The Greeks had several deities that were concerned with aspects of fertility: Aphrodite, Athene, Dionysus, Demeter and Persephone, Pan, and at a later date Adonis and Priapus.

The goddess Aphrodite emerged from the sea (off western Cyprus) from out of an open scallop shell. She was the prime fertility goddess who was particularly concerned with aspects of love and sexuality, but also of beauty and grace (the Graces were often seen as her attendants). Roses and violets were particularly associated with Aphrodite, she was often called 'violet crowned'. Aphrodite and Ares (the god of war) were lovers and produced a child called Cupid who had attributes of both: the power to incite love when he loosens his arrows from his bow. Aphrodite's other dalliance, with Dionysus (the god of wine), produced a misshapen child named Priapus. His overlarge phallus was seen with distaste and after birth his mother abandoned him on the mountains. He was found and raised by shepherds; therefore he became a well known figure in rustic areas and was a powerful fertility god in his own right. He became noted as a guardian of orchards, vegetable gardens and bees. His cult originated in Lampsecus in Asia Minor but spread in the 3rd century BC.

Athene was a goddess of war, having emerged fully armed from the head of her father Zeus (the chief of the Olympian Gods). She was also a goddess of handicrafts and was known for her wisdom. One of her myths concerns a competition to see which two deities would take precedence in the city of Athens: Athene or Poseidon who was god of the sea. The two rivals challenged each other to prove which would be most useful to man [the challenge recalls the Mesopotamian contest between the palm and the tamarix]. Athene won because she produced the olive tree. Thereafter she was associated with the cultivation of olives, which became such a vital resource for Greece; the olive became her

FIGURE 61. An olive tree sacred to the goddess Athena growing by the Erechtheion building on the Acropolis, Athens.

sacred plant. Athene had a long association with the city of Athens, and temples were built in her honour on the highest point of the Acropolis. As a mark of appreciation the Athenians built another sacred building the Erechtheion (next to Athene's great temple, the Parthenon) where they added a small sacred garden around the olive tree first planted by Athene.

Dionysus was the god of wine, and is always associated with over indulgence in drinking and feasting. He was also the god of drama and theatre productions. Dionysus was the result of the dalliance between Zeus and a beautiful mortal girl called Semele. Naturally Zeus's wife Hera was enraged when she learnt about their affair, and ensured her demise. Zeus hid the baby Dionysus in a cave on Mount Nysa where he could be looked after by three nymphs. While there Silenus acted as his tutor; Silenus himself was a demigod (sometimes thought to be the son of Pan) he was the wise drunken elder of the woodland satyrs, who undoubtedly initiated Dionysus into the joys of wine drinking. When Dionysus grew up he went to the east and to India, from where he returned in triumph, bringing back with him the cultivation of the vine. Because of this the

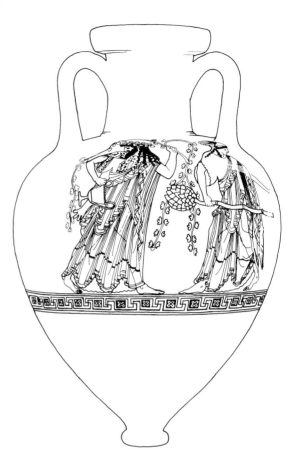

FIGURE 62. Detail showing Dionysus the god of wine, with a maenad carrying his thyrsus staff made from the stalk of the giant fennel and ivy leaves. Greek red-figure vase by the Kleophrades Painter, *c.*500–490 BC, Munich Museum.

vine and bunches of grapes are used as his symbol in art, and in some cases the vine appears to emanate from the god. Figs were also linked to the god mainly because they contained so many seeds, so they were seen as a symbol of fertility. Dionysus, or a member of his entourage, is often shown holding a *thyrsus*, a ceremonial staff. The *thyrsus* was made out of a long stem from the giant fennel (*Ferula communis*) topped with strands of ivy wound round and round to resemble a ball of ivy leaves; on top of which was a pinecone as a finial. The stem of the giant fennel was said to be softer than wood, if it hit you on the head during drunken revels. Also another reason for using fennel can be seen when you observe the emergence of this plant from the ground in spring: it is very phallic-like and this obvious connection to fertility will not have been missed. Ivy, like the vine, was also used as an emblem for Dionysus and his cult. In Classical representations of the god vine leaves and bunches of grapes were woven into a chaplet adorning his head, and ivy leaves and its flowers were used in crowns for members of his entourage which included Pan, Silenus, groups of satyrs (male woodland beings with pointed ears and tails) and maenads (female woodland nymphs). All of these are often seen on Greek vase paintings. One particular plant, the orchid became forever linked to the lusty satyrs mainly because of the shape of its roots: the ancient Greek word *orchis* implied a testicle! In ancient times like was used to cure like, so *orchis* was also in demand as an aphrodisiac. Some orchid flowers were even seen to bear a resemblance to the shape of a little satyr (especially *Orchis italica*; as its name implies it grows in Italy as well as in Greece).[4]

Pan was the son of Hermes and a nymph. He was originally a god from Arcadia, a mountainous area in the Peloponnese, where he presided over shepherds and their flocks. His worship spread across Greece in the 5th century BC. He is particularly noted for the fertility of animals and of mountainous and country districts in general. Herbs grown in pasture come under his care. Pan is often associated with caves, where he would rest from the midday sun, and often his shrines were located in a cave setting. He was half man half goat, and because of his lusty nature he was prone to chasing nymphs and maenads; therefore he is often included in Dionysus' throng.

From as far back as the Mycenaean era Demeter was the goddess associated with all aspects of growing corn, which was such a staple food in Greek diets. A recent study of the soils and plants around Classical temple sites of Greece has found that temples dedicated to Demeter (and Dionysus) were usually sited on land with good deep soil, and this is consistent with these deities' association with fertility.[5] One of her myths involves her daughter Persephone who one day was out gathering wild flowers when she was abducted by Hades (the god of the underworld) and was taken down to his realm. Hades wanted her to rule with him in the underworld, but she pined for sunlight. Her mother tried to seek her release, but all her entreaties failed. Her grief was so intense that the land became barren, the cereals would not grow and there was widespread famine. The gods were forced to act and a solution was found. Persephone could not return permanently to the land of the living because she had eaten some pomegranate fruit in her captivity, so she was forced to spend four (or six) months each year in the underworld. But for eight (or six) glorious months she was allowed to rejoin her mother in the light above ground. This myth attempted to explain why there were two very different seasons of the year; when Persephone was with her mother the land came to life once more, but when Persephone returned to her husband Hades winter approached and seeds became dormant in the ground. Because of this myth the pomegranate fruit was forever associated with Persephone. The cult of Adonis has a similar accounting for the seasons but will be mentioned later.

Greek myths concerning plants

There are 15 or more colourful Greek myths that weave a tale to give the origin of a plant/flower which we know as: olive, narcissus, hyacinth, crocus, smilax, bay, cypress, mint, heliotrope, fir tree, myrrh tree, tamarisk, helichrysum, achillea, adonis/anemone. The olive has already been mentioned. The myth associated with the narcissus flower is a sad one as the unfortunate youth

FIGURE 63. Narcissus hopelessly gazing at his own image, before turning into the narcissus flower. Seen in a Roman fresco from Pompeii.

Nárkissos (*Narcissus* in Latin), who had just turned sixteen, was so handsome that both girls and boys loved him, but he disdained them all. One day one of his thwarted lovers prayed that Nárkissos would share their same doomed fate of unrequited love. Nemesis, the goddess of fate, heard and granted this prayer ensuring that Nárkissos would fall hopelessly in love with the next person he saw. Nárkissos had been out hunting in the forest and came down to a pool to quench his thirst. He spied his own image reflected in the clear water and immediately fell in love with his own reflection. Every time he attempted to reach this image he failed and eventually he wasted away and died, to be replaced by the nodding yellow and white flowers that were thereafter given his name.

The hyacinth flower was named after Huakinthos (*Hyacinthus*) another handsome youth that was loved by two rival gods: Zephyrus the god of the West Wind and Apollo. Huakinthos however, favoured Apollo and one day while they were throwing discus the spiteful Zephyrus decided to blow a gust of wind to deflect Apollo's discus. Sadly the discus then hit Huakinthos on the head instantly killing him. Apollo could not revive him, so out of grief Apollo transformed Huakinthos's blood into a dark blue flower, named after his beloved, so that it would ensure the youth's immortality. However, in Greece the word for hyacinth was not specific to the botanical genus of that name, it encompassed several blue flowers including members of the scilla family, delphiniums and wild gladiolus. The latter bears the Greek sign of grief 'Ai Ai' on the lower lip of its flower which the ancients reckoned to be a mark of respect.

Another myth explains how the beautiful youth named Krokos (*Crocus*) became a flower. He was being pursued by the much besotted nymph Smilax. In desperation he pleaded with the gods to help him escape her persistent attentions. In answer the gods changed him into the crocus flower. Interestingly, Smilax who was a victim of her own hopeless passion was transformed into the prickly twining plant, forever clinging to others (*Smilax aspera*).

There is another sad story of how a beautiful shy girl called Daphne was transformed into a flowering bush. This myth was often reproduced in ancient art. The god Apollo fell in love with her, and was remorselessly chasing her everywhere. As in the myth of Krokos, Daphne despaired and prayed to the other gods to free her from his unwanted attentions, they heard her prayers and transformed her into the shrub we know as the bay tree. From then on the bay tree was associated with the god Apollo and it became his sacred plant.

Apollo was also fatally attracted to another boy named Kyparissos. The boy adored a tame stag that was sacred to the nymphs. One day Kyparissos was throwing his hunting spear but unfortunately it hit his pet stag that had been sleeping in the shade nearby. The boy was so heartbroken that he begged the gods to let him mourn for the stag forever. Apollo therefore transformed Kyparissos into a cypress tree (*Cypressus*), which became the classic symbol of eternal grief.

We can also consider the fate of the nymph Minthē (*Menthe* in Latin) who was the beautiful mistress of Hades (the god of the Underworld). When Hades' wife Persephone heard of their affair she trampled Minthē underfoot. But Hades

FIGURE 64. Apollo pursued Daphne so much that she implored the gods to save her, they responded by turning her into the bay tree. The scene is immortalised in a Roman mosaic from Antioch.

had the nymph transformed into the aromatic garden mint, so that when its leaves are bruised or trodden on the air is filled with fragrance and would be an eternal reminder of her.

FIGURE 65. Flowers depicted on 5th–4th century BC Greek coinage. *l to r:* rose or cistus of Megiste, styrax from Selge; a daisy-like flower from Erythrae; Silphium from Cyrene (after R. Plant, London, 1979

Clytie loved the sun god Helios. But, when he fell in love with another she was so upset that she spread tales against her rival. When her rival was killed, and Helios did not return, Clytie pined. She sat on the ground and would only gaze up at the bright face of her god as he traversed the sky. Slowly she was transformed into a violet-like flower whose head follows the passage of the sun. She became the heliotrope.

A nymph named Pitys was wooed by both the Acadian god Pan and Boreas the stormy north wind. Tragically she preferred Pan because he was gentler, and so in revenge Boreas blew her over a cliff. On finding her body Pan changed her into the fir tree, which then became his sacred tree. Following on from this tale, in autumn her tears of resin fall from the tree. Pan features in another plant transformation concerning the nymph Syrinx; but in this case she did not want Pan's attentions and was subsequently changed into the giant reed. Pan cut some stems and put them to his lips, to be as close to her as possible, and discovered the notes of what then became his syrinx/pan pipes. The giant reed (*Arundo donax*) is not actually a garden plant but Pan's syrinx is such an important symbol/motif of the god in classical art that its mythical origins have a place here.

It is immediately noticeable that many of these myths have tragic endings for the mortals involved. None more so than Smyrna/Murrha (*Myrrha* in Latin) who was the daughter of Crinas. Apparently she refused to honour Aphrodite, and in revenge the goddess made her fall in love with her father. In despair Murrha decided to disguise herself to reach her love, but when her father discovered that she was pregnant, and that he was the father, he was furious. He tried to kill her, but she ran into the woods. She prayed to the gods to save her, they took pity and turned her into a tree (the myrrh tree) and from its heartwood Adonis was born. Her teardrops form the resinous juice myrrh, today obtained from the Arabian bush *Balsamodendron myrrha*. Murrha's son Adonis was himself transformed into the adonis/anemone flower (the cult of Adonis will be discussed later). Another myth says that the sister of Adonis, Myriki, was changed into a tamarisk tree. The Greek word for tamarisk was *myriki*; the tree symbolised beauty and youth and became sacred to the goddess Aphrodite.

Other flowers are mentioned in myths: The helichrysum was named after the nymph Helichrsye who first picked its blooms. It translates as 'the flower

FIGURE 66. Rose flower depicted on the reverse of a coin from Rhodes (© Ashmolean Museum, University of Oxford).

of gold'. Achillea was named after Achilles the greatest of all Greek warriors. On his way to Troy he inadvertently mortally wounded Telephus (the son of Herakles). The oracle said that the wounder, meaning the spear, would be the healer. So Achilles scraped some rust off his spear and from this sprang the plant achillea which healed the wound.[6]

Another Greek flower mentioned in our sources is the dianthus. These were considered the flowers of Zeus '*dios anthus*'; *anthus* being the Greek word for flower. Roses and flowers in general were linked to the goddess Aphrodite. One myth implies that all roses were once white, but one day Aphrodite was running through the woods and a rose thorn scratched her. Some drops of her blood fell onto the rose flower turning it red. The rose concerned could be either *Rosa gallica* or *R. phoenicia*, both of which are ancient species.

Roses in ancient sources

Many ancient texts show that in Greece roses were picked for making garlands and also for making perfumed oils. Sappho, the 7th century BC poetess from the Island of Lesbos, informs us that the rose was her own favourite flower. It was universally counted as the most popular flower of ancient Greece, mostly on account of its wonderful scent.

The ancient Greek historian Herodotus in the 5th century BC mentions roses, and interestingly a 60-petalled rose that grew in an area of northern Greece/Macedonia.[7] A later writer, Theophrastus mentions a hundred-petalled rose 'most of such roses grow near Philippi [Macedonia]; for the people of that place get them on Mount Pangaeus, where they are abundant, and plant them. However the inner petals are very small.'[8] We can assume that these decorative strong smelling roses were planted in a form of garden. This is an important reference to the existence of gardens that are more than just a vegetable plot, but it refers to a practice in the 4th century BC (which will be dealt with later). The 'hundred-petalled' rose is not the centifolia rose we know of today for that was introduced to cultivation much later. The 'hundred-petalled' rose is now thought to have been a fully petalled form of *Rosa gallica* or alternatively *Rosa damascena,* or even a double form of *Rosa alba.*[9]

Flowers on Greek coinage

It was claimed that the rose grew prolifically on the Island of Rhodes or *Rhodos* (which was its Greek name meaning rose). Therefore the people of *Rhodos* decided to put this flower on the reverse of their coinage. The image does however bear some resemblance to a rock-rose (*cistus*) which also grows well on that island. In ancient times the term 'rose' could equally be applied to any flower that appeared similar to a true rose.

Several other Greek cities chose a plant or fruit as an emblem for their town,[10] for example Naxos chose a bunch of grapes, and Eretria on the Greek island of Euboea had a vine with two bunches of grapes. The Island of Melos and the Greek city of Side in southern Turkey both picked a pomegranate fruit as their identifying symbol on coins. Selinunte chose a celery plant (*Selinon* was the Greek for celery) which grew abundantly in that region; so this was in recognition of the plant's importance to their economy. Flowers of the beautifully scented storax (*Styrax officinalis*) were an emblem on the coinage of Selge, a Greek city in southern Turkey. Styrax shrubs grow wild in that region today. In ancient times the city was known for making perfumes from this flowering aromatic shrub (both styrax oil, and resin were used as incense). Styrax has a white flower that seems to resemble the equally highly scented *Philadelphus,* commonly known as mock orange.

Flower rosettes feature on some coinage: a simple eight-petalled flower was stamped on coins of Cyme, and a more distinct 12-petalled daisy-like flower was used on coinage of Erythrae in Ionia. Silphium was the enigmatic plant so important to the economy of the Greek city of Kyrene (Cyrene in Libya) and was therefore the identifying symbol on their coins. This plant appeared a bit like fennel and celery, but sadly in antiquity silphium was overpicked and became extinct. This was partly because it was a wild plant that resisted numerous attempts to cultivate it. The image on the city's coins (plus carved column capitals at Beida) is the only visual reminders of this once important plant.

Wild flowers as opposed to garden flowers

Flowers as such are rarely mentioned in gardens of this period. However wild flowers were abundant in spring, and several Greek texts mention how the Greeks enjoyed picking wild flowers to make chaplets and garlands. The Greek word for a garland/chaplet was *stephanos* which originates from the verb *stepho* (to put round). Wild flowers can still be seen growing between trees in olive groves and they make a glorious sight. Olives were and still are one of the main crops in Greece. They are very nourishing and they provide oil for cooking and lamps, and as we have seen cultivation of olives goes back to the Minoan Age. Olives were grown in groves and along the edges of fruit orchards.[11]

Literary evidence shows a great fondness for wild flowers, but there is little evidence for cultivated flowers in decorative gardens in ancient Greece. There are many reasons for this, firstly a large part of Greece is mountainous, and is hot and dry in summer. Also, rather crucially, Greek people in towns and rural areas could only rely on a limited supply of water drawn by bucket from local springs, public wells and cisterns. Another important factor to consider is that in ancient Greece individual city-states often fought with each other and so for safety reasons many people chose to live behind strong walls. For this reason cities tended to be sited on a prominent hilltop or on an acropolis. The Acropolis in Athens is an example, this later became a sacred area, but the name is used elsewhere to denote a hilltop fortified settlement – an 'acropolis site'. An example is Sillyon (a Greek city in Turkey) where the flat-topped hill, stands above the plain. There was once a large city on the top; on such a hill the ground is rocky and therefore houses could only have gravel or paved courts, as opposed to cultivated garden areas. These acropolis sites had no piped water, water had to be collected from a communal well or cistern. So with such a limited source this water was mainly reserved for human consumption.

Greek houses with courtyards

Plans of these towns show the density of housing on such an acropolis. Even at Olynthos in northern Greece the city was originally sited on a hill but when it expanded on the lower slopes of the hill in 432 BC, the highly planned and regulated rows of houses in the new section of the town were still small in size and close together. This was their preferred form of living. The city was conquered and not rebuilt so it has been possible to systematically excavate the site. Archaeologists have found that at Olynthos and elsewhere the Greek houses opened from the street into a courtyard which gave access to the rooms. The courtyards were not large, at Olynthos for example, the yards measured roughly only 51 m².[12] The surface of Greek courtyards was of gravel, or beaten earth. On occasion there may be a little altar located in the centre or to one side, there was no room for a garden.[13]

Archaeologists, however, found a couple of flower pots in one courtyard at Olynthos, indicating that at least a few potherbs may have grown there.[14] On several sites archaeologists have discovered an enigmatic pit in the courtyard of Greek houses. There has been speculation whether this was used as a form of latrine. However as there is often a channel directing water into the pit, and the finding of numerous potsherds within them, it has been suggested that they may in fact have been a pit for planting a tree, or perhaps a vine.[15] No botanical analysis has shown what species were involved.

Extramural gardens

Although ancient sources of the Classical period do not give any clues to indicate the existence of domestic town gardens in Greece, they do say that there were gardens outside towns. An example is quoted in Homer, Nausikaa says: 'there is my father's estate and his flowering orchard, as far from the city as the shout of a man will carry.'[16] A tradition became established where people went out of the city by day, to tend their fields or market-style gardens and returned at night or when alerted to danger. Several references, gleaned from the Laws recorded by Aristotle,[17] and from some of the comedy plays of Aristophanes (*c*.445–385 BC), indicate the existence of extra mural gardens. They mention that household refuse was regularly collected by civic dung collectors (from a large dolia kept just outside the front door!) and the contents were deposited just outside the town walls. This large heap could then be used as fertiliser by extramural gardeners.[18] These 'gardens' were mainly used to grow produce though, because agriculture and horticulture in Ancient Greece was really aimed at self sufficiency. Although there were no private domestic gardens, there was another form of garden that was open to all citisens: the sacred garden.

Sacred groves and gardens mentioned in Greek literature

Sacred gardens could be found in or outside cities. There are numerous Greek references to groves surrounding temples or shrines and these were in fact, considered by the ancient Greeks to be a garden. Sometime the word *alsos* (ἄλσος) was used to denote a grove of trees. They could be small areas, such as that surrounding the Temple of Hephaestus in the centre of Athens, or if they were in more rural situations there would be more space and therefore be correspondingly larger. The earliest reference mentioning a sacred grove is found in Homer's Odyssey 'You will find a glorious grove of poplars sacred to Athene near the road, and a spring runs there.'[19] In areas that were often ravaged by warfare, these places were all the more important, because by their very nature they were sacred, and so were regarded as sacrosanct. In fact there was a universal agreement that forbade the felling of trees in such sanctuaries – on penalty of death. So the tradition of having sacred groves or 'gardens' became well established. Apollonius of Rhodes mentions the Grove of Apollo at Kyrene with its myrtle trees.[20] The area around Apollo's temple today also has many fine bay trees, which were his sacred plant. The same city also had a Garden of Aphrodite, located near the spring, the myrtle which was her sacred plant must have extended into her garden area as well.

We also hear of the 'gardens of Aphrodite' at Athens, which surrounded her shrine. Such gardens needed water, and not surprisingly we tend to find that they are often located beside a stream. The Athenian 'Gardens of Aphrodite' are thought to have been close to the river Ilissos. To give an indication of what we might find within such sacred places Sappho provides a charming picture of the sacred grove around her local Shrine of Aphrodite (in the 7th century):

Come, goddess, to your holy shrine, where your delightful apple grove awaits, and altars smoke with frankincense. A cool brook sounds through apple boughs, and all's with roses overhung: from shimmering leaves a trancelike sleep takes hold.[21]

This idyllic setting can be compared with that of a much later Hellenistic pastoral poet, Theocritus, who was writing in the 3rd century BC:

Along that footpath, shepherd, past the oaks, you'll come across a statue, newly carved from fig, its bark still fresh... It's in a sacred grove, close by a spring forever flowing from the rocks round bays and myrtles and sweet-smelling cypresses. A vine spreads out its tendrils there, and bears its fruit; in spring, the clear-voiced blackbird sings his lively tune and lilting nightingales return the song in honeyed notes. Go there, sit down ...[22]

These extracts show a view of nature as a garden, but it is obviously not entirely a natural garden, because it contains a footpath, statue and a vine that is probably well tended. These sacred groves must have been enhanced as an offering to the deities who dwelt there, as well as being an attraction to visiting worshippers. You could say that the grand classical inspired gardens of places like Stourhead (in England) reflect this theme, of nature improved upon, and they help to recreate an ambience of the Greek sacred groves.

References indicate that offerings were sometimes hung on trees outside a sacred cave (usually ones that contained a spring) and as we have heard in some cases flowers were planted around the cave so that a little sacred garden would have developed nearby. This concept is recaptured in a Roman marble relief,

FIGURE 67. Landscaped gardens such as at Stourhead were inspired by the Classical world; they effectively recreate the ambience of a Greek sacred garden with temple, statues and grove of trees.

FIGURE 68. Roman marble relief depicting a lady making a sacrifice in front of a cave sacred to Pan. This scene evokes the sacred gardens around caves in Greece, Lateran Museum, Rome.

and it gives an impression of how such a sacred grove might have looked in this period. In the relief a lady makes an offering beside a statue placed in front of a cave, while a young pan plays his pipes in the cave entrance.

Sacred gardens discovered by archaeology

In the centre of Athens a grove was created around the Temple of Hephaestus, this is situated to one side of the Agora (the large central meeting square of a Greek city). Archaeological excavations around this temple showed that on three sides two rows of planting pits had been dug into the bedrock. The square pits were about 88 cm wide, and would have allowed a sufficient depth of good soil for each tree. Each pit was found to have a broken earthenware flower pot *in situ*, which at last is firm evidence for horticulture. The pots had been deliberately broken; Theophrastus the Greek botanist (of the Hellenistic period) mentions the practise of layering plants in pots,[23] these could then be used for transplanting trees. Sapling trees, still in their plant pots (but cracked so that root growth would not be held back) had been planted directly into their final positions around the temple. The orderly rows of plant pits were aligned with the columns of the temple. The size of the plant pits suggest that medium rather than large trees had been planted here giving a clue to its former appearance. Therefore when replanting the trees in the temple's sacred grove some years ago they decided to have myrtle in the 1st row and pomegranate behind. This combination would not become too overgrown quickly and would not obscure the temple, and they would add to its beauty. The sacred garden was also provided with small flower beds, found near the precinct wall of the temple, but we can only guess which species were planted there because no evidence was found.

Planting pits have been discovered in association with other temples providing further evidence for sacred groves. At Corinth seven plant pits were discovered on the north side of the Temple of Asklepios.[24] Twenty-three circular rock-cut pits were excavated by the Temple of Zeus at Nemea. The soil within these pits was analysed and has suggested that cypress trees once grew there.[25] This is supported by a passage in Pausanias that actually mentions a grove of cypress trees around the temple.[26] Evidence showed that the trees had been planted in the 4th century BC, but as earlier writers such as Pindar and Euripides mention sacred groves at Nemea it can be assumed that there had been an earlier sacred grove. To provide a link with the past cypress trees have been replanted around the temple site.

An interesting example for which some of the details are still preserved is the 'Garden of Herakles' on the Island of Thasos. This specific 'garden' included a special dining area for members of the cult. An inscription found nearby indicated that this particular 'garden' was apparently leased out, and would have supplied an income to maintain the cult. The terms of the lease stipulated that the trees (fig, nut and myrtles) should be tended, and that the lessee would be entitled to some of its produce.[27] So, it appears that in some cases it was permissible to make a profit from cultivating part of a sacred garden; this may have been the case in other forms of Greek 'gardens'. Vegetables would have formed part of the produce on leased plots and market gardens, but remains of vegetables and herbs are rare because they are so perishable. However, a rare waterlogged deposit found close to the Temple of Hera at Samos provided evidence

FIGURE 69. Archaeological excavations around the Temple of Hephaestus in Athens revealed two rows of tree pits with plant pots in each pit, alerting them to the presence of a sacred garden here, (American School of Classical Studies at Athens: Agora Excavations).

for the use of these plants by devotees: beet; blite (a spinach-like plant); caper; celery; coriander; dill; lettuce (a wild form *Lactuca serriola*); oriental poppy and purslane.[28] Pausanias (who had been travelling in Greece during the Roman period) mentions a venerable old willow growing in her sanctuary.[29] His brief descriptions of sacred gardens he saw in or around sanctuaries gives us an overall impression that they were shaded by rows of cypress, laurel or plane trees.

FIGURE 70. Myrtles and pomegranates have been replanted in the pits to recreate the effect of an Athenian sacred grove (photo: D. Bruff).

Tomb gardens

Another form of Greek garden is one that accompanied some of the important tombs, *kēpotaphia*. In general tombs lined the approach to a city. Heroes were particularly honoured in this way with a shrine (*heroon*). Often the tomb monument and its garden were enclosed, and were treated as sacred areas. Funerary gardens usually comprised just trees and large bushes making a small grove around the tomb, for the simple reason that mature plants would not require constant attention and watering in a dry climate.

Civic groves in Greek literature

Plutarch tells us that the earliest known attempt to provide shade giving trees in the heart of a city was by the Athenian statesman Kimon in the 5th century BC. He planted a series of plane trees in the Agora of Athens, and brought water to a fountain house at the edge of the square.[30] A mature plane tree has wide reaching branches and large leaves which creates excellent shade. Kimon also brought water to an area outside the city called the Akademy, so that a plantation could be established there. This measure led other later statesmen to make a similar gesture, for instance at Rhegion a Greek colony in southern Italy.

Three streams flow around Athens and along each of these there were groves of trees.[31] The Kephissos River watered the Akademy, the Eridanos watered the area around the Lyceum and the Ilissos flowed through the Kynosarges area. All three areas were kept as a place for recreation and were much frequented by the populace, these groves could be equated as a form of public garden. They were used by athletes in training and by the ephebes, the young adolescent men who were obliged to train for war. It was also the duty of all citizens to make sure they remained fit in readiness for war and so they would come to have races and exercise – under the welcoming shade of the trees. Each area had springs where the men and youths could quench their thirst after their exertions. Because these groves became so popular, Greek-style gymnasia were set up in each area. Between races and bouts of training the men would discuss the world at large, and philosophers joined in their debates. This led to the establishment of philosophy schools in all of these three areas. Plato formed his School in the Akademy, Aristotle in the Lyceum, and the Cynics in the Kynosarges. A later period mosaic, from Pompeii, shows Plato in the Akademy and is representative of this Greek form of park-like garden. The philosophers are shown discussing under the shade of a tree, a mere token that represented the grove, and of all the trees the wide branching plane tree epitomised the Akademy. Above them is a sundial, and in the distance (top right) are the city walls of Athens which illustrates its setting outside the city.

Literary references give a wonderful impression of the groves in and around the Akademy. One text is taken from a comedy play by Aristophanes it relates to the physical training contests that would have taken place there, but also names some of the trees that you would have seen:

> you'll go down to Akademe's Park and take a training run under the sacred olive trees, a wreath of white reeds on your head, with a nice decent companion of your own age; in autumn you'll share the fragrance of leafy poplar and carefree convolvulus [smilax], and you'll take delight in the spring when the plane tree whispers to the elm ...[32]

The second text about the Akademy comes from the ancient traveller Pausanias (writing much later in about AD 160) he was mostly concerned with statuary and monuments that he saw, but his description infers that these may have been a feature of other park like groves.

> Outside the city, too, in the parishes and on the roads, the Athenians have sanctuaries of the gods, and graves of heroes and of men... [he spied several of these on the way from Athens]. Before the entrance to the Akademy is an altar to love [Eros]... In the Akademy is an altar to Prometheus, and from it they run to the city carrying torches... There is an altar to the Muses, and another to Hermes, and one within to

FIGURE 71. Roman mosaic illustrating the eminent philosopher Plato discussing in his Akademy grove, from Pompeii.

Athene, and they have built one to Herakles. There is also an olive tree, accounted to be the second that appeared. Not far from the Akademy is the monument of Plato...[33]

These are just partial descriptions of what the area was like, but they help to furnish a picture of these park-like gardens.

Garden themes on Greek vase paintings

Another valuable source of information on life in ancient Greece can be found in the scenes painted on their distinctive pottery. Sadly, surprisingly few Greek vase paintings depict flowers, and none of gardens, this was mainly because the Greeks tended to concentrate on the human form rather than on landscape or gardens.

Some however depict trees, an example can be found inside a mid-6th century BC black-figure painted cup where there is a wonderful overall design with a man holding large branches of two trees with two birds and a nest, plus a cicada on one of the branches. It makes a nice verdant scene. The cup comes from the Eastern Greek world, and is now in the Louvre.

At least three vases and fragments show girls/women picking fruit from an orchard. A red-figure painted vase of *c.*480 BC shows two women holding baskets to collect the fruit from a centrally placed fruit tree. This vase is one of a few signed by the artist himself: Pistoxenos Syriskos (the Little Syrian). It may be

FIGURE 72. Red-figure
vase with girls picking
fruit, painted by
Pistoxenos Syriskos.

significant that the painter of this vase (like the previous example) may have been influenced by eastern horticultural ideas, because so few scenes depicting nature exist elsewhere. However, a similar red-figure vase with fruit pickers, painted by the Orchard Painter, can be seen in the Metropolitan Museum in New York. Here the overlap in this painting tends to give the impression of a fruit tree growing in the large pot between the fruit pickers, but the tree is actually behind the pot which was placed there specifically to contain all the collected fruit.

Some vase paintings show diners on a couch under a vine, but on inspection the vine is really a decorative device to indicate the presence of the god of wine: Dionysus. Often the vine is not supported at all. On other occasions the vine is shown growing out of the god, as a reminder of his association with the plant and its produce – wine.

Another Greek vase now in Florence (*c*.410 BC, painted by the Meidias painter) depicts the myth of Phaon playing the lyre in a bower. The bower is sketchily drawn, but it was seen as sufficient to signify an outdoor setting, presumably in a grove.

A 4th-century BC red-figure Sicilian vase portrays comic actors in a scene from a Greek play about Herakles and Auge. She was a priestess of the Temple of Athene at Tegea, and as he allegedly seduced her within the sacred precinct of the temple the stage scenery needed to include a representation of a sacred grove found within the temple confines. On this occasion a couple of tree branches placed on the temple's altar, acted as a more practical substitute for full sized trees.

In Greece it was the custom to cut branches of sweet smelling myrtle and bring them into the house of the bride prior to the marriage ceremony. Literary references mention this practise, and it is beautifully portrayed on a red-figure painted vessel in Athens Museum. Young women arrange the twigs in elegant finely decorated pots.

Adonis gardens

Broken pots/vases or broken amphorae were used as a planter for what is termed an Adonis Garden. A red-figure vase painting (now in the Karlsruhe Museum) shows three of these broken pots that constitute an important feature of the Greek and eastern cult of Adonis. The adherents of this cult and the planters of these pots were almost entirely married women and prostitutes, because it is primarily concerned with the cycle of vegetation and regeneration. Part of this cult involved sowing quick-growing seeds in old pots or broken amphorae, and after sprouting the pots were lifted onto the roofs of houses. The plants were not watered afterwards because they were destined to wilt and die in memory of the death of the god Adonis. In the vase painting Aphrodite is shown climbing half way up a ladder while her son Eros passes to her the 'Adonis Gardens' that were destined to be left on the roof.

One of the versions of this vegetation myth relates how Aphrodite had fallen in love with the beautiful youth Adonis. But he was mortally wounded by a wild boar while out hunting. Aphrodite was inconsolable and her grief stricken tears fell to the earth where they turned into the anemone flower. Both the adonis flower (*Adonis annua*) and red anemones (*Anemone coronaria*) are candidates for the flower concerned and both have a widespread distribution. Interestingly, in this tale (as with others) we find an occasion where Greek myths relate to each other, because while Aphrodite was rushing to the dying youth she scratched herself against a white rose bush, and her blood turned it red.

In the myth, Aphrodite was so distraught that she pleaded to the Olympian gods to have Adonis brought back to life. The story is touchingly recounted in Bion's *Lament for Adonis*. Her plea was partly successful for Zeus decreed that Adonis would spend six months in the underworld, and he could return to her for the remaining six months. This decision forms one version of Winter and Spring. Another myth (mentioned above) features Ceres and Persephone, and in fact one version of the Adonis myth is also linked to Persephone who also loved the young man. She wanted him to stay with her in the Underworld, but the tug of love was solved by decreeing that Adonis would stay six months with her and six months with Aphrodite!

So, in the Adonis rituals, the planted seeds reflect Adonis's short return to life, and his untimely death each year. Although this cult originated in Byblos it spread to Asia Minor and Greece. It is mentioned in one of Aristophanes comedy plays: The Lysistrata, so it was already in Athens by the 5th century BC. The cult later spread throughout the Mediterranean. It is a rather strange form of gardening, but could have appeared as a garden in miniature. The seeds planted in these gardens were of either: lettuce, fennel, barley or wheat (quick growing ones). Today in Malta they put pots of cress beside the altar in their Churches at Christmas, perhaps to reiterate that old sentiment: that the seeds like Christ's life would last but a short time.

FIGURE 73. Detail from a red-figure vase showing Eros offering a bowl of seedlings (an Adonis garden) to his mother Aphrodite who will place them on the house roof as part of the ritual in the cult of Adonis, Karlsruhe Museum.

Byblos, in Lebanon, was the ancient centre of the cult of Adonis. The cult ceremonies began when the water of the local river, the River Adonis, turned red. This was believed to be a sign that Adonis had died and his blood was being washed down river. This superstition came about through a phenomenon that still occurs after heavy equinox rainstorms wash the local red earth down river. In ancient times the people of Byblos then searched for his body. On finding a suitable log that could be substituted for his body, it was ceremoniously brought into the city and red flower petals would be strewn in his wake. There would be a day of lamentation following his death, and then the planting of the seeds.

It is possible that the Byblos cult of Aphrodite and Adonis could have arisen out of the Egyptian cult of Isis and Osiris translated into Greek myth. Isis and Osiris were connected to fertility and regeneration, and Byblos had many links with Egypt. A notable point is that Osiris' coffin was washed ashore there. Also the Osiris beds, those shallow receptacles that mimicked his outline and were sown with seeds of barley, do bear a marked resemblance to the later Adonis gardens. These cross cultural links are intriguing.

The Greeks of the Archaic and Classical periods were restricted by the rugged terrain and their dry summer climate which meant that they could only rely on springs and well water, and in some cases whatever could be stored in a cistern. In these periods Greeks were also hampered by social factors: people mostly lived in densely populated cities, with little space for gardens. There were no palaces here, as in Egyptian and Mesopotamian cultures, and no comparable aristocracy with large private houses and vast gardens. However, the Greeks made use of the abundant wild flowers in the countryside, by making chaplets to adorn their hair. They cultivated market gardens outside the city walls, and they had potager style gardens and orchards that appear to reflect Homeric

FIGURE 74. Adonis flowers (*Adonis annua*) in northern Cyprus (photo: B. Smith).

descriptions of the Garden of Alcinoös. But, their lasting legacy was their rich collection of Greek myths, which were largely assimilated into later cultures. In gardening terms their greatest achievement was the creation of sacred gardens and groves, in cities and in rural areas. These statuary filled groves were admired by later visitors to their shores, they were plundered, but we find that later cultures would develop further this Greek concept, especially of a philosophical garden area to recreate their own version of the Akademy groves.

Macedonian and Hellenistic Greek gardens

The resurgence and meteoric rise of the Kingdom of Macedonia in northern Greece during second half of the 4th century BC under Philip II and his son Alexander, and their subsequent domination of Greece, had tremendous repercussions for the art of gardening in that region. With the introduction of monarchies came the desire for palaces and correspondingly large dwellings for members of the new ruling class. Some of these may have contained garden areas, but as scholars believe the palaces were rebuilt during the Hellenistic age details of the earlier palace/house and garden may be masked.[34] It is possible that the gardens were inspired through contact with lands further east, such as southeast Thrace and Ionia that were at that time ruled by the Achaemenid Persians.

Gardens in Macedonia uncovered by archaeology

Aigai (Vergina, in northern Greece) was the traditional Macedonian capital city and a palace was built here by Philip II. The rooms of the palace were constructed around a large rectangular peristyle court (1600 m²), a smaller secondary court was added later. The two courts were open spaces and seem to have been kept as a garden, since there was no surface paving or other structures found within these areas. Stone rain water gutters survive in places along the edge of the colonnades, but no evidence was sought to find how the garden was planted as the site was excavated prior to the interests in garden archaeology. Previously Greek houses tended to have a form of portico (or *stoa*) on one side of their courtyard, but here the garden court was surrounded by four porticoes making a περίστυλον (*peristylon*); *Peri* means around, *stylon* relates to the columns. The *peristylon* is thought to have been a Greek invention but one has been discovered in the Persian palace at Vouni in Cyprus (*c.*500–450 BC).[35] The inspiration for this feature therefore, must be considered as coming from the melting pot of the Eastern Greeks and Persians. When there is more space it is a logical development to extend the stoa/portico to more than one side.

The Macedonian capital was transferred to Pella and another palace was built there by Philip II to replace a previous palace built by his predecessor Archelaos which had been destroyed by the Illyrians in 359 BC. The new palace and gardens were reconstructed on a lavish scale and included a series of colonnaded

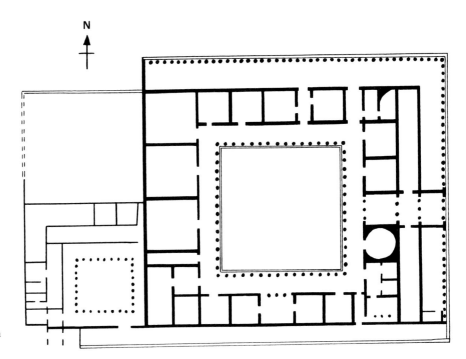

N

FIGURE 75. Plan of the Palace at Aigai, northern Greece, with two peristyle garden areas, 4th century BC.

peristyles. One of the gardens measuring 35 × 30 m (1050 m² in area) was found to have an altar in the centre, and the base of a semicircular seat on the western side. There was a pair of larger courtyards to the west of the residential section, and an even larger one beyond. The latter had a swimming pool on one side and has been identified as the palaestra/exercise area of the palace

There are also several large private residences at Pella that would have belonged to the faithful companions of the king; these were on a relatively smaller scale. One of the largest dwellings, the House of Dionysus, occupied a whole block of housing in the city; it had two rectangular peristyle courtyards, the smaller one was six columns wide (and can be compared with the peristyle garden at the palace at Aigai which was sixteen columns wide). The second colonnaded garden was 300 m² in area and was found to have sections of a wide stone drainage channel still in situ around the edges. Today the gardens at Pella and Aigai are covered with grass, but evidence of former plantings schemes is lacking for no garden archaeology was undertaken.

Hellenistic gardens

Alexander the Great famously set out to conquer the Persians in 334 BC, and in the course of his conquest he led his armies through modern Turkey, Syria, Lebanon, Egypt, Iraq, Iran and Afghanistan before returning through modern Pakistan. A campaign of twelve years throughout the region gave ample opportunity for his followers to absorb a range of ideas, including the eastern attitude to kingship and the level of luxury appropriate to royalty. The

Macedonians and Greeks in Alexander's army were amazed by the large well-stocked Persian gardens they saw. Alexander's retinue included a botanist who recorded many new plant species, some were sent back to Greece; these will be mentioned later.

After Alexander's death in 323 BC his empire broke up into a number of separate states ruled by his more powerful generals. After many years of war between them the survivors were: the Ptolemies who ruled Egypt, the Seleucid Empire that was centred on Syria, and the Kingdom of Macedonia itself which still dominated Greece. The period from the death of Alexander in 323–31 BC (being the end of the last of the successor kingdoms) is generally referred to as the Hellenistic Age. During this period the newly established royal families and their supporters had the wealth to support their ambitions for a luxurious lifestyle and one aspect of this was the possession of a Persian style *paradeisos*.

The garden areas are on the whole of a smaller scale than their Persian counterparts, but we can see that the Hellenistic concept of having a garden space in a palace was important. Instead of the palace being set within a large park-like garden, the Hellenistic palace often incorporated a rectangular or square garden area inside the palace itself. The Macedonians and Hellenes admired the way the Persians used porticoes for garden pavilions and this may have influenced the Hellenes to incorporate a version in their own gardens.

Peristyle garden courts were incorporated into palaces throughout the Hellenistic world, and we hear from Polybius that the Macedonian kings also had large well appointed game parks – also termed a *paradeisos*. As yet the only potential Hellenistic period game park that has been so identified is one at Aï Khanoum (see below).

Archaeological evidence for Hellenistic Gardens

Few Hellenistic buildings survive because most were destroyed and/or underlie later structures, so there are difficulties in distinguishing which part belongs to the earlier Hellenistic phase. However, a peristyle garden has been identified on the acropolis at Pergamon in Turkey, which was the seat of the Attalid Hellenistic rulers. In one section of the palace, built in the 2nd century BC, a number of large reception rooms were arranged around a square porticoed area that appears to have been kept as a garden. Grass is growing in the garden today, but as this was a rocky acropolis the soil would not have been deep enough to support large trees there, and at the time of excavation no note was made of plant material.

Further afield, at Aï Khanoum, a Hellenistic city founded by the Seleucid kings (beside the River Oxus in northern Afghanistan), the rebuilt 2nd century palace also included garden areas set within a porticoed peristyle. The largest garden (that was perhaps used as a forecourt) was traversed before entering the palace and would have been awe inspiring for visitors. It can be measured by the number of columns in the four surrounding porticoes: 34 wide and 27 deep.

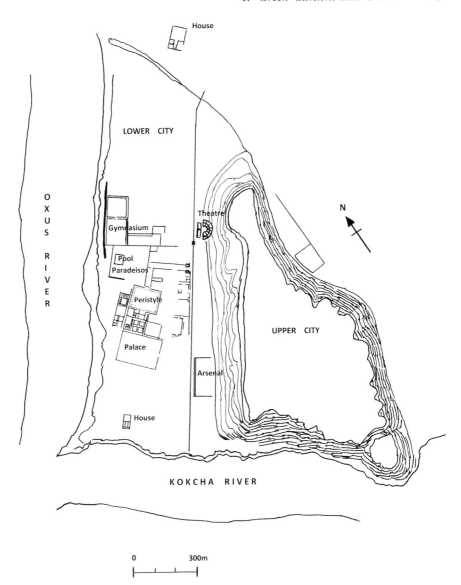

FIGURE 76. Plan of the Hellenistic palace at Aï Khanoum, 2nd century BC. The palace was provided with peristyle courtyards, garden areas, and a *paradeisos*.

A second peristyle of 16 × 16 columns may well have been a garden reserved for more private use. At Aï Khanoum another portion of this site has been recognised as a large park or Persian style *paradeisos* of the palace. This region retained strong Persian/Bactrian influences therefore the melding of ideas here are interesting.[36] The city fell to nomadic tribesmen *c.*145 BC and because of its remoteness the Hellenistic colony was not resettled or altered by successive cultures like the majority of other cities, therefore it gives a valuable insight into buildings and gardens of this period. Sadly no account was made of any garden features or paleobotany during excavation of the garden areas.

In Jordan there are rare remains of a Hellenistic palace at Araq el Amir (17 km west of Amman) which dates to the beginning of the 2nd century BC. The

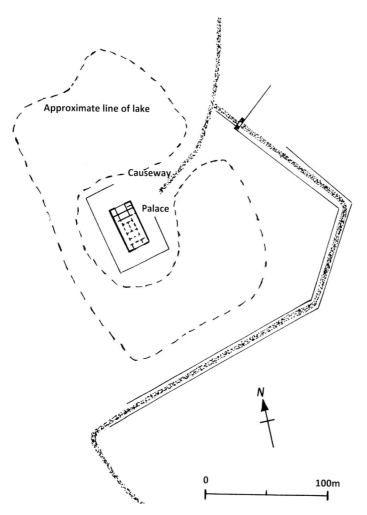

FIGURE 77. Palace of Hyrcanus at Araq el Amir, Jordan. According to Josepheus the palace was surrounded by a lake and was set in a *paradeisos* park with pavilions, 2nd century BC.

building is sometimes called the 'Castle of the Slave' because its owner Hyrcanus was descended from the local Tobaid priestly caste. His short lived palace was situated in its own little valley and is surrounded by a large enclosed park. We are fortunate that the Jewish chronicler Josepheus in his work on *Jewish Antiquities* gives a description. He mentions that there was a lake all around the palace, and that there were *aulai* (pavilions) placed in *paradeisoi* parks.[37] There is still a deep depression around the palace that corresponds with the artificial lake mentioned by Josepheus, and there was a causeway to gain access to the palace. Unfortunately the *aulai* have not been located, but these may have been largely made of wood and so would leave little trace. One rather charming feature that would have enlivened the gardens close to the palace itself was a pair of fountains that had been placed on both of the long side walls of the palace. About a quarter of the way along each wall there was a carved leopard, standing with one paw raised and with his tail curled around its hind leg. Water poured from the animal's mouth and gently flowed down into a shallow stone water trough. This enigmatic garden

FIGURE 78. Leopard fountain at the Palace of Hyrcanus at Araq el Amir, Jordan, 2nd century BC.

feature is a rare find in this period, but it shows that such items could have existed where there was a sufficient water supply nearby.

When King Herod's Winter Palace at Jericho in Judea (Palestine) was uncovered archaeologists carefully examined the garden areas (Herod reigned from 40–4 BC). Within the palace itself there were two peristyle courtyards that had been cultivated. In one of these, called the Corinthian peristyle, traces of plant bedding trenches came to light. The trenches had been neatly dug in rows, which is reminiscent of the orderly rows of Persian planting mentioned by Xenophon. However, no pollen was preserved to identify what species had been planted there. In the Ionic West Peristyle garden (B64, measuring 19.1 × 18.7 m, but with a planted area of 9.1 × 12.3 m) the straight rows of bedding trenches had been cut on a different alignment.[38] The north–south orientated trenches were 1.5 m apart. Here the soil was examined and pieces of charcoal were found, these may indicate what was growing in the garden or might just represent local species in the vicinity brought to the site as firewood and the remains subsequently used as fertiliser. They were mostly of native species: *Ficus sycomores, Olea europaea, Pistacia, Quercus, Tamarix, Ziziphus* (and *Juglans* the only non-native). Carbonised seeds included those from: the Geranium family, *Moraceae* (Mulberry), *Plantago indica, Trifolium, Lens* and *Triticum*.[39] A reconstruction of this garden was made showing a possible planting scheme where regular rows of balsam plants were laid out; these were highly prized plants specific to Judea (*Opobalsamum gileadensis*), and it is possible that they may have been grown in this garden at Jericho or nearby. We are reminded that in the Bible the prophet Jeremiah (8: 22) commented: 'Is there no balm in Gilead' because he knew that this was a major crop of that region.

Thirty-three flower pots have been found in the trenches of the Ionic garden at Herod's Winter Palace. The pots were rounded but tapered at the base; three holes had been made in the lower part of the pot before firing to ease drainage. The upper rim of each pot was on average about 11 cm in diameter. A latex cast was taken of one of the pots, which was found to have a root cavity in its ancient soil infill, this revealed that a former plant root went right through the pot.[40] Ancient sources (such as Pliny the Elder the great Roman natural historian) mention that these pots were used to make cuttings by air layering. To do this the pot is slipped over a young branch or shoot of a tree that you wanted to propagate, the pot was packed with soil, and then left to root for approximately two years. The pot is then cut off the parent tree and is ready to transport. The pots at Jericho had been planted straight into the ground, so must have already rooted. Some, evidently, had outgrown their pot because broken potsherds were also found. Tests revealed that these pots had been made locally.

Herod also constructed a large sunken garden at Jericho which lay on the opposite bank of the wadi. Next to this he placed a large rectangular swimming pool. His palace complex at Herodium also included a garden with another large pool, whereas two pools side by side were included in earlier Hasmonean palatial complexes at Jericho.[41] The precedent for these pools is thought to be Egyptian rather than Persian.[42] However, we need to consider the possibility that while previously living in Rome Herod may have been influenced by aristocratic garden designs he had seen, and these will be dealt with in the next chapter.

Apart from the royal palaces and dwellings of the elite, the average house of the Hellenistic Greeks was modest in size and they still preferred to have a practical paved court rather than a verdant garden. Examples of Hellenistic houses can be seen in the new residential area built at Priene (in Ionia), where the regularly planned houses were provided with plain courtyards as at Olynthus. However the average area of the open courts at Priene was originally 88.4 m[42] which was relatively more spacious that those of Olynthos. Some houses at Priene were later subdivided and the yards correspondingly shrank in size, whereas others such as House 33 were enlarged and the owners were able to construct a full peristyle around their open courtyard, but this area was not kept as a garden. On the Greek Island of Delos, some of the houses did have open peristyle courts, but they covered it with gravel or mosaic. Even in the western Greek site at Glanum in southern France, a small paved court merely acted as a light well for rooms around it.

Hellenistic gardens and groves mentioned by ancient writers

Few texts mention gardens of this period. We know of a palace at Antiochia, a city founded by Seleucus I *c.*300 BC. The city (more commonly known as Antioch) was sited next to the River Orontes and the Seleucid palace lay on the nearby island on the river. Apparently the palace occupied about a quarter of the island, which would allow sufficient space for a garden. This city became a metropolis but as the site has been continuously occupied all vestiges of the Hellenistic city are deeply buried.

Strabo mentions that at the nearby settlement at Daphne there was:

> a large shaded grove watered with springs, in the middle of which there is an inviolate enclosure and temple of Apollo and Artemis. It was the custom of the Antiochenes and their neighbours to hold a religious festival there.[44]

This was a large grove, but there was an important oracular shrine here and the area and its sacred groves were still treated with respect.

The luxurious life led by the Hellenistic rulers was often remarked upon by later writers, especially concerning the excesses in the city of Alexandria, named after the conqueror Alexander the Great. The city flourished under the Ptolemaic dynasty of kings. The city's position on the edge of the Nile delta ensured that there was a plentiful supply of water for gardens. The Ptolemaic Palace had several gardens; the area of the palace and its grounds totalled almost a quarter of the entire city. We hear of the *megiston peristylon* that was used for receptions. The palaces were extensive and were surrounded by an *alsos* (park) with several pavilions. There was room for a form of zoo for we hear that agents sent rare animals to Ptolemy II, and apparently Ptolemy VIII bred birds in the palace grounds (he wrote a treatise on the topic).[45] So the palace gardens incorporated some of the facets of a Persian *paradeisos* style of game park. There may have been botanical style gardens too. When Ptolemy II held a special feast in honour of Dionysus a large tent was erected in the grounds for entertaining, it was so large that 100 dining couches could fit into it, and statues were placed beside each wooden column supporting the pavilion.[46] Branches of myrtle, bay and other boughs were placed on the outside of the pavilion, and all sorts of flowers were strewn on the floors so that it formed a 'picture of an extraordinarily beautiful meadow.' Because of the climate the gardens of Egypt were said to be able to grow plants and flowers in abundance throughout the year, so we can visualise a fine verdant garden here.

There were many groves of trees in Alexandria, so the city could be likened to a garden city. There was a *museion* area and library which had 'a public walk, an exedra with seats' next to a building where people could study.[47] There was a sanctuary to Pan situated on an artificially made conical shaped hill. A spiral path led up to the summit from where there was an outstanding view of the whole city below. The Hellenes in Egypt were, of course, fortunate to have the benefit of centuries of Egyptian expertise in horticulture, and they may well have incorporated Egyptian features into their new gardens. Sadly none of these gardens are visible today because, due to changing ground levels, parts of the royal quarter are now below sea level, or are built over.

Records show that there were many *paradeisoi* in Ptolemaic Egypt, but on the whole this term was not confined to palm groves it was now used to describe utilitarian gardens including fruit orchards and for growing vegetables. The Fayum area in particular was developed into a series of farm and *paradeisoi* plots managed by Greeks, and interestingly some correspondence between officials and lessees has survived showing the management of these areas and the produce grown there.

Funerary gardens in Alexandria

Outside the city, to the west and east, there were large necropoli with numerous tomb monuments, Strabo said that there were numerous gardens in the suburb called Necropolis.[48] Some of the enclosed funerary gardens of the *kepotaphia* were rented out for fruit and vegetable growing like the *paradeisoi* mentioned above.

In contrast the 3rd century BC tombs within the Moustapha Pasha cemetery at Alexandria were largely dug out of the bedrock and four of these were fashioned to appear like houses/buildings with rooms leading off open courtyards. Tombs 1 and 4 were given a peristyle around their square court; each had an altar in the middle but the surface of the court was left bare. Tomb Three though was highly unusual it was constructed to resemble a theatrical stage with backdrop, the owner's funerary couch was placed in an alcove on centre stage; and the open area below (which would correspond to the theatre's orchestra) was turned into a form of garden. Here walkways surrounded two rectilinear plant beds of unequal size; each bed had been edged with low limestone blocks. The beds had been excavated further to provide a deep layer for planting.[49] Because these tombs were designed to resemble houses it seems possible that the garden plant beds reflect those seen in gardens of the living. These already pillaged tombs were uncovered during the 1950s prior to the emergence of garden archaeology and therefore an opportunity was missed to reveal evidence that could have informed us on the type of planting here, whether it was of vegetables, flowers, or a small grove of trees or shrubs.

A garden on a ship!

Hieron II of Syracuse (*c.*269–216 BC) had a stupendous ship constructed which became a classic sign of the excesses made during the Hellenistic period. Athenaeus gives us the details of this almost impossible feat of construction that was later presented as a gift to King Ptolemy and actually sailed to Alexandria.

> On the level of the uppermost gangway there were a gymnasium and promenades built on a scale proportionate to the size of the ship; in these were garden-beds of every sort, luxuriant with plants of marvellous growth, and watered by lead tiles hidden from sight; then there were bowers of white ivy and grape-vines, the roots of which got their nourishment in casks filled with earth, and received the same irrigation as the garden-beds. These bowers shaded the promenades. Built next to these was a shrine of Aphrodite large enough to contain three couches... There was also a water tank at the bow, which was kept covered and had a capacity of 20,000 gallons... By its side was built a fish tank enclosed with lead and planks; this was filled with sea-water; and many fish were kept in it ...[50]

This extract is the meagre surviving description of features that could have existed in Hellenistic gardens. However, the garden details given here may be a sign of over enthusiastic rhetoric in which Athenaeus was expressing ideas/features of his own time (*c.*AD 200) rather than earlier history.

Chaplets and garlands

The Hellenes continued to enjoy flowers woven into chaplets and garlands, which they wore when dining or celebrating in some way. Chaplets and wreaths were often composed of several different flowers and are mentioned by Athenaeus who often cited numerous earlier Greek writers. Here is an example that he found in *Mollycoddles* a play written by Cratinius:

> I crown my head, to be sure, with all sorts of flowers- narcissus, roses, lilies, larkspur, gillflowers, bergamot-mint too, and the cups of spring anemones, tufted thyme, crocus, squills, and sprays of gold-flower, drop-wort and day-lily so well beloved, chervil too ... tufts of narcissus, and with the perennial melilot I deck my head.[51]

We can speculate if all these flowers were included into one chaplet, or that these flowers were in different chaplets worn over the year. It remains an interesting list of plants that could be used for this purpose. Athenaeus reveals how some of the floral decorations were made and says that some wreaths were given special names, such as the one called *Heliktoi* (as mentioned by Chaeremon) it was apparently composed of 'Chains of twisted wreaths trice-coiled all about with ivy and narcissus ...'[52]

In some cases special chaplets to last an eternity were made of gold and placed in an aristocratic tomb to adorn the owner. One of the ones placed in the Tomb of Philip II of Macedon at Aigae comprised olive leaves and berries. Other golden chaplets have oak leaves and acorns; or myrtle flowers, leaves and berries. Such chaplets were also posthumously worn by influential women, such as the Hellenistic Carian princess from Harlicarnassus (Bodrum) who was given a gold myrtle chaplet to wear for eternity. These beautiful objects are finely made; they are light and delicate looking but have survived in an almost pristine condition. Such fine golden chaplets may also have been worn for special occasions in life.

Hellenistic Greek writers on plants

Callimachus, the poet and scholar from the Greek city of Cyrene, was given the enviable task of cataloguing all the books in the great Library of Alexandria (3rd century BC). During his time there he was undoubtedly influenced by the poetical works of earlier writers. Several of his hymns, epigrams, and fragments discovered on papyrus survive. One of the fragments, *Iamb 4*, is very interesting because it takes the form of a boastful contest between two trees: the olive and the laurel (bay). It is in a similar vein to the ancient Mesopotamian tale of rivalry between the palm and tamarisk trees, and we can wonder if Callimachus had heard of that earlier text. In this story the trees speak, and make much of their associations with deities: the bay was sacred to the god Apollo and the olive to the goddess Athene. The bay starts the contest by pointing out all the things in its favour: 'But what house is there where I am not beside the doorpost? What seer or what sacrificer carries me not with him?' the bay continued to extol its virtues and usefulness. But the olive tree's reply was crushing; an extract from this speech reveals one of the reasons why, she asks: 'What is the Laurel's fruit? For what shall I use it? Eat it not nor drink it nor use it to anoint. The Olive's fruit pleases in many ways: inwardly it is a mouthful ...'[53] not surprisingly she won the contest. Within this text is an interesting point showing how bay trees were regularly used in the home (probably as a pot herb) and were in a pot or in the courtyard itself 'beside the doorpost'.

As mentioned previously the Athenian Xenophon, c.401 BC had the opportunity to see at first hand the different and luxurious way of life in the East. Xenophon's account of his travels, the *Anabasis*, survives, written 30 years later, in which he spoke of the gardens of the Persian king. He also wrote the *Oeconomics*, a volume on the management of farms, but this says little on horticulture. Neither the writings, nor the experiences of those concerned in the expedition, seem to have affected the Greek form of gardening. But, during the conquests of Alexander the Great (from 334 BC onwards) a botanist took note of all the new plants they came across. Some of these were sent back to Greece and studied. This was a great period of discovery. The most influential man who made a study of botany and aspects of horticulture was the great philosopher Theophrastus.

Theophrastus had been a pupil of Aristotle, and became head of the Peripatetic School of Philosophy in the Lyceum area of Athens in 322 BC. The Peripatetic School derived its name from its *peripatos*, a shaded pathway; a reminder that the Lyceum would have been a green park-like area with paths. In those days philosophy included a study of topics now under the umbrella of Natural History, and one field of study in which Theophrastus excelled was in botany. His most famous work was his *Enquiry into Plants* which provides valuable information on a variety of cultivated and wild plants found in Greece (over 500 are mentioned). Theophrastus was known to have purchased a private garden close to his school, and he dedicated this garden to the Muses; sadly its whereabouts in or outside of the city is not certain. Theophrastus and his pupils studied a wide range of plants, and quite rightly he is sometimes referred to as being the 'father of botany'.

The majority of garden worthy plants he mentions are culinary, being herbs or vegetables. But, he does list a few cultivated flowers which he says 'are not numerous'. The flowers were: anemone, bergamot-mint, calamint, carnation, crocus, gillyflower, larkspur, lavender, martagon lily, narcissus, polyanthus, rose, sweet marjoram, southernwood, thyme, violet and wall-flower,[54] these were mostly used in making chaplets and garlands and of these the wall-flower was said to have been the most favoured. The gillyflower is an all embracing word for a sweet scented plant, the actual word used by Theophrastus was λευκόϊον which literally means white flowering plant. It was interesting to note that in this instance the Greek word he used for rose was that for a centifolia rose (ῥοδωνία). Theophrastus' research had shown that the roses in Greece had either five, twelve or 20 petals, and 'some a great many more than these ... however the inner petals are very small.' He also noted that some 'are not fragrant nor of large size.' Theophrastus carefully observed all Greek plants and those from further afield (such as the specimens sent back from Asia by Alexander's botanist). He gives great detail on each plant's appearance, its internal structure, reproduction capabilities and uses.

Theophrastus observed that 'Southernwood actually grows more readily from seed than from a root ... however it can be propagated by layering in pots in summertime, like the gardens of Adonis.'[55] *i.e.* grown in any form of pot. In contrast he mentions that thyme can be staked upwards against a wall but when it is layered downwards it 'is most vigorous when grown into a pit'. He says that the gillyflower/wallflower is the first to flower 'these, of all the flowers that the garland-makers use, far outrun the others.' In another chapter he lists the sowing times for garden vegetables, thereby providing a list of the range of plants cultivated in Hellenistic potager gardens at that time, although some such as radish and basil could have had several sowings:[56]

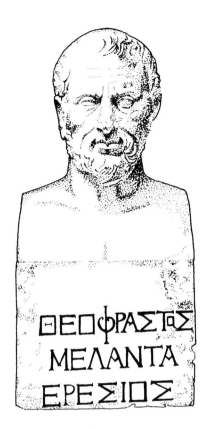

FIGURE 79. Bust of Theophrastus, Greek philosopher and 'father of botany' (Roman period), Vatican Museum.

1st period after the summer solstice [he probably means in the autumn]: cabbage, radish, turnip, beet, lettuce, rocket, monk's rhubarb, mustard, coriander, dill, cress.
2nd period after the winter solstice: leeks, celery, long onion, orach.
3rd period during the summer: cucumber, gourd, blite, basil, purslane, savory.

Theophrastus died *c*.287 BC. Fortunately Diogenes Laertius recorded the terms of his will and thankfully this has survived. The will gives a good impression of the Lyceum and its park. Theophrastus stipulated that some work should be done to the Museum, (the building dedicated to the Muses) and the grounds, following damage done during the revolt of Athens against the Macedonians. He said:

First they should be applied to finish the rebuilding of the Museum with its statues of the goddesses, and to add any improvements which seem practicable to beautify them. Secondly, to replace in the temple the bust of Aristotle with the rest of the dedicated offerings which formerly were in the temple. Next, to rebuild the small cloister adjoining the Museum at least as handsomely as before, and to replace in the lower cloister the tablets containing maps of the countries traversed by explorers. Further, to repair the altar so that it may be perfect and elegant... The garden and the walk and the houses adjoining the garden, all and sundry, I give and bequeath to such of my friends herein after named as may wish to study literature and philosophy there in common, ... Let me be buried in any spot in the garden which seems most suitable, without unnecessary outlay upon my funeral or upon my monument.[57]

Theophrastus did not forget his gardeners: 'And of my slaves ... to Manes and Callias I give their freedom on condition that they stay four years in the garden and work there together and that their conduct is free from blame.'

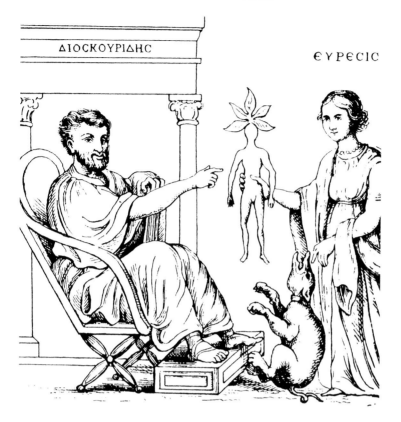

ΔΙΟⅭΚΟΥΡΙΔΗⅭ

ⲈΥⲢⲈⲤΙⲤ

FIGURE 80. Dioscorides examining a mandrake plant. From an early version of his herbal, *De Materia Medica.*

Yet another philosopher's school was established in Athens, in the house of Epicurus (*c.*250 BC) his pupils were taught communally in his small garden court. Pliny the Elder says that Epicurus was the first person to introduce a house garden in a Greek city,[58] but again there are no further details.

Greek herbals

Several Greek scholars made a study of plants and of these Diokles of Karystos, a physician working in Athens *c.*350 BC, was the first to compile a herbal. Sadly his work has not survived, but we know that he wrote a series of short descriptions of plants, their habitats and a list of their medicinal uses. There were a couple of Alexandrian herbals, one of these was Andreas the physician to the Hellenistic Egyptian king Ptolemy IV Philopater. Andreas was apparently murdered in 217 BC following a mistake! Nicander wrote a herbal *c.*200 BC called *Alexipharmaka* which read like a series of poems; it dealt mainly with animal and vegetable poisons and their antidotes. Some copies of Nicander have survived, mostly in the East where there is more danger of snake bites! The most influential herbal was by Krateuas, who was the physician to Mithridates VI of Pontus (120–63 BC). He was primarily a rhizotomist (a root cutter/herbalist), but wrote on the nature and uses of herbs. Importantly Krateuas was the first to include a drawing of each plant, so he is reckoned to be the father of botanical illustration.

Krateuas' manuscript does not survive, but we know that Dioscorides' work preserves many features of it, such as its use of drawings. Dioscorides held him in great respect.

Dioscorides was a Greek physician serving in the Roman army, he wrote his Greek Herbal in the 1st century AD (*c.*AD 65). He called his book *De Materia Medica* (On Medical Matters), it was partly a pharmacopoeia but it also contained much information on each plant, together with each plant's various names. In those days plant names were not standardised and a plant was known by one name in one locality and by another elsewhere, so Dioscorides preserves some of these early variants. Numerous copies of his herbal were made; the earliest surviving copy is now in Vienna. This copy is dated to the 6th century, but is believed to be a faithful reproduction of the earlier 1st century one. It was commissioned as a birthday present for the Byzantine Princess Juliana Anicia. One of the illustrations shows the princess in the centre escorted by allegorical figures. Another illustration portrays the great man himself – Dioscorides with a beard. The personification of discovery (H/Euresis) gives him a mandrake, a plant that was significantly shaped like a man and was known to have awesome powers, so was regarded with great superstition in the ancient world. Dioscorides' work has 383 botanic descriptions and many were accompanied by illustrations.

Many Greek writers and philosophers contributed to the knowledge accumulated by the Romans, and we hear that Pliny the Elder perused some of their texts for his own mammoth work. The conquering Romans took much from the Greeks, in all artistic fields, but perhaps less so in gardening.

Garden Plants of the Classical Greek and Hellenistic Era

Common name	Botanical Name	Literature	Archaeology	Archaic & Classical Greece	Hellenistic Period
Achillea/milfoil	*Achillea*	x		x	
Anemone	*Anemone coronaria* & *Adonis annua*	x		x	x
Apple	*Malus*	x		x	
Basil	*Ocimum basilicum*	x			x
Bay (Laurel)	*Laurus nobilis*	x		x	x
Beet	*Beta vulgaris*	x	x	x	x
Blite	*Amaranthus lividus*	x	x	x	x
Cabbage	*Brassica oleracea*	x			x
Calamint	*Calamintha incana*	x			x
Caper	*Capparis spinosa*		x	x	
Celery	*Apium graveolens*	x	x	x	x
Coriander	*Coriandrum sativum*	x	x	x	x
Cress	*Lepidum sativum*	x			x
Crocus	*Crocus sativus*	x		x	x
Cucumber	*Cucumis sativus*	x			x
Cypress	*Cypressus*	x		x	
Dianthus/pinks	*Dianthus* spp.	x		x	x
Dill	*Anethum graveolens*	x	x	x	x
Fennel	*Ferula communis*	x			x
Fig	*Ficus carica*	x		x	x
Fir	*Abies cephalonica*	x		x	
Garlic	*Allium sativum*		x	x	x
Gillyflower/*leukoion* (scented & white flowers)	*Leucojum aestivum*, *Mathiola incana*, also *Cheiranthus cheri*	x x			x x
Gourd	*Lagenaria siceraria*	x			x
Grape Vine	*Vitis vinefera*	x	x	x	x
Helichrysum	*Helichrysum*	x		x	x
Heliotrope	*Heliotropium europaeum*	x		x	
Hyacinth (blue flowers inc. larkspur)	*Scilla bifolia*, *Delphinium ajacis*, *Orchis quadripunctata*	x		x	x
Iris	*Iris* sp. *I.germanica*	x		x	
Ivy	*Hedra*	x		x	x
Lavender		x			x
Leek	*Allium porrum*	x		x	x
Lettuce	*Lactuca sativa* & *L.serriola*	x	x	x	x
Lily	*Lilium*	x			x
Marjoram, sweet	*Origanum marjorana*	x			x
Melilot	*Melilotus albus/M.indicus*	x			x
Mint & Water mint/ Bergamot-mint	*Mentha* sp. also *M. aquatica*	x x		x	x x
Mustard	*Sinapis alba*	x			x
Myrtle	*Myrtus communis*	x	x	x	x

Common name	Botanical Name	Literature	Archaeology	Archaic & Classical Greece	Hellenistic Period
Narcissus	*Narcissus tazetta/N.poeticus*	x		x	x
Olive	*Olea europaea*	x	x	x	x
Onion	*Allium cepa*	x			x
Orach	*Atriplex*	x			x
Parsley/chervil	*Petroselinum* spp./*Antbriscus cerefolium*	x		x	x
Pear	*Pyrus communis*	x		x	x
Plane	*Platanus orientalis*	x		x	x
Polyanthus		x			x
Pomegranate	*Punica granatum*	x		x	x
Poppy	*Papaver somniferum*		x	x	x
Purslane	*Portulaca oleracea*	x	x	x	x
Quince	*Cydonia oblonga*	x		x	x
Radish	*Raphanus raphanistrum/ R.sativus*	x			x
Rhubarb, monk's	*Rumex patientia*	x			x
Rocket	*Eruca sativa*	x			x
Rose	*Rosa*	x		x	x
Savory	*Satureja*	x			x
Smilax	*Smilax aspera*	x		x	
Southernwood	*Artemisia*	x			x
Styrax	*Styrax officinalis*		x		
Tamarisk	*Tamarix*	x		x	
Thyme	*Thymus vulgaris*	x			x
Turnip	*Brassica rapa*	x			x
Violet	*Viola odorata*	x		x	x

Notes

1. Homer, *Odyssey* V, 68–74. trans. R. Lattimore, New York, 1975. Celery (*selinon*) rather than parsley appears in the original Greek text, therefore I have included it here.
2. Homer, *Odyssey* XXIV, 245–247. trans. R. Lattimore, New York, 1975.
3. Homer, *Odyssey* VII, 112–132, trans. R. Lattimore, New York, 1975.
4. Baumann 1993, 210–211.
5. Retallack, G. J., 'Rocks, views, soils and plants at the temples of ancient Greece', *Antiquity* 82, 2008, 640–657.
6. Further myths concerning plants are found in Baumann 1993; Bernhardt, P. *Gods and Goddesses in the Garden*, London, 2008; Giesecke, A. *The Mythology of Plants*, Los Angeles, 2014.
7. Herodotus, *Histories* VIII, 138. trans. A. Sélincourt, London, 2003.
8. Theophrastus, *Enquiry into Plants* VI, 6.4. trans. A Hort. London, 1916.
9. Phillips, R. and Rix, M. *The Quest for the Rose*, London, 1993,16.
10. Several are identified in Plant, R. *Greek Coin Types and their Identification*, Seaby, London. Nos 1813–39.

11. Foxall, L. *Olive Cultivation in Ancient Greece: Seeking the Ancient Economy*, Oxford, 2007, 221–223.
12. Carroll-Spillecke 1989, 80; figs 4 and 5.
13. Carroll-Spillecke 1992, 86, figs 3–5; Wycherley, R. E. *How the Greeks Built Cities*, London, 1976, 177.
14. Foxall, L. *Olive Cultivation in Ancient Greece: Seeking the Ancient Economy*, Oxford, 2007, 242; Robinson, D. M. *Vases Found in 1934 and 1938, Excavations at Olynthus* 13, Baltimore, 1950, 396–425, pls 250–252.
15. Foxall, L. *Olive Cultivation in Ancient Greece: Seeking the Ancient Economy*, Oxford, 2007, 239.
16. Homer, *Odyssey* VI, 293–294. trans. R. Lattimore, New York, 1967.
17. Athenian Constitution 50, 2b.
18. Vatin, C. 'Jardins et Services de Voirie', *Bulletin de Correspondance Hellenique* 100, 1975, 555–654.
19. Homer, *Odyssey* VI, 291. trans. R. Lattimore, New York, 1967.
20. Apollonius of Rhodes, *Argon* II, 505. trans. W. H. Race, London, 2008.
21. Sappho, 2, trans. M. L. West, *Greek Lyric Poetry*, Oxford, 1994, 36.
22. Theocritus, *Epigrams* IV, trans. A. Holden, Harmondsworth, 1974.
23. Theophrastus, *Enquiry Into Plants* VI, 7, 3. trans. A. Hort, London, 1916.
24. Carroll 2003, 68; Roebuck, C. *The Asklepeion and Lerna. Corinth 14*, Princeton, 1951, 41.
25. Miller, S. G. (ed.) *Nemea, A Guide to the Site and Museum*, Athens, 1990, 157–158. Miller, S. G. 'Excavations at Nemea 1976,' *Hesperia* 46, 1977, 11.
26. Pausanias II, 1,7. trans. W. H. S. Jones, London, 1959.
27. Carroll-Spillecke 1992, 90.
28. Megaloudi, F. 'Wild and cultivated vegetables, herbs and spices in Greek Antiquity (900 BC to 400 BC),' *Environmental Archaeology* 10, 2005, 73–82. p. 74.
29. Pausanias XXIII, 5. trans. W. H. S. Jones, London, 1959.
30. Plutarch, *Life of Cimon*, 13. trans. J. W. Longthorne, London, 1838, 342.
31. Carroll 2003, 29.
32. Aristophanes, *Clouds*, 1005–1009, trans. A. H. Sommerstein, Oxford, 1982.
33. Pausanias XXIX, 2. trans. W. H. S. Jones, London, 1959. I have used Greek 'k's instead of Roman 'c's to keep the Greek spelling tradition.
34. Nielsen 1994, 81.
35. Neilson 1994, 60.
36. Neilson 1994, 127–128; see also Bernard 1994, 72.
37. Josephus, *Jewish Antiquities* XII, 233–34. trans. R. Marcus, London, 1958.
38. Gleason 1988, 21 & 30, fig. 4; Gleason, K. L. 'Towards an archaeology of landscape architecture in the ancient Roman World,' unpublished doctoral thesis, University of Oxford, 1989, 236–247, figs 92–93.
39. Gleason 1988, 28.
40. Gleeson 1988, 28–30, fig. 6.
41. At the Palace of King Hyrcanus I and of King Alexander Jannaeus, Evyasaf, R.-S. 'Gardens at a Crossroads: The influence of Persian and Egyptian Gardens on the Hellenistic Royal Gardens of Judea'. *Bollettino di Archeologica* (online) 1, 2010 (Vol.D.D9/5), 2010, 32.
42. Bedal 2003, 174; Evyasaf 2010, 35. However, no comparable contemporary Egyptian gardens have survived. The 18th Dynasty examples cited by Bedal and Yvyasaf are from a considerably earlier period, thus suggesting that the style of gardening did not change over the centuries that intervened.

43. Konstandopoulos, A. (ed.) *Priene*, trans. F. Stefani, Athens, 2000, 180.
44. Strabo XVI, 2, 6. trans. H. L. Jones, London, 1996.
45. Athenaeus, *Deipnosophistae* XIV, 654, c. trans. C. B. Gullick, London, 1957.
46. Athenaeus, *Deipnosophistae* V, 196–197. trans. C. B. Gullick, London, 1928.
47. Strabo, *Geographica* XVII, 1, 8. trans. H. L. Jones, London, 1996.
48. Strabo, *Geographica* XVII, 1, 10. trans. H. L. Jones, London, 1996.
49. Venit, M. S. *Monumental Tombs of Alexandria*, Cambridge, 2002, 63.
50. Athenaeus, *Deipnosophistae* V, 207d. trans. C. B. Gulick, London, 1928.
51. Athenaeus, *Deipn* XV, 685, trans. C. B. Gulick, London, 1957.
52. Athenaeus, *Deipn* XV, 679f., trans. C. B. Gulick, London, 1957.
53. Callimachus, *Iambi 4, fr.*194. trans. C. Whitman, London, 1989.
54. Theophrastus, *Enquiry into Plants* VI, 6. trans. A. Hort, London, 1916.
55. Theophrastus, *Enquiry into Plants* VI, 7, 3. trans. A. Hort, London, 1916.
56. Theophrastus, *Enquiry into Plants* VII, 1, 1–3. trans. A. Hort, London, 1916.
57. Diogenes Laertius, *Lives of Eminent Philosophers*, Theophrastus V, 51. trans R. D. Hicks. London, 1972.
58. Pliny, *Naturalis Historia* XIX, 19, 51. trans. H. Rackham, London, 1971.

CHAPTER FIVE

Etruscan Gardens

The Etruscans are believed to de descended from the earlier Villanovan culture in Italy which commenced *c*.900 BC, but the distinctive Etruscan civilisation is traditionally dated from the 7th to the 1st century BC. Their heartland was Etruria, a region named after these enigmatic people. This region is now in part of Tuscany and northern Lazio, but at one stage the Etruscans ruled a far greater area: as far north as Bologna and the Po Valley, and in the south as far as Cumae; their influence may have reached further. At one time the Etruscans even ruled Rome (*c*.616–510 BC). However, Rome eventually conquered Etruria and the much weakened Etruscans were amalgamated into the Roman way of life. Etruscan culture has had to be reconstructed from their rich remains discovered by archaeology because sadly their language (which was a non Indo-European one) has not been fully deciphered. Most Etruscan texts that have survived are fairly short, and can only hint at aspects of their mythology, religious practices or society. The Roman Emperor Claudius wrote a history of the Etruscan people, and this could have been a huge source of information on these enigmatic people, but sadly this has not survived. However, at times the Romans and Greeks (their rivals) have furnished small titbits of information on the Etruscan way of life in their own writings. So, it is largely through Classical literature and by the artefacts that the Etruscans left behind in their tombs that a picture of their culture can be assembled.

Etruscan deities with links to horticulture

Each Etruscan city may have had its own special deities, but there was one god that was important to them all: Voltumna. Every Spring there was a pan-Etruscan religious festival held at his great sanctuary at *Fanum Voltumnae* (near Orvieto) but only recently has the whereabouts of this special place been located.[1] Here the Etruscans would consult and elect a new high priest and a supreme king over the chief twelve cities of Etruria;[2] afterwards there would be great festivities and games. Voltumna was primarily a god associated with vegetation and the seasons. It appears that Voltumna later became the Roman god Vertumnus (his role in the Roman World is discussed in the next chapter).

    Some gods had male and female counterparts like Cel and Cilens who were, respectively, the earth mother and father. Selvans was the god of boundaries and fields, and the countryside in general; the Romans adopted him into their own pantheon and gave him the name Silvanus (but the Roman Silvanus was notably a rustic god associated with woodlands). Over time many cultures adapt their ideas to outside influences and we also find that several Etruscan deities became equated with similar Greek gods; of these Fuflans took on aspects of the Greek Dionysus. Therefore Fuflans was associated with gaiety and vitality as well as wine and fertility. Turan was an Aphrodite-like goddess connected to love, fertility and health, and Atunis was an earth god who appears to have resembled the Greek Adonis. A more direct assimilation is noted in the Etruscan Phersipnai who is similar to the Greek goddess Persephone.

The town of Hortanum (Orte) may have been named after an Etruscan goddess called Horta, who was believed to be associated with Summer. Little is known about her, but she is thought to have been connected to agriculture and gardens, and her name may have led to the origin of the Latin word for a garden: *hortus*.

The Etruscans were known to be deeply religious and would readily seek help from their gods and priests on all matters. To the Etruscans the most important figure connected to agriculture was the mythical man-child Tages. The legend says that one day a man ploughing the soil by Tarquinia dug more deeply than was usual and from the earth emerged this little man who looked like a child but had the wisdom of a sage. Tages imparted his knowledge of agriculture to all the people who gathered around him, and disclosed the secrets of what became the *Etrusca disciplina*, the Etruscan art of divination.[3] This great teacher is almost a god, and is commemorated on many Etruscan engraved mirrors. He appears as a small naked child, often below the groundline of the main scene, recalling the myth of his miraculous appearance; this is seen in the first mirror from the British Museum mentioned below.

Book three of the *Etrusca disciplina* (the *libri rituales*) was devoted to all forms of religious ritual. One of these interestingly gives advice to agri-horticulturalists to beware of certain plants in their orchard. If you would see any of the following ill-omened plants you would need to get rid of them immediately: a briar-rose, a fern, wild pear, black fig or red dogwood.[4] These plants could soon take over and could indicate the loss of fertility in the soil, which would need remedial action. The books also indicates instances where the interpretation of omens could be sought in all facets of life; the flight path of birds could have significance for instance, and apparently there was even a work on prophesying from trees.[5] Such comments may seem strange to us today, but nevertheless they do indicate that the Etruscans had some form of a garden, be it an orchard or a potager style garden.

Temple sanctuaries and groves

Several Etruscan cities had a temple sanctuary, such as the so-called Belvedere Temple at Orvieto which was sited towards the rear of a square enclosure. The Portonaccio sanctuary at Veii was triangular to suit the contours of the hilltop town, but there was a large space on the southern sector of the temple precinct. Each of these had areas that were possibly sufficient for sustaining shade trees. There was probably a sacred grove associated with the important cult centre of the *Fanum Voltumnae* (*fanum* means shrine). However at Marzabotto in northern Etruria, the Etruscan city with a regular planned layout was more spacious and the main sanctuary area with its temples was placed on two terraces of the acropolis above the city. The sacred sector of the town incorporated a nearby spring which was given its own shrine. Today this part of the site is covered with trees and gives the impression of a sacred grove.

Garlands

The Etruscan tomb paintings give a wonderful insight into Etruscan life, by depicting fashions and furnishings. Some of the frescoes show the owners enjoying their last feast and in some cases they hold a garland in their hands, or garlands are being made to give to the participants at the feast, as in the Tomb of Hunting and Fishing at Tarquinia (*c.*530 BC). In a number of frescoes painted garlands appear to be hung as if from a picture rail running along the upper part of the frescoed walls. The garlands are usually painted a uniform colour red, but in the Tomb of Hunting and Fishing the numerous garlands were differentiated. There are four different forms of garland repeated around the room: blue ones with red dots, red with dark red dots, yellow with a fringe of black lines, and purple with dark red dots. These may represent garlands comprising different flowering plants that unfortunately are unidentifiable. However, when garlands are carved on stone sarcophagi and funerary urns, they are often shown draped around the neck of the tomb owner reclining on his couch. These garlands show more details, often individual petals can be distinguished, sufficient to indicate that the majority of the garlands consisted of roses.

Tomb paintings and reliefs used as evidence for Etruscan flora

The Etruscans appear to have appreciated plants, for several frescoes depicting everyday scenes on the interior walls of their tombs use plant motifs as a border device running along the top of the wall. In the Tomb of the Triclinium at Tarquinia (*c.*470 BC) the painter chose a long sinuous stem of ivy, with periodic clusters of ivy flowers. In the tomb of the Bulls (*c.*540 BC) there was a row of pomegranate fruits. Many frescoes also frequently use trees to separate different figures or animals. An example is in the archaic period fresco in the Tomb of the Baron also at Tarquinia (*c.*510 BC). The trees were painted green but are stylised; we can make out that three different species were intended, but they are difficult to identify. A columnar tree could represent a cypress and another may have been intended as a laurel/bay which has alternately placed lanceolate leaves. In the frescoes of the Tomb of the Leopards (*c.*480–470 BC) the trees have similar shaped leaves but they are arranged in an opposite pattern along the branches which would indicate myrtles. Myrtles produce small black berries and these trees were also shown laden with black fruit (their identification is speculative because bay trees also bear black fruit, but are olive shaped).

A veritable grove of trees is depicted in the first chamber of the Tomb of Hunting and Fishing, garlands and scarves drape from their branches. There are also numerous trees in the Tomb of the Bulls in the two superimposed scenes. The upper scene recreated an episode of Greek Homeric mythology. On the right Troilus the young Trojan prince approaches a sacred shrine and fountain outside Troy, but in the reeds behind the fountain lies the Greek warrior Achilles ready to ambush him. In this unusual rendition of the myth there is a dwarf fruiting date palm tree, and a lily-like plant behind one of the horse statues on the fountain and altar. There are also olive or myrtle-like sprigs nearby, perhaps to indicate a sacred grove. The seven trees in the lower section of this fresco have been carefully differentiated by their pattern of leaves and branching habit. The central one could be a broadleaf tree with a wide girth, but again they are schematic as are the other plants depicted in this particular fresco therefore the species intended cannot really be identified. One of the few flowers that are clearly depicted is the poppy, which has such a distinctive seed head. A bunch of three poppy stems are held by one of the ladies in the processional scene painted on the 6th century BC Boccanera panels (from Cerveteri, now in London). The lady behind her holds another bunch of flowers.

A flourishing grapevine features in the pediment and along the roof beam of the Tomb of the Triclinium, a figure on one side leans out as if to pluck one of the many bunches of grapes. The proximity of this scene to the diners below could be interpreted as reflecting a vine trained to grow next to their homes, in a garden area perhaps. Fruit are often included in frescoes and carved reliefs, where they are shown ready to eat, piled onto a dining table in banquet scenes. The most common species represented are bunches of grapes and pomegranates.

Plants depicted on Etruscan Mirrors

The mirrors are believed to have been a gift on a girl's marriage; on the reverse side they often depict scenes from mythology and therefore floral elements are seldom shown. However there is often an outer frame of ivy around scenes engraved on the back of Etruscan bronze mirrors; alternatively a laurel wreath or trailing vine framed the picture. The main focus though is the figured scene in the centre, and on a 6th century mirror from Tarquinia (now in Berlin) the ivy seems to make a bower for an encounter/marriage between a young couple. Foliage rises behind the youth, and a small plant of ivy springs up between them. The young girl holds out a flower to her lover.

Another mirror from Tarquinia (now the British Museum) is framed by laurel, distinguished by its alternate leaves and berries. The main theme is of an augur or priest giving a blessing to another young couple. The groom carries a

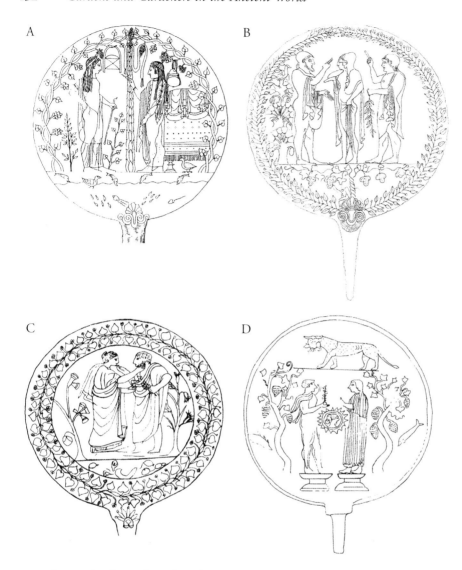

FIGURE 81. Garden scenes engraved on Etruscan bronze mirrors. A. from Tarquinia, now in Berlin; B. from Tarquinia, now in the British Museum; C. now in Florence; D. now in Paris.

sprig from a bush, perhaps laurel or myrtle. Behind the augur there are three trees with a bird perched on top. The bird could relate to a garden setting but could also refer to one method of divination used by augurs based on the direction of a bird's flight. Hopefully the auguries would be favourable for the young couple. A flourishing vine tree is featured below, with large bunches of grapes. The scene does give the impression of a garden or orchard.

A mirror now in Florence, with a wide ivy border, portrays an interesting scene with a couple about to embrace. She holds a flower in the fingertips of her left hand. He holds a twig, again perhaps myrtle, but all around them are flowering plants, again indicating a verdant outdoor setting such as a garden.

One Etruscan mirror (now in Paris) features a man and a woman on pedestals, perhaps to signify they are deities. On either side is a vine tree laden

FIGURE 82. Detail of a stylised plant, possibly an arum. From an Etruscan mirror, Tarquinia, 4th century BC.

with fruit. The man holds out his hand and in the palm of the proffered hand is a plant. The closely spaced leaves on the straight stalk could indicate a lily bulb with its growing stem. This is a highly scented plant and could have held some significance to the Etruscans, but sadly ancient sources are silent on this issue. A similar scene features on a mirror in the British Museum,[6] here Turan and her winged son Eros offer each other gifts: a dove from Turan and a lily-like flower from Eros. Meanwhile a winged victory (Meanpe) flies above to crown Turan with a wreath of laurel or myrtle.

Medicinal plants

It is believed that the Etruscans used a form of Herbal. Occasional references by ancient writers gave the Etruscan name for certain plants, and glosses comparing these names with Greek and Latin were made. These were used in antiquity by an anonymous lexicographer/physician to add the Etruscan names of some plants to the Herbal manuscripts of Dioscorides. Of these, 11 names of plants are undoubtedly Etruscan and can be described as having a religious or medicinal use: arum, feverfew, gentian, helichrysum, henbane, madder, pimpernel (scarlet and blue), smilax, thyme, tuberous thistle and valerian.[7] These plants can cure or ease symptoms of a variety of ailments, from toothache and eye problems, snake bite, for healing wounds, and even for ridding man and beast of internal parasites. The latter was a particularly debilitating problem and preventative measures were sought for in the Brontoscopic Calendar, a surviving text on Etruscan divination (thankfully copied and recopied). This important text highlighted the times of the year when heavy rains following thunderstorms could lead to an outbreak of liver fluke.[8] Research into this infection has shown that a number of the plants mentioned above proved to be efficacious as a vermifuge (they contained toxins that could expel/destroy internal parasites). Several other plants identified on Etruscan sites would have been resorted to as a cure/preventative, amongst these are: chamomile, centaury, herb Robert, pomegranate rinds and roots, flax seed, ranunculus, wormwood and incense.[9] Some of these plants are still used in various herbal remedies (except madder which was found to have carcinogenic properties);[10] apparently the bark of Pomegranates is still used as a vermifuge in country districts in central Italy.[11] It is therefore most likely that Etruscans, or the augurs and physicians at least, would have had an area of their garden plot devoted to medicinal plants.

Archaeological evidence for garden plants

Most of the botanical investigations on Etruscan sites has concentrated on discovering what they had been eating, rather than what they had been planting. However, studies have shown that besides cereals their diet included chickpeas, lentils and peas that were discovered at Acquarossa; hazelnuts, walnuts, pine nuts, grapes, plum and other seed-bearing fruits, broad beans, lentils and peas at Verucchio;[12] and olives, grapes, figs, pear, wild cherries and hazelnuts at Blera.[13] These could well have been planted in a kitchen garden/orchard. The sweet cherry was unknown at this time so the Etruscans would have utilised their native species. The investigations of a 6th century BC farmhouse at Pian D'Alma discovered pollen, seeds and charcoal samples of a number of plant species,[14] one of these was vetch (*Vicia sativa*). Six remains from spent fruit stones of cornel (*Cornus mas*) were identified; the cornel's fruit is edible and until recently they were regularly harvested. Sadly though, in many cases only the genera of plant species can be identified, such as *Rubus, Malus, Rosaceae, Liliaceae, Asteroideae, Caryophllaceae, Boraginaceae* and *Labiatae*. Many of the species found at this site have been interpreted as being woodland plants, and some are certainly from weeds (such as *Urticaceae* – nettles) although they can be edible. You might also find them on cultivated land, perhaps even a garden plot that needs weeding from time to time.

An Etruscan agriculturalist

Latin sources reveal the existence of an agriculturalist named Saserna in the 2nd century BC, whose work was continued by his son. His name is Etruscan and apparently he lived in the north of Italy, but only tantalising relics of his writings on agriculture have survived in the works of others. As garden culture is akin to some of the practises performed in agriculture his books on the subject could have revealed interesting ideas. Apparently Saserna was given praise in some quarters, Columella said he was 'no mean authority on husbandry.'[15] In a surprising instance of an earlier global warming Saserna was said to have believed that the weather was getting warmer and this would enable people to produce larger crops of olives and grapes[16]. Pliny the Elder mentions that Saserna and his son disapproved of growing vines supported on trees.[17] He was mostly praised for his advice on vines, and his methods of ensuring the survival of cuttings was heeded by later agriculturalists.[18] Besides making wine at home for friends and family the Etruscans were known to have cultivated extensive vineyards and were skilled at making their wines. They exported their surplus, and we hear that Tuscan wine was appreciated in Greece.[19] In fact Etruscan wine amphorae have even been discovered on sites in southern France, Spain, Sicily and Greece. A number of ancient shipwrecks have been discovered off the French coast, and by Cap d'Antibes divers found a cargo of around 180 Etruscan amphorae.[20] This shipwreck was dated to the mid-6th century BC. The wine of Etruria (or Tuscany) is still well thought of.

Saserna also recommended using plants that could enrich the soil such as lupine, beans, vetch, bitter vetch, lentils, the small chickpea and peas.[21] However, he was at times mocked for resorting to superstitious methods. For instance Varro recalls the method used by Saserna to disinfect things, he recommended people to 'Soak a wild cucumber in water, and wherever you sprinkle the water the bugs will not come.'[22]

FIGURE 83. detail from an Etruscan mirror depicting crown grafting on a tree, now in Florence.

Evidence illustrating the skill of Etruscan aboriculturalists is found on an Etruscan mirror depicting a scene from the Myth of Bellerophon. On either side of the hero there appears a heavily pruned tree. The trunks of these trees have been cut off and two scions have been grafted onto the trunk of the parent tree. This could be interpreted as crown grafting which is done to rejuvenate an old fruit tree.

Etruscan gardens

No direct evidence for a garden space has been discovered archaeologically, as yet, although the large early form of peristyle courtyard within the 7th–6th century BC Palace of Murlo may have had at least some trees for shade. The archaic houses at Acquarossa (*c.*600 BC) were grouped around a central communal area but two of the houses also had a rear doorway which the excavators have suggested led to a back court or garden.[23] Around 550 BC the houses at Acquarossa were enlarged and were given larger courtyards, but evidence is lacking to determine if part of this could have been used as a garden.

At Marzabotto the regularly planned houses within the Etruscan city had a prototype *atrium Tuscanum* (this feature is discussed in the next chapter) but no garden. The difficulties in searching elsewhere for evidence of gardens in this period is complicated by the fact that the Etruscans generally lived in communities sited on defensible hilltop places, and many of these sites are still occupied as towns today, which hampers any archaeological excavation there. Hill top towns tend to be densely populated and although there may have been some garden areas inside the town walls most gardening/horticulture would have been outside the walls. Therefore the enigmatic scenes depicted on the Etruscan bronze mirrors and tomb walls can only give some hint of the nature of horticulture practised in this period. The Romans so effectively took over the Etruscan people that after a while their language and their distinctive culture died out. But over the years of living in close proximity to Etruria there were inevitably cultural exchanges, and the Romans benefited from the rich legacy left by the Etruscans.

Garden Plants of the Etruscans

Common name	Botanical name	Fresco, relief or sarco- phagus/urn	Mirror	Literature	Botanical remains
Apple	*Malus*				x
Arum	*Arum italicum*			x	
Aster	*Asteroideae*				x
Bay	*Laurus nobilis*	x	x		
Blackberry	*Rubus fruticosus*				x
Borage	*Boraginaceae*				x
Broad bean	*Vicia faba*				x
Cherry, wild	*Prunus avium/Cerasum Apronianum*			x	x
Chestnut	*Castanea sativa*				x
Chicory	*Cichorioideae*				x
Cornel	*Cornus mas*				x
Elderberry	*Sambucus nigra*				x
Elm	*Ulmus* sp.				x
Feverfew	*Chrysanthemum parthenium*			x	
Fig	*Ficus carica*				x
Gentian	*Gentiana* sp.			x	
Grape Vine	*Vitis vinefera*	x	x	x	x
Hazelnut	*Corylus avellana*				x
Helichrysum	*Helichrysum stoechas*			x	
Henbane	*Hyoscyamus niger*			x	
Ivy	*Hedra helix*	x	x		x
Lentil	*Lens esculenta*				x
Lily	*Liliaceae*		x		x
Lime	*Tilia* sp.				x
Madder	*Rubia tinctorum*			x	
Myrtle	*Myrtus communis*	x	x		x
Olive	*Olea* sp.				x
Pea & grass pea	*Pisum sativum* & *Lathyrus sativus*				x
Pear	*Pyrus communis*				x
Pimpernel (red & blue)	*Anagallis arvensis* & *A. caerulea*			x	
Pine	*Pinus* sp.				x
Plane	*Platanus*				x
Plum & Sloe	*Prunus domestica* & *P. spinosa*				x
Pomegranate	*Punica granatum*	x		x	
Poppy	*Papaver somniferum*	x			
Ranunculus	*Ranuncukaceae*				x
Rose	*Rosa* sp.	x			x
Scabious	*Knautia* sp.				x
Smilax	*Smilax aspera*			x	
Strawberry tree	*Arbutus unedo*				x

Common name	Botanical name	Fresco, relief or sarco-phagus/urn	Mirror	Literature	Botanical remains
Tuberous thistle	*Cnicus tuberosus*			x	
Thyme	*Thymus vulgaris/T.serpyllum*			x	
Valerian	*Valeriana officinalis*			x	
Vetch	*Vicia sativa*				x
Vibernum	*Vibernum tinus*				x
Walnut	*Juglans regia*				x
Wormwood	*Artemisia absinthium*			x	

Notes

1. Stopponi, S. 'Orvieto, Campo Della Fiera – *Fanum* Voltumnae', in Macintosh Turfa 2013, 632–654.
2. The venue is mentioned by Livy 4, 23,5; 4, 25,7. trans. A de Sélincourt, London, 1971.
3. Cicero, *De Div*, 2, 23. trans. W. A. Falconer, London, 1923.
4. Thulin, C. O. *Die Et. Disciplin*: 3, 1909, 86, cited by Heurgon, J. *Daily Life of the Etruscans*, London, 1964, 112.
5. de Grummond, N. T. 'Haruspicy and augury,' in MacIntosh Turfa 2013, 544.
6. B.M. Number GR 1840.2–12.8. Swaddling, J. *Etruscan Mirrors*, London, 2001, 52–53, fig. 32b.
7. Johnson, K. P. 'An Etruscan herbal?', *Etruscan News* 5, 2006, 1 & 8.
8. Harrison, A. P. and Turfa, J. F. 'Were natural forms of treatment from Fasciola hepatica available to the Etruscans?', *International Journal of Medical Sciences* 7(6), 2010, 16–25.
9. Harrison, A. P. and Turfa, J. F. 'Were natural forms of treatment from Fasciola hepatica available to the Etruscans?', *International Journal of Medical Sciences* 7(6), 2010, table 1.
10. Harrison A. P. and Bartels, E. M. 'A modern appraisal of ancient Etruscan herbal practices,' *American Journal of Pharmacology and Toxicology* 1(1), 2006, 21–24.
11. Guarrera, P. M. 'Traditional antihelmintic antiparasitic and repellent uses of plants in Central Italy,' *Journal of Ethnopharmacology* 68, 1999, 83–192.
12. Macintosh Turfa, J. *Divining the Etruscan World*, Cambridge, 2012, 155.
13. Baker and Rasmussen 2000, 184.
14. Lippi, M. M. *et al.* 'Archaeo-botanical investigations into an Etruscan farmhouse at Pian D'Alma (Grosseto, Italy),' *Atti della Soceità Toscana de Scienze Naturali de Pisa Memorie*. Series B 109, Pisa, 2002, 159–165.
15. Columella, *De Re Rustica*, I, 1, 5. trans. H. B. Ash, London, 1993.
16. Columella, *De Re Rustica*, I, 1, 5. trans. H. B. Ash, London, 1993.
17. Piny, *Naturalis Historia* 17, 199. trans. H. Rackham, London, 1971.
18. Columella, *De Re Rustica* 3, 17, 4. trans. H. B. Ash, London, 1993.
19. Athenaeus, *Deipnosophistae* 15, 702, b. trans. C. B. Gullick, London, 1957.
20. Gran-Aymerich, J. and MacIntosh Turfa, J. 'Etruscan goods in the Mediterranean world,' in MacIntosh Turfa 2013, 395.
21. Columella, *De Re Rustica* 2, 13, 1. trans. H. B. Ash, London, 1993.
22. Varro, *De Agri Cultura* 1, 2, 25. trans. W. D. Hooper and H. B. Ash, London, 1979.
23. Rohner, D. D. 'Etruscan domestic architecture,' in Hall, J. F. (ed.) *Etruscan Italy*, Utah, 1996, 120–121.

CHAPTER SIX

Roman Gardens

The Romans originated from the Latin peoples of Latium in Central Italy, over time they conquered all of their near neighbours, including the Etruscans, and the increasingly powerful city of Rome grew to dominate all of Italy. The traditional founding of Rome was said to have occurred *c*.753 BC. As previously mentioned Rome was ruled by Etruscan kings (616–510 BC), but after the deposition of the last king the Roman people voted to establish a republic which lasted until Augustus took power in 27 BC. Over centuries the Roman Empire expanded and eventually conquered all the lands around the Mediterranean Sea. Provinces were formed from *Hispania* (Portugal and Spain) in the far west to *Syria* in the east, and from northern *Britannia* to *Africa* (the northern part of Africa). The Roman Empire finally ended in AD 476 in the west, but continued longer in the eastern provinces under the aegis of Byzantium. However, the Roman way of life continued in north Africa until the Arab Invasions of the 7th century AD.

Evidence for gardens during the long period of Roman rule is enhanced by the wealth of Classical literature that has survived, and by a large number of sites discovered by archaeology. Most of all, we are very fortunate that the catastrophic volcanic eruption of Vesuvius (in AD 79) covered the cities of Pompeii and Herculaneum with a thick blanket of ash and pumice, thereby preserving a time capsule for posterity. Here studies could be made on all facets of the Roman way of life, including their houses and gardens.[1] This vital information can be compared with material found elsewhere in Italy and from Rome's provinces.

The Roman *Hortus* and agri-horti-culturalists

By at least the 2nd century BC a Roman estate and garden was called a *hortus* (plural: *horti*); Cato was the first known person to use this term. This word has given rise to our own word Horticulture meaning the culture of the Hortus. In the early days of the Roman Republic the *hortus* garden was primarily a utilitarian area mostly used for growing vegetables and herbs, but it also included fruiting trees.

We are very fortunate that four Roman agricultural/horticultural manuals survive. Although these works are primarily on farm management and husbandry they also include sections devoted to arboriculture and the culture of the *hortus* as part of the farm and villa estate. The earliest was written by Cato (2nd century BC), then Varro (*c.*36 BC), Columella (*c.*AD 60) and Palladius (4th century AD). Cato's manual *De Agri Cultura* is brief and succinct but is very informative of early practices. Varro's *Rerum Rusticarum* (on rustic matters) also gives advice on profitable occupations such as bee-keeping, the management of fish stocks, aviaries and game preserves. In the process he gives examples where these can be made into decorative elements in a garden. Columella, who was a farmer from Gades (Cadiz in Spain), compiled a very thorough manual on all aspects of agri/*horti*-culture which extended to twelve books. Book 10, dealing specifically with gardens, was written in verse. Columella's great work was used extensively in the later manual *De re rustica* written by Palladius.

Pliny the Elder also describes agri-horticultural practises. He compiled a great encyclopaedia on Natural History of which books 12–27 concerns plants, their origins, habits, cultivation and uses.[2] His prodigious work is the most informative on Roman gardens. His nephew, known as Pliny the Younger, wrote numerous letters, some of which describe gardens.

Roman deities connected to gardens

The Romans were a very superstitious people and they had numerous deities. When they conquered another city or region, they tended to amalgamate the local deities into their own pantheon, partly because the Romans feared upsetting any deity that could turn against them. Therefore the Romans absorbed *Voltumna* from the Etruscans, in the process his name changed to Vertumnus,[3] his functions in the Roman world are mentioned below. *Demeter, Gaia* and *Herakles* originated from Greece, they respectively became Ceres (the goddess of cereal crops), Tellus (the Mother Earth goddess) and the latter was re-named Hercules.

After prolonged exposure to Greek culture we can identify other Roman deities that had a Greek counterpart, but often foreign deities underwent an evolutionary change during the process of Roman assimilation. The pre-existing Roman goddess Minerva took on several attributes of the Greek Athena; Juno is like Hera; Mars the god of war is similar to Ares but has a link to agriculture; Bacchus the ever popular god of wine takes over from Dionysus, *etc*. Over time many Greek myths were so well known and universally accepted that they became woven into the pre-existing Roman pantheon, and often then further embellished. One such is the Greek Cronos who the Romans believed had fled from Greece to Latium in Italy, but once there was known as Saturn. Saturn was in fact an ancient Italic god (origins otherwise obscure). To the Romans he was credited with bringing the art of agriculture to Italy.[4] He was commonly known as 'the sower'. Saturn is usually shown as an old man wearing a veil over his head and a sickle or scythe in his hand. His great feast day was celebrated with much merriment in the Saturnalia on 17–23 December.

FIGURE 84. Venus, the prime Roman deity associated with the garden's fertility, accompanied by cupids and her sacred flowers roses. Demi-lune mosaic, Macktar Museum, Tunisia.

Bacchus merged with Liber the old Italic male god of fertility. Bacchus was forever associated with wine and merry making, therefore his sacred plant was the vine often shown with large bunches of grapes. His symbol was either vine leaves, a bunch of grapes, or a wine drinking cup. Before a feast a libation of wine would be poured to honour the god. Bacchus retains Dionysus' links to the theatre and therefore theatre masks were also used as an allusion to this god.

Venus was the most important of all the Roman garden deities, she was an ancient Latin goddess who was noted as a 'protectress of the garden.'[5] Venus was primarily concerned with the garden's fertility, but increasingly she became associated with man's fertility after her syncretism with the Greek Aphrodite. Venus was known for her great beauty and her capacity for pleasure; her associates are the three Graces. Her sacred animal was a hare (and the rabbit). Of the birds the dove, swan and sparrow were sacred to her, and her sacred flowers were the rose and myrtle. The apple also became a symbol of the goddess after she was awarded one as a prize in the mythical beauty contest between herself, Juno and Minerva.

Flora was originally a Sabine (Italic) goddess of Spring and flowers, and all blossoms; she was introduced to Rome in their earliest days. The Roman poet Ovid wove a Greek-style myth around her.[6] He recounts how after her union with Zephyrus (the west wind) Flora's breath clothed the ground and the trees with flowers. Flora was given eternal youth and thereafter she cared for young people in the flower of their youth. She was generally worshipped by all who wanted to ensure that flowers would blossom on their trees, and on their vegetables, herbs and crops, as well as garden flowers. Flora had a festival of her own, the *Floralia*, which lasted 6 days, 28 April–3rd May. During the rather licentious festival every man and beast wore garlands of flowers, mostly of roses. In art Flora is represented bedecked with flowers.

Pomona was a Latin goddess of fruit trees, she had no Greek counterpart. Her name derives from the Latin *poma* meaning fruit, the *pomarium* being a fruit-garden or orchard. Her role was in the care of fruit trees; from their cultivation, welfare and fruit gathering to grafting and pruning. Ovid weaves a wonderful myth about how Pomona was a young virgin who spurned all male advances, until Vertumnus finally wooed her after trying numerous disguises.[7] Vertumnus's name is said to have come from the verb *vertere*, which means to turn or change, and this partly explains his ability to change shape and guises. He also presided over the change of the seasons and horticulture. After their union Vertumnus takes on many of Pomona's attributes. They are both represented as figures carrying fruit (either in a basket or by holding them in the folds of their drapery) while in their other hand is a pruning hook, which serves as a reminder of their craft. Over the centuries a certain amount of syncretism took place, and we find that both Flora and Pomona were later absorbed into the cult of Venus.

Priapus took over the role played by Vertumnus, and the two minor gods Mutunus and Tutunus. Mutunus and Tutunus (the two are usually grouped together) were ancient Roman phallic gods who could ensure fertility; and their emblem, the phallus, was a potent symbol used to avert the evil eye of malice and jealousy. The Eastern Greek god Priapus was first worshipped at Lampsacus (northern Turkey) but his cult spread through Greece during the Hellenistic era and from there to Rome. He was said to have been the grossly deformed son of Venus and Bacchus who was abandoned soon after birth. He was taken to be exposed on the mountains, but shepherds took pity on him and reared him; partly because of this Priapus was known to be a rustic god. His huge phallus ensured his association with procreation and fertility but was the cause of numerous ribald poems; eighty of these Latin verses were collected in the *Priapeia* dated to the 1st century AD. In Italy this rustic god took over the care of vegetable gardens and orchards. All owners of produce gardens would put up a wooden statue to represent Priapus who would then protect their garden, as long as he was given all due offerings and prayers. He was often depicted as a grossly ithyphallic figure brandishing a pruning hook in one hand, both in recognition of his potent powers of fertility and in the art of horticulture. These symbols/weapons were also used to avert the evil eye and to scare away destructive birds from crops, and most importantly to stop or deter potential thieves from stealing produce from the garden. Humorous poems by Martial and others highlight the dangers of owning a wooden statue.

> In Spring I am worshipped with roses, in autumn with apples, in summer with corn-wreaths, but winter is one horrid pestilence for me. For I fear the cold, and am apprehensive lest I, a wooden god, should in that season afford a fire for ignorant yokels.[8]

But there was potentially a greater danger in possessing a marble one which could be stolen. In both cases the owner would be vulnerable if left without a Priapus to care and watch over their garden. Priapus was later included in the Bacchic entourage and therefore was often crowned with vine leaves. On occasion he wears a crown of wheat ears, or spikes of rocket flowers which were sacred to him. His sacrificial animal was the ass, which was known to be a lusty animal. A Roman myth explains an alternative reason for his association with the ass. Apparently Priapus lusted after a nymph called Lotis, and one day decided to creep up to her while she was sleeping. An ass brayed and woke her just in time and she fled. To ensure her protection the gods transformed Lotis into a lotus tree. This would be the southern Nettle Tree (*Celtis australis*) a very elegant tree of the elm family that was a Roman introduction to Italy from the north African provinces. It produces edible berry-like fruit and was considered highly garden worthy.

The Romans had a surprising number of minor divinities that presided over all manner of events. Before embarking upon a task, a prayer and offering to a particular god would have been required. This is even more evident for agricultural and horticultural tasks, but considering that the Romans initially sprang from a rural community, and traditions have deep roots in the countryside, it is perhaps understandable. We find that there was a deity for almost every stage of preparing plant beds, and for each stage of plant growth. For instance Proserpina was in charge of germinating seeds, Seia for looking after it in the ground, Segetia while it was ripening, Nodutus was in charge of the joints and knots of the stems (he was generally known as the knotted one), and Tutilina when the crop was harvested and stored (she was also known as 'she who keeps safe'). The poet Servius names some that were mainly applicable to agriculture but would also have been invoked for vegetable plots:

> It is quite obvious that names have been given to divine spirits in accordance with the function of the spirit. For example, *Occator* was so named after *occatio* (harrowing); *Sarritor*, after *sarrito* (hoeing); *Sterculinus*, after *stercoratio* (spreading manure); *Sator* after *satio* (sowing).[9]

By the 1st century BC, one of the great Roman agriculturalists (Varro) provides a definitive list of deities that he says, would be advisable for all husbandmen to invoke. They are all paired, often with a male and female counterpart, and he usefully gives the reasons for their inclusion:

> First, then, invoke *Jupiter* and *Tellus*, who, by means of the sky and the earth, embrace all the fruits of agriculture; and hence, as we are told, that they are the universal parents, Jupiter is called 'the Father', and Tellus is called 'Mother Earth'. And second, *Sol* and *Luna* [the sun and the moon], whose courses are watched in all matters of planting and harvesting. Third, *Ceres* and *Liber*, because their fruits are most necessary for life; for it is by their favour that food and drink come from the farm. Fourth, *Robigus* and *Flora*; for when they are propitious the rust will not harm the grain and the trees, and they will not fail to bloom in their season; wherefore, in honour of Robigus has been established the solemn feast of the Robigalia, and in honour of Flora the games called Floralia. Likewise I beseech *Minerva* and *Venus*, of whom the one protects the oliveyard and the other the garden; and in her honour the

rustic Vinalia has been established [on 19 August]. And I shall not fail to pray also to *Lympha* and *Bon Eventus*, since without moisture all tilling of the ground is parched and barren, and without success and 'good issue' it is not tillage but vexation.[10]

The Romans always feared a failed harvest; so all measures possible were taken to avert this. Therefore in rural communities these rustic deities held sway, and accordingly altars where sacrifices were made would be set up on every farm and villa estate. Gardens in urban sites are still essentially places where plants are grown, so this is another area where we find altars placed so that the household could perform all their necessary rituals.

Sacred gardens

The earliest record of altars in a rural sacred enclosure dates back to 250 BC, in the bronze tablet from Agnone that was written in Oscan (an anc. Italian language). The deities worshipped here were: Ceres, Flora, Genita, Hercules, Lympha, nymphs, Prosperina, and possibly Venus.[11] We hear that shrines and altars were built on country estates, Statius mentions a small shrine of Hercules in the grounds of his friend Pollius Felix. After a sudden rainstorm his guests and their garden furniture couldn't all fit into it so he resigned himself into building a larger temple for the god![12] In cities space is more limited, but at Alba Fucens, an ancient city in central Italy dating back to the 3rd century BC, a shrine dedicated to Hercules was given a large rectangular sacred precinct. The central part appears to have been tended as a garden, but no botanical studies have been made here. We can however speculate whether this vast space contained a sacred grove with plants specific to the god because Pliny the Elder mentions that in some cases plants associated with certain gods were planted around their respective temples: 'the chestnut-oak to Jove, the bay to Apollo, the olive to Minerva, the myrtle to Venus, the poplar to Hercules.'[13]

Archaeological evidence for sacred gardens

A possible sacred grove (a *nemus*) has been discovered in the precinct of the Temple of Juno at Gabii which was rebuilt in the 2nd century BC. Here archaeologists found three rows of rock-cut tree planting pits in the north-east corner,[14] but in the dry conditions of late summer a number of matching dark green squares were visible making a pronounced contrast with the parched grass within the precinct. The deep pits had kept the grass moist, and made them quite clear, showing that the three rows of tree plant pits also continued along the north side of the precinct.[15] A total of 27 pits were revealed, 24 in a quincunx-like formation. Planting trees in a *quincunx* (spaced out like the number five on a dice with one in the middle) was recommended by Roman agriculturalists so that the trees would have sufficient root space; they would create a more pleasing diagonal view and from 'whatever direction you look at the plantation a row of trees stretches out in a straight line.'[16] Rock-cut plant

FIGURE 85. Detail of a sacrifice before an altar and statue of a goddess, from a mosaic depicting rural tasks of the calendar year, from Vienne, now in St Germaine-en-Laye, near Paris.

pits have recently been discovered in the enclosure of the Temple of Venus at Pompeii along with a series of terracotta plant pots,[17] and evidence suggesting a sacred grove was also discovered in the sacred precinct of the East Temple at Thuburbo Maius (in modern day Tunisia).[18] Here a row of root cavities revealed the presence of the former trees. The trees had been spaced 50–70 cm apart.

In Rome fragments of an ancient map of the city engraved on marble (dated *c*.AD 200) was found to give details of a number of buildings and some of these were temples, each located in a rectangular sacred enclosure. Two of the temples on this Severan Marble Map were the *Adonaea* (for the worship of Adonis) and the *Divus Claudius* (a temple dedicated to the deified Emperor Claudius).[19] For both of these a series of dots and dashes within the garden space indicated the ancient planting scheme. These rare examples give the impression of a sacred grove. For the latter there were four rows of lines on three sides of the rectangular garden space and seven rows on the fourth side. The lines rather than dots have been interpreted as indicating a series of topiary hedges. For the *Adonaea* there were four rows of dots signifying trees, and a symmetrical pattern of four broken lines and plant beds on either side of a centrally placed elongated water basin.

Rural gardens

At Boscoreale, a rustic Roman villa (*villa rustica*) uncovered from the same volcanic fallout that covered nearby Pompeii, archaeologists have discovered that the land surrounding the villa was used to grow vines; but there was also a *hortus*, located close to the villa. This was customary partly so that valuable produce and beehives could be protected more easily; *horti* were usually enclosed by a hedge or ditch to keep livestock away from tasty produce. Within the *hortus* at Boscoreale plant beds were clearly defined; around each bed soil had been heaped up into a ridge (a method mentioned by Pliny the Elder) so that when watering the bed the ridge would prevent precious water from seeping away from the plants being tended. A cistern/well had been sited close by so that the gardener did not have to go far to fetch a bucketful of water. Rustic gardens were really designed to provide enough to make the family self-sufficient, but as Virgil's delightful poem about the old man from Tarentum shows a simple rustic garden could also have a space somewhere to include a few flowering plants too.

> he laid out a kitchen garden in rows amid the brushwood,
> bordering it with white lilies, verbena, small-seeded poppy.
> He was happy there as a king. He could go indoors at night
> To a table heaped with dainties he never had to buy.
> His the first rose of spring, the earliest apples in autumn ...[20]

Poppy seeds would be harvested to sprinkle on top of newly made bread. Normally the womenfolk of a rural villa would weed the *hortus* between doing chores in the house, stray finds of lost hairpins in plant beds confirm this.[21] It was however, the duty of the *Matrona* (mistress and housekeeper) of the house to ensure that the household was sufficiently provisioned from the *hortus*.[22] Men would perform the heavier tasks in the garden, orchard and field.

An interesting poem (an extract from a less obscene text in the *Priapeia* (51)) gives an indication of the plants that could be present in a rustic *hortus* that was undoubtedly carefully watched over by the god Priapus. In this case he vigorously complains about the thieves coming into his domain:

> The fig tree here is no better than my neighbour's, nor are the grapes such as golden-haired Arete gathered [she was the wife of the mythical Alkinoös]; nor are the apples meet to be the produce of the trees of Picenum. Neither is the pear, which at such hazard you try to pilfer; nor the plum, more mellow in colour than new wax, nor the service-apple which stays slippery stomachs. Neither do my branches yield an excellent mulberry, the oblong nut, [a filbert], nor the almond bright with purple blossom. I do not, more gluttonously, grow divers kind of cabbage and beet, larger than any other garden trains, and the scallion with its ever-growing head; nor think I that any come for the seed-abounding gourd, the clover, the cucumbers extended along the soil, or the dwarfish lettuce. Nor that any bear away in the night-time lust-exciting rockets, and fragrant mint with healthy rue, pungent onions and fibrous garlic. All of which, though enclosed within my hedgerow, grow with no sparser measure in the neighbouring garden, which having left, ye come to the place which I cultivate, O most vile thieves ...

There were always rustic villas and farms in the countryside, but by the late 2nd–1st centuries BC we find that some grew into large country houses that were increasingly embellished with decorative elements. Large villa estates tended to grow into three distinct groups of buildings. These were: the rustic portion that still contained a *hortus rusticus*; then there was a storehouse the *villa fructuaria*; and there would now be a separate house for the owner, a *villa urbana* which was furnished to a higher standard. The *villa urbana* often included an ornamental garden. Cicero, the great statesman and lawyer, indicates when this development began when he mentions that in his grandfather's lifetime the family home was small, but during his father's occupancy it was 'rebuilt and extended' into a *villa urbana*.[23] An example is the 1st century BC villa complex at Sette Finestre, near Cosa, where the three parts of the villa have been identified together with at least three enclosures for *horti*.[24] The walls of the main garden were embellished with small turrets with rows of niches at the top of each one; it has been suggested that they mimicked the town walls of a town, or alternatively they may have served as a series of miniature dovecotes (in Latin a *columbarium*).

The change of villa design was partly influenced by an increase in wealth stemming from Roman conquests in Sicily and the east. Booty brought back to Rome after these conquests included sculpture that was sent to beautify public buildings and these indirectly triggered a desire to beautify people's own home and garden as well. One of the returning generals, Lucullus, was especially influential in this movement because he partly emulated the opulence of eastern rulers and his subsequent hedonistic lifestyle became proverbial. Around 60 BC he built a grand villa with landscaped gardens on the Pincio, one of the hills overlooking Rome, this was the first project on such a scale, and its beauty was greatly admired, although censured by some. The new garden form contained elements derived from Persian and Hellenistic *paradeisoi*, those pleasure gardens and game preserves of eastern rulers, as well as elements borrowed from the sacred groves of Hellenistic Greece. Many Romans aspired to own something grand and they tended to emulate some of these features in their own villa/house and garden, albeit on a smaller scale. Gardens within the estate of a *villa urbana* could be extensive, but there were also smaller areas of greenery in courtyards inside the villa itself, and these would be closer to what was possible in an urban domestic garden. Pliny the Younger reveals in one of his letters how one of his internal gardens was shaded by four plane trees and in the centre a fountain played in a marble basin.[25] Such details can now be matched by archaeology (see below). Internal gardens were on occasion termed a *viridarium*, meaning a place of greenery.

Urban domestic gardens

In urban situations there was less space and houses were fitted cheek by jowl in blocks in a grid of streets. But many Romans, unlike the Greeks, opted to have a garden of some kind within their allotted plot. The earliest Roman houses (a *domus*, pl. *domi*) to incorporate a garden have been found at: Cosa, a Roman colony in Etruria; at Fregellae a Latin city south of Rome, and at Pompeii. At Cosa the 3rd century houses were each given a *hortus* that was roughly equal in size to the house.[26] The early *domi* found at these sites are what is often termed an atrium style house. The first phases of this early form (Type A) dates back from the 4th to the beginning of the 2nd century BC.[27] Atrium-houses were

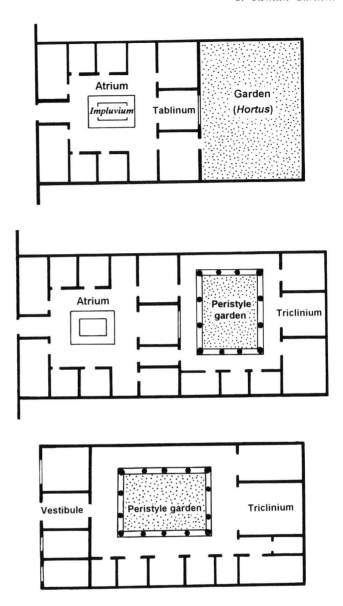

FIGURE 86. Plan showing three different forms of a Roman house (*domus*) with garden.

usually axial in plan, and often comprised a passageway leading into an *atrium* hall. The partly open roof above the atrium was inclined inwards so that falling rainwater could be captured in the *impluvium* basin below. From there rain water was channelled into an underground water storage cistern. Water could then be drawn for the family's needs and to water plants in the garden when necessary. The garden or *hortus* was usually sited to the rear of the house and would be as large as space would allow; for security there would be high walls around the garden.

Over the centuries the layout of the Roman *domus* changed after eastern elements – such as a colonnaded peristyle – were incorporated into the house plot

(Type B). This had the benefit of allowing more rooms to be added around the peristyle. The Romans again preferred to cultivate this open space as a true garden. This popular style appears to have come in fashion during the 2nd century BC.

In the Type C *domus* the garden itself became the heart of the house. This type is more often found outside of Italy, and there were a number like this in Roman Britain (such as at Gloucester, Caerwent and Silchester).[28] There are a few Type C houses at Pompeii, so this form can be said to date from the 1st century AD at least, but type A and B were still current elsewhere.

The House of the Vettii at Pompeii displays many features that you might find in a Roman peristyle garden. Ideally, as here, the garden is surrounded by a peristyle comprising four porticoes, again enabling rainwater to be collected from the roof. In some houses there was insufficient room for a complete peristyle so two or three porticoes were built instead (as in the House of the Tragic Poet at Pompeii). Sometimes the remaining solid garden walls had applied stucco to make imitation columns and were painted so that the illusion of a peristyle was created. On these occasions the spaces between the imitation columns of the

FIGURE 87. Full-scale reconstruction of the peristyle garden at the House of the Vettii, Pompeii, which was a rare opportunity to appreciate the spectacular effect of the jets d'eau, and the full complement of the garden's sculptural furnishings. Made for the *Il Giardino Antico Da Babilonia A Roma* 2007 exhibition in Florence.

pseudo-peristyle could be painted to appear like a garden or a landscape, or even as a window through which you could see a garden beyond. These *trompe l'oeil* works of art would help to give the impression of a much larger garden area. At Pompeii we can see that even the owners of small dwellings could beautify their home with a garden, even if the only space available was a mere strip.

Other forms of Roman gardens: Public gardens (*porticii*)

Gardens were created to adorn many public buildings, such as libraries, bath complexes, and temple precincts. Sources suggest that plantations in these gardens were mostly of evergreen shrubs and trees. Public gardens were often enclosed by a large rectangular peristyle, and therefore they came to be known as a *porticus* (pl. *porticii*). Pompey the Great was the first wealthy Roman to create a 'porticus garden' (in 55 BC) to form a beautifully verdant entrance to the magnificent new theatre that he was building on the Field of Mars at Rome. The porticoes and tall shade trees planted in this garden gave shade from the sun and space for spectators to gather before and after plays. Propertius provides an indication of the appearance of this garden, he says it had an 'avenue thick-planted with plane trees'.[29] He also implied there were two fountain figures beside a pool in this welcoming public area. Martial mentions that the garden of the *Porticus Pompei* had a *nemus duplex* (a double grove of trees)[30] so the plane trees could well have been placed on either side of the central path that is shown on the relevant fragment of the Marble Map. The garden plan also shows that there were a series of semicircular and rectangular recesses along the margins of the garden to provide seating areas.

We also hear of the *Porticus Liviae*, a garden that had been donated to the populace by the Empress Livia; the garden walks here were said to be shaded by a huge grape vine that produced large quantities of wine every year.[31] Plantations of box were a feature of 'sun-warmed Europa', a public garden mentioned in passing by the poet Martial.[32] The donation of public gardens was seen as a great act of benevolence, but also it was very good propaganda for the individual concerned. Not to be outdone by Pompey, in his will Julius Caesar left his own gardens to all the citizens of Rome; and later Augustus planted the *Nemus Caesarum* for public use and also his *silvae et ambulationes* (woods and promenades) that were created around his mausoleum. Others followed suit, such as Agrippa who donated his bath complex and associated gardens (the *Porticus Vipsania*) which were said to be planted with laurel bushes.[33]

The concept of Portico gardens was not confined to the metropolis, several have been found in cities throughout the Roman world. At Italica and Merida in Spain the theatre was provided with an adjacent portico garden, at the latter the garden has now been replanted with trees and green hedges on either side of a wide central path.

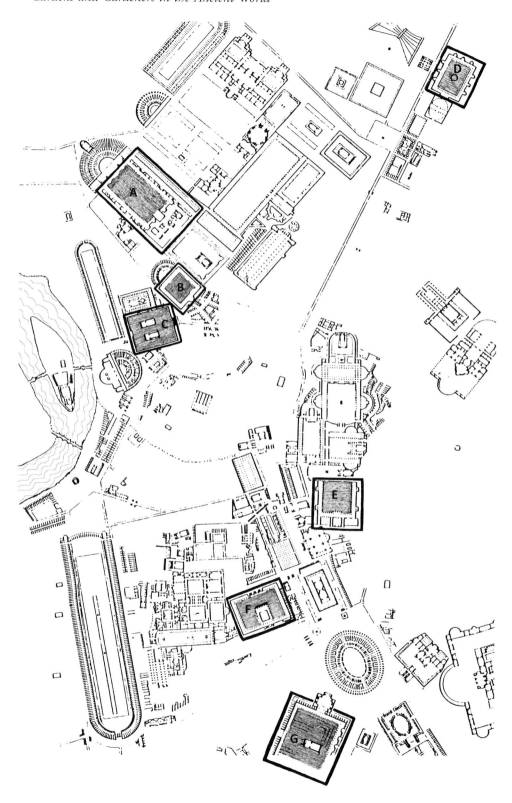

Corporate gardens and those associated with inns and taverns (*tabernae*)

Gardens were also created on the premises of private clubs and guilds, as seen at Ostia in the House of the Triclinia, where numerous dining rooms opened onto the porticoes surrounding the garden. The garden of the guildhouse at Tarraco (Tarragona) in northern Spain was highly ornamental with two marble nymph fountain figures besides a pool. Inns and taverns often had an open garden area (a version of our beer gardens) where drinking parties could take place. Virgil tells of an innkeeper whose staff would stand outside and tempt any passerby to sample their wares in pleasant surroundings: 'There are garden nooks and arbours, mixing-cups, roses, flutes, lyres and cool bowers with shady canes [trellises] ... come; rest here thy wearied frame beneath the shade of vines.'[34] Such dining establishments have been discovered by archaeology at Pompeii, Ostia and elsewhere.

Market gardens and plant nurseries

Literary evidence for these is provided by Pliny the Elder who mentioned visiting a nursery garden so that he could inspect the variety of medicinal plants growing there. He also discusses how to create a nursery bed, and to make cuttings in plant pots.[35] Both Cato and Varro state how useful it would be if market gardens were sited on the outskirts of cities so that fresh produce could easily be brought to a ready market.[35] A few *Hortuli* (the specific term used for market gardens) were located in the more spacious south-east part of Pompeii. On excavation one of these proved to be a commercial garden for growing flowers. Part of the site of the Garden of Hercules was found to have well preserved soil contours showing a network of wide plant beds separated by water channels.[37]

In the dry conditions of Egypt ancient letters and contracts of leases written on papyri during the Roman period have miraculously survived in the Fayumn area and at Oxyrhychus. Some attest to the existence of market gardens where vegetables were the prime source of income, but we also hear how some gardeners specialised in cucumber growing, or in providing flowers. One letter asked for 2000 narcissi and roses to be sent for a wedding celebration.[38] Archaeological evidence for a huge commercial plant nursery has been discovered at Abu Hummus in the Western Delta area of Egypt.[39] The complex dates to the 1st century BC–3rd century AD. Here plants had been propagated from cuttings in clay receptacles. The proprietors had made use of a supply of used wine amphorae and cut them into two halves. The bottom half of the amphora had its pointed end cut off to create a drainage hole, while the upper half of the amphora was inverted so the neck of the vessel could provide a convenient drain hole. An astonishingly huge quantity of used amphorae were found here in numerous rows, stacked carefully beside a path in eight baked-brick propagating bays. Each bay had water channels. To give an indication of

FIGURE 88 *(opposite)*. Map of central Rome showing the location of several public portico gardens. A: *Porticus Pompei*, the first such garden built *c.*55 BC by General Pompey the Great to form a pleasant adjunct to his new theatre building; B: *Crypta Balbi*; C: *Porticus Octavia*; D: *Templum Soli*; E: *Templum Pacis*; F: *Adonaea*; G: *Templum Divus Claudius*, a portico garden surrounding the temple of the deified Emperor Claudius. The Temple of Peace (E) was judged to be the most beautiful building in Rome, aided no doubt by the lush garden forecourt (map after MacDonald 1986, fig. 206).

the scale of the enterprise each row had approximately 27 amphorae, and there appears to have been four rows on each side of the path in each bay. The portion of the complex uncovered is therefore thought to have held *c.*4928 amphorae. The staggering quantity of plants being propagated here is not just to supply local orders but has been assumed to be for the export market. When the scions had sufficiently rooted they could have been shipped to Rome or elsewhere. Earlier Ptolemaic papyri from the Zenon archive suggests orders for a variety of fruit trees: apples, apricots, figs, olives, peaches, pears, plums, walnuts, laurels and roses. At times large quantities of trees were requested, such as 200 pear trees, 500 pomegranates, 10,000 vine shoots,[40] and there may have been similar orders at the site of Abu Hummus.

Tomb gardens

Tombs were normally located on roads leading out of the city, for reasons of hygiene. Romans aimed to have an impressive monument that would be noticed, therefore they themselves would be remembered. Occasionally rich people would opt to have an adaption of the Hellenistic style *cepotaphia*, a monumental tomb surrounded by a garden enclosure. A satire by Petronius gives the scenario of a fictitious parvenu freedman Trimalchio discussing his own funerary monument which would include a plot containing fruit trees and vines.[41] Usefully, he also suggested how large it would be, which gives an indication of the scale of these plots; it was envisaged to be 'a hundred feet facing the road and two hundred back into the field'. This would be sufficiently large to provide his shade with the customary offerings in his honour and any surplus produce could usefully provide an income for any heirs. For example a number of funerary inscriptions stipulate that their descendents should give the deceased his customary tipple of wine. In these cases a pipe would be fitted next to the tomb so that a libation could be poured down to sustain his shade (or soul) below. Another inscription asked that profits could be used so that his survivors would offer him roses on his birthday, forever.[42] Banqueting facilities were often included in the garden so that family and friends could come out to dine with the departed, and the deceased would be able to retain that vital link with the living.

FIGURE 89. Two miniature frescoes depicting trellis fences forming 'garden rooms'. Upper from Herculaneum, lower from Pompeii.

Fresco paintings depicting gardens

Frescoes reveal many aspects of garden art and the key feature is that it is a verdant scene,[43] with trees and flowering plants, but many also feature decorative elements that must have been current in gardens of that time. We see trellis fences, decorative low marble walls, fountain bowls in a variety of shapes, and sometimes sculpture in their garden setting. The frescoes on the rear garden wall of the House of the Marine Venus at Pompeii (*in situ*), and those of Livia's Garden Room at Primaporta (now in the Massimo Museum, Rome; see Fig. 106) are examples. There seems to be a delight in illustrating their gardens filled with a variety of birds and prized species of plants, but we can also notice that the artist has depicted plants flowering and trees fruiting all at the same time regardless of their season. The scenes may be a real-life representation of a garden, or a desire to depict an ideal garden, but they also invoke a literary comparison. The Romans liked to show their knowledge of classical Greek culture, and Homer's myths were very popular. In this case the myth where Odysseus describes a mythical never-endingly fruitful, abundant garden belonging to Alkinoös, King of the Phakians is brought to mind, and on occasions the Romans actually compared their own garden with this mythical one.[44] So these frescoes adapt this Greek myth into an ornamental Roman ideal. The frescoes certainly show that Romans aimed to nurture a fertile garden.

At Primaporta the Empress Livia had a wonderful cool underground room (for use in high summer to avoid the searing heat above), this room was covered with beautiful garden frescoes, she obviously wanted to be reminded of the greenery and fresh air outside. A low yellow lattice fence forms a dado-

like zone around the base of all the walls, and then as if behind this, we can see a low white marble wall comprised of different decorative panels. In the centre of each frescoed wall this low wall forms a recess so that a specimen tree could be displayed to greater effect. As with many Roman frescoes the plants are painted with care and we are able to determine the species depicted, and gain an insight into which plants were cultivated in that period. Clumps of low growing plants are shown in front of the low wall, with mid-height flowers and shrubs behind it, forming an underplanting for the trees and taller shrubs behind. An amazing variety of birds are illustrated in these frescoes (70 in all) some are flying above while others alight on a branch or stand on the edge of the wall and fence; the myriad of birds reinforce the idea that what we are seeing is a welcoming real garden.

A wide range of plants is painted in frescoes, in the House of the Fruit Orchard at Pompeii there were a number of fruit bearing trees (apple, cherry, fig, lemon, pear, yellow and blue plums and peach or pomegranate).[45] More decorative species were chosen for the frescoes in the House of the Golden Bracelet. There were laurustinus (*viburnum tinus*), bay, oleander, dwarf oriental plane trees and palms, strawberry trees, pink flowering rose bushes, variegated ivy, white flowers of feverfew or chamomile, golden flowers of chrysanthemum segetum, white drooping flowers of Solomon's seal, blue flowers of periwinkle, opium poppy, and white Madonna lilies. In the dado zone there were hart's tongue ferns, iris and rounded clumps of ivy. Many of these plants are depicted in frescoes elsewhere, and apart from the rose, bay, and pine trees, the most popular perennial plants depicted in garden frescoes were acanthus, and the hart's tongue fern. Other flowers and bushes can be identified in frescoes such as the grey-leaved aromatic bush of southernwood, in the House of the Marine Venus.

On occasion ivy is shown growing in a mound supported by a reed stick (bamboo had not yet been discovered), some of these feature in a fresco in the House of Ceii and in a dado in the House of the Vettii. This is valuable information on an aspect of Roman horticultural practice that could not be found by archaeology.

Several miniature frescoes illustrate features found in larger gardens, such as wooden arches, or a pergola (in Latin *pergula*) and trellis fences that formed enclosures.[46] The Romans were the first to create 'garden rooms', and as these frescoes show the Romans enjoyed creating architectural decorative effects by having semicircular and rectangular recesses to give more variety. A niche would make a perfect backdrop for a special sculptural item or urn fountain bowl. The permutation of Roman trellis design is endless, they were of varying height, however they were usually in a diamond lattice pattern. Several miniature frescoes have been found at Pompeii and Herculaneum, but also at Rome and Alba Fucens.[47] In the latter, figures stand under the arched entrance of three long *pergulae*. In between each *pergula* there are enclosures edged with green clipped hedges; in the centre of these there is a rectangular blue pool.

Pergolas and trellises could be used to grow vines, and an example is the fresco from Boscoreale (now in the Metropolitan Museum in New York) but they also were used to train roses, ivy, and even gourds (as seen in a 4th-century AD fresco in the Via Latina Catacomb at Rome).

Archaeological discoveries of ornamental garden features

Sadly only the post-holes of a pergola and trelliswork can be discovered by archaeology, the upper portion would have rotted away long ago leaving little trace. So we are very fortunate that frescoes illustrate their appearance, and indicate how the garden space was used. Archaeological evidence for *pergulae* have been discovered in several Pompeian gardens; a fine example is in the House of Loreius Tiburtinus where the pergulae extend along both sides of an elongated water feature in the lower garden. Root cavities beside each post of the *pergulae* indicated that vines had once shaded the walkways beneath. However, another house provided evidence for a simple fence (in this case made of reed) that delineated a path in the garden of the House of the Chaste Lovers at Pompeii. The paths were made of hard beaten earth, and showed clearly against the friable dark enriched soil of the plant beds. Garden paths elsewhere were found to be of sand or gravel.

Wooden seating would also have rotted over the centuries leaving perhaps only a stain to mark its former position in the garden, as found at the House of Bacchus and Ariadne at Thuburbo Maius where just the supports were detected. However without further indications the supports by themselves could relate to either three wooden benches or tables, or even a mixture of both.[48] The poet Martial mentions how his wooden garden seats had deteriorated badly, so it is perhaps not surprising that many householders decided to have a more permanent garden seat made of stone or marble. Also al fresco dining areas were constructed in gardens, and these were especially favoured in summertime when it would be too hot indoors. They were often shaded by a vine covered pergola to filter the sun's rays and shade diners reclining on their couches below.

Many examples of masonry outdoor dining couches have been discovered in cities and villas around the Roman world. There were three forms, a *biclinium* (*bi*=two, *clini*=couch) these could be sited in an L shape or facing each other as at the House of the Thunderbolt at Ostia. The *triclinium* (*tri*=three) comprised three couches that were usually designed in the form of a U shape; nine diners could fit onto a *triclinium* each facing inwards when reclining. This was the type most favoured during the Roman period. At least two residents of the excavated part of *Vienna* (modern Vienne/St Romaine en Gal, France) had a vine covered outdoor *triclinium* couch in their peristyle gardens; as did an inhabitant at Russellae in Etruria. The third form of dining couch current during the Roman period was the *stibadium*, which was a large semicircular couch. Often these were provided with a little semicircular water basin where

fingers could be washed during meals. A good example is the one found in the middle of a peristyle garden at Italica in Spain; similar couches were even fitted into gardens in North African provinces such as in the House of Hesychius at Cyrene (Libya). In both of these cases a pool was sited adjacent to the couch, perhaps so that dishes of food could be floated on the water's surface to keep cool, as in a delightful scenario recounted by Pliny the Younger.[49]

At Pompeii more evidence of garden furnishings survive simply because citizens left quickly or were engulfed by the cataclysmic volcanic eruption of Vesuvius. Shrines, altars, sundials, statuary and sculpture were left behind; there was precious little time to save their own lives. It was their misfortune that has aided our knowledge of their daily lives. Complete sculptural collections survive in some houses whereas in most cases elsewhere survival depends on chance, such as if items were thrown into a pool (as at Welschbillig in Germany where 68 herm statues from a decorative wall once lined the pool).[50] The Romans admired Greek sculpture and many copies and versions were made (of varying standards) so that those affluent enough could display them in their homes and gardens. Statuary and sculpture were expensive items so owners would site them carefully to capitalise their effect.

FIGURE 90. Simple reed fences line a garden path in a pattern discovered by archaeology at the House of the Chaste Lovers, Pompeii. A full scale reconstruction of this garden was made for the *Il Giardino Antico Da Babilonia A Roma* 2007 exhibition in Florence.

FIGURE 91. Outdoor dining couches. Left: the *biclinium*; centre: *Triclinium*; right: *stibadium*.

FIGURE 92. Beyond the rectangular raised pool are the remnants of a *biclinium* al fresco dining area and shrine. The two couches are placed so that the diners reclining there could face each other to converse. Mattresses would have made the couches more comfortable, House of the Thunderbolt, Ostia.

One of the ideal locations was in the garden where guests would be able to admire them, so many were actually placed in direct line of sight of diners reclining on their dining couches in a grand reception/dining room. Statuary was seen as decorative yet they also embodied the deity portrayed, so they were treated with due respect.

The most popular items of statuary found in Roman gardens were statues of water deities (in proximity to water features) or deities closely associated with nature who would be considered at home in the greenery of the garden. Silvanus the god of woodlands sometimes makes an appearance; but the rustic god Pan, and those boisterous woodland revellers the satyrs, were frequent visitors in sculptural form; as were all of the Bacchic entourage. Members included: Ariadne the consort of Bacchus, his drunken foster father Silenus, maenads who were frequently being chased by satyrs, Pan, fauns, centaurs, bacchantes, and Priapus. Bacchic statuary is often humorous, at times perhaps irreverent, but was in keeping with the carefree attitudes of Bacchus himself. Large versions of Bacchic wine cups (a *cantharus*) were made in marble and these served to form an association with the god in the garden. Many were turned into a fountain, as seen in the beautiful Pompeian frescoes where birds come to drink water at the edge of the bowl.

Statues of Venus were also popular in gardens, her lover Mars (the god of war) was on occasion found in garden contexts due to his liaison with Venus but also because he had a connection to agriculture. It was also no surprise that their mischievous son Cupid was a popular figure in garden statuary. Winged cupids and statues of children, with or without animals were understandably favourite subjects being a reminder of youth.

Certain myths could be re-enacted in the garden in a statuary form: a statue of Hercules could recall the myth of the hero's exploit in the Garden of the Hesperides. Diana and animals, such as boars and stags, could allude to many Romans favourite sport – hunting; while statues of the Muses and Apollo could foster contemplation and inspiration in the garden.

However, herms were the most popular items of sculpture in Roman gardens. These were simply a bust on a shaft. Cicero owned a couple of bronze herms, but these would have been very costly items and the majority were made of marble. The busts often portrayed the god Hermes (after whom they were named) or a Bacchic figure. Herms sometimes represented an emperor or philosopher, and could even be made in the likeness of a member of the household; they were a very versatile form of ornamentation in the garden. There were even janiform herms: these were co-joined busts that like the god Janus had one face looking forward while the other looked back. The paired faces were sometimes male and female so there might be a satyr and maenad, or alternately the facial features reveal a young and old Bacchus. The latter were the most popular choice for a janiform herm.

Gardens (in Italy and Spain in particular) were adorned with one or more *pinakes* (sing. *pinax*); these were rectangular marble plaques placed on top of a short marble post. They were carved on both sides generally with Bacchic iconography, paired theatre masks were favoured. Ornaments were also suspended from the architrave of the garden's surrounding porticoes, these were *oscilla* (sing. *oscillum*). Their name suggests that they would oscillate with a breeze, but in reality these marble discs were too heavy to do this, because on average they were *c.*30 cm in diameter. Frequently traces of the iron suspension hook is still detectable. *Oscilla* were also carved on both sides so they would be seen and admired to good effect from the peristyle and from in the garden itself. Gardens would contain more than one *oscillum*, and if a house had more than one peristyle, as at the House of the Citharist at Pompeii, then as many as twelve could be possible hanging from their porticoes.[51] The majority of these decorative items were circular, but there were some small rectangular ones, and some were shaped like a theatre mask, others represented a semicircular pelta. The latter form mimicked the shape of a *pelta* shield belonging to the mythical Amazons. The most commonly encountered *oscillum* is a circular or pelta shaped one, and these have been discovered in gardens in the provinces as well as in Italy. *Oscilla* often feature in the garden frescoes of Pompeii where they hang suspended from a line along the top, or they are shown hanging from an archway in some of the miniature garden enclosure scenes.

FIGURE 94 *(above left)*. An *oscillum* which mimics the form of a *pelta* shield carried by an Amazon. There are griffin heads on either side and a palmette on the top, which is the point of suspension. The main scene features a satyr and a *pedum* stick used by shepherds, Cordoba Archaeological Museum.

FIGURE 95 *(above right)*. On a Roman sundial a metal gnomon pointed out the hours on a concave inner surface of a fan-like dial. The length of a Roman hour varied throughout the year therefore the long summer hours were read from the wider placed lines on the lower section, and the shorter winter hours from the upper portion. The curved line crossing over the hours marks the equinoxes, Larino, Italy.

FIGURE 93 *(above)*. Terminal busts of a janiform herm. Like the god Janus one head looks forward and the other back. This form can show a combination of young and old faces or male and female, Alexandria Archaeological Museum.

Another item that was specific to this period (although invented by late Hellenistic Greeks) was the sundial. These stone objects usually had a concave dial[52] and a metal gnomen that created a shadow pointing to the approximate hour. What better location could you find to be able to read the time of day than a sunny spot in a garden.

Garden pools

The construction of aqueducts to cities, and the diversion of streams to country properties meant that the inhabitants could now add water features to their gardens. Many Romans chose to construct an ornamental pool, although not all were used to contain fish. On occasion evidence for fish keeping was confirmed by finding a row of fish refuges that had been inserted into the side walls of the pool. Some were of stone but many were in fact terracotta amphorae inserted with the neck of the vessel flush with the side wall of the pool, examples of these were found in the rectangular pool of the House of the Triconch Hall at Ptolemais in Libya.

The majority of Roman garden pools were rectangular in shape or semicircular as these shapes were easier to construct. Most were found to fall into seven different types that reflect a change in fashion or taste.[53] The simple rectangular pool at Ptolemais was classified as a Farrar Type A. All Roman pools were based on geometric shapes; there was never a desire to have an irregular shaped pool. The interior of pools were sometimes painted blue, or had fish painted on the

sides, any movement of the water would then make them look to be swimming about. Another form of decoration was to line the pool with a beautiful mosaic, which could have fish or suitable aquatic scenes (this was particularly favoured in shallow examples of the semicircular pools of Farrar Type E).

In some gardens the gutters around the peristyle were replaced by a narrow elongated pool that ran continuously around three sides, leaving one open for access, this form was favoured at *Vienna* (Vienne in France) but less so elsewhere. More interesting shapes of pool were attempted and we find that some had either semicircular niches added to the exterior of the rectangular pool (Types B and C), or they had a combination of semicircular and rectangular niches made in the interior of the pool (Type D). More complex water basins appear to have had little islands of greenery in their midst (Type F). This was achieved by constructing several watertight caissons that could be filled with soil and planted. A number of houses in Conimbriga, Portugal,

FIGURE 96 *(above left)*. A row of terracotta amphorae were used to provide fish refuges in a Type A rectangular pool at the House of the Triconch Hall, Ptolemais, Libya.

FIGURE 97 *(above right)*. Typology of Roman pools.

FIGURE 98. Restored garden with a gutter water-basin running around three sides. The clean lines and the blueness of the water give a wonderful indication of how they once might have appeared, House of the Five Mosaics, *Vienna* (modern Vienne/St Romain-en-Gal, France).

FIGURE 99. A water garden, Type F pool. Water-tight caissons allow islands to be planted inside the pool; 400 water jets create a stunning spectacle, House of the Water Jets, Conimbriga, Portugal.

FIGURE 100. Three intercommunicating pools with central fountain in the garden of the Villa at Piazza Armerina, Sicily (photo: M. Morley).

have a pool of this kind, each with differently shaped caissons. At the House of Swastikas the rectangular water basin had four symmetrically disposed quarter-circle islands of greenery, while the House of the Water Jets had six. A later style saw the introduction of intercommunicating pools (Type G) and is typified by the three pools seen in the peristyle at the Villa of Piazza Armerina, Sicily.

Fountains and *nymphaea*

Water could be brought to the pools by employing a fountain fed by gravity. Single or multiple fountains played into pools. At the House of the Water Jets at Conimbriga there were 400 small bronze fountain jets, these were sited around the rim of the water basin and around each of the 'islands' to make quite a spectacle, and what is astounding is that they are still in working order today. The jets make just a gentle arc because of low water pressure, but the overall effect is amazing; and that was the intention. Romans wanted and needed to display their wealth, and this is another method of doing so. At times you see a conspicuous consumption of water (for fountains) simply to tell their world that they were important influential people.

Water outlets were often fashioned of bronze, some were plain as at the House of the Water Jets, but elsewhere ones fashioned in the shape of a dolphin or bird have been found. The desire for ornamentation was great, and we find that a lion's mask, or head of a fluvial deity, were very popular devices used to direct water from a wall mounted fountain. Marble statues were bored through so that water could pour out of the mouth of an animal; or alternatively water would be made to trickle out of an urn or wineskin carried on the shoulder of a figure, the viewer was meant to interpret this as wine pouring. The tinkling sound of water enlivened a garden and fountains were positioned carefully to maximise their effect. Even if you only had a small light-well court it could be made attractive with a central fountain. One option was to have a quasi-pyramidal marble fountain sculpted with panels of shallow steps so that water could flow through a shell at the top then tumble down the short flights of steps into a catchment basin below.

Elaborate fountain houses, or *nymphaea*, were built in a prominent position in gardens.[54] These were imagined as being the home of a nymph and were meant to invoke a cave setting where nymphs abide, so accordingly a pumice panel was often inset into their design if possible. The shrine-like *aedicula nymphaeum* were usually sited against a garden wall; they had either a pediment or rounded roof, and a statue recess. Several were painted, but a number were encrusted with beautifully decorated mosaic and shell work. Shells were strongly suggestive of water domains and here they fulfilled a double connection: to the nymph who was seen as the source of the water, and with Venus who was born from the sea and also happens to be the prime goddess of gardens. These highly decorative architectural garden features were not just confined to Pompeii, for

FIGURE 101. A freestanding water-stair fountain would enliven a small garden court or lightwell. Water slowly trickled through the holes in the shells and masks down the stairs and into a shallow catchment basin below, Aquileia Museum.

FIGURE 102. Mosaic and shell covered shrine to a water nymph, a *nymphaeum*, House of the Great Fountain, Pompeii.

similar ones, although less well preserved have been discovered at Hadrian's villa and on the Palatine.[55] Some Romans decided to construct larger *nymphaea* that comprised several niches so that they resembled the facade of a Roman theatre, as in the House of the Bull at Pompeii[56] and the House of Cupid and Psyche at Ostia. If you had a large villa you might want to erect a building with an interior that was meant to resemble a grotto. Water was brought to feed fountains inside, and this type of *nymphaeum* made suitably cool settings for feasting. The frescoed walls of the Auditorium of Maecenas in Rome is a good example with garden scenes painted in niches inside, this was of almost basilica-like proportions.

Those who were fortunate to have a cave on their estate could enhance it as seen in a fresco from Boscoreale (now in New York). Some Romans even converted a cave for dining parties, as mentioned by Seneca (see below). At Sperlonga (ancient *Speluncae* near Tarracina, Italy) the garden ran right up to the sea and a natural sea cave on the shoreline was converted into a superb grotto visited by Emperor Tiberius, it is a historical site described by Tacitus.[57] The dining area was sited on a little island and sea water had been funnelled around it to make a large pool (which had several fish refuges set into its sides). The diners faced into the cave itself, and would have gazed upon a mythical pageant in over life-size sculptural form portraying Odysseus and his men blinding the giant Polyphemus, this made a fantastic backdrop. Fragments of this, and other sculptural groups, were discovered in the water

FIGURE 103. A garden by the sea shore had a nearby sea cave that was converted into a luxury dining area for the Emperor Tiberius; scene of a dramatic event in AD 26 mentioned by Suetonius. Sperlonga, ancient *Sperluncae* (meaning the cave).

where they had toppled or been thrown down at the end of antiquity. On the other side of the cave a chamber had been converted into a room where guests could sleep off their excesses. Pliny the Younger mentions such a garden room in his large garden.[58]

Novelty devices such as automata became fashionable among the wealthy and Hero of Alexandria's book *Pneumatics* gives several detailed designs for their use in a garden. These ingenious devices were partly made of bronze and worked by means of running water, vacuum, levers and siphons. Some featured birds singing and moving and the bronze birds sitting on branches found at the luxurious House of Fabius Rufus at Pompeii are believed to have been part of one of these ancient devices.[59]

Descriptions of Roman gardens

Most contemporary Latin descriptions of actual gardens are short passages, but they give titbits of garden art in this period. Most quotations concern large properties which were of more interest to writers at that time. Cicero shows what would be ideal in a garden when he describes one in a letter to his brother who had been searching for a new villa:

> I proceeded straight to your Fufidian estate, which we purchased for you in the last few weeks from Fufidius for 100,000 sesterces … A more shady spot in summer I never saw, water gushing out in lots of places … you will have a marvellous charming villa to live in, with the addition of a fishpond with jets d'eau, an exercising-ground, and a plantation of vines ready staked …[60]

Varro mentions that he had a stream running though his estate with bridges to cross over to an island, nearby there was a *museum* (this was similar to a nymphaeum) and further down there was an ornamental aviary which he describes in great detail.[61] It included dining facilities so you could watch birds perched in tiers as if seated in a theatre. There were even two fish pools nearby with ducks swimming about. Seneca gives a partial indication of what he thought were luxurious additions in the garden at Vatia's villa which was by the sea near Baiae, in what was a desirable sea-side location:

> I could not describe the villa accurately; for I am familiar only with the front of the house, and with the parts which are in public view and can be seen by the mere passer-by. There are two grottoes, which cost a great deal of labour, as big as the most spacious hall, made by hand. One of these does not admit the rays of the sun, while the other keeps them until the sun sets [these would have been used as dining rooms, the former in the summer and the latter for winter months]. There is also a stream running through a grove of plane-trees, which draws for its supply both on the sea and on Lake Acheron; it intersects the grove just like a *euripus*, and is large enough to support fish.[62]

The *euripus* mentioned here was a fashionable water feature; one can be seen in the House of Loreius Tiburtinus at Pompeii. These were narrow elongated rectangular pools that sometimes have little bridges over them like the famous one built in the Campus Martius in Rome in 19 BC. These *euripii* alluded to the original Euripus, a celebrated narrow channel between mainland Greece and the island of Euboea that periodically had a tidal race. Romans liked to make such an association and large sheets of water were regularly named after water channels of antiquity or famous rivers, such as the Nile or the Canopus canal.[63] The latter was in a notoriously liberal area near Alexandria in the Nile delta.

The *Historiae Augusta* reveals that the emperor Hadrian named different parts of his fabulous villa and gardens at Tivoli after some of his favourite places in the Empire that he had seen on his travels, and one of these was Canopus. His version of Canopus was a fabulous dining area placed at the edge of a vast sheet of water which was lined by an elegant colonnade and statues. A crocodile, in statuary form, furthered the tenuous connection with the Nile delta, and two river god fountain statues completed the scene. A narrow plant bed with a row of amphorae type plant pots was found on one side of this large pool. Hadrian also named an area after the *Poikile* a painted colonnade in Athens which he recreated as a magnificent long covered walkway overlooking a large garden. Here he could walk in his colonnade '*in circuitum*'; other wealthy Romans followed fashion and we find inscriptions about garden colonnades in a similar situation stating that a number of turns of the circuit could make a *stade* (625 Roman feet).[64] Another area was landscaped to reflect the Vale of Tempe, a particularly beautiful spot in Thessaly. A cave was enhanced to suggest Hades, and there was an area to evoke the Academy of Athens. Hadrian was not alone in naming areas within gardens; Cicero called one part of his garden 'the Academy'. When searching for statues to ornament this particular garden he requested muses, herms and philosophers, but not bacchantes (wanton female attendants of Bacchus) which would have spoilt the atmosphere he hoped to gain. Themed and period gardens are not new; Caligula had Egyptian statues brought from Egypt, and had copies of pharaohs made with his own features added so that he could adorn an 'Egyptian' pavilion and create a little Egypt for himself in the *Horti Sallustiani* at Rome.

We are very fortunate that Pliny's nephew, known as Pliny the Younger, left two lengthy descriptions in letters inviting a friend to visit him and see the beauties of his villa and extensive gardens. He had a maritime villa at Laurentum, near Ostia, and a villa at Tifurnum. He relates how at the former, which was on the seashore, two prospect towers provided a view of the sea, his gardens, the woods and mountains. Statius and others also mentions how a fine view was much appreciated,[65] and carefully landscaped gardens could enhance this. One part of Pliny's garden at Laurentum had a circular drive (a *gestatio*) that was really a wide pathway or alley where people could go for litter-borne walks:

> All around the drive runs a hedge of box, or rosemary to fill gaps, for box will flourish extensively where it is sheltered by the buildings, but dries up if exposed in the open to the wind and salt spray even at a distance. Inside the inner ring of the drive is a young and shady vine pergola ... The garden itself is thickly planted with mulberries and figs.[66]

There was also 'a terrace scented with violets' at Laurentum, and a well stocked rustic kitchen garden. Pliny gives a fuller picture in words when speaking about his Tuscan villa. It was built on a sloping hillside so the gardens were designed on a series of terraces, he also included a *gestatio* which he likens to a Roman circus race-track:

> In front of the colonnade is a terrace laid out with box hedges clipped into different shapes, from which a bank slopes down, also with figures of animals cut out of box facing each other on either side. On the level below there is a bed of acanthus so soft one could say it looks like water. All around is a path hedged by bushes which are trained and cut into different shapes, and then a drive [*gestatio*], oval like a race-course, inside which are various box figures and clipped dwarf shrubs. The whole garden is enclosed by a dry-stone wall which is hidden from sight by a box hedge planted in tiers; outside is a meadow, as well worth seeing for its natural beauty as the formal garden I have described; then fields and more meadows and woods …[67]

Another section of these extensive gardens concerns his so-called *hippodromus*. This was an interesting garden form that is also found at Hadrian's villa and in the imperial palace on the Palatine in Rome. The design of a *hippodromus* (sometimes called a stadium) again mimicked a race track and accordingly was made to resemble the long rectangular shape with a curved end to mark the turning point of the track. However, instead of staging horse races in these places there were promenades. Sidonius described an alternative option to have a large lake on his property (in Gaul) that could be turned into a boat racing venue. The island in the middle of this lake was fitted with turning posts and was the scene 'of jolly wrecks of vessels which collide at the sports.'[68] The huge pool found at Welschbillig (mentioned above) provides an actual example, but this particular pool had a long thin island in the centre just like a *spina*, the central reservation, seen in chariot racing tracks. Therefore the Welschbillig pool may have provided many happy hours of fun for staged boat races. Romans loved to make such allusions, boat races or promenades instead of race tracks. Pliny was rightly proud of this part of his garden because he careful details all its many parts. These insights into the highly developed art of Roman gardening are extremely valuable, and helps to visualise such a setting. The text is so vivid you can actually feel you are taking a stroll around the garden with him. He says that:

> The design and beauty of the buildings are greatly surpassed by the riding-ground [*hippodromus*]. The centre is quite open so that the whole extent of the course can be seen as one enters. It is planted round with ivy-clad plane trees, green with their own leaves above, and below with the ivy which climbs over trunk and branch and links tree to tree as it spreads across them. Box shrubs grow between the plane trees, and outside there is a ring of laurel bushes which add their shade to that of the planes. Here the straight part of the course ends, curves round in a semicircle, and changes its appearance, becoming darker and more densely shaded by the cypress trees planted round to shelter it, whereas the inner circuits-for there are several-are in open sunshine; roses grow there and the cool shadow alternates with the pleasant warmth of the sun. At the end of the winding alleys of the rounded end of the course you return to the straight path, or rather paths, for there are several separated

by intervening box hedges. Between the grass lawns here and there are box shrubs clipped into innumerable shapes, some being letters which spell the gardener's name or his master's; small obelisks of box alternate with fruit trees, and then suddenly in the midst of this ornamental scene is what looks like a piece of rural country planted there. The open space in the middle is set off by low plane trees planted on each side; farther off are acanthuses with their flexible glossy leaves, then more box figures and names.

At the upper end of the course is a curved dining seat of white marble, shaded by a vine trained over four slender pillars of Carystian marble. Water gushes out through pipes from under the seat as if pressed out by the weight of people sitting there, is caught in a stone cistern and then held in a finely-worked marble basin which is regulated by a hidden device so as to remain full without overflowing. The preliminaries and main dishes for dinner are placed on the edge of the basin, while the lighter ones float about in vessels shaped like birds or little boats. A fountain opposite plays and catches its water, throwing it high in the air so that it falls back into the basin, where it is played again at once through a jet connected with the inlet. Facing the seat is a bedroom ... Here too a fountain rises and disappears underground, while here and there are marble chairs which anyone tired with walking appreciates as much as the building itself. By every chair is a tiny fountain, and throughout the riding-ground can be heard the sound of the streams directed into it, the flow of which can be controlled by hand to water one part of the garden or another or sometimes the whole at once.[69]

Pliny's text serves to invoke the true spirit of a Roman garden. His clear descriptions and those of other authors allow a great understanding of the Roman way of life; it is also interesting that Romans viewed a garden as a subject worthy of discussion. Contemporary sources and archaeology combined allow us to appreciate the advances made in the art of garden landscaping during the Roman period.

Roman gardeners and topiary

There is no all embracing term for a gardener in the Roman period, for horticultural workers were named after the task they performed. Therefore there was a *vinitor* who trimmed vines, both in a vineyard and on garden pergolas covered by vines. An *arborator* (*arbor* means tree) was needed to trim and graft fruit trees and generally took care of large trees, lopping branches when needed. Someone who tended vegetables was called an *olitor* or *holitor* (both spellings exist) the word came from the Latin *holeris* which means vegetables. An *aquarius* was a water carrier, and he would be needed to water seedlings in nursery beds, and plants elsewhere in the garden. There was also a *hortulanus* who was someone involved in market gardening. The names of some of these 'gardeners' are preserved on a series of funerary inscriptions.[70]

There was however a specialist gardener a *topiarius* (pl. *topiarii*); their skilful work clipping hedges and bushes was referred to as *opus topiarii* and this led to our word topiary. The art of topiary was in fact invented by the Romans, Pliny the Elder credits Gaius Matius as the inventor during the reign of Augustus

FIGURE 104. Detail of an *arboritor* grafting trees in a mosaic depicting rural tasks of the calendar year, from Vienne, now in St Germaine-en-Laye, near Paris.

FIGURE 105. Sinuous architecturally inspired lines of the topiary hedge bordering a wide path at Fishbourne Roman Palace, southern Britain.

(27 BC–AD 14).[71] The *topiarius* created *topiar* which means landscape, so he was also a landscape gardener and was known to design gardens. Both Pliny the Elder and Cicero show that *topiarii* were admired for their creativity. They were often highly skilled and there are several references to how box hedges could be trimmed into tiers, even obelisks, figures of 'various shapes', or they could spell out names in the well clipped hedges. Pliny the Elder mentioned that hedges were even made into representations of 'hunting scenes or fleets of ships and imitations of real objects,' such was the inventiveness of *topiarii*.

Through archaeology we have evidence of the layout of hedges and some of the designs were quite intricate, such as those discovered bordering a wide path at the Palace at Fishbourne (Britain) dated AD 75. At Fishbourne the soil was poor and stony so the Romans dug deep bedding trenches and filled the trenches with good enriched dark soil so that the hedges would stand a better chance of survival. The contrasting colour and texture of the soil was immediately noticed by the excavators and revealed that the bedding trenches were in a classic architecturally inspired pattern: the straight lines were enlivened by alternating semicircular and rectangular recesses. The topiary hedge has been replanted at Fishbourne using box as archaeologists found remains of box nearby. Box was generally used when making a topiary hedge, we also hear of cypress and rosemary, but yew was never used in the garden at all because it was considered very poisonous.

Roman gardeners used tools such as a hoe (*sarculum*), pruning hook (*falx arboraria*), rake (*rastrum*), fork (*ferrea*). A spade (*pala*) was usually made of wood but had an iron shoe as a cutting blade, this type was called a *palas lignea*. A *bidens* was a form of hoe with two teeth. There was also a special twin headed tool called an *ascia-rastrum* this incorporated a *bidens* on one side and a *sarculum* on the other. All of these tools have been discovered on archaeological sites and some even appear in frescoes and mosaic. The tool most frequently shown in use by a horticulturalist is the *bidens*, they often feature in mosaics depicting tasks associated with the seasons of the year.

Plants were nurtured and transported in distinctive terracotta pots (*ollae perforatae*) which had at least three holes on the side as well as on the bottom. Two of these flower pots were found in the garden at Fishbourne. In Rome as one might expect a great number of flower pots have been unearthed, for instance in the small garden at the Villa of Livia at Primaporta 19 *ollae perforatae* had been placed around the edge of the small peristyle garden and a further three in the middle.[72] In 1875 74 were discovered in other *horti* on the Esquiline, and so many were found at Nero's Golden House that they gave up counting! As already mentioned, on occasion reused amphorae cut in half were an alternative form of plant pot, and in the Severan garden phase of the Vigna Barberini on the Palatine a variety of forms were used, some originally from Africa.[73]

Cato and Pliny mention that gardeners used *ollae perforatae* to propagate fruit trees and other plants by air layering.[74] Baskets were sometimes used instead of a pot when layering a plant on the ground. Numerous sources mention how gardeners also made cuttings of perennial plants and herbs as well as bushes (from violets to southernwood). They grafted trees to improve fruiting and they also experimented to produce different flavoured fruit, *e.g.* by grafting plums onto apples and peaches on plums. We even hear of two or more fruit branches grafted onto one tree. Pliny the Elder also reveals that produce could be forced into early growth to bring forward the flowering of rose bushes or fruiting of fruit trees, to achieve this hot water was poured into a trench around the bush/tree.[75] Martial hints that wealthy individuals may have had a form of conservatory where transparent stone was used to protect precious fruit trees from frost.[76] Columella records the use of a *specularium*, miniature greenhouses made of transparent stone, which was wheeled around to take advantage of the sun's heat so that early cucumbers could be grown for Emperor Tiberius; Seneca mentions that they were also used to force early blooms of lilies.[77]

Pliny also discusses some of the more decorative plants 'that the topiarius cultivates,' such as the acanthus, Romans apparently preferred the smooth leaved variety (*Acanthus mollis*). We also hear of the periwinkle (*Vinca minor*). Both of these were used as ground cover plants and the acanthus in particular was said to cover the banks of borders and raised portions in gardens.[78] While the cynoglossos was said to be 'a most attractive addition to ornamental gardens.' Pliny also speaks about the Jupiter's beard (our *Anthyllis barba-jovis*) which he says was 'used in ornamental gardening and is clipped into a round bushy shape and has a silvery leaf.'[79] There are many such interesting titbits and such comments hint of the advances in horticulture during the Roman period.

Romans sought new or better plants from all around the Empire and these were introduced to Italy. We hear of the Jujube (*Zizyphus jujuba*) and lotus tree (also known as the nettle tree *Celtis australis*) that were discovered in north Africa and made attractive garden trees, they also had edible berries. The lemon and citron (*Citrus lemon*; *C. medica*) were also new introductions to Italy and were prized for their health giving properties, both feature in a mosaic in Rome.[80] The name of the peach (known as *malus persica*) shows that it was believed to originate in Persia. It arrived in Italy in the 1st century AD at least, for peach remains were discovered in a waterlogged site in a *domus* at Privernum dating to AD 50–100.[81] Because peaches were new and exotic they feature in several Pompeian frescoes; often a slice of the fruit is cut out so you can see their distinctive large nut inside. One of the earliest fruit tree introduced to Rome was the sweet cherry in about 60 BC, which General Lucullus brought back from Pontus (on the Black Sea coast of Turkey) after his campaigns against Mithridates. The fruit was so widely acclaimed that it was subsequently introduced to other provinces, and we hear that the sweet cherry became established in Britain by AD 46. Many useful plants were introduced to Britain[82] and the early dissemination of plant species is a great legacy we owe to the Romans.

Pliny the Elder's lifetime work (*Naturalis Historia*) contained much of his own observations and the accumulated wisdom of numerous great authors (many whose work no longer survives). It was the first encyclopaedia, a vast compilation of '20,000 noteworthy facts' in 37 books. Books 12–27 are of especial note as they deal with botany and pharmacology, but he also included sections on cultivated trees, shrubs, herbs and vegetables. He lets us know which plants were used as ornamentals, and those for making chaplets, as well as culinary plants and those necessary for beekeeping or for making cordials and medicines; a table of these garden plants was provided in my earlier book on *Ancient Roman Gardens*.[83]

In the present table of garden plants of the Roman period (based on those mentioned by Pliny the Elder) I have included the Classical name for each one because we can often trace the nucleus of these in the modern botanical names. I have listed the Latin names for plants used by Pliny and Greek names from the

works by Dioscorides and Theophrastus. For plants that were known to have a Greek name I have added a G. For the Latin names I have added a R (not an L for Latin), this is to save confusion with the modern universal botanical naming system invented by Carl Linaeus in AD 1737, because scholars put a L after the name of each of the plants he classified. When Linaeus compiled his plant lists he decided to use (where possible) the ancient name which was still current in many cases. For instance, Roman texts show that box trees were called *buxus* and therefore our modern botanical name for this shrub is now *Buxus sempervirens* the ancient name is preserved in the first part of the name, the second part is a descriptive element so that a precise species can be identified. In the case of the laurustinus, *Vibernum tinus*, the last part of this plant's name is the ancient name of what Pliny described was a kind of laurel, called *tinus*. The modern Latin botanical naming system preserves a marvellous link with the past. In the table of Roman garden plants there are also two columns on the right to indicate if a particular plant species was identified in frescoes, mosaics or in reliefs (F/M/R); the A stands for whether they were present in archaeological contexts. The plants in this list are all mentioned by Pliny the Elder.

FIGURE 106. The verdant frescos from Livia's Garden Room at Primaporta, near Rome, reveal elements of garden landscaping art. A trellis fence and decorative low marble wall provide strong horizontal lines to counter the strong vertical forms of the trees and bushes, but the severity of the wall is broken by forming a recess to create a more pleasing effect, and also to highlight a specimen tree. On other occasions a statue or urn could be placed there, *c*.20 BC (Museo Nazionale Romano, Rome, Italy. The Bridgeman Art Library)

Archaeology of Roman gardens and botanical remains

At Pompeii archaeologists have been able to trace plant pits and root cavities, contours of plant beds or cultivation trenches, and where possible pollen and macrofossils were extracted for analysis.[84] Like today, some people lovingly tended their garden and others less so. Therefore gardens were found to comprise the utilitarian, as well as informal ones and formal designs.

FIGURE 107.
Reconstruction of
a gardener's bench
with facsimile Roman
flowerpots, Fishbourne
Roman Palace, Britain.

FIGURE 108. The sweet rocket or dame's violet
(*Hesperis matronalis*) was much appreciated by the
Romans for its wonderful strong scent at night,
hence its ancient name *hesperis*, the evening star,
photographed in my old garden.

The layout of an informal garden was revealed in the House of Polybius which had been densely planted.[85] There were numerous small root cavities at the east and south edges of the pseudo-peristyle suggesting shrubs. Eight tree root cavities beside the west wall were interesting because a number of nail holes above them indicated that these trees had been espalier trained against the wall. Five of these planting pits still had fragments of the broken flower pot with them from when they had first been planted out. The form of the five larger tree roots within the garden resembled fig, pear and olive, and stake holes near some of these showed that some of the branches had become so laden with fruit that they needed supporting. The outline of a tall narrow ladder for fruit picking was still preserved on the garden soil in this house. However the only conclusive evidence for fruit trees in this garden came from macrofossils of fig and pollen of olive. The majority of other pollen grains came from windblown trees flowering at the time of the eruption (such as hazel, oak, pine, lime and walnut) and were not necessarily in this particular enclosed spot. Some of the perennials and weeds present here included members of the *caryophyllaceae* family and *chenopodiaceae, ericaceae, geranium, gramineae, plantago*, a type of potentilla and some ferns: *dryopteris* type*, polypodium* and *pteridium.*

A plan of a formal garden was revealed at Cosa in the House of the Skeleton which was dated to the 1st century BC. The rectangular garden was on sloping ground and two diagonal paths met then continued until reaching a parapet, beyond which was found a number of tree plant pits. Another path ran at right angles on the upper part of this garden and led up to an al fresco triclinium dining area.[86]

At Pompeii on the edge of the town, the large House of the Golden Bracelet had a luxurious dining room facing onto a formal garden which was at a lower level. The first sight that greeted anyone looking down into the garden was a decorative pergola shading a Farrar Type B pool that had 28 water jets around its rim, and one in the centre, these would have created a fine spectacle for dining parties.[87] Further into the garden there was evidence for topiary hedges on either side of a central path that widened into a large oval in the middle. Forty-three root cavities along the rear and north wall of this garden were believed to be of vines trained to grow upwards thereby clothing the walls.

The layout of the garden in the relatively more modest House of the Chaste Lovers at Pompeii was similar to that of the House previously mentioned as the paths followed the margins of the garden and then bisected the garden. Again there was a wide oval space in the centre of the path. However, this smaller garden had a reed fence surrounding the plant beds rather than a hedge. Two species of reed had been used, the giant reed (*Arundo donax*) for the fence supports and the smaller *Phragmites australis* simply placed diagonally into the soil for the main part of the barrier. Interestingly pollen and macrofossils detected in the plant beds has shown that plants were deliberately chosen for colour and effect, and on either side of the path juniper bushes alternated with

FIGURE 109. Hadrian's luxurious dining area beside a vast pool recreated the atmosphere of dining beside the Canopus canal that he had admired when in Egypt. Two river gods representing the Nile and the Tibur are placed at the entrance to this part of his villa at Tivoli.

roses and artemisia.[88] Pollen grains also confirmed the presence of campanula, cerastium, lychnis, malva, myrtle, plantago, and *polypodium australe*. Plants that were in the genus *asteraceae* and *caryophyllacae* are also represented here. Sadly some pollen grains of species within a genus are too similar to distinguish apart and so we cannot be more precise.

Outside of Pompeii evidence of garden plans is more limited, but excavations at Hadrian's Villa at Tivoli has revealed numerous garden areas. In the peristyle of the Grand Vestibule, for instance, the contours of the plant beds were preserved revealing a similar symmetrical arrangement of a path bisecting the plant beds into two halves, here though the path widened into a large circular recess with a plinth for a decorative feature in the centre.[89] In the Piazza d'Oro area an elongated water basin bisected the peristyle garden (instead of a path). A number of planting pits (*c*.80 cm deep) had been cut into the rocky tufa of the beds.[90] These were linked to a network of trenches but were found to continue under the shallow pool and proved to be an ingenious labour saving plant watering system. Water was directed to a series of ducts on the western side and irrigated the first plant bed, then water filtered through the trenches, which were at an even slope of 3%, to water the plants in the second eastern bed. Sadly the soil in this garden was too acidic for the preservation of pollen or seeds, so we can only speculate as to the planting scheme there.

It is noticeable that many formal gardens were designed using symmetrical principles and Roman garden design can be assumed from a number of sites.

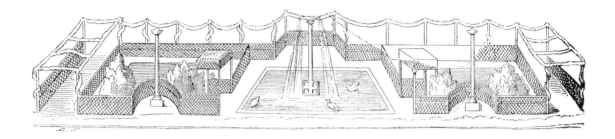

At Conimbriga for instance, a range of water gardens give an indication of the patterns created in the 3rd century AD.[91] In several houses a Farrar Type F pool dominates the garden, but these pools have decorative islands of greenery that mimic planting beds in a 'normal' garden. The water around and between these water tight caissons take the place of paths. At the House of Cantaber the water like paths divided the garden into four large segments, each L shaped plant bed was given a semicircular recess on two sides. While at Luni (northern Italy) the Type F pool resembled a quadripartite garden, but each of the four quadrants were roughly octagonal. Eight fountains played into the water channels and one in the centre. The island beds however might have been covered by grass as the depth of soil was minimal, but as numerous vase fragments were found here a more interesting suggestion is that the area was used for potted plants.[92]

As discovered around the Empire, there were public and private gardens, and Roman gardens could be small or large; such as those confined in a peristyle *viridarium* that could be contrasted with the often extensive landscaped grounds that surrounded a country villa. Roman gardens became ornate with Greek inspired statuary and sculptures. Urns and bowls were both seen as works of art and were used as fountains. Pergolas, bowers and trellises usefully provided shade and were a support for vines allowing wine to be made on the premises; they also added to the overall charm of the garden, and combined with a wooden archway they could make garden rooms, and close or open up different sections of a garden. Pools of increasing complexity were added to many gardens, and water features from jets d'eau to *nymphaea*. A wide range of plants were grown in Roman gardens, scented flowers and aromatic leaved plants were especially favoured. Plants were sought from across the Empire to provide new or better garden worthy varieties. Gardens were places of work for some (such as *topiarii*) but were a place of relaxation and contemplation for others. In short, Roman gardens were a prime location for displaying the owner's wealth (to keep up their social standing), and ultimately they were an ideal location where they could entertain guests dining al fresco under the cool shade of a vine covered pergola.

FIGURE 110. Drawing of a miniature fresco where climbing plants are trained to form garlands trailing from post to post and across pergolas around garden enclosures. In the centre a tall fountain plays water into a rectangular pool. Auditorium of Maecenas, Rome (Daremberg and Saglio 1900, 3, 288).

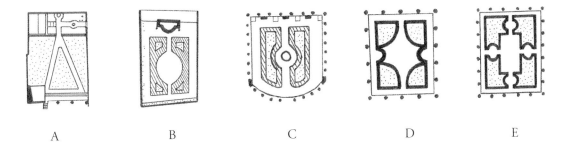

A   B   C   D   E

FIGURE III. Garden Plans. A. The House of the Skeleton, Cosa; B. The House of the Golden Bracelet, Pompeii; C. The Grand Vestibule, Hadrian's Villa, Tivoli; D. The House of the Swastikas, Conimbriga; E. The House of Cantaber, Conimbriga (the stippled areas represent plant beds and the diagonal hatching are garden hedges).

What is so different about the Roman period is that gardens were now no longer the prerogative of the few but were enjoyed by the populace as well. In previous eras gardens, as we have seen, were reserved for the king, high priests and ruling elite. However, at Pompeii and elsewhere in the Roman world, it was not only the rich elite who could afford to own a garden, but now shop keepers and anybody else who had the will to have a small bit of nature beside their home could cultivate a garden, even if it was just a small corner or strip. If this small area was placed in front of a wall then with a suitably painted verdant backdrop the impression of a much larger lush garden could be achieved. Roman inventiveness in garden art has to be admired.

Garden Plants of the Roman Period

Common name	Classical name	Botanical name	F/M/R	A
Acanthus	*Akantha G. Acanthus R.*	*Acanthus mollis*	x	x
Alexanders	*Ipposelinon G. Olusatrum R.*	*Smyrnium olusatrum*		x
Almond	*Amugdale G. Amygdala R.*	*Amygdalus communis Prunus dulcis*	x	x
Anemone	*Anemone G. Anemones R.*	*Anemone coronaria*		x
Anise (aniseed)	*Anicetum R. Anesum R.*	*Pimpinella anisum*		
Anthyllis (barba-jovis)	*Barba Iovis R.*	*Anthyllis barba-jovis*		
Apple	*Melea G. Malus R.*	*Malus domestica*	x	x
Apricot	*Armeniaca G. & R. Praecoqua R.*	*Prunus armeniaca*		
Asparagus	*Aspharagos G. Asparagus R.*	*Asparagus officinalis*	x	x
Aster	*Asteriskos G. Aster R.*	*Aster amellus; Aster* sp.		x
Azarole & Hawthorn	*Mespilon G. Mespila R. Oxyacantha R*	*Crataegus azarolus C. oxyacantha* (hawthorn)		x
Balm	*Melissophullon G. Melissophyllum R./Apiastrum R.*	*Mellisa officinalis*		
Basil	*Okimon G. Ocimum R.*	*Ocimum Basilicum Acinos arvensis*		
Beans (broad bean)	*Kuamos G. Faba R.*	*Faba vulgaris; Vicia faba*		x
Beet	*Teutlon melan G. Beta R./Beta aestate R.*	*Beta vulgaris B. maritima*		x
Blite/Good King Henry (spinach-like)	*Bliton G. Blitum R.*	*Blitum Bonus-Henricus Chenopodium bonus-henricus*		
Box	*Pusos G. Buxus R.*	*Buxus sempervirens*		x
Brussels Sprout	*Cyma R.*	*Brassica cymosa*		
Butcher's broom	*Chamaidaphne G. Ruscus R.*	*Ruscus aculeatus*		x
Cabbage	*Krambe emeros G. Brassica R.*	*Brassica oleracea*		x
Caper	*Kapparis G. Capparis R.*	*Capparis spinosa*		x
Cardoon & artichoke	*Kaktos G. Carduos R.*	*Cynara cardunculus/ C.scolymus*	x	
Carnation	*Diosanthos G. Iovis flos R.*	*Dianthus* spp. *D.caryophylleus*	x	x
Carob	*Keratia G. Ceratia R./Ceronia R.*	*Ceratonia siliqua*	x	x
Carraway	*Karos G. Careum R.*	*Carum carvi*		
Carrot	*Daukos G. Staphylinus R.*	*Dracus carota*	x	x
Catmint/Calamint	*Elenion G. Nepeta R.*	*Calamintha nepeta*		x
Cedar	*Kedron G. Cedrus R.*	*Juniperus oxycedrus*		
Celery	*Selinon G. Helioselinum R.*	*Apium graveolens*		x
Cerintha	*Telephion G. Cerinthe R.*	*Cerinthe major*		x
Chamomile	*Anthemon G. Anthemis R. Leucanthemis R.*	*Anthemis nobilis*	x	x
Cherry	*Kerasia G. Cerasus R.*	*Prunus cerasus*	x	x
Chervil	*Caerefolium R.*	*Anthriscus cerefolium*		
Chestnut	*Kastana G. Castanea R.*	*Castanea vesca*	x	x
Chicory	*Kikhorion G. Cichorium R.*	*Cichorium intybus*		x
Chrysanthemum	*Chrusanthemon G. Chrysanthemum R.*	*Chrysanthemum segetum & C. coronarium*	x	x

F/M/R = fresco/mosaic/reliefs; A = present in archaeological contexts

Common name	Classical name	Botanical name	F/M/R	A
Citron	*Persica mela G. Citrea R. Citrus R./Malus Medica R.*	*Citrus medica*	x	x
Convolvulus	*Smilax leia G. Convolvulus R.*	*Convolvulus sepium*	x	x
Conyza (ploughman's-spikenard)	*Arktion G. Conyza R./Cunilago R.*	*Inula conyza*		
Coriander	*Koriannon G. Melanthium R/ Git R.*	*Nigella sativa*		x
Cornel tree	*Krania G. Cornus R.*	*Cornus mas*		
Cornflower (Cyanus)	*Cyanus R.*	*Centauea cyanus*	x	x
Cress	*Kardamon G. Nasturtium R.*	*Lepidium sativum*		
Crocus & saffron	*Krokos G. Crocus R.*	*Crocus odorus & C. sativus*		
Cucumber	*Kolokuntha G. Cucumis R.*	*Cucumis sativus*		x
Cumin	*Kuminon G. Cuminum R.*	*Cuminum cyminum*		
Cyclamen	*Kuklaminos G. Cyclaminus R. (2 kinds)*	*Cyclamen coum & C. neapoli- tanum*		
Cypress	*Kuparissos G. Cupressus R.*	*Cupressus sempervirens*	x	x
Dame's violet (sweet rocket)	*Hesperis R.*	*Hesperis matronalis*		
Damson	*Kokkumelia G. Damascena R.*	*Prunus insititia*		x
Date Palm	*Phoinix G. Palma R.*	*Phoenix dactylifera*	x	x
Dill	*Anethon G. Anetum R.*	*Anethum graveolens*		x
Dittany (pepperwort)	*Diktamnon G. Lepidium R.*	*Origanum dictamus [Amarcus dictamus]*		
Elecampane	*Panakes kheironeion G. Inula R.*	*Inula helenium*		
Endive	*Kikhorion G. Seris R./Intybum R.*	*Cichorium endivia*		
Fennel & giant fennel	*Marathron G./Ippomarathron G. Feniculum R. & Ferula R.*	*Foeniculum vulgare Ferula communis*		x
Feverfew (parthenium)	*Parthenion G Leucanthemum R. Anthemis R*	*Chrysanthemum parthenium* or *C. leucanthemum*		
Fig	*Sykon G. Ficus R.*	*Ficus carica*	x	x
Garlic	*Skorodon G. Alium R.*	*Alium sativum*		x
Gentian	*Gentiane G. Gentiana R.*	*Gentiana lutea/ asclepiadea*		
Germander	*Chamaidrus G. Teucrion R. olium R.*	*Teucrium polium/ T.chamaedrys*		
Gourd/ marrow & possibly melon	*Sikuos emeros G. Pepon G. Cucurbita R. & Pepones R Melopepo R.*	*Lagenaria siceraria; Cucurbita pepo*	x	x
		Cucumis pepo; C.melo	x	x
Grape Vine	*Amelos G. Vitis R.*	*Vitis vinifera*	x	x
Hart's tongue fern	*Phullitis G. Lingua R.*	*Asplenium scolopendrium*	x	
Hazelnut	*Karua Pontika G. Abellana R.*	*Corylus avellana*	x	x
Helichrysum	*Elichruson G. Heliochrysus R.*	*Helichrysum italicum; H.stoechas*		x
Heliotrope (blue flowers)	*Eliotropon G. Heliotropium R.*	*Heliotropium europaeum?*		
Holly	*Kelastros G. Aquifolia R.*	*Ilex aquifolium*		x
Horehound	*Prasion G. Marruvium/Marrubium R.*	*Marrubium vulgare*		x
Hound's tongue	*Kunoglosson G. Cynoglossos R.*	*Cynoglossum officinale*		
Houseleek	*Aeixoos G. Sedum R./aizoum R.*	*Sempervivum tectorum*		
Hyacinth (inc. Scilla, Delphinium & larkspur)	*Delphinion G. Uakinthos G. Hyacinthus R.*	*Scilla hyacinthoides; S.bifolia; Delphinium ajacis; D.peregrinum; D.consolida*		

Common name	Classical name	Botanical name	F/M/R	A
Hyssop	*Ussopos G. Hysopum R.*	*Hyssopus officinalis*		
Jujube tree	*Paliouros G. Ziziphus R.*	*Zizyphus jujuba*		
Juniper	*Arkeothos G./Kedros G. Iuniperus R.*	*Juniperus communis*		x
Iris	*Iris G. Iris R.*	*Iris germanica; Iris pallida*	x	
Ivy	*Kittos G. Hedera R.*	*Hedera helix*	x	x
Laurel (bay)	*Daphne G. Laurus R.*	*Laurus nobilis*	x	x
Laurustinus	*Tinus R.*	*Viburnum tinus*	x	x
Lavender	*Stoichas G. Stoechas R.*	*Lavendula stoechas*		
Leek	*Prason G. Porrum R.*	*Allium porrum*		x
Lemon	*Citrus R.*	*Citrus lemon*	x	x
Lettuce	*Thridax G. Lactuca R.*	*Lactuca sativa*		
Lily	*Krinon basilikon G. Emerokallis G. Lilium R.* (4 kinds)	*Lilium candidum; L.martagon*	x	x
Lovage	*Ligusticum R.*	*Levisticum officinale*		
Lychnis	*Luchnis stephanomatike G. Lychnis R./Phlox R.*	*Lychnis coronaria/L. flos-jovis*		x
Maidenhair & spleenwort	*Trichomanes G. Adianton G. Adiantum R.*	*Adiantum capillus-veneis; asplenium trichomanes*		
Mallow	*Althaia G. Malakhe G. Althaea R. Malva R. Hibiscus R.*	*Althaea officinalis; Malva*		x
Tree mallow	*Malakhe G. Arbor Malva R.*	*Lavatera arborea/L.olbia*		x
Mandrake	*Mandragoras G. Mandragora R.*	*Mandragora officinarum*		
Marjoram	*Amarakos G. Amarcus R.* (sweet marjoram); *Origanon G. Origanum R.* (wild marjoram)	*Origanum marjorana [Marjorana hortensis];* *O. onites; O. vulgare*		x x
Mastic tree	*Pistakia G. Lentiscus R.*	*Pistacia lentiscus*		x
Medlar	*Mespilon eteron G. Mespila R.*	*Mespilus germanica*		x
Melilot	*Melilotus R.*	*Melilotus albus*		x
Mint	*Minthe G. Menta R.*	*Mentha spicata*		x
Mulberry	*Morea G. Morus R.*	*Morus nigra & Morus alba*	x	x
Mustard	*Sinepi G. Sinapis R.*	*Sinapis alba*		x
Myrtle	*Mursine G. Myrtus R.*	*Myrtus communis*	x	x
Narcissus(3 varieties)	*Narkissos G. Narcissus R.*	*Narcissus jonquilla; N. poeticus; N. tazatta*	x	
Nettle tree	*Lotos G. Lotos R./Celthis R.*	*Celtis australis*		
Oleander	*Nerion G. Rododaphne G. Rhododendron R./Nerium R.*	*Nerium oleander*	x	x
Olive	*Elaia G. Olea R.* (*oliva R.* = its berry)	*Olea europaea*	x	x
Onion	*Kromuon G. Cepa R.*	*Allium cepa*	x	x
Orache/ orage	*Alimos G. Atriplex R.*	*Atriplex hortensis*		x
Parsnip	*Sisaron G. Pastinaca R.*	*Pastinaca sativa*		
Parsley	*Oreoselinon G. Apium R.*	*Petroselinum sativum*		x
Partridge plant (pellitory or polygonum)	*Perdion G. Helxine R.* or *Perdicium R./Sideritis R.*	*Parietaria diffusa; Polygonum romanum?*		
Peach	*Persica R.*	*Prunus persica*	x	x
Pear	*Apion G. Pira R.*	*Pyrus communis*	x	x
Pennyroyal	*Blekho G. Puleium R.*	*Mentha pulegium*		

Common name	Classical name	Botanical name	F/M/R	A
Periwinkle	*Klematis G. Vicapervica R.*	*Vinca minor*	x	
Pine (stone pine)	*Penke emeros G. Pinus R. & Picea R.*	*Pinus pinea; Pinus halepensis*	x	x
Plane tree	*Platanos G. Platanus R*	*Platanus orientalis*	x	x
Plantain	*Arnoglosson G. Plantago R.*	*Plantago major*	x	x
Plum	*Kokkumelia G. Prunus R.* (many kinds)	*Prunus domestica*	x	x
Pomegranate	*Rhoa G. Punica R.*	*Punica granatum*	x	x
Poppy	*Mekon G. Rhoeas G. Papaver R.*	*Papaver somniferum; P. rhoeas*	x	x
Purslain	*Andrachne agria G. Porcillaca R.*	*Portulaca oleracea*		x
Quince	*Kudonia G. Cotoneum R./ Cydonea R.*	*Cydonia oblongata*	x	x
Radish	*Raphanis G. Raphanus R.*	*Raphanus sativus*	x	x
Reed (used in the garden)	*Kalamos G. Harundo R./Calamus R.*	*Arundo donax*	x	x
Rocket	*Euzomon G. Eruca R.*	*Eruca sativa*		x
Rose (12 varieties)	*Rhodon G. Rodonia G. Rosa R. Centifolia R*	*Rosa gallica; R. damascena; R. moschata; R. alba*	x	x
Rosemary	*Libanotis G. Rosmarinus R.*	*Rosmarinus officinalis*		x
Rue	*Peganon G. Ruta R.*	*Ruta graveolens*		x
Sage	*Sphakos G. Salvia R.*	*Salvia officinalis*		
Savory/Cunila? (summer savory)	*Thumbra G. Satureia R. Cunila R.*	*Satureia hortensis*		x
Service tree (Sorbus)	*Oua G. Sorbus R.*	*Sorbus domestica*	x	x
Smilax	*Smilax tracheia G. Smilax R /Milax R.*	*Smilax aspera*		x
Soapwort	*Strouthion G. Radicula R.*	*Saponaria officinalis*		
Sorrel	*Rumix R./Lapathum R.*	*Rumex acetosa*		
Southernwood (silver leaved)	*Abrotonon G. Habrotonum R.*	*Artemisia arborescens*	x	x
Spikenard/Gallic nard (Valerian)	*Nardos G. Saliunca R.*	*Valeriana celtica*		
Squill (sea squill)	*Skilla G. Scilla R.*	*Urginea maritima*		
Strawberry tree	*Komaros G. Arbutus R./Unedo R.*	*Arbutus unedo*	x	x
Terebinth	*Termithos G. Terebinthus R.*	*Pistacia terebinthus*		
Thyme	*Erpullos G. Thymus R./Serpyllum R.*	*Thymus vulgaris; T.serpyllum*		x
Tree medick	*Kutisos G. Cytisus R.*	*Medicago arborea*		
Tuber apple (introduced from Syria)	*Tuberes R.* (red & white forms)	unknown		
Turnip	*Gongulis G. Rapa R.*	*Brassica rapa*	x	x
Vervain	*Peristereon orthos G. Sacra herba R. Verbenaca R.*	*Verbena officinalis*		x
Vetch	*Orobos G. Ervum R. Ervilia R./Vicia R.*	*Vicia ervilla; V.sativa; V. villosa*		x
Violet/gillyflower (includes wallflower & stocks)	*Ion G. Leukoion G. Viola R.* (violet, yellow & white forms)	*Viola odorata; Cheiranthus cheiri; Matthiola incana*	x	x
Walnut	*Karua basilika G. Iuglans R.*	*Juglans regia*	x	x
Wormwood	*Apsinthion G. Absinthium R.*	*Artemisia absinthium*		x

Notes

1. Wilhelmina Jashemski made a study of 450 gardens at Pompeii and the area covered by Vesuvuis, published in 2 volumes in 1979 & 1993.
2. c.f. Farrar, 2001b, 1053–1055.
3. Propertius, *Elegies*, IV, 2. trans. G. P. Goold, London, 1990.
4. And of grafting Macrobius, *Saturnalia* I, 4, 25, trans. P. V. Davies, Columbia, 1969.
5. Jashemski 1979, 124.
6. Ovid, *Fasti* V, 195. trans. J. G. Frazer, London, 1989.
7. Ovid, *Metamorphose* XIV, 623–771. trans. D. Raeburn, London, 2004.
8. *Priapeia,* 86, trans. L. C. Smithers and R. Burton, Ware, 1995. cf. Martial *Epigrams* VI, 73. trans. W. C. A. Ker, London, 1943.
9. Servius, *On Virgil's Georgics* I, 21. trans. M. Dillon and L. Garland, Abingdon, 2005.
10. Varro, *Rerum Rusticarum* I, 1, 5–7. trans. W. D. Hooper and H. B. Ash, London, 1979.
11. Bonfante, L. *Etruscan*, London, 1990, 57.
12. Statius, *Silvae* III, 1, 82f. trans. J. H. Mozley, London, 1928.
13. Pliny, *Naturalis Historia* XII, 2,3, trans. H. Rackham, London, 1986.
14. Coarelli, F. *Ditorni Di Roma*, Rome, 1993, 169–170; Lauter, H. 'Ein Tempelgarten?', *Archaeologischer Anzeiger* 1968, 626–631.
15. Private observation in September.
16. Pliny, *Naturalis Historia* XVII, 15, 78. trans. H. Rackham, London, 1971.
17. Carroll, M. '*Nemus* and *templum*. Exploring the sacred grove at the Temple of Venus in Pompeii', in Guzzo, P. G. and Guidobaldi, M. B. (eds) *Nuove richerche nell'area vesuviana (scavi 2003–2006)*, Rome, 2008, 37–45.
18. Jashemski 1995, 573.
19. Shown as F and G on the Map of Central Rome illustrated in this chapter. Map after Macdonald, *The Architecture of the Roman Empire II, An Urban Appraisal*, Yale, 1986, fig. 206.
20. Virgil, *Georgics* IV, 127ff, trans. C. Day Lewis, Oxford, 1983.
21. For instance at Frocester Court in Britain. Gracie H. S. and Price, E. G. 'Frocester Court Roman Villa, second report 1968–77: the courtyard', *Transactions of the Bristol and Gloucestershire Archaeological Society* 97, 1979, 13.
22. Pliny the Elder, *Naturalis Historia* XIX, 57. trans. H. Rackham, London, 1971.
23. Cicero, *De Legibus* II, 2, 5. trans. C. Walker Keyes, London, 1988.
24. Potter, T. W. *Roman Italy*, London, 1987, 105–107.
25. Pliny, *Epistles* V, 6,20.
26. Brown, F. E. *Cosa, the Making of a Roman Town*, Michigan, 1980, 64.
27. Farrar 1998, 15–17; Jashemski 1979, 16; Carroll-Spillecke 1992, 94.
28. Farrar 1996, 5; McWhirr, A. *Roman Gloucestershire*, Gloucester, 1986, 43; Boon, G. C. *Silchester the Roman Town of Calleva*, Newton Abbot, 1974, 189.
29. Propertius, *Elegies* II, 32, 12. trans. H. E. Butler, London, 1912.
30. Martial, *Epigrams* II, 14, 10. trans. W. C. A. Ker, London, 1943.
31. Pliny, *Naturalis Historia* XIV, 11. trans. H. Rackham, London, 1986.
32. Martial, *Epigrams* II, 14, 15. trans. W. C. A. Ker, London, 1943.
33. Martial, *Epigrams* I, 108, 3. trans. W. C. A. Ker, London, 1943.
34. Virgil, *Minor Poems, Copa*, 7f and 31. trans. H. R. Fairclough, London, 1946.
35. Pliny, *Naturalis Historia* XVII, 11, 65–66. trans. H. Rackham, London, 1971.
36. Varro, *de Re Rustica* I, 16, 3. trans. W. D. Hooper and H. B. Ash, London, 1979.
37. Jashemski 1993, 94.
38. Rea, J. R. *The Oxyrhynchus Papyri* 46, London, 1978, 100, letter 3313.

39. Kenawi, M., Macaulay-Lewis, E. and McKenzie, J. E. 'A commercial nursery near Abu Hummus (Egypt) and re-use of amphoras for the trade in plants', *Journal of Roman Archaeology* 25, 2012, 195–225.

40. Kenawi, M., Macaulay-Lewis, E. and McKenzie, J. E. 'A commercial nursery near Abu Hummus (Egypt) and re-use of amphoras for the trade in plants', *Journal of Roman Archaeology* 25, 2012, 196–197.

41. Petronius, *Satyricon* XV, 71. trans. J. P. Sullivan, Harmondsworth, 1986.

42. *Corpus Inscriptionum Latinarum* V, 7454. Berlin, 1863–83.

43. For those of Pompeii see the catalogue of paintings and mosaics in Jashemski 1993, appendix II, 313–404. c.f. Settis, S. *Le Pareti Ingannevoli,* Milan, 2002.

44. *E.g.* Martial, *Epigrams* XII, 31, 9–10. trans. W. C. A. Ker, London, 1920.

45. Jashemski 1993, 318–322.

46. Farrar 2001a. cf. Daremberg, C. H. and Saglio, E. D. M. *Dictionnaire des Antiquités Grecques and Romaines*, Paris, 1900, 4, 392–93.

47. Campanelli, A. *Effetto Alba Fucens*, Pescara, 2002, 65.

48. Jashemski 1995, 563.

49. Pliny, *Epistles* V, 6, 36–37. trans. B. Radice, London, 1972.

50. Farrar 1998, 124–5; Wrede, H. *Die Spätantike Hermengalerie von Welschbillig*, Berlin, 1972, 20–21, figs 1–53.

51. Jashemski 1993, 30; Dwyer, E. J. *Pompeian Domestic Sculpture*, Rome, 1982, 92–95.

52. There were spherical, conical, cylindrical and horizontal or vertical plane sundials. Some relied on the sun shining through a hole on the upper overhanging surface, as at Aquileia. cf. Gibbs, S. L. *Greek and Roman Sundials*, London, 1976.

53. Farrar 1998, 72–82.

54. A study of those in Italy was made by Neuerburg, N. *L'Architettura delle Fontane e dei Ninfei nell'Italia Antica*, Naples, 1965.

55. Tomei, M. A. 'Nota sui Giardini Antichi del Palatino', *Mélanges De L'École Française De Rome, Antiquité* 104(2), 1992, 921–922.

56. Andersson, E. B. 'Fountains and the Roman dwelling', *Jahrbuch des Deutschen Archäologischen Instituts* 105, 1990, 207–236.

57. Tacitus, *Annales* IV, 59. trans. M. Grant, Harmondsworth, 1966; Suetonius, *Tiberius,* 39. trans. R. Graves, London, 1991.

58. Pliny, *Epistles* V, 6, 38. trans. B. Radice, London, 1972.

59. di Pasquale, G. and Paolucci, F. (eds) 2007, 220–223.

60. Cicero, *Fratrem* III, I, 3, trans. W. G. Williams, London, 1929.

61. Varro, *de Re Rustica* III, 10–17. trans. D. Hooper and H. B. Ash, London, 1979.

62. Seneca, *Epistles* LV, 6, trans. R. M. Gummere, London, 1925.

63. Cicero, *De Legibus* II, 1, 2. trans. C. Walker Keyes, London, 1988; *Ad Fratrem* III, 9, 7. trans. G. Williams, London, 1919.

64. Grimal 1969, 255; one was found at Tarracina, Lugli, G. *Forma Italiae Reg.I Latium et Campania,* 1, Rome, 1926, 142, no.90.

65. Statius, *Silvae* II, ii, 33ff. trans. J. H. Mozley, London, 1928.

66. Pliny, *Ep.* II, 17,14ff. Reprinted by permission of the publishers and the Trustees of the Loeb Classical Library from P*liny: Letters, Books 1–7. Panegyricus*, trans. B. Radice, Loeb Classical Library® Vol. 55, 137–139, 343, 349–353, Cambridge, Mass. Copyright © 1969 President and Fellows of Harvard College.

67. Pliny, *Ep.* V, 6, 16ff. Reprinted by permission of the publishers and the Trustees of the Loeb Classical Library from P*liny: Letters, Books 1–7. Panegyricus*, trans. B. Radice, Loeb Classical Library® Vol. 55, 137–139, 343, 349–353, Cambridge, Mass. Copyright © 1969 President and Fellows of Harvard College.

68. Sidonius, *Epistles* II, 2, 19. trans. W. B. Anderson, London, 1956.

69. Piny, *Epistles* V, 6, 32ff, Reprinted by permission of the publishers and the Trustees of the Loeb Classical Library from *Pliny: Letters, Books 1–7. Panegyricus*, trans. B. Radice, Loeb Classical Library® Vol. 55, 137–139, 343, 349–353, Cambridge, Mass. Copyright © 1969 President and Fellows of Harvard College.

70. Preserved in the *Corpus Inscriptionum Latinarum*, (CIL) VI, 2, 9457–9; CIL. VI, 2, 9473.

71. Pliny, *Naturalis Historia* XII, 6, 13. trans. H. Rackham, London, 1986.

72. Liljenstolpe, P. and Klynne A., 'The Prima Porta Garden Archaeological Project. Investigations of the Imperial Gardens at the Villa of Livia at Prima Porta', in *Proceedings of the XVth International Congress of Classical Archaeology*, Amsterdam, 1999, 235, fig. 91.

73. Villedieu, F. *Il Giardino dei Cesari*, Rome, 2001, 98.

74. Cato, *De Agri*, CXXXIII. trans. W. D. Hooper and H. B. Ash, London, 1979; Pliny, *Naturalis Historia* XVII, 21, 97. trans. H. Rackham, London, 1971.

75. Pliny, *Naturalis Historia* XXI, 10, 21. trans. W. H. S. Jones, London, 1989.

76. Martial *Epigrams* VIII, 14.. trans. C. A. Ker, London, 1920.

77. Columella, *de Re Rustica* XI, 3, 52–53. trans. E. S. Forster and E. H. Heffner, London, 1993; Seneca, *Epistles* CXXII, 8. trans. R. M. Gummere, London, 1925.

78. Pliny, *Naturalis Historia* XXII, 34, 76. trans. W. H. Jones, London, 1989.

79. Pliny, *Naturalis Historia* XVI, 31, 76. trans. H. Rackham, London, 1986.

80. Therme Museum, Rome, inv. no. 58596; Jashemski 2002, 102.

81. Sadori, L. *et al.* 'The introduction and diffusion of peach in ancient Italy', in *Plants and Culture: seeds of the cultural heritage of Europe*, Bari, 2009, Edipuglia, 46. A peach stone has also been discovered at Pompeii in deposits from the House of the Vestals (Ciaraldi 2007, 124).

82. A list of these is given by Cunliffe, B. 'Roman Gardens in Britain' in MacDougall and Jashemski 1981, 98.

83. Farrar 1998, 206–208, table II; 139 Roman plants are listed under six headings to indicate their use.

84. Jashemski, W. F. and Meyer, F. G. *The Natural History of Pompeii*, Cambridge, 2002; Jashemski 1993.

85. Jashemski 1993, 249–251.

86. Brown, F. E. *Cosa, the Making of a Roman Town*, Michigan, 1980, 69, figs 89–91.

87. Jashemski 1993, 166–167.

88. Ciarallo 1993, 110–116; 2000, 39.

89. Ricotti, E. S. P. 'Adriano: Architettura del verde e dell'acqua', in Cima, M. and Rocca, E. (eds) *Horti Romani*, Rome, 1998, 364–366.

90. Jashemski and Ricotti 1992, 586.

91. De Alarcão, J. and Etienne, R. '*Les Jardins à Conimbriga (Portugal)*', in Macdougall and Jashemski 1981, 69–74.

92. George, M. *The Roman Domestic Architecture of Northern Italy*, Oxford, 1997, 52 and fig. 103.

CHAPTER SEVEN

Byzantine Gardens

In the late 3rd century Emperor Diocletian split the Roman Empire in two halves (East and West) mainly for administrative reasons. Each half was given an emperor to govern it. The capital of the Western Empire was later moved to Ravenna. In AD 330 Emperor Constantine sited his capital at the Greek city of Byzantium which was renamed Constantinople (now Istanbul). Constantine encouraged Romans to come to the east to his 'New Rome', however, the main language used in the East was Greek not Latin. The term 'Byzantine Empire' is a modern one for its citizens still referred to themselves as Romans '*Rhomaioi*', but this appellation helps to separate the two halves of the empire. All dates after this point are AD.

By 476 the last Western Emperor was deposed at Ravenna and the Western Empire ceased to exist. There was a brief re-conquest of Italy and North Africa by the Eastern Emperor (under Justinian) and some of the church decorations at Ravenna date to this time, but the power base was now in the East. The Byzantine Empire lasted until 1453 when Constantinople finally fell to the Ottoman Turks.

After Constantine gave his support to Christianity (in 313) we find that the period of Late Antiquity and the Early Byzantine era is increasingly associated with Christian elements that required a different iconography to depict this 'new' religion, and some Christian passages were seen to relate to gardens.

Byzantine saints associated with gardens

St Thecla from Iconium (Konya, southern Turkey) was converted by St Paul, and is believed to have become one of his disciples. She retired to Meriamlik in Cilicia and was known to have performed many miracles of healing in the gardens of her shrine. The site became a place of pilgrimage. Her feast day is the 23 September.

St Phocas who lived *c.*303 at Sinope (on the southern shore of the Black Sea, northern Turkey), was a market gardener who worked just outside the city. His martyr story relates how soldiers called at his home looking for a man called Phocas. He invited them to stay for supper and said he would direct them to him in the morning. Understanding the implications of their visit, Phocas later went outside and dug his own grave in his garden! In the morning, Phocas led the soldiers out into his garden and the soldiers although reluctant were obliged to execute him. His martyrdom is celebrated on 22 September. A large 5th-century church was built outside Sinope that may have been dedicated to their local saint Phocas. Sinope was a base for both the Roman and later the Byzantine Navy so St Phocas was adopted by sailors as their patron saint, therefore sometimes he is depicted in art carrying a large ship's steering oar.

Helena (the mother of Constantine) became an important early Byzantine saint because she travelled to the Holy Land searching, and finding, holy relics and sites associated with the bible. Soon afterwards these places were visited by pilgrims. St Helena died *c.*330; her feast day is celebrated on 18 August. One of the sites along the circuit of pilgrimage was St John's garden (near the spot where Christ was baptised); this holy area was visited by the pilgrim nun Egeria in 384. She informs us that the 'garden' (or *Kepos* in Greek) appeared to comprise an apple orchard.[1] Sites were still visited in later periods and we hear of the Church of the Shepherds near Bethlehem which was visited by the pilgrim called Peter the Deacon (1137). He said 'A big garden is there now, protected by a neat wall all round,'[2] sadly he didn't elaborate further on the garden's appearance.

St Anne (the mother of the Virgin Mary) and Mary herself are at times linked to gardens, mainly in association with both of their Annunciations. In art this scene often portrays them standing or sitting in a garden (for details of the garden of St Anne see below). Several flowers were used as a symbol of Mary, such as the white Madonna lily and the rose.

Saints venerated in the Western Empire will be mentioned in Chapter 9.

FIGURE 112. St Phocas, the market gardener from Sinope, northern Turkey. Fresco, St Mark's Basilica, Venice.

Christian churches and gardens

Numerous Christian churches were constructed throughout the Empire; some were built at new locations, or on a site associated with a martyr or saint, but in the densely populated towns another solution needed to be found. One answer was to utilise a large or public garden, it is at present unknown if these were donated by wealthy individuals or were requisitioned by the community. Another solution was to convert some of the pagan temples that abounded throughout Roman cities, because many had fallen out of use in the 4th century.

At Sufetula (Sbeitla, Tunisia), which was a major Christian centre in Roman North Africa, two such churches have been discovered. One church was built in the centre of the former sacred precinct/grove of a pagan temple. The church (dedicated to St Servus) was sited roughly east–west on a different alignment to the temple. The pagan temple itself was turned into a Christian baptistery in the 5th century. A second newly built church, the Basilica of St Vitalis at Sufetula, was however, constructed within a large pre-existing domestic garden. Archaeologists discovered some fragments of a marble edged path and a decorative mosaic lined fishpond from the former garden below the church's nave. The subject of the mosaic was suitably aquatic: it was covered with fish swimming on a white background.

Church atrium gardens

Many Early Christian Churches were provided with a forecourt, called an *atrium*. The name was originally used in a domestic Roman context to describe a large partly roofed reception hall of a house or villa, but now it was used to describe a large open reception area where large groups of people could gather before hearing mass. It was also where the catechumens (people who were striving to become Christians) could stay and pray until they were baptised into the faith. Unlike today, you could not enter a church if you had not been christened, so Church atria were much frequented.

In many ways the Early Church atrium was remarkably similar to the public portico gardens associated with Roman pagan temples. The old concept of a precinct containing a sacred grove was given a new perspective: atria were now often treated, or likened to, a 'Paradise' or a 'Garden of Eden'. An example is the imposing Church of St John at Ephesus (Seljuk in Turkey) which was given a new rectangular porticoed atrium positioned as a forecourt to the church. The atrium garden is at present covered with grass. However a later text from the 15th century concerning the Church of St Mary Peribleptos at Constantinople gives some indication of what could be expected in such places. The Spanish ambassador Clavijo said that 'the entrance of this church is a great courtyard in which are cypresses, walnut-trees, elms and many other trees ...'[3] these would create sufficient shade for the populace gathering to attend church services.

Plants are mentioned in association with the area around the 5th century Shrine and Basilica of Saint Thecla at Meriamlik (near Silifke in southern Turkey) which was often referred to as a paradise. Mosaics discovered in her basilica further this concept. Saint Thecla's life story and miracles were recorded in the fifth century. Apparently a number of miracles took place in the gardens at Meriamlik, in the atrium of the church and just outside. Some passages refer to a myrtle wood which the Virgin was believed to frequent. This sounds familiar because myrtle groves were previously sacred to the Greek Aphrodite and the Roman Venus, but now they have been Christianised. Ancient descriptions of the shrine reveal that there was a well in the atrium of her church. Also we hear that pilgrims brought in grain to feed the numerous birds that were bred in the atrium gardens, such as doves, swans, geese and pheasant. In miracle 26, which possibly reflects the gardens outside, numerous trees are mentioned, all in flower, all in fruit, and streams watered the trees.[4] Parts of these extensive gardens sound like a flowery mead, where families could rest and have picnics, and where the sick would recover their health. The site became an important healing shrine, and was visited by Gregory of Nazianzus in 374, and by the pilgrim Egeria who said that the church was very beautiful.[5] Saint Thecla is still remembered in the cathedral at Barcelona (Spain) where its cloister garden has been turned into a giant aviary filled with ducks and numerous birds, all dedicated to this enigmatic saint.

Archaeological discoveries of atria gardens

A remarkable survivor of a garden-like Early Church atrium can be seen at Theveste (Tebessa in Algeria) in the huge late 4th century Basilica complex of St Crispina which was constructed outside the ancient town. It was a great pilgrimage centre so the site included a hostel as well as a large formal garden. Like several church atria a covered walkway or portico surrounded the garden area. However here three sides of the portico were at a

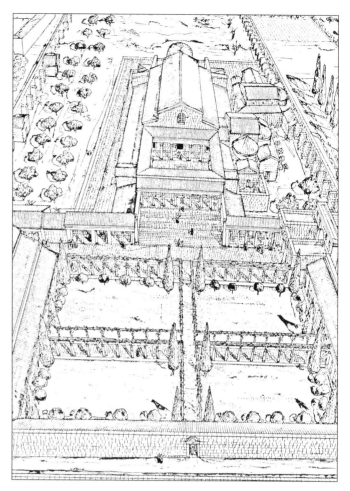

FIGURE 113. Early Christian Church with *atrium* garden. The garden had elevated walkways on three sides; from there three staircases led down to paths that crossed in the centre. Each path and walkways were delineated by an ornamental stone wall. The garden effectively formed a cross shape, Basilica of Saint Crispina at Theveste (Tebessa in Algeria), 4th century (after J.-C. Golvin in Blas de Roblès, J.-M. and Sintes, C., Aix-en-Provence, 2003, 227).

higher level and three staircases led down into an impressive sunken garden.[6] The garden was designed so that four paths met in the centre, effectively forming a cross; this created a garden of four quadrants. Large sections of the path's paving survive, and each path was edged on both sides by a low ornamental marble wall. Numerous marble posts of this wall remain in situ and give a tantalising impression of the decorative aspect of church atria gardens.

There were also atria (reception areas) associated with many Jewish synagogues of a comparable date. This form of atrium usually had a fountain for ablutions, often placed centrally, as at Sardis in Turkey, although in this case the atrium was paved.

One of the holy Pilgrimage sites in Palestine was Terebinthus (Elonei Mamre, near Hebron) which developed around the terebinth tree under which the biblical figure Abraham met the three angels. A simple garden developed around Abraham's well and this holy tree. The terebinth is a member of the pistachio family, and has red berries/fruit. It has a distinctive smell, but is chiefly noted because it produces a gum resin that had healing properties and was used for purification purposes. The terebinth has a long history of being classed as a sacred tree in the East (and in Crete).[7] Constantine constructed a basilica for pilgrims to this holy site, and it appears on the Madaba mosaic map (of *c*.560). Excavations have shown that there was a well-built stone wall defining the rectangular temenos measuring 49.35 × 65 m. The basilica was sited in the eastern third of the sacred enclosure, the remainder of the temenos then became the church's atrium. A well (Abraham's well) was found to be in the south-west corner of the atrium, and the former position of the terebinth tree was deduced by a gap in the paving to the north of the well.[8] This holy site was visited by the Bordeaux Pilgrim (in 333), Antonius of Piacenza *c*.570, and Peter the Deacon (1137).[9] Unfortunately so many pilgrims wanted to commemorate their visit by taking a souvenir that by the 7th century only a stump of the tree was left and naturally the tree succumbed and died! It is not known if there were other plants in association with the venerable tree in the atrium.

Monastic gardens

Several Byzantine monasteries, churches and hermit cells had garden areas, be it a vegetable garden or orchard to provide food for the monks. A few have been discovered archaeologically in Israel near Jericho,[10] and even in desert places where isolation could aid their devotion. This self sufficiency is still practised in surviving monastic communities in Egypt, Sinai and Greece.[11] In places hillsides around monasteries were terraced to provide more productive planting areas, and these monasteries (especially those on Mt Athos in Greece) preserve the semblance of earlier Byzantine monastic gardens. Byzantine sources give an indication of the plants grown in monastic gardens: there were vegetables collectively termed *lakhana* (greens), beet, broad bean, carrot, chickpea, cucumber, garlic, leek, onion, squash, apple, olive, peach, pear, fig, mulberry, cherry, grape, melon, pomegranate, and citrus (which were mentioned as growing in Greece and Turkey).[12]

Monastic communities also formed in quiet areas close to major cities, texts mention those in proximity to Constantinople. They would have incorporated orchards and vegetable plots within or nearby. However, over time some of the monasteries in the metropolis were embellished, and we hear that the monastery of Kosmidion was provided with 'numerous fountains, beautiful lawns, and whatever else can delight or attract the eye.'[13]

Depictions in mosaic and frescoes of garden elements

Mosaics covered walls and ceilings as well as floors in some prestigious buildings. Luckily, the beautiful mosaic encrusted ceilings of the circular mausoleum of Constanza, the daughter of Emperor Constantine (in Rome) have survived because it was later turned into a church. One panel depicts a wonderful vine harvest. These mosaics are one of the earliest Christian examples (they are dated to the 4th century), at that time Christians no longer wanted to display overtly pagan themes. Geometric designs and vintage scenes were considered acceptable, the latter remained popular because of familiarity, many people would have been still engaged in grape picking on their estates or in their own gardens. Now, however, a vintage scene could be seen to reflect the biblical passage referring to 'Christ being the true vine'. A second delightful mosaic in Constanza's mausoleum displays numerous branches of fruit trees, birds and ritual objects. One wonders if there was a desire to depict every known fruit at that time. You can clearly identify branches laden with grapes, apples, pears, pomegranates, figs, medlars, and branches with pine cones (that produce edible pine nuts). But, there were also fruits that are harder to specify, such as crab apples, rose hips, cherries and other cherry/berry-type fruits. Some of the smaller fruits may belong to the sorb family, and are a reminder that the greenish-red fruits of the service tree (*Sorbus domestica*) were still favoured at that time, as were those of the Azarole (*Crataegus azarolus*) with its orange edible fruit.

Mosaics inside Early Churches (and some synagogues) often depict 'Paradise', or elements of this Biblical theme; there was one on the floor of St Thecla's basilica. In the 6th-century Church of St Apollinare in Classe, at Ravenna, the mosaic in the conch of the apse portrays a somewhat stylised version of paradise composed of two tiers of trees and flowers amongst a rocky landscape. The flowers are of white daisies, white lilies, and various red and white unidentifiable flora. Multi flowering white lily plants separate a row of twelve sheep walking along the base of the scene; the sheep represented the twelve apostles.

Another new feature in scenes of Paradise is the inclusion of four rivers. This is seen in the apse mosaic at the Church of St Vitale (also at Ravenna) where a young Christ is seated with angels and Church donors in a flower filled paradise. Below Christ's feet flow the Four Rivers of Eden/Paradise: the Tigris, Euphrates, Gehon and Pishon. The inclusion of four rivers in a mosaic or fresco now becomes an identifiable indication that the subject of the scene was intended to be of Paradise. A later example of this theme from the 12th–13th century can be seen on one of the frescoed walls of the Monastery Church of St Stephen at Brajcino in Macedonia (FYROM).

In floor mosaics Paradise could take the form of a row of trees, as at Hérakléa Lynkestis (in Macedonia (FYROM), dated to the early 6th century). Here, there are eight different trees that are shown 'blossoming in all seasons alike' which is how the Byzantine historian Chorikios praised a similar mosaic from Gaza.[14] Such scenes are reminiscent of the age-old Classical ideal of an ever-fruitful garden, like the mythical Homeric garden of Alkinoos; old sentiments remain popular. The long scene, *in situ* in the narthex of the ruined church at Hérakléa Lynkestis is a real tour de force. The central panel depicts the true vine emerging out of Christ's wine-cup. It is flanked by deer and peacocks, and is framed by two large fronds of foliage. From left to right the trees depicted are: a pine tree, cherry tree, apple tree, a sorb-like fruit tree, cypress, a date palm tree with bare looking branches but two bunches of pendulous fruit, a citron tree, fig tree and finally a pomegranate tree. The scene is reminiscent of a paradise teeming with all creatures and plants. Roses and lilies spring up below the tree canopies, and animals emerge between the trees, birds fly off in alarm. The wide border around this mosaic comprises little scenes of birds and fish, making the whole representative of all the animals of God's creation. This became a popular new Christian theme, especially during the later period of iconoclasm (726–843). Another floor mosaic in the same town features panels of trees, birds and animals, so you could recite 'and on the third day trees were created, on the fifth fish and fowl, on the sixth animals ...' Such designs owe something to the pagan Orpheus myth, where he tamed the birds and beasts with his fine music, and was previously depicted in the midst of these creatures.

Another popular Early Christian theme was to recount the story of Jonah and the whale. Jonah was seen as a hero who survives the ordeal of being swallowed alive, and was later spat out. He therefore was also seen as a symbol of resurrection. There is a marvellous floor mosaic re-enacting this miraculous feat, in the 4th century Basilica at Aquileia in northern Italy. There is however a third scene where Jonah is shown reclining under a climbing gourd plant that God had caused to grow after Jonah had complained about the fierce sun. This vegetable plant seems to be an unlikely shade giving tree for a garden but we can see that in a 4th century catacomb painting Jonah's gourd tree is supported by a full pergola frame. A climbing gourd could therefore form an alternative (or be supplementary) to a vine covered pergola in a garden of this period. The gourds of the Roman and Byzantine periods originated in Africa and would have been *Lagenaria siceraria*. Cucumbers were also grown on a pergola. Trellises would be used for growing the maximum of crops from climbing plants in a *hortus*, but in a more luxurious villa they could easily be used in a more decorative fashion.

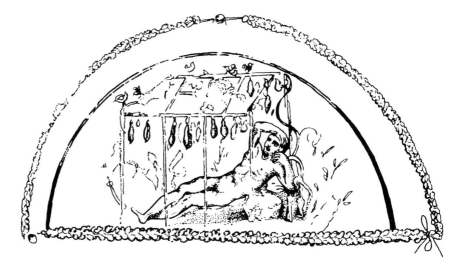

FIGURE 114. Fresco of Jonah reclining under a gourd tree, here supported by a pergola frame, Via Latina Catacomb, Rome, 4th century.

A more decorative garden is implied in a series of paired scenes appearing behind the stylised columned recesses and projections in the dome mosaic of the Orthodox Baptistery at Ravenna. The garden scenes suggest a decorative garden lay beyond the highly ornamental low white marble walls. Each of the paired scenes show a tree directly behind the open-work wall and there is an arch of foliage hinting at an arbour beyond. The panels of the painted ornamental walls show an amazing variety of decorative patterns such as: overlapping fishscale, an elaborate cross in circle design and a floriate star-like pattern. Marble walls such as these would have been very costly, but simpler designs could have been used elsewhere. Their use, however, does illustrate that fashions in Roman gardening continued into Late Antiquity. Also, herms were evidently still popular because several Byzantine relief carvings and ivory plaques show a series of herm headed finials employed as a decorative device on pillars supporting low marble walls. An example can be seen in the relief of Theodosius in the Hippodrome at Istanbul.

Fountains of all forms remained popular, and a scene of stags drinking at a fountain was another Early Christian motif. This image recalled the words of Psalm 42: 'As the deer pants for streams of water, so my soul pants for you, O

FIGURE 115. Detail from a mosaic depicting a Paradise filled with trees and animals, *in situ* in the narthex of the Basilica at Hérakléa Lynkestis (Macedonia, FYROM), early 6th century.

FIGURE 116. Mosaic detail showing the use of decorative white marble walls in a garden setting with a tree, and arching foliage behind, Orthodox Baptistry, Ravenna, Italy, 5th century.

FIGURE 117. Pinecone fountain in a marble cantharus bowl. The cone was pierced to allow four streams of water to trickle down to the basin below, mosaic in the Baptistry of the Episcopal Basilica at Stobi, Macedonia (FYROM), 6th century.

FIGURE 118. Mosaic showing Isaac blessing his son Jacob in his garden, Church of Santa Maria Maggiore, Rome, 5th century.

God.'[15] But, in this period a new highly fashionable form emerged: the pinecone fountain. The pinecone acted as a finial on a stout shaft, all made of bronze. The cone was perforated with several holes so that when water was directed up, it would let out streams of water. Numerous pinecone fountains feature in floor mosaics in Macedonia (FYROM); they were especially favoured in baptisteries (as at Stobi and Ohrid), but also in Bishop's palaces (as at Hérakléa Lynkestis). Often the pinecone is shown as having four streams of water jetting upwards before it cascades down into a large cantharus cup, but at Plodiv (in southern Bulgaria) there are six full streams with an equal number of intermittent streamlets in between. At Hérakléa Lynkestis the mosaicist humorously included a pair of ducks swimming in the water beside the pinecone fountain in the cantharus! At Stobi the pinecones feature in four alternating scenes, set into either a cantharus or a tall stemmed wide dished urn, both being forms that were highly popular during the Roman period. Archaeologists working in the baptistery at Stobi actually discovered a large marble cantharus that mirrored the image seen in the mosaic below it. Pinecone fountains remained popular through to the Late Byzantine period and can be seen in manuscript paintings, and in the beautiful 15th century fresco in the Church of the Virgin Pantanassa at Mistra in Greece. A similar bronze pinecone fountain head mounted on a long shaft (53.5 cm tall) has been discovered archaeologically and is now displayed in the British Museum.[16]

Scenes of actual gardens, of Late Antiquity, are rare in the west; one of the most notable in mosaic is placed alongside other biblical scenes high up in the nave of the Church of St Maria Maggiore in Rome (dated *c.*432–440). This amazing scene depicts Isaac reclining on a couch in his garden, where he is ready to bless his son Jacob. The garden itself is however simply shown with a few trees, flowers and birds. At St Vitale in Ravenna a wall mosaic has Abraham

FIGURE 119. Rebecca at the well. The water source is personified as a water nymph pouring her water from an upturned urn, *Genesis* manuscript, Vienna, 6th century.

and his wife Sarah being hospitable to three visiting angels in their garden (prior to him sacrificing his son Isaac). The angels sit under the canopy of a large tree, bushes are hinted at behind them, and a few flowers spring around their feet.

Manuscript illustrations of Byzantine gardens

Manuscripts paintings and texts give a fuller picture of Late Roman and Byzantine gardens. One theme that had a garden context is the Biblical story of Rebecca at the well. This can be seen in a 6th century Genesis, now in Vienna. Rebecca is shown twice, walking towards the well and giving Eliezar, a camel driver, and ten camels a drink from the well.[17] Rebecca walked beside a three sided colonnade (providing a suggestion that they surrounded a garden). The water source is personified as a reclining nymph pouring her water from her upturned urn to create the stream (and water for the well). Nymphs pouring water, and river gods, were popular images in the pagan world but the concept of a personification was evidently still current in Byzantine times. It is noticeable that in scenes of Christ's Baptism it was also deemed appropriate to include the figure of a river god to personify the River Jordan. This is seen in mosaics and frescoes.

Many versions of the theme of Paradise and Eden existed. The 12th century *Homilies* of Jacob Kokkinobaphas (now in Paris) illustrates multiple scenes of the Adam and Eve story. The snake is pictured in the tree tempting Eve, and lower down the page this act is followed by their expulsion from the beautiful garden paradise of Eden. The four rivers of Eden surge forth with gusto; but it was still thought necessary to depict the source of these great waters as a personification of a man with a giant water vessel over his shoulder, which is so reminiscent of a pagan river god.

A 10th century Psalter depicts King Hezekiah, sick and healed. The painting shows him reclining in front of his palace and in his gardens, but just a few bushes are shown in the background. Similarly in the *Paris Psalter* 'The Prayer of Isaiah' the event takes place in the open, perhaps the garden, for there are red flowers around the praying figure. A dark figure nearby is a personification representing night. In the Bible he says: 'and the daughter of Zion is left as a cottage in a vineyard, as a lodge in a garden of cucumbers.'[18] Later he says 'as a garden that hath no water,' the Bible has several analogies to gardens.

More details are depicted within the garden appearing in an 11th century illumination showing the Biblical scene of scribes standing before Caiaphas seated in front of what may be a garden pavilion.[19] In the garden heavily pruned trees appear to the left of the group of men, and also to the right behind a simple decorative fence. On the far right is a superb two-tiered fountain with a pinecone spouting streams of water into the two bowls below.

In the 12th century *Vatican Octateuch*, a page features the House and garden of Egdon, King of Moab. He is shown larger than life on the left, and dwarfs the house. What is of note here (on the right) is the animal's head fountain mounted on the garden wall. Water pours out of its smiling mouth into a circular mottled marble basin below, its overflow pours onto the ground and out of view. A variety of trees grow behind the wall, and are represented by three different forms, one a tall slim cypress, another a dense leaved species that formed tiers of foliage, the third sported clusters of leaves at the end of its otherwise bare branches.

Another architectural design is shown in the Sinai Codex of the *Homilies* of Gregory of Nazianzos.[20] This page highlights the figure of Gregory who is given pride of place in the centre, writing his homilies inside his Bishops palace, but below there are elements of a grand garden. His garden is defined by what appears to be a nymphaeum, a masonry wall with three small niches above and two large

FIGURE 120. A deputation of elders meet Caiaphas in his ornamental garden which has a two-tiered fountain with a spouting pinecone, 11th century.

recesses containing fountains. Both are pinecone fountains, the one on the left is set into a three-tiered basin and on the right the pinecone has been placed in a circular bowl from which the water trickles down into a square basin. On either side of the nymphaeum is a variety of trees and flowers behind a decorative low wall. Of the trees four are cypresses and two are carefully tonsured into two-tiered small trees. Topiary was evidently still in favour, but now seemingly only to produce tiered bushes and trees.

Garden elements are often included at the top or around pages listing the Canons of the Gospel (especially during and after the 9th century). The most colourful ones with greater floral additions are actually in Armenian manuscripts;

FIGURE 121 *(left)*. House and garden of Egdon, king of Moab. His garden is filled with trees, seen behind a wall with an animal mask fountain, *Vatican Octateuch* (Vat. gr. 746. fol. 473v), 12th century.

FIGURE 122 *(below)*. Gregory's garden. An architectural garden backdrop, or nymphaeum, with two recesses for fountains. On either side are ornamental walls with trees and flowers behind, detail from *Homilies* of Gregory of Nazianzos (Cod.Sinaiticus 339, fol. 4v).

they include fountains, roses, trees and birds in an amazingly variety. An example is in the Zeytun Gospels of *c.*1256.[21]

Ancient descriptions of gardens

Life in Constantinople was similar to that of Rome, for many aristocrats from Italy had been encouraged to settle there, and presumably they built luxurious houses with gardens. Several ancient texts indicate that they even had summer residences on the Bithynian coast, which always had a pleasant climate (in northern Turkey). Some references mentioning these gardens survive in biographies of the Emperors, or the Lives of the Church Fathers. Now, however, texts are couched in biblical terms, but they do sometimes include pagan terminology that survived from classical literature.

An informative text of Late Antiquity comes from a letter written by Gregory of Nyssa (*c.* 395). It is in many ways reminiscent of the letters of Pliny the Younger because he describes the estate and gardens of a villa belonging to his friend Adelpius at Vanota in Galatia (Turkey).

> Straight before us ... were the beauties of the house, where one part is marked out from another by some delicate invention. There were projecting towers, and preparations for banqueting among the wide and high-arched rows of trees crowing the entrance... Then about the building are the Phaiakian gardens; rather let not the beauties of Vanota be insulted by comparison with those Homer never saw 'the apple with bright fruit' as we have it here, approaching the hue of its own blossom ... he never saw the pear whiter than new-polished ivory. And what can one say of the varieties of peach, diverse and multiform, yet blended and compounded out of different species? For just as with those who paint 'goat-stags' and 'centaurs', and the like, commingling things of different kind, and making themselves wiser than Nature, so it is in the case of this fruit: Nature, under the despotism of art, turns one to an almond, another to a walnut, yet another to a 'Doracinus', mingled alike in name and flavour ... And in all these the number of single trees is more noted than their beauty; yet they display tasteful arrangement in their planting, and that harmonious form of drawing – drawing, I call it, for the marvel belongs rather to the painter's art than to the gardener's ... So readily does Nature fall in with the design of those who arrange these devices, that it seems impossible to express this by words. Who could find words worthily to describe the road [path] under the climbing vines, and the sweet shade of their cluster, and that novel wall-structure [a trellis or pergola] where roses with their shoots, and vines with their trailers, twist themselves together ... and the pond at the summit of this path, and the fish that are bred there? ...[22]

We can see that Gregory reaffirms the fashion of comparing a beautiful garden with those of the mythical Homeric King Alkinoös, King of the Phaiakians. The fruitful trees in this text imply that many were grafted, producing fruit from compatible species. The Doracinus is a named new variety that was produced at that time. When Gregory refers to the painter's art this was probably an allusion to the art of a *topiarius* (a landscape gardener) who would have created a fine setting for a garden 'tableau'.

The reference to banqueting outside must relate to an al fresco dining area. One is mentioned in a text by St Methodius who talks of a banquet in a walled garden where ten guests could recline on an outdoor *stibadium* (a semicircular couch). This type of dining couch remained in use through the Early Byzantine era, and this was the form depicted in Biblical scenes of Christ and the Apostles at the Last Supper (such as in the 6th-century Rossano Gospels, and in a mosaic at St Apollinare in Classe at Ravenna, Fig. 122), where they are shown reclining on a *stibadium* couch, not the long rectangular table we see in the more familiar illustrations of the medieval period.

In Constantinople itself, we hear that a new garden was made in the Great Palace for Basil I (*c.*867–886) called *Mesokêpion*.[23] This simply translates as middle garden, in Greek, it was so named because it was bounded by buildings on either side. It was said that it was well-watered and 'blooming with all manner of plants', however, which plants are not specified! Another text describes the area around the palace: 'Round about were houses such as benefited the condition of noble men, and very serviceable too. There were also gardens of delightful beauty and ever-flowing fountains gushing forth, fed from outside by well-built conduits.'[24] This shows the owners had access to aqueducts so that extra water would be supplied for these fountains.

Fortunately, John Geometres names some of the plants that you would have been able to see in a 10th-century imperial garden (believed to have been within the Aretai Palace near Constantinople):

> laurels ... with vines, with ivy clusters, with fruit-bearing trees ... rose beds, lilies, scented violets, chrysanthemum, sweet narcissus and crocus, the sweeter purple hyacinth and the more conspicuous flame-coloured variety. Nothing is absent that would be better present; nothing is present that ought to be absent ...[25]

The flame coloured plant could be *Gladiolus byzantinus* a native species of gladiolus. In those days (as in the earlier Graeco-Roman period) the term hyacinth was generally used to denote a blue flower, which could be anything from a delphinium to a scilla.

The garden must have been a large one because there was an interesting addition to this text: 'Do you see the multitude of creatures ... running together to the beauty of its lord, as formerly to the melody of Orpheus, they stay there ...' John Geometres acknowledges that the myth of Orpheus is no longer current, for it was now considered pagan, but for completeness he includes it all the same. There was still a need to make references to classical texts which revealed that you were well educated. But, over time the Christian Byzantines preferred to liken their own gardens to a Biblical one, the Garden of Eden. This new style can be noted in the panegyric verses of John Geometres when talking about the imperial garden at Constantinople: 'four springs flowing from the old Eden water the new Eden ...' The four springs could be seen as a means to replicate (in the garden) the image of the 'Four Rivers flowing out of Paradise' which are often depicted in Byzantine art.

Other writers were more inclined to describe the fountains to be seen there (often in great detail). Many were very elaborate, such as his Peristyle of the sigma. *Sigma* is the Greek word for a semicircular *stibadium* dining couch:

> The latter [the peristyle of the sigma] gives on to an open terrace in the middle of which is a bronze fountain having a rim crowned with silver and a gilded cone. This is called the Mystic Fountain of the Triconch... There too, next to the long side of the Sigma have been erected two bronze lions with gaping mouths. These spouted water and flooded the entire hollow area of the Sigma, thus providing no small amount of pleasure. At the time of receptions the fountain was filled with pistachios and almonds as well as pine-nuts, while spiced wine flowed from the cone for the enjoyment of all those that stood there and were desirous of partaking...[26]

In the *Life of St Basil* two elaborate fountains are mentioned in the atrium:

> The southern one is made of Egyptian stone [porphyry] and is encircled by serpents excellently carved. In the middle of it rises a perforated pine-cone ... [water also spouted from a white marble upper section] the northern fountain is of Sagarian stone ... it too has a perforated pine-cone of white stone projecting from the centre of its base while all around the upper rim of the fountain the artist has fashioned, cocks, goats and rams of bronze, and these, by means of pipes, vomit forth jets of water ...[27]

Apart from novelty fountains, we learn that automata were still fashionable in wealthy households. A famous one, was noted by Liudprand in the court of Constantine VII (*c.*949) it comprised a gilt-bronze tree in whose branches birds 'emitted cries appropriate to their different species.'[28] There was also a lion that roared.

There is an interesting description of a painting on a ceiling in an imperial palace, written by Manuel Philes (*c.*1300) which in flowery language describes what appears to be a *paradeisos*, in this case a game park form of garden.

FIGURE 123 *(left)*. Christ and Apostles reclining on a *stibadium* dining couch, in a Last Supper scene in the Church of St Apollinare Nuovo, Ravenna, 6th century.

FIGURE 124 *(right)*. *Gladiolus byzantinus*, Crete (photo: J. Farrar).

Where has this luxurious garden been planted? Do you not see it above ground ... What moisture have the roots absorbed to have produced such delicate shoots on the plants? For the painter, no matter how exactly he imitates nature, is unable to pour in water. Whence has the warmth of vegetation crept through to put forth flowers that adorn the boughs, to make leaves with their hidden shadows? Who has gone by and painted, next to the lilies, all those colours of the beautiful grove? ... See how the painter has shown himself an excellent caretaker of the grove: for he has depicted the carnivorous animals pursuing only those which by nature feed on herbs, so that the meadow should not be given over to grazing to be ravaged all too soon. And lest the fowl devour the grass, he has confined them in circular pens. And the foursome of hares, fashioned so fitly, he has gathered in a single group least they be parted from one another, and one of them, rushing out into the meadow, be immediately seized by the jaws of those bloodthirsty animal-stalkers ... As you see, he has also painted a female lion and given her a fixed abode that she might feed her cubs, and fenced her with a woven barrier, least she boldly sally forth and chase away the roe with her young ...[29]

The Byzantines copied many earlier Greek and Roman texts which has helped to preserve these valuable manuscripts. Works such as Vergil were carefully copied and many editions were illustrated. Hesiod's *Works and Days,* which was an ancient Greek text on agriculture, included illustrations of Byzantine period agricultural tools (see below). A variety of Herbals was also copied – such as those of Dioscorides and Nikander. The latter's work was primarily concerned with antidotes to snake bites, and in a 10th century copy there is a finely drawn, somewhat Roman-looking, scene of a shepherd walking in a tree filled area.

There was an amusing late Byzantine book, the *Porikologos* (often translated as the *Fruit Book*, *Porika* indicates fruits). This was written in the form of a satire where fruits and vegetables were personified. The satire was set in the court of Emperor Quince. Grape, a high ranking fruit, accused Pepper of plotting high treason, but the latter's lawyer succeeded in finding him blameless. So the accuser – Grape – was then condemned to be forevermore trodden upon to provide wine, and its residue must. This trial between two plants has in some ways echoes of the earlier Greek contest between the Laurel and the Olive, and the even earlier Mesopotamian contest between the Tamarix and Date palm.

The garden of St Anne, mother of Mary

One of the most popular garden themes of the Byzantine period was taken from the apocryphal story of the Annunciation to St Anne (from the Gospel of St James: 2–3), where she was miraculously informed in the garden that she would at last have a child – the Virgin Mary. An 11th-century mosaic in a Church at Daphni (nr Athens) depicts this event in a wonderfully sensitive way. Three aspects are shown, in one a servant looks on from the doorway of the house (on the left) while Anne's husband Joachim is seated in bushes on the right where an angel appears to him to explain what has just happened. The main part of the narrative concerns St Anne who stands in the centre of the garden with hand held aloft,

FIGURE 125. The Garden of St Anne, mother of Mary. St Anne stands beside a highly decorative three-tiered fountain with a pierced pinecone finial. Birds rest in the tree nearby, mosaic in the Church of the Dormition, Daphni (nr Athens), late 11th century.

beside her is a very decorative fountain. Garden fountains are often included in this scene, but on occasion there is a simple well rather than a fountain, but both reaffirm the impression in the viewer's eye that the event is taking place in a garden. Again the Byzantines chose to depict a pine-cone fountain, at Daphni it is placed in a three tiered water basin made of an expensive mottled marble. The Byzantines did not have rules of perspective as we understand them today so the basins appears a bit distorted, but this allows us to notice that the middle basin is of a quatrelobe form while the lower one is square. Trees are sited behind and to the side of the fountain, one of which is presumably the laurel mentioned in the Gospel text; six doves are shown roosting in its branches.

The same theme adorns a wall in the narthex of the Kariye Camii church at Istanbul, here the scene includes the bird's nest that St Anne had noticed in the nearby tree. The fountain pool though is less ornamental, it comprised two solid-looking shallow rectangular tiers instead of the three tiers seen at Daphne. A small lion's mask water outlet feeds water from the upper pool down to the lower one. A similar rectangular box-like fountain is depicted in a 13th-century fresco in the Church of Clement Peribleptos at Ohrid in Macedonia (FYROM), but in this case there is a pair of lower basins. Again a lion's mask water outlet allowed water to flow from the upper to the lower basins. The fountains from Istanbul and Ohrid seem to indicate a different style that was current alongside the slender versions.

Frescoes of the Annunciation of St Anne at St Pantelemon Church at Nerezi and at the Church of St George at Kurbinovo, both in Macedonia (FYROM), place her garden on top of a columned structure, perhaps a cryptoporticus to create a level garden area. The garden is surrounded by a light fence to stop people from falling if they walked too close to the edge. Trees behind the fence hint at a larger

FIGURE 126. A two-tiered shallow, rectangular, box-like fountain seen in a mosaic in the narthex of the Kariye Camii Church, Istanbul, early 14th century.

garden beyond. In the fresco at Kurbinovo a stone garden urn was placed just behind the metal fence. Such fresco and mosaic illustrations appear to reflect the decorative items you would see in a small garden of the period, as opposed to a palatial one.

Images of St Anne's garden are augmented by a lengthy description by Theodore Hyrtakenos (14th century), but this is essentially an imaginary garden. The text implies that Theodore had envisaged St Anne's garden to be circular because he mentions how it was enclosed by a 'wall in the shape of a ring'. The wall was high and well secured to stop thieves from entering, and would give privacy. Inside there was a dense ring of cypresses, he specifies that these were heavily pruned 'sufficiently stripped of stems in their trunks, and from there grew straight, so that they shot up … shaped like a cone'. This is a feature we see in many contemporary illustrations. Other trees were planted, again in a circular pattern around the garden, each species being planted together. Although 'all kinds of trees' are mentioned none apart from cypress are actually specified. However seven flowers were named as being present in the garden: roses, lilies, violets, narcissus, lotus, crocus and hyacinth. In pride of place in the centre of this garden was a highly ornamental fountain bowl made from light green stone. It was decorated with carved leopards, bears, and other wild animals, and around the rim the craftsman had shaped and positioned carved birds as if coming to drink. Positioned within the fountain itself was a pine cone:

> pierced with as many holes as there are on a head, three plus four. From the holes darted up as many jets of water as there are veins … [the cone] was hewn in porphyry, while the tube was constructed from a different, gleaming stone … linen-colour …[30]

A garden would not be complete without birds flying about and Theodore mentions a nightingale singing in the garden, and elsewhere there is a bright green parrot, a peacock and a swan. The water for the garden was said to have come from their own Eden and the Euphrates, and at one point he adds that he prefers this garden to 'that silly little garden of Alkinoos'.

'Sophrosyne's garden' a 14th-century allegorical poem

The description of St Anne's garden and the allegorical poem by Theodore Meliteniotes on '*Sophrosyne's garden*' give a marvellous insight into the minds of the Byzantine people and of what they aspired to in what were essentially imaginary gardens. We can wonder if these descriptions reflect similarities to their own gardens. The wealth of details in the poem on Sophrosyne's garden gives further clues on aspects of Byzantine garden design. The poem ends with a eulogy to God and a reminder that the Garden of Sophrosyne was Paradise. The actual word used was *paradeisos*. One abiding note is that again trees were planted in rows, and that special measuring cords were used in the spacing of plants. The poem is so evocative of this period that the following extracts provide the essence of a Byzantine garden. Sophrosyne translates as either 'moderation or chastity'; she allows access to her garden where she says there are birds and animals in the garden, and fish in the pool.

> look at the pleasant site of this garden, its valley, the position of the place, the fragrance of the flowers that are in the garden, the unusual beauty and colours of the herbs, the meadows [implying grassed areas] ... the ineffable and divine beauty of the shrubs ... all around, near the enclosing wall, non-fruit bearing trees were standing in rows, as if they were a first chorus. Then, a second chorus, that of evergreen trees, was standing within ... The fruit-bearing trees were standing as a third chorus ... Seeing the compactness of those trees, one would think that he was looking at a very dense mountain inside the garden. At the very edge of this garden innumerable kinds of shrubs were planted ... The craftsman had pitched the trees in such rows, and had positioned the chamber in such a straight line that he managed to please everybody by the view alone ... all kinds of herbs, as well as various flowers that adorned the place ... [they were of all colours and heavily perfumed]. In the very middle of this plain, on an elevation, there were fragrant, novel, and strange garden beds ... Amidst the continuous trees, violets and lilies, as well as balsam trees and basil, together with roses, were sprouting in the garden ... The garden also had several springs and fountains jetting forth from the ground and outpouring around in a circle, much cooler than melted snow ...
>
> In the very middle of this garden there was a pool of generous width, having little depth towards the bottom. It was an indescribable structure made with rock crystal [marble?] of the most pure whiteness. [there were numerous carved birds and animals on the edge of this pool]. The mouths of these animals and birds were opened by some kind of mechanical device. Some were receiving the streams of water in their feet through some pipes, and were again spitting them forth through their mouths inside the pool, pouring like a spring. These offered immeasurable delight with their abundance ...
>
> I even saw a grapevine all around the pool, bearing many diverse and enormous grapes ... Could the garden beds of those fragrant flowers, which were filled with plants breathing sweet unguents, be easily described by anyone? I do not think so. For who could outline with words their composition, order, and beauty, as well as their ultimate symmetry? Their skilful gardener seemed to have used measuring cords of equal length. Some beds were growing roses, others were bringing myrtles to bloom, and yet others narcissus, violets and lilies together with balsam trees, different beds were bringing forth different flowers ... The colour of the flowers was seen all-variegated. For the swarm of roses stood purple, the myrtles possessed an emeraldlike appearance, the narcissus seemed from afar as platinum [probably a cream-coloured species], and the dark blue of the violets like the colour of the sea ...[31]

It is clear that the Byzantines enjoyed their gardens, whether they were large or small. The recurring features mentioned in descriptions of a Byzantine garden are that their walled enclosures contained trees that were grown in rows and that flowers were grown between the rows under the shade of the trees. This seems to be true of both a utilitarian garden and pleasure garden and is actually recommended in the Byzantine *Geoponika* which says:

> [the garden] should be entirely surrounded by a wall or other enclosure. Do not plant it at random or in a confused way, relying, so to speak, on the contrasts between the plants to lend beauty. Instead, put each kind in its own place, so that the smaller are not overpowered or deprived of nourishment by the larger. Fill the spaces between the trees with roses, lilies, violets and crocus, plants that are most pleasant and inviting in appearance, aroma and use – and are also useful to bees. [32]

Byzantine agri/horticulturalists

In the 10th century a Byzantine opus on agriculture was produced for Emperor Constantine VII Porphyrgenitus called the *Geoponika* (which could be translated as Agricultural pursuits). It had been compiled using a number of reedited earlier works, many of which no longer survive. This great undertaking was produced in twenty books, and includes sections covering horticulture and the *paradeisos*. It says that:

> Gardening is essential to life. For health and convalescence a garden should be developed not at a distance from the house but in proximity to it, where it will give enjoyment to the eyes and pleasure to the sense of smell ...[33]

Some books deal with specific topics such as Book three which is a month by month calendar of work. Books four to seven deal with various aspects of viticulture. Book 8 gives recipes for a variety of health giving wines, from fruit, flowers and herbs. Book 9 advises on the cultivation of olives. But books 10–12 are especially useful to horticulturalists. Book 10 deals with fruit and nut trees, giving information on all aspects of their growth, whether from seed or cuttings, time of planting, to methods used if they need protection in winter (for citrons). Advice is given on how to successfully store the picked fruit; and how to graft and create hybrids (although some of the hybrids seem improbable). If you wanted to create a novelty shaped fruit, such as a citron or quince with a human or animal face then this book explains how to do so using moulds.[34]

Book 11 details the more decorative plant species, such as myrtle and rose, for the latter the book tells you how to make them more aromatic. We also hear that roses could be planted in tubs and pots to produce flowers earlier, or you could dig a trench around the bush and pour warm water into it twice a day.[35] Interestingly numerous plants in this section have been provided with a short passage on their mythical origins. Apparently the white lily (*Lilium candidum*) acquired its pure white colour after Zeus placed his mortal born baby son, Herakles, to Hera's breast while she was asleep. After he drank his fill Hera's milk still flowed and created the 'milky way', and 'what fell to earth and spread over the soil gave a colour like milk to the flower of the lily'.[36]

Book 12 concerns the vegetable garden, including what soil and manure is best suited, and methods to eradicate vegetable pests. A wide range of vegetables

FIGURE 127. Aspects of agriculture and horticultural husbandry in the *Homilies* of Gregory Nazianzos. The upper scene shows the art of grafting, below beekeeping, using hexagonal wooden hives, 11th century.

and herbs are included, and apart from informing on the correct time to sow them, there are instructions on their medicinal use. There are many interesting extra tips on their use and the following was said about rocket, because if 'mixed with honey, it cleans up spots on the face. Drunk in advance with wine it lessens the pain of a whipping ... Rocket helps with smelly armpits.'[37] Book 13 deals with the eradication of various pests.

The plants (trees, flowers, herbs and vegetables) that are mentioned in the three relevant books of the *Geoponika* provide a good indication of the species thought garden worthy during the Byzantine period, they are listed below in this order:

In Book 10: Grape vine, date palm, citron, pistachio, peach, apples, pears, quinces, pomegranates, plum, cherry, jujube, fig, almond, chestnut, walnut, hazelnut, mulberry, medlar, cornel.

In Book 11: Laurel, cypress, myrtle, box, Aleppo pine, mastic/lentisk tree, willow, holm oak, rosemary. rose, lily, iris, violet, narcissus, crocus, marjoram, costmary, balm, basil, ivy.

In Book 12: Mallow, lettuce, beet, cabbage, asparagus, gourd, melon/pumkin, cucumber, turnip, radish, celery, mint, rue, rocket, cress, chicory/endive, leek, garlic, onion, hartwort, pennyroyal, dill, spearmint, grape hyacinth bulbs, squill, sorrel, artichoke, purslane, mushrooms.

The 11th-century *Homilies* of Gregory Nazianzos (Paris, MS. gr.533) contained several delightful scenes showing life on a large country estate that would have benefitted from the knowledge contained in the *Geoponika*. One page illuminated six aspects of agricultural and horticultural husbandry.[38] Two of the scenes show a pastoral ideal: shepherds tending their flock of goats, and a shepherd watching over two cows which no doubt represented a herd. The third vignette represented the art of grafting trees, the gardener is poised with a pruning blade in hand, to either prune or cut off a scion to graft onto another tree. Another scene depicts someone relaxing under a shaded canopy waiting to see if his bird-catching traps succeeded. Some birds may have been sold as pet songbirds, but the majority would have been caught to supply food for the dinner table. The fifth scene illustrates fishing on a lake within the estate, while the sixth illuminates methods of beekeeping. In this case the hives appear to be semicircular and made of wood, although in the text Gregory mentions that hives were in fact hexagonal. The trees in this rural scene are heavily pruned and this reminds us that in hot countries the lower branches of trees were either grazed by sheep/goats and/or were regularly removed so that the leaves could provide an alternative fodder for animals when grass was too parched for cattle to eat.

Occasionally horti-agricultural workers are depicted in mosaics and manuscripts, an example in mosaic is the gardener using a two pronged hoe in the Palace mosaic at Istanbul (sixth century). The Byzantines called this form of drag hoe a *dikella*, while two-pronged digging forks were given the name *lisgarion*.[39] Several workers are illustrated in an 11th century-manuscript which shows them using the *lisgarion* bident fork and pruning hooks in a vineyard.[40] The vine dressers tool was called a *kladeuterion*.[41] Apparently in this period vines were regularly grown next to olive trees so that they could provide some support, and this may be what we are seeing in the Paris manuscript.[42] The *drepanon* was a sickle for harvesting crops, and a bramble slasher was a *batokopin*. You would hope that the latter was not needed in a small domestic garden, although it could be handy in larger ones.

FIGURE 128. Detail from a manuscript showing horticultural workers using bident forks and pruning hooks. (Mss. Gr. 74, Paris), 11th century.

A gardener was called a *kepouros*, in this period there were also specialists such as vinedressers. Apparently the latter working at the Lavra Monastery on Mt Athos were provided with extra rations of wine on the days when they pruned vine branches.[43]

Archaeological remains of Byzantine gardens

The remains of gardens of this period are elusive. Contemporary literature shows they existed but after the conquest by the Turks in 1453 the palaces and gardens would have fallen out of use or been obliterated by later buildings. The location of several former palace gardens and parks of Constantinople have been identified by studying descriptions in written sources, however they could only be deduced by the line of certain terraces, a wall and cisterns.[44] Also a relief of a goose reused in an Ottoman fountain may have once belonged to the Aretai gardens,[45] a tiny fragment of the sculpture and fountains that once enriched this once splendid suburban garden. The only garden area to survive the centuries is a courtyard in front of the remains of a three-storey 13th-century Palaiologan palace now called the Palace of the Sovereign (Tekfur Sarayi, Istanbul). Here the colonnaded facade would have provided easy access to what could have been a garden haven. Until recently this area had been used as a vegetable garden, providing evidence for the fertility of the soil within the area concerned, but sadly no garden archaeology has been undertaken here as yet. During the later period of Byzantium areas outside the walled city of Constantinople suffered from the perpetual wars and therefore there would have been few country houses and gardens there.

However recent excavations on an undisturbed site at Sparta in southern Greece have provided environmental evidence dated to the Byzantine period, from just before the site was abandoned in the 13th century. Here archaeologists found pips of fig, grape and olive, and seeds of *Atriplex, Cicer arietinum, Lens culinaris, Malva, Pisum sativum, Vicia ervilia, Vicia faba, Chenopodium album, Cerastium* and *Polygonum*; they were also able to identify the charred macrofossils of *Brassica campestris ssp. Rapifera* (a form of Turnip).[46] There were no species here that could be considered ornamental.

All indications (from literature and art) show that plants of this period were similar to those used by the Romans, therefore to save duplication no separate plant list has been provided for this particular chapter. The Roman period plant list can be used if needed. What appears to differ between the Roman and Byzantine periods is that the Byzantine gardens contained trees that were clearly heavily pruned, and their art shows that they favoured clipping bushes and trees into tonsured tiers. The display of water features were important and Byzantine fountains feature in numerous descriptions and images of gardens, and many of these fountains comprised two or three tiers. But, perhaps the abiding feature of this particular period is the image of a pinecone, within the fountain, pierced with four or more holes to direct water upwards then down into a basin below.

Notes

1. *Egeria's Travels*, 15.2–6; Wilkinson, J. *Egeria's Travels*, London, 1971, 111.
2. Peter the Deacon's Book on the Holy Places, L1; Wilkinson, *Egeria's Travels*, London, 1971, 185–186.
3. *Clavijo*, 37ff; trans. C. Mango, New Jersey, 1972, 217.
4. Dagron, G. ed. *Vie et Miracles de Sainte Thècle*, Brussels, 1978, 357
5. *Egeria's Travels*, 23.2–4; Wilkinson, *Egeria's Travels*, London, 1971, 121–122.
6. Blas de Roblès, J.-M. and Sintes, C. *Sites et Monuments antique de L'Algérie*, Aix-en-Provence, 2003, 226–28.
7. Beckmann, S. 'Terebinth in Eastern Mediterranean Bronze Age Crete,' *Athanasia* 2012, 30.
8. Avi-Yonah, M. and Stern, E. (eds) *Encyclopedia of Archaeological Excavations in the Holy Land* 3, 1977, 777–778.
9. Pilgrim of Bordeaux, 599; *Itinerarium* of the Piacenza Pilgrim; Peter the Deacon *Book on Holy Places*, N1. Wilkinson, *Egeria's Travels*, London, 1971, 163–165; 188–189. The site is also mentioned by Sozomen in the 5th century (*Historia Ecclesiastica* II, 4–54).
10. *E.g.* at Chariton, Talbot, A.-M. 'Byzantine monastic horticulture: the textual evidence,' *Byzantine Garden Culture* 2002, 50.
11. Littlewood (2013, 54–55) mentions Coptic monks working in the garden of the Monastery of St Paul, Egypt and (p. 148) a monk on Mt Athos.
12. Talbot, A.-M. 'Byzantine monastic horticulture: the textual evidence,' in Littlewood *et al.* 2002, 52; Littlewood 2013, 57. Both mention 'oranges' but I believe that at this date they were citrus, lemon or citrons, as listed in the *Geoponika* 10, 7.
13. Renauld, E. (ed.) *Michel Psellos, Chronographie* 1, Paris, 1926, 72; cf. Talbot, A.-M. 'Byzantine monastic horticulture: the textual evidence', in Littlewood *et al.* 2002, 63.
14. Choricus, *Laudatio Marciani* I, 17ff. trans. C. Mango, New Jersey, 1972, 63.
15. Psalm 42.1, NIV.
16. Inv. No. 1856, 1226, 1007. This was from Pompeii, but is similar to those depicted in Late Antiquity and Byzantium.
17. *Genisis* 24.11.
18. *Isaiah* I,8.
19. Now in the Bibliothèque Nationale, Paris. Cod. Par. Gr.74, fol.52R.
20. Codex Sinaiticus 339, fol.4v. 11th–12th century.
21. Several decorated headpieces are illustrated in Littlewood 2013, 98–105. Of these, eight include an image of a pinecone fountain.
22. Gregory of Nyssa, Letter XV; *Nicene and Post-Nicene Fathers of the Christian Church* 5. trans. W. Moore, Michigan, 1976.
23. *Vita Basilii*, 86. trans. C. Mango, New Jersey, 1972, 195.
24. Renauld, E. (ed.) *Michel Psellos, Chronographie* 1, Paris, 1926, VI, 186; Mango 1972, 219.
25. Trans. H. Maguire: Maguire 1990, 210.
26. Theophanes Continuatus *On the buildings of Theophilus* 829–42 AD, 139ff. trans. C. Mango, New Jersey, 1972, 162.
27. *Vita Basili*, 86, trans. C. Mango, New Jersey, 1972, 194.
28. Liudprand, *Antapodosis*VI, 5, 8. trans. C. Mango; Mango 1972, 209.
29. Manuel Philes, Poem 62, Cod. Paris; Mango 1972, 248.
30. Trans. M.-L. Dolezal and M. Mavroudi. The full text can be found in Littlewood *et al.* 2002, 143–150.
31. Littlewood *et al.* 2002, 151–158. trans. M.-L. Dolezal and M. Mavroudi.

32. *Geoponika* 10.1. trans. A. Dalby; *Geoponika, Farm Work*, 2011, Totnes.

33. *Geoponika* 12.2. trans. A. Dalby, Totnes, 2011; cf. Rogers, R. 'Κηποποιΐα: Garden making and garden culture in the Geoponika', in Littlewood *et al.* 2002, 173.

34. *Geoponika* 10.9; 10.27, Totnes, 2011.

35. *Geoponika* 11.18, Totnes, 2011.

36. *Geoponika* 11.19, Totnes, 2011.

37. *Geoponika* 12.26, Totnes, 2011.

38. Bibliothèque Nationale, Paris. Ms. Gr. 533, fol.34.

39. Bryer, A. 'Byzantine agricultural implements: the evidence of medieval illustrations of Hesiod's *Works and Days*,' *Annual of the British School at Athens* 81, 1986, 50, 70.

40. Bibliothèque Nationale, Paris. Ms. Cod. Par. Gr.74, fol.39v.

41. Bryer, A. 'Byzantine agricultural implements: the evidence of medieval illustrations of Hesiod's *Works and Days*,' *Annual of the British School at Athens* 81, 1986, 78.

42. Bryer, A. 'Byzantine agricultural implements: the evidence of medieval illustrations of Hesiod's *Works and Days*,' *Annual of the British School at Athens* 81, 1986, 50.

43. Talbot, A.-M. 'Byzantine monastic horticulture: the textual evidence,' in Littlewood *et al.* 2002, 53.

44. Maguire 2000, 251–262. Four gardens in Istanbul (anc. Constantinople) were considered: Philopation, Aretai, Mesokepion and Mangana.

45. Maguire 2000, 257.

46. Hather, J. G. *et al.* 'Turnip Remains from Byzantine Sparta' *Economic Botany* 46(4), 1992, 397.

CHAPTER EIGHT

Islamic and Persian Gardens

In the 7th and 8th centuries Arab Muslims from southern Arabia spread the Islamic faith over large swathes of Christian Byzantium and the resurgent Persian Empire in the East (that had been ruled by the Sassanian Dynasty). The Sassanid Persian Empire was replaced with the Islamic Umayyad caliphate. The Islamic Empire soon extended from central Asia to the Atlantic. Therefore evidence for early Islamic gardens is stretched over several countries in the West as well as in the East.

Early Islamic gardens in the East

Damascus, in Syria, was made the first Islamic political capital; it was a city surrounded by desert but its springs irrigated palm groves and gardens that were much admired. These gardens may be the inspiration for the beautiful paradise mosaics adorning the walls of the large forecourt of the Umayyad mosque (dated to 705–715). The mosaics depict a wonderful idealised landscape with buildings, pavilions, bridges over streams, fountains and an abundance of trees (including a citron). These mosaics are often thought to have similarities with those of Byzantium, and the new Islamic rulers would have made use of whatever skilled craftsmen they could find, whether Christian or Muslim. These mosaics are one of the earliest depictions of an idealised Islamic garden.

The mosaics at the unfinished Umayyad palace built *c.*724–743 at Khirbet al-Mafjar, 2 km north of Jericho, are also of interest because, although most of its mosaics were of geometric designs, an apse of one room was decorated with a skilful composition comprising a lion and deer under the canopy of a large tree, recalling a *paradeisos* hunting park. The depiction of images (in human form) were officially banned in 721, but an alternative was to have the geometric patterns or to depict nature, often in the form of trees and flowers. Interestingly though, near life-size human figures in plaster were recovered from the entrance passage to this palace. Although the palace has been excavated not much is known about its gardens, beyond that one courtyard was constructed in the form of a Roman peristyle. A possible garden nearby contained a large elaborate square fountain pool with an octagonal pavilion in the centre.[1] With water all around, it would have provided a refreshingly

cool resting place in high summer. Gardens were seen as a welcoming area of retreat.

The Umayyads were succeeded by the Abbasids, a dynasty based in Baghdad. In 849 they built a new palace at Samarra (Iraq) close to the Tigris River. The Bulkawara Palace is one of the earliest known Islamic palaces and the largest ever constructed, it covered 1.33 km². Its plan has survived almost unaltered because it was abandoned during another dynastic squabble about 50 years after it was built. The plan reveals numerous garden areas and the proximity of this great river ensured that they could be well irrigated. Arab sources mention that plants for these gardens were imported from all corners of their territories. The main gardens of the palace were designed as a series of three large rectangular intercommunicating areas. The archaeologist who excavated this site interpreted the areas as gardens with pathways in each section that had been laid out in a cross pattern which effectively divided each garden into four compartments.[2] This was to become a standard plan of the Islamic Persian style of garden, called a *chahār bāgh* (which means four gardens).

FIGURE 129. Paradise as a garden, in mosaics around the courtyard of the Umayyad mosque Damascus, AD 705–715.

The Chahār Bāgh and other names for gardens

Bāgh is the Persian word for garden, and a garden plant bed was called a *bāghca*. The *chahār* denotes that it was divided into four parts, usually by pathways, one running down the centre of the garden and the other bisecting it half way down, thus creating the four elements of the iconic Islamic garden. However, as we have seen, its origin goes back further in time. The classic four-part garden had been used at times by the Romans, but the design dates back even further for it was noted at the ancient Persian Palace of Cyrus at Pasargadae in 546 BC. Later this simple garden layout was further enhanced with water features. There were several different forms of *bāgh*. We hear of a *Chenār Bāgh*, the *chenār* is the oriental plane so these large shade trees in this type of garden would be ideal for a picnic under their wide canopy. Another form of garden was the *Gul Bāgh* which means a rose garden, in this period roses retain their position as the most favoured of all flowers. The first rose was said to have formed from the beads of perspiration from the prophet's brow.

In the Islamic holy book, the *Koran*, the Arabic word used for a garden was *janna* (pl. *jinān*); and this word was also used to imply 'Paradise' which everyone aspired to reach. Their paradise was like the earlier *Paradeisos*, it was effectively a garden. They envisaged the garden containing two fountains and date palms, pomegranates and other fruit trees, as well as beautiful maidens. The Koranic Paradise garden had rivers flowing through them, four rivers were named,[3] the number four could be linked to the idea of a four-part garden, and the *chahār bāgh* would be perhaps a realisation of this concept. There are similarities between the Jewish and Christian concepts of Eden and Heaven, as both have the four rivers of Paradise flowing out of Eden. Islam absorbed many ideas from civilisations current at that time, and this is an example of the continuity of imagery. A quotation from the Koran also includes more decorative elements within their Paradise garden:

> It is He who grew the gardens, trellised and bowered, and palm trees and land sown with corn and many other seeds, and olives, and pomegranates, alike and yet unalike. So eat of their fruit when they are in fruit, and give on the day of harvesting ...[4]

Besides the four gardens of Paradise, Muslims have 'Seven Heavens' (seven levels of paradise). The Persian word for paradise is *bihesht*, and interestingly some Persians decided to name their own garden '*Hasht Bihesht*', which means 'the eighth paradise'. Scholars and poets liked to make comparisons between earthly gardens and the heavenly paradise promised by the Koran, so these garden owners were likening their own garden to a paradise on earth, making it an eighth paradise. As the supreme model the poets took the Garden of Eram (or Iram). This legendary garden was built in Yemen by Shaddad to rival paradise in splendour, but it brought divine retribution on the patron for being too presumptuous. The moral in this tale was that it was alright to compare your garden with that of paradise, but take care because anything made by man cannot equal, or excel, that created by God.

Most of the terminology for Islamic gardens is either Arabic or derived from Persian, so we also hear of a *bustan* (an Arabic term) which was an orchard or grove, this replaced both the old Persian *pairidaeza* and Greek word *paradeisos* but was still in effect a verdant walled enclosure. The *bustan* would contain not only a variety of fruit trees, but also shade trees to allow plants to grow below in dappled light rather than be burnt by the fierce relentless sun of summer.

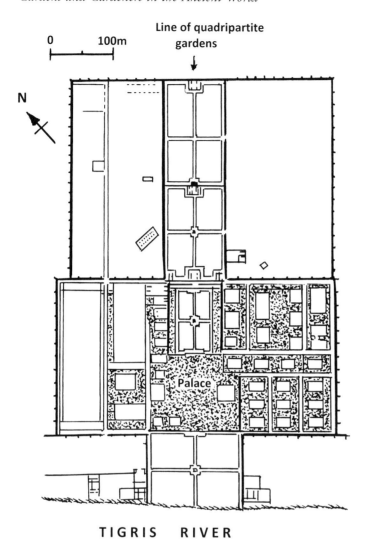

FIGURE 130. Abbasid Palace beside the River Tigris, Samarra (Iraq). A series of interconnecting gardens was designed so that paths formed four garden compartments, a *chahar bagh*, AD 849.

Some of these trees were also selected because they were known to be good for timber, as mentioned by Islamic agriculturalists.

Agriculturalists, gardeners and botanists

A gardener in the Islamic world was called a *bāghbān*. Several rose to become well regarded in their profession. In Spain, Abū'l-Khayr was noted as 'the tree planter' who worked in the royal gardens of al-Mu'tamid at Seville (*c*.1085–1100). While based in Seville Abū'l-Khayr wrote a book on agriculture that included sections on horticulture.

Six other agricultural treatises were produced in Moorish Spain these were by: Ibn Wāfid, Ahmed Ibn Hajjaj in Seville (*c*.1074); Ibn Bassāl in Toledo (*c*.1074–1085); Al-Tighnarī in Granada (*c*.1107–1110); Ibn al-Awwām wrote the celebrated *Book of Agriculture* in Seville (*c.*1180); and *c.*1348 Ibn Luyūn from Almeria wrote a treatise that was later dubbed 'the Andalusian Georgics' when it was recently translated from the Arabic into Spanish. In these great works we notice that the number of plant species mentioned increases over the centuries, and by 1348 we learn that there were around 160 species growing in the gardens of Moorish Spain. The agriculturalists elevated the study of plants to a science, they were given a special name *shajjar*, and we hear that botanists (*nabati*) were employed with a *shajjar* in princely entourages.

Famous Islamic botanists working in Spain were: Ali Ibn Farah, also known as Al-Shafran (12th century) working in Guadix, Abu Ja'far Al-Ghafiqi (d. 1165); Al-Rumiyya (d. 1240) and Ibn Al-Baytar of Malaga (d. 1248).[5] These botanists were also concerned with pharmacology, and Baytar went on to write a book on herbs and introduced many new drugs. Apparently as early as *c.* 756–788 a botanical garden was created in Al-Andalus for Al-Rahman the first, in the grounds of his palace of Al-Rusafa. He wanted this garden to be stocked with plants that were familiar to him from his eastern homeland, so he sent two gardeners as ambassadors to Syria, Yazid and Safar, to bring back seeds and precious seedlings.[6] Safar was known for developing pomegranates in Islamic Spain. We even hear that a 9th-century emissary from Cordoba was sent to Byzantine Constantinople to smuggle out a special variety of fig that they wanted.[7] Botanical gardens and nursery beds were created to try to acclimatise and naturalise a range of plant species new to Spain (plants and seeds were sought from Syria, Persia and north Africa). After time these were propagated and disseminated throughout the western Islamic world, and ultimately to medieval Europe.

In Persia Rashīd al-Dīn who worked in Yazd and Tabriz was noted for his advice on arboriculture which was included in his agricultural manual the *Āthar wa ahyā'* (*c.*1310). Chapters 8–11 are of particular interest because they concern gardens and horticultural practises. He also included information on plants and practises from distant countries: within central Asia, India, and even the different climatic regions of northern and southern China.[8] In his book he informs that:

> If anyone ... plants trees or brings different kinds of trees and seeds to a province where they had not been found before, plants and sows them and teaches people how to do so and encourages them to cultivate such trees and seeds, many people will benefit from his efforts and guidance for years to come and reward will accrue to him in the next world.[9]

Rashīd al-Dīn comments on the skill of gardeners in Isfahan who were adept at tending and pruning fruit trees, especially noted was their care of quince trees. A later Persian agriculturalist was Qasim B. Yusef Abu Nasri who wrote his *Ishad al-zira-a* in 1515 in Herat.[10] Although of a slightly later date it imparts relevant information compiled under the Timurid dynasty. Chapters 5–8 cover horticulture and arboriculture, this work includes advice on vegetables, herbs,

aromatics, fruit trees, ornamental trees bushes and flowers
(chapter 8, which gives details of an ideal garden's layout and
its suggested plantings, will be discussed later).

Of the Persian gardeners we hear of Al-Zardakāsh who
worked for Timur at Samarqand, then (*c*.1490) Maulānā Hājji
Qāsim is mentioned in connection with cultivating different
varieties of grapes, also at Samarqand.[11] However the most
highly respected gardeners of this period were the family of at
least three generations working for Sultan Husain in Herat.
The elder was known as Sayyid Ghiyās al-Dīn Muhammad
Bāghbān (d. *c*.1499). His son Sayyid Nizām al-Dīn Amīr
Sultān-Mahmūd, usually referred to as Mirak-I-Sayyid
Ghiyas (*c*.1476–*c*.1559) became famous as a great landscape
architect, gardener and agriculturalist. His speciality was in
the construction and overseeing of the *chahār bāgh* form of
garden and pavilions.[12] Mirak's son Muhammad continued the
family tradition of being a master gardener and later worked
for Babur and the Mughal court in India, his greatest work
was building Humāyūn's tomb (in 1562) where the garden was
an integral part of the funerary complex.[13]

Occasionally a gardener is portrayed in Persian manuscripts,
he is often shown in the background working in the garden
area. He is usually depicted with his foot on a spade, several
of these spades appear to have a bar just above the cutting
blade of the spade. The spades all have long shafts with no
cross handle, and apparently the shaft was made from wood
of the white poplar tree.

FIGURE 131. Detail of a
Persian gardener using a
long handled spade with
foot rest. *Shahnama*, *c*.AD
1420.

Islamic gardens in Spain discovered by archaeology

Evidence of further early Islamic gardens now shifts to Spain because, in
the 13th century, the lands of the Middle East were devastated by Mongol
Invasions. Sites became ruined and later built over obscuring evidence for the
earlier gardens, this catastrophe caused a great gap in time when searching for
evidence of Islamic gardens.

In Spain, however, after the initial Islamic conquests, conditions were more
settled, and by chance there are some interesting surviving gardens from the
10th–14th centuries. There is also some evidence of continuity in Spain for the
Moors took over a region that had been occupied by the Romans and Visigoths.
Some cities such as Cordoba (the former Roman capital of *Baetica* province in
southern Spain) had many gardens that had been commented on by Roman
writers. Eleventh century sources indicate that the Muslims had appropriated
the Visigothic/former Roman Palace, which now became their Alcazar,[14] new
buildings were added later. In cities like Valencia archaeologists have recently

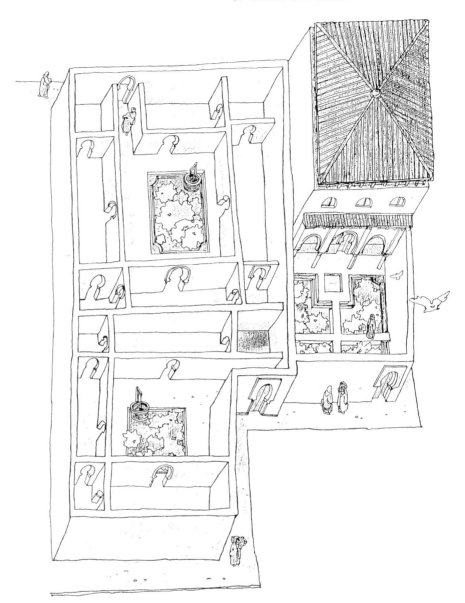

FIGURE 132. Plan of
an Islamic house with
courtyard gardens at
Valencia (after S. C.
Gimeno and E. D. Cusi
in Garcia, I. L. *et al.*
1994, fig. 161).

discovered a house of the Islamic period that directly overlies a Roman
dwelling.[15] They discovered that the Islamic house preserved much of the earlier
Roman one. Each had internal light-well garden courts, and a larger garden
because the Roman garden peristyle had been replaced by only one portico. This
short colonnade had three Islamic arches. Archaeologists discovered that two
distinct levels of garden survived at Valencia, and the Islamic one is believed to
have had a design with cross paths to reflect the *chahar bagh*. In Islamic Spain,
though, one Moorish/Spanish name for a garden was *huerta*, which basically
derived from the Latin *hortus*.

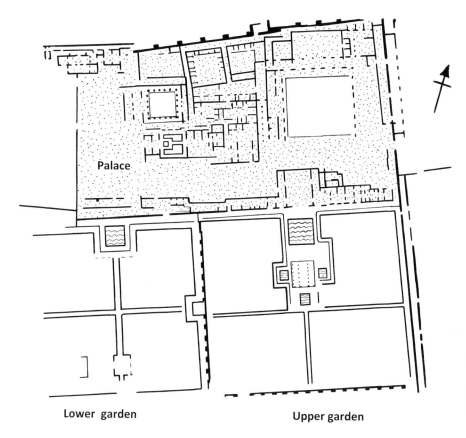

Palace

Lower garden

Upper garden

FIGURE 133. Umayyad palace at Madinat al-Zahra, near Cordoba. The large gardens have traces of cross paths, pools and pavilions which would have made refreshing places to relax surrounded by lush vegetation, AD 936–1010.

Cordoba became the capital of Islamic Spain under the Umayyad dynasty that had fled the dynastic infighting within Syria. In 936 the first Caliph of Al-Andalus, Al-Rahman III, built the Moorish palace of Madinat al-Zahra (also known as Medina Azahara) just outside Cordoba. However, the palace was sacked by Berber rebels in 1010 after only 74 years of use. So this site, like Samarra, was destroyed and never rebuilt, thereby preserving details of a richly decorated building and its well furnished extensive gardens. When excavated archaeologists found that the palace was provided with pleasant internal courtyard gardens, and two large terraced gardens with pools and pavilions. The pair of large gardens measured approx. 163 ×144 m.[16] These two gardens (called the upper and lower gardens) had both been constructed using the four part design. Each dividing path was bordered by narrow irrigation channels. In the upper garden a pavilion was constructed on a raised platform, this was sited off centre in the garden and had paths and four rectangular pools surrounding it, making this location a veritable garden room, a cool space to relax amidst lush vegetation. How this garden was originally planted is not known, but we can infer from poetry and later manuscripts that it would have been well stocked with seasonal flowers, roses, trellised vines, shrubs, fruit trees and cypress trees. The renowned poet and gardener Ibn Luyün actually said that an ideal garden should have a pool and evergreens.[17] These would provide

FIGURE 134. A woman looks out over her garden, represented by a pool with horse head fountains, a tall cypress tree and vine arbour, manuscript painting from the *Bayad was Riyad* Cordoba, now in the Vatican.

a framework throughout the year that could be enlivened with flowering plants in their season.

Garden pools were often fitted with a fountain to circulate and aerate the water; archaeologists have found a number of zoomorphic garden fountain outlets in Spain. A bronze deer was actually discovered at Madinat al-Zahra, and we can speculate if this was one of the animal figures spouting water on each side of a faceted basin mentioned in a text by Al-Maqqart; sadly he didn't actually say which species of animals were present.[18] A rather sweet stone elephant was found near Cordoba, its trunk functioned as the fountain spout, the elephant hunches his back and lowers his head and trunk, so he appears to reach down and drink the water from a pool. However, the most popular form was that of a lion – either seated or standing. A roaring lion was recorded at Madinat al-Zahra, whereas the lion fountain at the Munyat al-Naūra gardens in Cordoba was said to have had jewelled eyes.[19]

Contemporary illustrations of gardens from Al-Andalus (Andalucia)

Simple illustrations of Hispanic Islamic gardens survive in the *Bayad was Riyad* (now in the Vatican) an illuminated manuscript retelling a love story set in the East but was written in Cordoba. The lively scenes portrayed could reflect the gardens of Cordoba and give some indication of life in these gardens. In one scene we see a musician and court ladies singing in a garden. Another shows a duck pond with a slender tree (perhaps a cypress) standing in the middle of a lawned area behind the pool.[20] On one side a vine climbs up a trellised arbour, and on the other two women look out over their garden. In the bottom right hand corner an iris plant grows in a niche; and a hare, or perhaps what is more appropriate – a rabbit, is shown about to climb up some stairs. The rabbit was endemic to Spain and was particularly noted by the Romans who used it as one of their symbols for their province of *Hispania*, the new Muslim overlords were continuing this idea. The pool in this garden was ornamented with paired fountains in the form of a horse's head, the water spouting from their mouths.

A poem commemorating a garden in Spain

We can picture in our minds another garden, called Al-Amiriya, that lay alongside the river in Cordoba. This garden was mentioned in an evocative poem composed by Sa'id (*c*.978) a poet sent from Baghdad to commemorate al-Mansur's new gardens that had been given as a wedding gift by his father:

> Behold the river nearby, gliding like a snake,
> While the birds sing praises, in the shelter of the trees' limbs.
> And the branches drunkenly embrace in the swaying of their boughs.
> And the gardens reveal the splendour of the daisy's smile.
> And the tender narcissus gazes at the anemone's cheek,
> While the gentle wind bears the scent of sweet basil.
> May you pass an eternal lifetime here in happiness and peace![21]

Surviving Islamic gardens of Al-Andalus

Fortunately there are comparable Islamic palaces in Spain that are less ruinous, although these have later additions. Three gardens within the Alcazar of Seville, the palace of the Almohad caliphs retain elements of their original 12th century design. The garden now called the Patio del Crucero (which was a large courtyard of 47.40 × 34.40 m)[22] and that of the Casa de Contratación both featured the familiar cross-axial plan. This basic design was however modified to create two levels, the raised pathways created four sunken garden areas. This development would help to retain moisture for bushes and/or trees planted there. Any deluge of rain would immediately wash away and keep the paths dry. In the Patio del Crucero garden, a circular fountain basin had been placed at the centre of the cross-axial paths, water would pour over its sides into its surrounding circular water basin from which water flowed through intercommunicating water channels along the four paths radiating outwards, making the whole garden visually appealing. Small trees, such as the oranges that are flourishing there at present, would have their canopy at a lower level and at a glance would resemble bushes. You would be able to pick the fruits more easily at this level and the beautifully scented flowers of these trees would more easily be appreciated when strolling in the garden. The third courtyard garden was the Patio del Yeso, which consisted of a rectangular pool presently flanked by narrow beds planted with orange trees under planted with sweet violets.

A palace had been constructed in Granada in the 11th century by the vizier, but with the rise of the Nasrid dynasty a great building program was began at the Alhambra palace by sultan Muhammad I (1232–1272). His descendents added numerous features, but the lions in the Fountain Court are survivors from the earlier days of these gardens.[23] The garden in the Court of the Lions was divided into four quadrants by paths which had a rill, a narrow shallow water channel, running down the centre of each path. The water of the fountain poured from the mouths of twelve lions facing outwards, down into a shallow circular basin beneath them, then along each of the four rills. The 12 lions spouting water in the Court of the Lions were arranged to appear as if they were shouldering the weight of a huge water bowl. The text inscribed on the rim of this fountain bowl is engaging: 'Truly, what else is this fountain but a beneficent cloud pouring out its abundant supplies over the lions underneath?' Water was always an important feature in Islamic gardens, as they were in Byzantine gardens. The sound of water playing in a fountain is very soothing and peaceful, it also helps to muffle conversations you did not want other people to overhear, so in certain places a fountain could also create a semblance of privacy.

It seems that at the end of the 13th century (in the Nasrid period) the layout of Islamic gardens in Spain changes; the familiar quadripartite design seems to be replaced by gardens with large or elongated pools.[24] A good example of this new form is seen in the Court of the Myrtles at the Alhambra constructed by Yusuf I (1333–1354). Myrtle bushes have been planted in a strip on either side of the central large rectangular pool, and as far as we know this has always been the case because myrtles (and oranges) were noted in this garden just after the Christian conquest of Granada in 1492.[25] The pool of this beautiful garden provided a sheet of still water which has the effect of a mirror by reflecting the architecture around it on its surface; this is an excellent example of what is termed a reflection pool. It gives a wonderfully calm atmosphere to the area. Two circular fountains were placed at either end of the long length of the glistening pool, they serve to break the otherwise severe straight lines of this garden's design and they add life to the otherwise placid environment.

In the early 14th century Muhammad III built a sumptuous summer palace, the Generalife, to catch the breezes higher up on the hill above the Alhambra at Granada. The most celebrated garden here was the Acequia Court (or Canal Court) which because of its terraced location was designed as a long narrow garden. It has an elongated narrow water channel along the centre of the garden that is divided into two parts by a cross path. Circular water basins have been placed at the beginning, middle and end of its course. The break in the middle of the two pools allows for a four part garden design although here four elongated octagonal plant beds were created. Excavations in this area found details of the original garden design 70 cm below the present pavements. Deep plant pits were discovered suitable for planting shrubs and small trees. We can envisage the scene because contemporary sources noted myrtles and orange trees growing there.[26] Sadly the series of water jets that line the two halves of the long water feature in this garden were not part of the original design, and are later additions.

The Islamic architects often incorporated prospect balconies called a *manzar*, in Spanish a *mirador* (meaning a place for looking), so you could gaze down and enjoy the view over a garden below. The walls of the mirador overlooking the Lindaraja Gardens of the Alhambra were covered with poetic inscriptions in stucco. In one of these, the poet Ibn Zamrak says: 'In this garden I am an eye filled with delight and the pupil of this eye is, truly, our lord.' He therefore informs us that the mirador could be likened to an eye allowing a view of the garden.[27]

Mosque gardens

Gardens were sometimes constructed in the forecourt of mosques, like earlier atrium gardens, but these were predominantly filled with trees not flowers. The earliest is attached to Cordoba's Great Mosque (the Mezquita). The altered courtyard garden (measuring *c*.120 × 60 m) was laid out under al-Mansur in 987–988. The former great mosque of Seville was similarly provided with a tree planted forecourt. These gardens were basically a *bustan*, a grove of trees to shade believers as they congregated for prayers. Today they are both planted with orange trees and are known as the Patio de los Naranjos, the trees are neatly aligned in rows. Originally the ground was of beaten earth but it is now paved, except for a reserved section for each tree.[28] A regular network of stone-lined narrow irrigation channels supply water to each individual tree. These gardens also contain a water basin where worshippers could perform their ablutions.

Plants grown in Islamic Spain

Several Islamic manuscripts from Spain mention garden plants, and together with surviving treatises on agriculture/horticulture they can give an indication of what was grown in the gardens there. The earliest is *Le Calendrier de Cordoue* by Arīb b. Sa'īd, which dates from 961–976. This lists about 100 plants, mostly fruit trees and crops that were growing in Cordoba; it also gives the dates for sowing, planting and harvesting. Later works such as *The Book of Agriculture* by Ibn al-Awwām writing in Seville *c*.1085 and Ibn Luyūn from Granada in 1348 (mentioned earlier) give a larger number of plants, and the rising number of garden-worthy plants reaches 160.[29] Some of the plants and trees are species that would be classed as tender in more northerly climes, and are therefore less familiar to us. Also several cannot be fully identified in translations from the Arabic originals into Spanish. A large proportion of the plants were already known from Roman times, but there were notable introductions to the country such as the banana (*Musa paradisiacal*) then known as *mūz*, and the Seville orange (*Citrus aurantium*) in Arabic it was called *nāranj*. The latter was first recorded in Spain by Ibn Bassāl *c*.1080. The grapefruit (*zanbū*) is mentioned at a later date. We also hear for the first time about the Judas tree which was much admired for its coloured flowers, and the bead tree (*Melia azederach*) with its panicles of attractive lilac flowers followed by yellow berries.

In the work by Ibn Luyūn he specified that 'numerous plants are cultivated for the delight of sight and smell, or to be used as ornamentation.'[30] These

FIGURE 135. Walkways surround an elongated pool flanked by sunken garden beds. Patio del Yeso, Seville Alcázar, 12th–13th century.

FIGURE 136. Reflecting pool, Court of the Myrtles, Alhambra, Granada, 13th century (photo: © 2010 G. Farrar).

plants, he says, were planted in the *bustan*; in this case he uses the Arabic term used for an enclosed orchard or grove, but these were clearly also treated as a domestic garden. He shows that at least one part of the *bustan* would have been reserved for leisure purposes. What is clear is that colourful flowers were sought for and that aromatic plants were highly favoured. In many cases the texts mention digging up wild plants to transplant into the garden/orchard. Some of the comments made by Ibn Luyūn and others are informative on plant usage in the garden. The lily they say 'is planted in those areas of the orchards where no labour is made, and next to the ponds. It is planted in gardens and houses because of its beauty.'[31] The colocasia was used for its beautiful foliage effect, it was apparently 'planted next to water flows'; this plant seems to have taken over the role played by the *acanthus mollis* (favoured by the Romans) which is not mentioned at all. Other flowers planted in gardens/orchards are water lilies (especially the white ones), yellow narcissus, violets, wallflowers, stocks, vinca, camomile (or similar daisy-like species), anemones, mallow, rose, red flowered hibiscus, butcher's broom, oleander, strawberry tree, lavender, rosemary, basil and aromatic herb species simply identified as 'incenses'. Of the trees mentioned the spiny azarole was used in making hedges around vineyards and gardens. Several trees were useful giving much needed shade, such as the elegant nettle tree (*Celtis australis*) which was planted by garden walls. The stonepine and the cypress were noted as suitable for planting around the *bustan* walls 'in order to beautify them'. The texts also say that if the stonepine 'is planted in the middle of a pool or pond, it causes delight with its beauty and shade.'[32] This must mean that it was planted on an island. The cypress was also used for lining pathways in gardens. Myrtle was used 'surrounding the pavilions in gardens'. Oleaster and service trees were referred to as beautiful trees and together with pomegranates were planted near wells and pools. The citron, lemon, orange and grapefruit were planted where they would be sheltered by garden walls, especially from cold north winds. Ivy was apparently allowed to grow on reed lattices to create shade for other plants, and could provide an architectural element within gardens.

Ibn Luyūn also provides a useful summary in verse explaining how large decorative gardens should be laid out and makes suggestions as to how it should be planted:

> Then next to the reservoir plant shrubs whose leaves do not fall and which rejoice the sight; and, somewhat further off, arrange flowers of different kinds, and further off still, evergreen trees. And around the perimeter climbing vines, and in the centre of the whole enclosure a sufficiency of vines; and under climbing vines let there be paths which surround the garden to serve as a margin. And amongst the fruit trees include the grapevine... [also] arrange the virgin soil for planting whatever you wish should prosper. In the background let there be trees like the fig or any other which does no harm; and any fruit tree which grows big, plant it in a confining basin so that its mature growth may serve as a protection against the north wind without preventing the sun from reaching [the plants]. In the centre of the garden let there be a pavilion in which to sit, and with vistas on all sides, but of such a form that

no one approaching could overhear the conversation within and whereunto none could approach undetected. Clinging to it let there be [rambler] roses and myrtle, likewise all manner of plants with which a garden is adorned.[33]

Surviving Islamic gardens in Morocco and Sicily

In Morocco large gardens were constructed in association with the sultan's palaces. In Marrakech there are two gardens of note: the Agdal and the Menara (both date to *c.*1157). The former gave its name to a special type of garden seen in this country. The Berber name *agdal*, like its namesake, was applied to large walled gardens predominantly stocked with trees planted in regimented rows. These gardens contained one or more rectangular huge water basins that were used as reservoirs to irrigate the gardens. To make this easier there was an extensive network of water channels and several enclosures within these vast gardens. The Islamic agriculturalists of the west were well known for their ground breaking knowledge and application of hydraulics. Sources suggest that the Agdal and Menara gardens were stocked with numerous trees, among which the following were named: apricots, grape vines, olive trees, oranges, and aromatic plants.[34] Today many varieties of fruit trees are planted there, and the pathways between enclosures are even shaded by trellises of jasmine and roses. These historic gardens are thought to have been created by Al-Hāj Yaʿīsh, an outstanding landscape architect working for the Almohad rulers.

In Norman Sicily there was a palace and gardens in Palermo that were greatly influenced by Islamic stylistic ideals (built *c.*1155 by Arab-Normans), it is now called La Zisa, which derives from the Arabic *aziz* meaning precious). An inscription in Kufic script above an archway says: 'This is the earthly paradise which opens to the regard; this is the *Mustʾazis* and this is the *Aziz*.' The gardens were greatly admired by later visitors to Palermo (inc. Alberti), they mentioned a pavilion beside a pool, fountains and groves of oranges and lemons. A French count, Robert II of Artois was so impressed by what he had seen (in 1270) that on his return he tried to recreate the water features in his own garden.[35]

Garden poetry and literature in the Eastern Islamic/Persian world

In the 10th century Baghdad was considered the wealthiest city in the eastern Islamic world, it was the setting of the fabulous *Tale of Arabian Nights*. Visitors to the city describe palm filled gardens with pools and pavilions, perhaps like those of Spain mentioned above. Early writers in Spain often compared their homes and gardens to those in their eastern homeland.

The name of this city is descriptive for *bagh* means gardens; it was once literally a city of gardens. Several Persian poets praised gardens and the beauty of nature, the first was Firdausi, the great epic poet of Iran who wrote his *Shahnama* (History of Kings) *c.*1010. In this verse he recalls the garden of the daughter of Afrasiyab.

> It is a spot beyond imagination
> Delightful to the heart, where roses bloom,
> And sparkling fountains murmur – where the earth
> Is rich with many-coloured flowers; and musk
> Floats on the gentle breezes
> And lilies add their perfume – golden fruits
> Weigh down the branches of the lofty trees.[36]

In the 12th–13th centuries the greatest poets were Hafiz and Sa'di from Shiraz. They are often quoted today because of the timeless quality of their work. Hafiz often included a line or two on flowers, as well as incorporating the joys of life, women, and merry making. Here is an example:

> Let's go to the garden and have some fun,
> Let's sing like the birds and sit in the sun
> let's look at the colours, red, blue, and pink
> by the beds of flowers let's sit and drink.[37]

Another verse from Hafiz is understandably a favourite one; it has a resonance to today for who wouldn't like to do the same:

> Oh! Bring thy couch where countless roses
> The garden's gay retreat discloses;
> There in the shade of the waving boughs recline
> Breathing rich odours, quaffing ruby wine![38]

Sa'di wrote two books of poems, the *Bustan* and the *Gulistan* the Rose Garden. In these he writes moralistic stories and poems that are compared to a collection of flowers in a garden, hence the title. Here is a telling verse:

> What use to thee that flower-vase of thine?
> Thou would'st have rose-leaves; take then, rather, mine.
> Those roses but five days or six will bloom;
> This garden ne'er will yield to winter's gloom.[39]

The roses in Sa'di's *Gulistan* garden would, metaphorically, continue to bloom because they were written words and the written word lives long. Sa'di loved his garden so much that he chose to be buried in his own at Shiraz. His next poem shows that Islamic gardens could be colourful with many hued flowers:

> A garden where the murmuring rill was heard;
> While from the trees sang each melodious bird;
> That, with the many-coloured tulip bright,
> These, with their various fruits the eye delight.
> The whispering breeze beneath the branches' shade,
> Of bending flowers a motley carpet made.[40]

Omar Khayam (*c.*1048–1125) is famous for his *Rubáiyát* which is full of emotion and has a haunting quality. In verse five he reminds people of the fabled gardens of Iram (mentioned earlier):

> Iram indeed is gone with all its rose
> And Jamshyd's Seven-ringed Cup where no one knows;
> But still the Vine her ancient Ruby yields,
> And still a Garden by the Water blows.[41]

The rose is often mentioned and in verse eighteen it is used to dramatic effect:

> I sometimes think that never blows so red
> The Rose as where some buried Caesar bled
> That every Hyacinth the Garden wears
> Dropt in its lap from some once lovely Head.[42]

Omar Khayam's tomb is at Nishapur in Iran in a region where a distinctive rose blooms. As a mark of respect to his translator a specimen of one of these roses was collected and planted on the tomb of Fitzgerald in 1893. This rose is now cultivated under the name *Rosa 'Omar Khayam'*. It is a light pink rose with a semi-double quartered head, and greyish foliage.

Persian poetry shows there was a special attachment to the rose, above any other flower, its scent is often mentioned with nostalgia. Roses grow well there, and their damask rose (*Rosa damascena*), also known as the Muhammadan rose, was also used for making rose water and attar rose oil. Apparently the mythical king Jamshid was attributed with discovering the use of aromatic plants and the distillation of their prized rose oil. The particular form of rose used is so quintessentially associated with Iran that it was generally referred to as the 'Persian rose'. As mentioned earlier the rose was called *gul*, but this word was also used for flowers in general. Often a flowering plant would have a *gul* prefix *e.g. gul-i-narges* which can be translated as 'narcissus flower'. There were names for different species of rose. They had a hundred-petalled rose which was known as *gul-i-sad barg*, and a musk rose that was called *mushkīn*.[43] Beside pink and red roses there was also a yellow Persian rose, known as *gul-i-zard*. There was even a name for people who so admired roses, or flowers, they would call themselves a *gulbaz*.[44]

Nizami wrote his *Khamseh* (a book of five poems) c.1209, this extract provides more information on gardens during his period, and an indication of some of the flowers and plants that these eastern gardens could contain. The poet rejoices that the garden is reawakening in Spring:

> Come, gardener! Make gladsome preparation,
> The rose is come back, throw wide open the gate of the garden.
> Nizami hath left the walls of the city for his pleasure ground;
> Array the garden like the figured damask of China.
> Dress up its beauty with the ringlets of the violet;
> Awaken from its sleep the tipsy narcissus.
> Let the lip of the rosebud inhale a milky odour;
> Let the tall cypress spread wide its branches,
> Tell the news to the turtle dove, that its bough is again green...
> The lip of the pomegranate stain with red wine;
> Gild the ground with the safflower.

Give to the lily a salutation from the Judas tree;
Direct the running streamlet towards the rose-bush.
Behold again the newly-risen plants of the meadow!
Draw no line over that delicate drawing!
Others like me are inspired with the love of the verdant;
Bear my salutation to every green thing.
How the mild air of the garden is attractive to the soul!...
The trees are blossoming by the edge of the garden.[45]

Islamic scholars studied Graeco-Roman texts and were particularly interested in medicine and the use of herbs grown in gardens. Many surviving manuscripts have Arabic notations alongside the Greek or Latin, and of course copies in Arabic were made. It is perhaps rather surprising that one of the earliest surviving copies of the Herbal of Dioscorides is in fact an Arabic one. In some versions, illustrations of Dioscorides now show him wearing Islamic dress rather than his Roman toga! Roman manuscripts written by Galen were also studied, and his *Book of Antidotes* was popular. One of the remedies was for snakebite and as with others an illustration accompanied the text. In this case a man is depicted with the offending snake, but a doctor arrives on horseback to provide a timely antidote, this involved drinking a concoction of crushed leaves and flowers of oleander. Therefore an oleander plant was shown in flower nearby, other trees are in the background. Oleander is poisonous so the dose needed to be mixed carefully, apparently it was more affective if some rue was added. Oleander was often included into gardens despite its toxicity, it is nevertheless a decorative plant and as we have seen it has its uses.

Funerary gardens

The great poets Sa'di and Hafiz were both honoured by the construction of a memorial at the site of their tomb in Shiraz. The city of Shiraz has long been known as a garden city because of its regular water supply. In the 15th century the area around each tomb was beautified by the creation of gardens. The Sa'diyya (or Arāmgāh-e Sa'dī), the funerary garden of the celebrated poet Sa'di is located in a narrow valley with a spring flowing through, it is shaded with cypress and pine trees. Sa'di's tomb is about a mile north-east of the Hafiziyya which commemorates the much loved Hafiz; both were buried in their native city. Hafiz's tomb garden has two pools and the pleasant park-like surroundings are shaded by trees, and adorned with numerous plant pots filled with flowers. These gardens have been enhanced in recent years and there are now pavilions where people can read the verses of these great poets.

Descriptions of gardens in the Eastern Islamic World

As a consequence of the invasions of nomadic Mongols in the 13th century, cites throughout Persia and the Middle East were pillaged and plundered, there was widespread destruction in town and country. Irrigation canals were severed and this led to large areas reverting to desert. When the land became more settled the new Mongol overlords made use of the remaining *chahar bagh* gardens but in a different way. Early Islamic gardens were mainly designed to be looked at, but now the grassed areas were seen as ideal places to erect tents or to create a kiosk (an open pavilion) where they could rule and be entertained in fresh air. One of the most fearsome rulers was the mighty Timur (who we know as Tamerlane) who became lord of Samarqand in 1369. A series of military campaigns enabled him to establish a vast territory under his control, from the Mediterranean to the Himalayas and from northern India to Russia. Fortunately three writers documented this period, one of them being a Spanish ambassador called Clavijo who provides valuable descriptions of audiences and festivals held in the ruler's gardens:

> We were come to a great orchard … [various members of the court were seated on a dais under an awning] Then coming to the presence beyond we found Timur and he was seated under what might be called a portal … He was sitting not on the ground, but upon a raised dais before which there was a fountain that threw up a column of water into the air backwards, and in the basin of the fountain there were floating red apples.[46]

Timur brought in architects from far and wide to construct new garden areas, and was justifiably proud of them. We hear of six different garden zones, one of these was the *Dilgusha* garden (which means Heart's Ease) this was the first garden Clavijo entered. Then there was the *Bagh-i-Maidan* (garden of the square), *Bagh-i-Shimal* (northern garden), the *Bagh-i-Naw* (new garden), a *Gul Bagh* (a rose garden), and a *Chenar Bagh* (a garden with plane trees); the oriental plane provides ample shade and would make ideal places for al fresco dining under its wide canopy. These elements are seen in some of the Persian miniature paintings. Clavijo gives another description of one of these Timurid gardens at Samarqand:

> We found it to be enclosed by a high wall which in its circuit may measure a full league around, and within it is full of fruit trees of all kinds save only limes and citron-trees which we noted to be lacking. Further, there are here six great tanks, for throughout the orchard is conducted a great system of water, passing from end to end: while leading from one tank to the next they have planted 5 avenues of trees, very lofty and shady, which appear as streets, for they are paved to be like platforms. These quarter the orchard in every direction, and off the five main avenues other smaller roads are led to variegate the plan.[47]

The paved 'platforms' mentioned here could well be raised walkways. The lack of citrus trees in this unnamed garden could be due to cooler winters in the region of Samarqand.

Fortunately a detailed description of the layout of a Timurid garden is preserved in the *Ishād al-zirā-a* an agricultural manual written by Qasim B. Yusef Abu Nasri. In this book the eighth chapter deals with the laying out and planting of a garden.[48] This great work was written in 1515 for the new Safavid rulers, but it relates the expertise of the preceding Timurid dynasty. Nasri had consulted Mirak-I Sayyid Ghiyas of Herat (born *c.*1476), who was the most knowledgeable horticulturalist at that time and was one of three generations of notable gardeners.

When the measurements given are translated we find that this Timurid garden was *c.*133 m wide, and the whole rectangular walled garden would be about 2.4 ha. Nasri suggests that there should be a raised walkway on either side of a water channel running through the length of the garden leading to a raised platform, a dais, with a pavilion and a pool. These elements effectively cut the garden into two halves. Poplar trees were planted around the perimeter garden wall with irises below, next to a path that follows the circuit of the walls. The interior of the garden is divided into three areas reserved for rows or squares of one or two species; these were aligned symmetrically in the garden on both sides of the central path. The first part comprised fruit trees; you would encounter rows of apricots and plums, but there was a space for red roses in the upper corner. Next came eight paired squares, two for quince, two for nectarine and peach, two for pomegranate and two for pear. The middle section comprised 18 square flower beds and four elongated plant beds with trefoil (clover) and a narrow strip of calendula that were sited alongside the central path. The remaining third that was closer to the dais was planted in rows, there were dog roses, figs, cherry, flowering Judas tree, sour cherry, mulberry, apple and surrounding the dais they planted cucumber.

The 18 paired flower beds contained the following plus some unidentified flowers:

1. blue violet, iris, 'hundred-petaled' rose and wild saffron.
2. Saffron crocus, narcissus and 'six-petaled' rose.
3. Tulip, iris, and common anemone.
4. 'Blue' jasmine, 'yellow' Judas tree, yellow violet, 'two-tiered' tulip and stocks.
5. Red rose, yellow rose, jonquil.
6. Rose interspersed with red poppy.
7. Yellow jasmine, 'six-month' rose, waterlily, pinks, lemon-yellow iris and hollyhock.
8. Hollyhock, white jasmine.
9. Oriental tulip and amaranths. And by the pool there were dog roses or eglantine.

Nasri makes this comment: 'Be sure to take good care of your trees and flowers, In short, don't be idle for a moment!'[49]

Depictions of Islamic Persian gardens

A collection of manuscripts was assembled by Timur's son Shah Rukh and others in Herat (the new Persian capital, 1408–1447), and fortunately a few from this period survive. The famous epic by Firdausi, the *Shahnama*, was copied and the greatest painters of the day were commissioned to make illustrations to accompany this much revered text. A later version was given 258 miniature paintings. Other famous books were treated similarly with several illustrations to

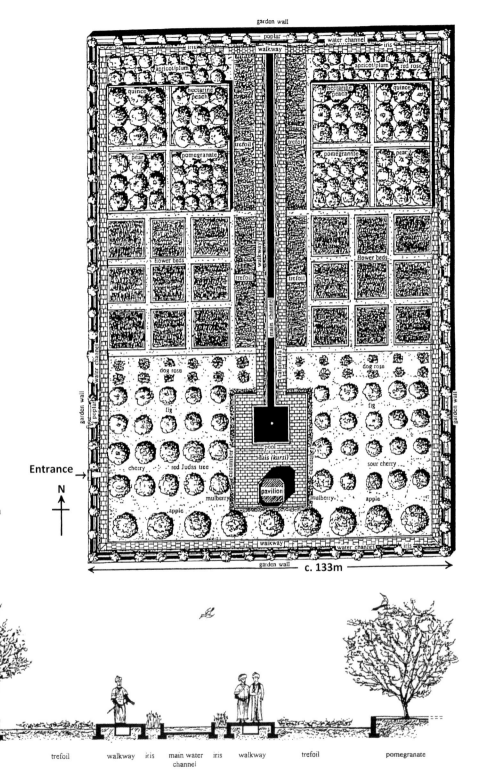

FIGURE 137.
Reconstruction (plan and cross-section) of the layout of a Timurid garden of the 15th century, based on descriptions in a Persian agricultural manual written by Qasim B. Yusef Abu Nasri, the *Irshad al-zira*.

match key points in the text, of these Nizami's *Khamsa* was also well illustrated. Some scenes show events taking place in a garden and these can be helpful when trying to visualize gardens of the period.

One of the earliest Persian miniatures painted by Jonayd (*c*.1396) that depicts a garden rather than a landscape is found in the romance story of *Humay va Humayun* in the *Divan* of Khvaju Kirmani of Baghdad. This retells the tale of the Persian prince Humay meeting the beautiful Humayun, the daughter of the Mongol Emperor of China. This story highlights the links Persia had with other cultures mainly via the Silk Road (another miniature featured a delegation from the ruler of Hind in northern India). The tale was retold many times over the centuries. In the version illustrated here Humayan watches from an upper floor of the palace as Humay approaches on his horse. The palace and its garden resemble that of a modest Persian house, and we see the typical high walls that protect the property and its garden from the elements and marauders. Tall trees border the garden with flowers at their base. We can make out a white lily, red carnations, mallows/hollyhock and a pale pink rose bush within this delightful garden. Another scene from this romantic story shows the two lovers seated on a dais taking tea in the middle of what appears to be a large garden bordered by flowering trees, that include cherry blossom, hibiscus and roses. Servants pick rose buds from a tall bush. A multitude of low growing flowers covered the ground. Each flower had been painted with care, but we note that there was a predominance of red and pink flowered species depicted here for effect.

The Teheran copy of the fables of *Kalila and Dimna* (1420–1425) has a frontispiece illustrating the presentation of the manuscript to its patron seated on a dais in his garden. The dais was set on what appears to have been an octagonal platform surrounded by a decorative low wall. One of the court officials is shown walking through its arched entrance. In front of the throne on the dais there is a fountain set in the centre of an ornamental pool, its outline mimicking that of a ten- petalled flower. Ducks swim in the pool, the water is now grey because the original silver has tarnished.[50] In the background there are flowering bushes and flowers; with fruit trees shown in full blossom, one pink and two with white flowers. In between are four tall slender cypresses standing in pairs, the cypress was much admired for its elegant form. There were also two tall white stemmed poplar trees that had been carefully clipped into tiers. The most popular trees depicted in Persian miniatures are: the ubiquitous cypress, cherry blossom trees or blossom trees in general, plane trees, poplar and willow.

Scenes from the *Khamseh* written by Nizami were painted by numerous artists over the years, but Aga Mirak from Herat was an artist who was working for the Timurid dynasty. One of his miniatures (of *c*.1494) illustrates the tale of Shirin and Khusraw, another famous Persian love story that relates to a much earlier date. Mirak painted Shirin seated on a carpet, on a plant filled green sward, in what could be a *Chenar Bagh*. Three tall trees and a willow hint at what could be a shady picnic spot. Music and refreshments were at hand. Shirin who was a beautiful Armenian princess is shown contemplating a portrait of her

FIGURE 138. A prince seated in his garden, from the frontispiece of the Fables of *Kalila and Dimna*, Teheran, *c.*AD 1420–1425.

intended, Khusraw. Khusraw was a much earlier great Sassanian Persian king, who led a fearsome army up to the gates of Istanbul in 608 (the Byzantines called him Chosroes II). To the Persians he was a hero and often featured in their legends.

Another memory that has survived and was passed through succeeding generations is the special paradise garden depicted on Persian carpets. They preserve the story of a very famous carpet owned by the Sassanian King Khusraw I. The original carpet was said to have graced the floor of the king's audience hall so everyone of rank would have been familiar with it. This carpet was known as the 'Winter Carpet', it had been specially designed to depict the king's fabulous garden as it would have appeared in Spring. He had regarded this garden as his own paradise, and therefore this carpet would be a reminder to Khusraw and his courtiers of their beautiful verdant garden until Spring returned. The later paradise carpets show what is basically a *chahār bāgh* (a four part garden)

FIGURE 139. A Timurid walled garden, trees border the garden with flowers at their base, *Humay va Humayum*, by Khvaju Kirmani, Baghdad, *c.*AD 1396 (© British Library Board. All Rights Reserved. Add 18113 f.18v).

divided by four broad water channels, although some carpets have more garden areas and water channels. Water is usually indicated by wavy lines and fish swim along the watercourse, sometimes ducks swim alongside them. The number and width of these channels emphasis how water is all important in these arid lands. The centre of the composition has a shaped pool or a decorative device to simulate the position of a central dais and pavilion. There is usually a border of specimen plants/trees and the remainder is filled with square or rectangular plant beds. In some versions the flowers and trees are depicted schematically, in others the plants are more defined, the most accomplished also include garden fauna, a variety of birds and even rabbits, foxes and deer. There is a conspicuous profusion and the aim was to show an imagined paradise.

Surviving Eastern Islamic/Persian gardens

Although several named gardens are known, these have not survived the vicissitudes of time. In 1941 archaeologists working in Samarqand discovered a garden built for Ulugh Beg, Timur's grandson. They unearthed a number of ceramic pipes and evidence for irrigation channels within and around the garden, and brick and marble paving.[51] Sadly at that time no record was made of any botanical evidence.

Near Herat, a city once famed for its gardens, only two Timurid period gardens survive. One of these is the funerary garden of Gazar Gar, an 11th-century saint favoured by Shah Rukh who ordered the garden to be made in 1428.[52] The second garden is now ruinous, but was noted in Soviet aerial photography in 1946. The garden was defined by a walled rectangular enclosure and a familiar quadripartite designed garden plan. It may have been part of the *Bāgh-i Jahān-ārā* of Sultan Husain that was recorded as being approximately 132 acres (c.53.4 ha).[53] In 1933 Robert Byron wrote that the ruined garden he saw here was on terraces, there had once been a pavilion and water features, and 'from the empty tank at the top, a line of pools and watercourses descends from terrace to terrace.'[54] This region has been a war-zone for a number of years and therefore no garden archaeology was possible.

The majority of surviving Islamic gardens in the East belong to the next dynasty, the Safavid, who rose to power in 1502 and are therefore out of the scope of this book, as are many of the beautiful Persian miniature paintings of this era. The earliest of the Safavid gardens, the Bagh-i Fin, dates to 1590, but the walls of the enclosure are earlier as they are mentioned in sources in 1504,[55] so there may have been a pre-existing garden there. The Bagh-i Fin is believed to preserve the spirit of Timurid gardens. It is predominantly a plantation of cypress trees and comprises a series of square and rectangular planting areas divided by a network of paths and water channels or rills. A pavilion and water basins were sited off centre inside this enchanting *chahār bāgh* style of garden. Water was provided by a *qanat*, a tunnel dug into the hillside until it intersects with a water bearing strata. The water sourced from this spring would then flow continually. *Qanats* were used throughout Persia and the Middle East and also have been discovered in Morocco to supply the gardens of Marrakech with water.

Babur and the birth of Mughal gardens

Babur was the grandson of Timur (b. 1483–1530), he was 12 years old when he inherited on the death of his father. However, there was great upheaval at this time and the Safavid rulers gained control. Babur lost his base in Samarkand, so he travelled south over the Hindu Kush mountains and made Kabul his new capital. He made glorious gardens there. Fortunately his memoirs are preserved in the book called the *Babur-Nama*. In his youth Babur had either stayed or visited some of the Timurid palaces and gardens, and had been entranced by the gardens of his homeland in Samarkand as well as in Herat. In many ways he wanted to recreate them and the familiar *chahār bāgh* design in his new gardens. His journeys and conquests in Afghanistan and India are well documented, and he reveals in the memoires that wherever he went he preferred to rest in a garden. If there was not one nearby then he would have one made! Fortunately some of Babur's gardens are described in this outstanding documentary book. For instance in 1504 he created a garden at Istalif where he realigned the stream and built a platform so that he could look over the plane trees, holm oaks and Judas trees growing on the slopes below. He was so overwhelmed by its beauty that he said 'if, the world over, there is a place to match it when the Judas trees are in bloom, I do not know it.'[56]

His most celebrated garden was the *Bagh-i-Wafa* believed to be near Jalalabad, he says:

> I laid out the Four-gardens, known as the *Bagh-i-Wafa* (Garden of Fidelity), on a rising ground, facing south ... There oranges, citrons and pomegranates grow in abundance ... I had plantains [bananas] brought and planted there; they did very well ... The garden lies high, has running-water close at hand, and a mild winter climate. In the middle of it, a one-mill stream flows constantly past the little hill on which are the four garden plots. In the south-west part of it there is a reservoir, ten by ten, round which are orange-trees and a few pomegranates, the whole enriched by a trefoil-meadow. This is the best part of the garden, a most beautiful sight when the oranges take colour. Truly that garden is admirably situated![57]

Babur founded a new dynasty in India, the Mughal, a name derived from their Mongol background. His descendants continued to create gardens, their gardens in India formed an integral part of the design of buildings, of palace or funerary monument. Babur had requested that he should be buried in Kabul, in the grounds of one of his beloved gardens. His wish was honoured and the gardens surrounding the tomb are now called the Bagh-e-Babur (the original name of these gardens is not known). Babur's tomb and remnants of these gardens have survived.[58] The walled gardens covered about 11.5 ha, and were designed on 15 terraces. It retained the geometric Timurid layout with a central axis, water channels and pools. It originally had a pavilion, but there were alternations over the years by later Mughal princes who came to honour their founder's memory, this ensured that the tomb continued to be a place of veneration.

In the Islamic period (in the east and west) gardens were essentially walled enclosures which could include shady groves laid out in a symmetrical way. Planting included aromatic species and those that would please the eye. Pavilions were erected within to make the most of refreshing breezes and to enable the soul to relax amid the calming effect of surrounding flora. Above all, the Islamic garden is epitomized by the use of water, in pools or water channels and where possible with fountains playing. These elements, in hot climates were all the more admired and appreciated.

Garden Plants of the Islamic Period

Common name	Botanical name	Painting	Literature	West	East
Almond	*Prunus communis*	x	x	x	x
Amaranth	*Amaranthus*		x		x
Anemone	*Anemone*		x	x	x
Anise	*Pimpinella anisum*		x	x	
Apple	*Malus domestica*		x	x	x
Apricot	*Prunus armeniaca*		x	x	x
Artichoke	*Cynara scolymus*		x	x	
Ash	*Fraxinus excelsior*		x	x	
Asparagus	*Asparagus officinalis*		x	x	
Azarole	*Crataegus azarolus*		x	x	
Balm	*Melissa officinalis*		x	x	
Balsam-tree	*Commiphora opobalsamum*		x	x	
Banana (*mūz*)	*Musa paradisiaca*		x	x	x
Basil	*Ocimum basilicum*		x	x	x
Bay	*Laurus nobilis*		x	x	
Bead tree/Persian Lilac	*Melia azedarach*		x	x	
Bean (Broad)	*Vicia faba*		x	x	
Bean (Kidney)	*Vigna cylindrica*		x	x	x
Beet	*Beta vulgaris*		x	x	x
Blite	*Chenopodium capitatum*		x	x	
Boxthorn	*Lycium europaeum*		x	x	
Butcher's broom	*Ruscus aculeatus*		x	x	
Calamint	*Calamintha nepeta*		x	x	
Calendula/ Marigold	*Calendula officinalis*	x	x	x	x
Camomile	*Anthemis nobilis*		x	x	
Caper	*Capparis spinosa*		x	x	
Caraway	*Carum carvi*		x	x	
Carob	*Ceratonia siliqua*		x	x	
Carrot	*Dracus carota*		x	x	
Cauliflower	*Brassica oleracea cauliflora*		x	x	
Celery (wild/smallage)	*Apium graveolens*		x	x	
Cherry	*Prunus cerasus*	x	x	x	x
Chestnut	*Castanea sativa*		x	x	x
Chicory	*Cichorium intybus*		x	x	
Chufa	*Cyperus esculentus*		x	x	
Citron	*Citrus medica*		x	x	x
Clover/Trefoil	*Trifolium alexandrinum*		x	x	x
Colewort/cabbage	*Brassica oleracea*		x	x	
Colocasia	*Colocasia antiquorum*		x	x	
Colocynth	*Citrullus colocynthis*		x	x	x
Cordia/Sebesten	*Cordia myxa*		x	x	
Coriander	*Coriandrum sativum*		x	x	
Cornflower	*Centaurea cyanus*		x	x	
Cress	*Lepidium sativum*		x	x	

Common name	Botanical name	Painting	Literature	West	East
Crocus (Saffron)	*Crocus sativus*		x	x	x
Cucumber	*Cucumis sativus*		x	x	x
Cumin	*Cuminum cyminum*		x	x	
Black cumin	*Nigella sativa*		x	x	
Cypress	*Cupressus sempervirens*	x	x	x	x
Date-palm	*Phoenix dactylifera*		x	x	
Delphinium/stavesacre	*Delphinium staphisagria*		x	x	
Dianthus/Pink	*Dianthus* spp.	x	x		x
Dill	*Anethum graveolens*		x	x	
Dragon arum	*Dracunculus vulgaris*		x	x	
Egg-plant/ Aubergine	*Solanum melongena*		x	x	x
Elecampane	*Inula helenium*		x	x	
Endive/chicory	*Cichorium endivia*		x	x	
Fennel	*Foeniculum vulgare*		x	x	
Fenugreek	*Trigonella foenum-graecum*		x	x	
Feverfew	*Chrysanthemum parthenium*		x	x	
Fig	*Ficus carica*		x	x	x
Fumitory	*Fumaria officinalis*		x	x	
Garlic	*Allium sativum*		x	x	x
Germander	*Teucrium chamaedrys*		x	x	
Gourd	*Lagenaria vulgaris*		x	x	
Grape Vine	*Vitis vinifera*		x	x	x
Grapefruit/ Shaddock	*Citrus maxima/ C.grandis*		x	x	
Hartstongue Fern	*Phyllitis scolopendrium*		x	x	
Hawthorn	*Crataegus monogyna*		x	x	
Hazelnut	*Corylus avellana*		x	x	
Henbane	*Hyoscyamus niger*		x	x	
Hibiscus	*Hibiscus rosa-sinensis*	x	x	x	
Hollyhock	*Althaea (Alcea) rosea*	x	x	x	x
Horehound	*Marrubium vulgare*		x	x	
Houseleek	*Aeonium arboreum*		x	x	
Iris	*Iris* spp.	x	x	x	x
Ivy	*Hedera helix*		x	x	
Jasmine (white)	*Jasminum officinale, J.sambac*		x	x	x
Jasmine (yellow)	*Jasminum fruticans*		x	x	
Judas tree	*Cercis siliquastrum*		x	x	x
Jujube	*Zizyphus jujuba*		x	x	x
Juniper	*Juniperus communis*		x	x	x
Lavender	*Lavandula* spp. (inc. *L. stoechas*)		x	x	
Leek	*Allium porrum*		x	x	
Lemon	*Citrus limon*		x	x	
Lentil	*Lens esculenta*		x	x	x
Lettuce	*Lactuca sativa*		x	x	x
Lily	*Lilium candidum*	x	x	x	x
Lucerne	*Medicago sativa*		x	x	
Lupine	*Lupinus albus*		x	x	

Common name	Botanical name	Painting	Literature	West	East
Mallow (garden, shrub, tree, mashmallow)	*Malva neglecta, Hibiscus syriacus, Lavatera arborea, Althaea officinalis*	x	x	x	x
Mandrake	*Mandragora officinarum*		x	x	
Maple	*Acer* spp.		x	x	
Marjoram	*Origanum vulgare*		x	x	
Marjoram (Sweet)	*Origanum majorana*		x	x	
Mastic tree	*Pistacia lentiscus*		x	x	
Medlar	*Mespilus germanica*		x	x	x
Melilot	*Melilotus officinalis*		x	x	
Melon	*Cucumis melo*		x	x	x
Milk-vetch	*Astragalus lusitanicus*		x	x	
Mint	*Mentha* spp.		x	x	
Mulberry (Black)	*Morus nigra*		x	x	x
Mulberry (Silk)	*Morus alba*		x	x	x
Mung bean	*Phaseolus aureus, P.mungo*		x	x	
Mustard	*Sinapis alba*		x	x	
Myrtle	*Myrtus communis*		x	x	
Narcissus	*Narcissus* spp.	x	x	x	x
Nectarine	*Prunus* var. *nucipersica*		x		x
Nettle tree	*Celtis australis*		x	x	
Holm oak	*Quercus ilex*		x	x	
Oleander	*Nerium oleander*		x	x	
Oleaster	*Elaeagnus angustifolia*		x	x	
Olive	*Olea europaea*		x	x	
Onion	*Allium cepa*		x	x	x
Orach	*Atriplex hortensis*		x	x	
Orange (Seville)	*Citrus aurantium*		x	x	x
Oregano	*Origanum vulgare*		x	x	
Parsley	*Petroselinum crispum*		x	x	
Parsnip	*Pastinaca schekakul*		x	x	
Pea	*Pisum sativum*		x	x	
Peach	*Prunus persica*		x	x	x
Pear	*Pyrus communis*		x	x	x
Peony	*Paeonia* spp.	x	x	x	
Periwinkle	*Vinca pervinca, V.minor*		x	x	
Pine	*Pinus pinea*		x	x	x
Pistachio	*Pistacia vera*		x	x	x
Plane	*Platanus orientalis*	x	x	x	x
Plantain	*Plantago* spp.		x	x	
Plum	*Prunus domestica, P.cerasifera*		x	x	x
Pomegranate	*Punica granatum*		x	x	x
Poplar (black & white)	*Populus nigra, P.alba*	x	x	x	x
Poppy	*Papaver somniferum, P.rosea*	x	x	x	x
Privet	*Ligustrum vulgare*		x	x	
Purslane	*Portulaca oleracea*		x	x	
Quince	*Cydonia oblonga*		x	x	x

Common name	Botanical name	Painting	Literature	West	East
Radish	*Raphanus sativus*		x	x	x
Reed	*Arundo donax*		x	x	
Rocket	*Eruca sativa*		x	x	
Rose	*Rosa* spp.	x	x	x	x
Rosemary (*rūmīrū*)	*Rosmarinus officinalis*		x	x	
Rue	*Ruta graveolens*		x	x	
Safflower	*Carthamus tinctorius*		x	x	x
Savory	*Satureia* spp.		x	x	
Service tree	*Sorbus domestica*		x	x	
Sesame	*Sesamum indicum*		x	x	
Southernwood	*Artemisia abrotanum*		x	x	
Spanish broom	*Spartium junceum*		x	x	
Spinach	*Spinacia oleracea*		x	x	x
Squill	*Urginea maritima*		x	x	
Stock	*Matthiola incana*		x	x	x
Strawberry tree	*Arbutus unedo*		x	x	
Sumach	*Rhus coriaria*		x	x	
Sycomore Fig	*Ficus sycomorus*		x	x	
Tamarisk	*Tamarix* spp.		x	x	x
Terebinth	*Pistacia terebinthus*		x	x	
Thyme	*Thymus* spp.		x	x	
Tulip	*Tulipa* spp.		x		x
Turnip	*Brassica rapa*		x	x	
Violet	*Viola odorata*	x	x	x	x
Wallflower	*Cheiranthus cheiri*		x	x	
Walnut	*Juglans regia*		x	x	x
Waterlily	*Nymphaea alba*		x	x	x
Watermelon	*Citrullus vulgaris*		x	x	
Whitebeam	*Sorbus aria*		x	x	
Willow	*Salix* spp.	x	x	x	x
Wormwood	*Artemisia absinthium*		x	x	
Yew	*Taxus baccata*		x	x	

Notes

1. Hamilton, R. W. 'Al-Mafjar, Khirbet,' in *Encyclopedia of Archaeological Excavations in the Holy Land* 3, Oxford, 1977, 754–765; Grabar, O. 'Mafjar, Khirbat Al-', in Meyers, E. M. (ed.) *The Oxford Encyclopedia of Archaeology in the Near East*, Oxford, 1997, 3, 397–399.
2. This site was excavated by Herzfeld (published 1912) and some doubts have been raised about his interpretations.
3. These were: Al Cawthar, a River of Life, Salsabil and Tasnim (Ch. 75).
4. Koran 6: 141.
5. El Faïz, M. 'Horticultural changes and political upheavals in middle-age Andalusia,' in Conan, M. and Kress, J. (eds) *Botanical Progress, Horticultural Innovations and Cultural Changes,'* Dumbarton Oaks, 2007, 120; Ruggles 2000, 18.
6. Al-Maqqari, *Analectes* I, 304, cited by Ruggles 2000, 17.

7. El Faïz,M. 'Horticultural changes and political upheavals in middle-age Andalusia,' in Conan. M. and Kress, J. (eds) *Botanical Progress, Horticultural Innovations and Cultural Changes,*' Dumbarton Oaks, 2007, 120; Sanchez, E. G. and Lopez, A. 'The botanic gardens in Muslim Spain,' in Tzon Sie, L. and deJong, E. (eds) *The Authentic Garden: A symposium on gardens*, Leiden, 1991, 79.

8. Lambton, A. K. S. 'The *Athār wa Ahyā* of Rashīd al-Dīn Fadl Allāh Hamadāni and his contribution as an agronomist, arboriculturist and horticulturalist,' in Amitai-Preiss, R. and Morgan, D. O. (eds) *The Mongol Empire and its Legacy*, Leiden, *c.* 2004, 134.

9. *Waqf-nāma-i Rabʿ-i Rashīdī*, 15, cited by Lambton *c.* 2004, 135.

10. Subtelny, M. E. 'Agriculture and the Timurid *Chaharbagh*: the evidence from a medieval Persian agricultural manual,' in Petruccioli 1997, 110–111.

11. Subtelny, M. E. 'Mīrak-I Sayyid Ghiyās and the Timurid Tradition of Landscape Architecture,' *Studia Iranica* 24, 1995, 20, n.4.

12. Subtelny M. E. 'Agriculture and the Timurid *Chaharbagh*: the evidence from a medieval Persian agricultural manual,' in Petruccioli 1997, 112.

13. Subtelny, M. E. 'Mīrak-I Sayyid Ghiyās and the Timurid Tradition of Landscape Architecture,' *Studia Iranica* 24, 31.

14. *Akhbar majmua* (Ruggles 2000, 40).

15. Garcia, I. L. *et al. Hallazgos Arqueológicos en el Palau de les Corts*, Corts Valencianes, 1994, plan 10, figs 160–161.

16. Ruggles 2000, 81; Ruggles, D. F. 'Madinat al-Zahra', in Shoemaker, C. A. (ed.) *Encyclopedia of Gardens: History and Design*, Vol. 3, London, 2001, 839.

17. Ruggles 2000, 183.

18. Al-Maqqari, *Analectes* I: 371, 374. cited by Ruggles 2000, 210.

19. Al-Maqqari, *Analectes* I: 371, 374. cited by Ruggles 2000, 210.

20. Ruggles 2000, 196–197.

21. Al-Maqqari, *Analectes* I: 384, trans. D. F.Ruggles, in Ruggles 2000, 113–114.

22. Almagro, A. 'An approach to the visual analysis of the gardens of Al-Andalus', in Conan 2007, 65.

23. Acedo, A. C. *The Alhambra and Generalife In Focus*, trans. J. Trout, Granada, 2000,106.

24. Almagro, A. 'An approach to the visual analysis of the gardens of Al-Andalus', in Conan 2007, 69.

25. Navagero, *Viaje* 46, cited by Ruggles 2000, 183.

26. Navagero, *Viaje* 47, cited by Ruggles 2000, 170.

27. Ruggles 2000, 203.

28. Ruggles 2008, 91.

29. 176 are listed by Harvey (1992, 78–82); this included several herbs and crop plants. His list features plants from six individual manuscripts. Ornamental species are listed by Sánchez and Bermejo (in Conan 2007,75–93) taken from eight Andalusian agronomists and botanists.

30. Sánchez, E. G. and Bermejo, E. H. 'Ornamental Plants in Agricultural and Botanical Treatises from Al-Andalus', in Conan 2007, 77.

31. Mentioned by Abu'l-Khayr and Ibn al-Awwäm; Ibn Luyūn said that it was for decoration (Sánchez, E. G. and Bermejo, E. H. 'Ornamental Plants in Agricultural and Botanical Treatises from Al-Andalus', in Conan 2007, 79).

32. Sánchez, E. G. and Bermejo, E. H. 'Ornamental Plants in Agricultural and Botanical Treatises from Al-Andalus', in Conan 2007, 78.

33. Grabar, O. *The Alhambra*, London, 1978, 123.

34. El Faïz, M. 'The garden strategy of the Almohad Sultans and their successors (1157–1900),' in Conan 2007, 96.

35. Rawls, W. (ed.) *Gardens Through History, Nature Perfected*, New York, 1991, 73.

36. Firdausi, *Shahnama*, trans. D. N. Wiber; in Wilber 1979, 17.

37. Hafiz, 191, trans. K. H. Shaida, Charlestown, 2010.

38. Hafiz, trans. D. N. Wiber; in Wilber 1979, 17.

39. Sa'di, *The Rose-Garden of Shekh Muslihu'd-Din Sadi of Shiraz*, trans. E. B. Eastwick, 1979, 14.

40. Sa'di, *The Rose-Garden of Shekh Muslihu'd-Din Sadi of Shiraz*, trans. E. B. Eastwick, 1979, 13.

41. Omar Khayam, *Rubáiyát* 5, trans. E. Fitzgerald, London, 1995.

42. Omar Khayam, *Rubáiyát* 18, trans. E. Fitzgerald, London, 1995.

43. Subtelny, M. E. 'Visionary rose: metaphorical interpretation of horticultural practise in medieval Persian mysticism,' in Conan. M. and Kress, J. (eds) *Botanical Progress, Horticultural Innovations and Cultural Changes*,' Dumbarton Oaks, 2007, 14–15.

44. Wilber 1979, 6.

45. Nizami, *Khamseh, Iqbalnama*, trans. H. Wilberforce-Clarke. Cited in N. M. Titley, London, 1979, 6.

46. Wilber 1979, 26.

47. Wilber 1979, 28.

48. Subtelny, M. E. 'Agriculture and the Timurid *Chaharbagh*: the evidence from a medieval Persian agricultural manual,' in Petruccioli 1997, 117; Subtelny, M. E. 'Mīrak-I Sayyid Ghiyās and the Timurid Tradition of Landscape Architecture,' *Studia Iranica* 24, 39–45.

49. Subtelny, M. E. 'Agriculture and the Timurid *Chaharbagh*: the evidence from a medieval Persian agricultural manual,' in Petruccioli 1997, 118.

50. Ruggles, private communication.

51. Moynihan 1979, 75.

52. Moynihan 1979, 52.

53. Subtelny, M. E. 'Mīrak-I Sayyid Ghiyās and the Timurid Tradition of Landscape Architecture,' *Studia Iranica* 2, 39–40; c.f. Ball. W. 'The remains of a monumental Timurid garden outside Herat,' *East and West* 31(1–4), 1981, 79–82.

54. Moynihan 1979, 52.

55. Hobhouse, P. *Gardens of Persia*, London, 2003, 94.

56. Titley 1979, 24.

57. Trans. A. S. Beveridge, The *Babur-Nama in English*, London, 1969, 208–209.

58. It is now a UNESCO site; cf. UNESCO website, World Heritage Centre.

CHAPTER NINE

Medieval Gardens

When the Western Roman Empire crumbled in the early years of the 5th century AD Britain and western Europe entered the so-called Dark Ages. In general towns shrank and lost their earlier importance, some were abandoned. In southern Europe Christianity and the Christian Church organisation continued to develop and maintain a place in the new political structures that developed, and Christian leaders were still figures of authority especially after immigrant barbarian groups adopted Christianity. Latin continued to be used as the language of Church literature.

Apparently the royal and noble families of the Goths and Franks came to appreciate certain aspects of the earlier cultured society, and this appears to have included a respect for a fine pleasure garden. One of the earliest recorded gardens of the Post-Roman period is mentioned in the verses of Venatius Fortunus (530–609) who said that one of the widowed queens of the Franks created a convent garden, near Poitiers, in which there were fruit trees. He specifies 'an apple and a tall pear.'[1] Another garden near Paris was apparently noted for its fragrant roses.

Sources

Apart from archaeology, evidence for gardens in this period is found in Church documents, contemporary literature, herbal books, illuminated manuscripts, tapestries and embroideries. A number of Herbals and lists of garden/medicinal plants have survived from this period including that made for Charlemagne (800), the St Gall Monastery list of 820, Walafrid the monk (840), Aelfic (995), Hildegard of Bingen (1150), Garlande (1225), Albertus Magnus (1260), Crescentiis (1305), Friar Henry Daniel (1375) and Jon Gardener (1400). John Harvey in his book on *Mediaeval Gardens* compiled all of these into a table listing over 250 species of garden plants. In this period many of these plants were in fact herbs, for medicinal use, but some were also included into a garden so that there would be a supply of scented flowers and foliage to use when strewing on floors (to freshen the air inside buildings). In secular society there was over time a greater interest in possessing decorative plants, these will be mentioned later. Medieval Herbals often contained drawings of the plants, mainly for identification purposes, and many were based on the earlier works of Dioscorides, and especially Apuleius Platonicus.

Arabic and Classical texts were also studied, and a monk at Monte Cassino, Constantine the African (1020–1087) is known for his translation of a number of Arabic medical and herbal texts into Latin, these were instrumental in reintroducing knowledge. In England Gilbertus Angelicus wrote his *Compendium* (*c*.1230) which was the first English text to incorporate some of these Arab authorities. But from the 12th century onwards there was a renewed interest in Classical manuscripts; they were studied in depth and many were translated. Among these were the Latin works of Pliny the Elder, Cato, Varro, Columella and Palladius. Palladius was translated into medieval English *c*.1420, this was a popular edition often called the Colchester Palladius.[2]

Bishop Isidore of Seville (d. 636) wrote a book called *Etymologies*, a work that was partly encyclopaedic and a lexicon combined, containing origins of particular words. The 17th chapter of this book was concerned with 'rural matters' that included over 200 plant names of trees, herbs, vegetables and aromatics. Some entries are longer than others, this is one of the shortest: 'French lavender (*stoechas*) grows on the Stoachades islands, whence it is named.'[3] These are the French Iles d'Hyères near Marseille.[4] Nineteen vegetables are mentioned by Isidore including: 'The carrot (*pastinaca*) is so called because its root is an excellent nourishment (*pastus*) for humans, for it has a pleasant aroma and is delectable as a food.'[5]

Medieval patron saints of gardeners

St Dorothy was a virgin who was martyred *c*.303; her feast day is on 6 February. She came from Caesarea in Cappodocia. On her way to be executed (under Diocletian) a lawyer named Theophilus mocked her, suggesting that she could send him flowers and fruit from the heavenly garden. Miraculously a child then appeared with a basket of apples and roses, which Dorothy gave to Theophilus. Thereafter Dorothy's emblem in art was a laden basket.

St Maurilius came from Milan; where he studied under St Ambrose. Apparently he followed St Martin to Tours, in France, and was ordained by St Martin. Maurilius (or Maurille, which is his French name) was sent to Chalons to convert the heathens there; afterwards he was made Bishop of Angers, but he felt that this was too great an honour for him so he fled incognito to Britain. Maurilius wore humble clothes and presented himself to one of the British rulers, requesting to serve as a gardener. He continued until a visitor to court recognised him, and he was persuaded to return to his Bishopric in Angers. St Maurilius is depicted in a celebrated tapestry from Angers, in France dated 1460. In the tapestry he wears a violet-coloured robe, and is working with a long-handled spade. An enclosure garden nearby is planted with fruit trees, gooseberry bushes and a small bed of flowers.

St Fiacre was a hermit who lived around the 7th century. His feast day is celebrated on 1 September. He was originally from Ireland, but went to Meaux in France where he built a hermitage. He was known for the fine vegetables he grew around his humble abode; a spade is used as his emblem in art.

Monastic gardens

Evidence suggests that a form of Roman-style garden appears to have survived, but in a completely different context within monasteries. The square/rectangular columned cloister formed a garden enclosure that harkens back to the Classical peristyle garden. In fact these can be dated from as early as *c*.560, for within the Monastic Rules of St Isidore (Bishop of Seville), there was a stipulation to have such a garden. In Britain these gardens were often called a cloister garth. Many cloister gardens can still be seen next to cathedrals or within monasteries throughout Europe; they often have a well in the centre, as at Gerona in northern Spain. An alternative was to place the well in one corner of the garden. Space was also reserved for a herbarium, where medicinal herbs could be cultivated to provide remedies that could relieve sick monks and lay people.

During the 7th century the rule of St Benedict became established throughout the west, and he initiated not only the desire for self sufficiency, within the monastic community, but also that there should be areas/gardens where monks could go for privacy, study or contemplation.

Documents giving details of monastic gardens

A plan for the monastery of St Gall, Switzerland (*c*.820) has survived and this gives a good indication of what these early establishments comprised, especially as all of the buildings are named. This plan is a valuable tool for reconstructing the actual appearance of early medieval monastic gardens. The monastery church was unusually designed with an apse at either end. The cloister garden (marked A) is adjacent to the Church, the surrounding covered walkways gave access to the monks dormitories, refectory and cellar. The colonnades/porticoes of the cloister are represented on the map as a number of arches. Four taller arches in the centre of each row mark the main points of entry into the garden. It is noticeable that four paths form a quadripartite plan, here they led to a fountain or well in the centre of the garden.

The buildings of the monastery were well spaced, and those that were directly associated with garden areas are located on the top portion of this plan. Starting from the left the monastery provided a separate house for a physician, which was close to his physic garden (marked B). Here 16 rectangular plant beds were labelled to indicate which plant species should be grown there, each species was given a separate bed. In the eight plant beds in the centre there were: sage, mustard, rue, cumin, gladiolus/iris, lovage, pennyroyal and fennel. Then, to save wasting space, plant beds were also made alongside the walls of the physic garden, these contained: mint, rosemary, fenugreek, costmary, savory, beans,

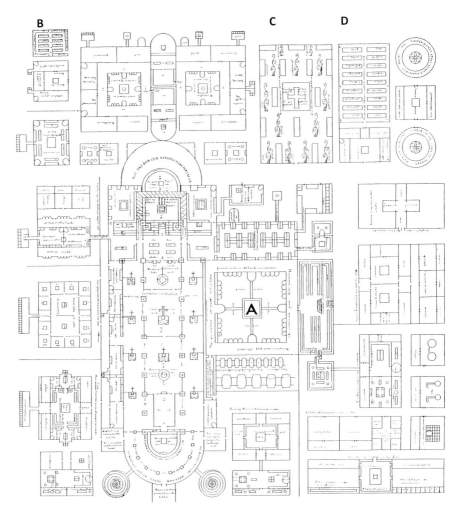

FIGURE 140. Part of the plan of the monastic gardens at St Gall, Switzerland, *c*.AD 820. The cloister garden is marked (A), the physician's house and garden is located top right (B), the cemetery with its orchard trees (C) had 15 fruit and nut trees in it: apple, pear, medlar, mulberry, peach, plum, quince, service tree, bay, almond, chestnut, fig, hazelnut and walnut. The next building (D) was the lodgings of the gardener, positioned close to his vegetable plot (after Gothein 1966).

rose and lilies. An infirmary was conveniently sited next to the physic garden. This building was provided with smaller cloister gardens; these were necessary to bring clean fresh air to very ill patients. The cemetery was located nearby (C) this would be well kept and made pleasant by being in an orchard garden setting. Thirteen trees were schematically drawn in this orchard, of which there were: apple, pear, mulberry, peach, plum, service, medlar, chestnut, fig, quince, hazel, almond and walnut. The next building was reserved for the gardener, who would be close to the large vegetable garden under his care (D) which is referred to as a *hortus*. Like the physic garden, cultivation of vegetables took place within rectangular plant beds aligned in two rows. Fortunately, as in the physic garden, all the plant beds in the vegetable garden were labelled in Latin. There were: onions, garlic, leeks, shallots, celery, parsley, coriander, chervil, dill, lettuce, poppy, savory, radish, parsnip, carrot, cabbage, beet and an unrecognisable species. These show a good range of plants were grown that could supply the needs of the community, both medicinally and for sustenance.

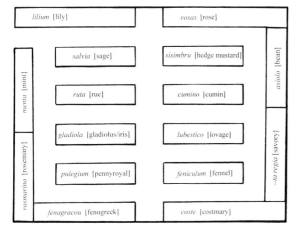

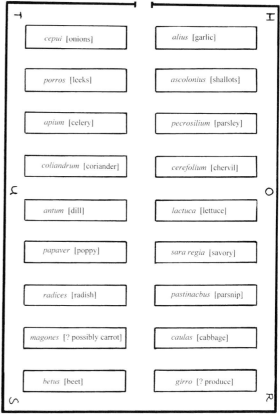

FIGURE 141 *(above)*. The Physic garden at St Gall. Individual plant beds are drawn and labelled indicating the plants used at that time.

FIGURE 142 *(right)*. Eighteen plant beds in the vegetable garden at St Gall (*c*.AD 820).

Of necessity other plants would have been cultivated, or were gathered, outside the confines of the monastery. Lay brothers would have toiled in these areas for the benefit of the cloistered community.

Details of another important garden survives in a descriptive poem about an abbot's little garden (which he called a *Hortulus*). The garden was made by Abbot Walafrid Strabo *c*. 840, of the Benedictine Abbey of Reichenau in southern Germany. Again each species of plant was planted into individual rectangular beds; there were 24 of them in all. The plant beds around the perimeter of the *hortulus* were occupied by: poppy, lily, rose, radish, calamint, ?ambrosia, agrimony, betony, clary, costus, horehound, wormwood, marrow, gourd, mint and southernwood. The central beds contained: sage, chervil, rue, parsley, gladiolus, lovage, pennyroyal and fennel. The accompanying text is full of interesting observations on the plants and contemporary horticulture, the following excerpt sheds light on aspects of Walafrid's garden:

> I plant my seeds and the kindly dew moistens them. Should drought prevail, I must water it, letting the drops fall through my fingers, for the impetus of a full stream from the water pot would disturb my seedlings. Part of my garden is hard and dry under the shadow of a roof; in another part a high brick wall robs it of air and sun. even here something will at last succeed! ...[6]

Another passage dwells on the virtues of roses and lilies above all other flowers to decorate the church. We must not forget that monasteries also liked to cultivate a variety of decorative flowers that could be picked for decorating the Lady Chapel. Scented flowers and foliage were also needed to strew onto the floors of churches, to combat the rather rancid smell of the populace, and especially of the sick coming to monasteries hoping for a cure.

In England a plan was made for Prior Wibert (*c*.1165) of the Benedictine monastery and cathedral at Canterbury. This plan included little drawings of stylised flowers in garden areas. One corner of the enclosure had been selected for the monk's cemetery, which again was also an orchard. But within this area there was a large decoratively shaped fishpond (labelled *piscina*) thereby turning this relatively sombre site into a pleasant area for contemplation. The fishpond may have had an ornamental appearance, but it was large enough to supply a stock of fish as an alternative food source. The route of a number of water conduits are shown on the plan, leading to and from the pool, a well, and to the herb garden (*herbarium*) and large cloister garth. The plan shows that the herbarium appears to have been bordered, by a pergola-like trellis.

Accounts from Glastonbury Abbey reveal that the gardens supplying the Abbey had 23 plant beds of leeks, other beds were devoted to garlic, onions, beans, herbs, madder, flax and hemp.[7]

Monastic gardens discovered by archaeology

At Haverfordwest Priory in Wales excavations have revealed a large garden of about 50 × 20 m. The garden was arranged symmetrically and paths subdivided the garden into four pairs of large rectangular bedding areas of unequal size, each were bordered by low walls.[8] One of the plots was more differentiated by having a form of an arbour fitted into the centre, with a path leading to it from the lodging.

Different requirements were needed for monks of the Carthusian order. These monks belonged to a silent order that chose to live communally, but separate. Therefore each monk's cell was accompanied by its own walled garden to promote prayer and minimise distractions from contact with others. The remains of a 14th century Carthusian Monastery has been discovered at Coventry, in central England, and at Mount Grace in Yorkshire. In such establishments the monks cells are like a detached two-storey house sited at one corner of its individual garden plot, but all the houses were arranged around a large open cloistered garden. Each monk could tend his own garden, and it depended on the individual if he chose to cultivate it for growing vegetables and herbs, or if he wanted to make a more decorative garden, both were allowed. Food was brought to each monk, so they did not need to be self sufficient from their own gardens. The provision of garden spaces allowed monks fresh air, and did not compromise their self-imposed solitude. At Coventry there are thought to have been thirteen monk's cells with garden plots.[9] Archaeologists found that the monk's gardens were approximately 14.3 m (16 yd) long and 10.9 m (12 yd) wide, and they discovered paths and roof tiles used as edging for raised plant beds.[10] At Mount Grace there were fifteen individual monk's gardens, one of which has been reconstructed. Sadly, there are no botanical records to indicate how the gardens were planted.

During the excavations at the Dominican Priory in Oxford however, evidence from the 15th-century drains has provided some information on what the nearby gardens would have contained. The species discovered there included: marigold, opium poppy, henbane, greater celandine, wild strawberry, black mustard, box, walnut, apple, cherry, pear, plum and almond.[11] The excavator notes that some of these may have originated from a physic garden, but the finding of box could imply a more ornamental area. It is impossible to tell however if the fruits came from their own orchards, or had been purchased from elsewhere.

Rustic gardens

In this period a garden could be defined as being an area that could be dug with a spade, as opposed to using a plough. In rural areas people carefully tended plots close to their house, where the womenfolk could look after the small kitchen garden while their menfolk worked in the fields. Evidence from deserted medieval villages in England has shed some light on these otherwise unrecorded humble abodes. Many peasant house and garden plots (and especially those at Wharram Percy, in Yorkshire, which was extensively studied by archaeologists) appear to have been defined by ditches and banks topped by hawthorn hedges, an alternative was to surround the plot with a rustic fence. Paths were generally narrow and made of beaten earth; paving would have been too costly. One of the common names for an Anglo-Saxon peasant garden gives an insight into the main crop grown there. Their '*leac tun*' was primarily a leek garden, although it would not necessarily be the sole vegetable grown there. Leeks can be cropped one at a time when you are ready for them, so this invaluable crop would last throughout the lean winter and early spring months. Leek beds would not have been swept clear of weeds though (as we do today) because some garden weeds are edible, and might have been left as a secondary crop to add variety to their diet (*e.g.* fat hen, chickweed and dandelion). At the Weald and Downland Open Air Museum, in southern England one such rustic garden has been recreated beside a humble

FIGURE 143. Recreated rustic garden at the Weald and Downland Open Air Museum.

cottage, and this is helpful to visualise how such gardens could have appeared. Nearby, there is a yeoman's house, called 'Bayleaf', with a correspondingly larger garden plot. Bayleaf was also given an orchard, and a hazel coppice that could be cropped regularly to provide a good supply of withies to make fencing and basketry.

Urban gardens

Many English towns and villages were laid out with long narrow burgage plots that provided substantial land to the rear of the house. Apart from a working and storage area, there could have been space for a kitchen garden,[12] in some cases a small orchard, and the ubiquitous pigsty. The plots varied in length depending on the character of the town, but at Eynsham, a new borough created in 1215, the plots were between a quarter of an acre and an acre (0.1–0.4 ha).[13] The rear yards could be separated by ditches, fences or hedges. Two interesting court cases at Bradford came about because one man had enclosed his plot and another had not.[14] In the former, Adam Notebroun (in 1342) had damaged his neighbour's crops of herbs and peas when he laid down a hedge. In the latter, Robert Dikson's pigs escaped and ate his neighbour's herbs, leeks and grass! Fortunately a bird's eye plan of the village of Wilton survives. Although this is later in date (mid-16th century), it can still provide relevant information as it illustrates how the plots were laid out and this could reflect earlier practices.[15] Hedges appear to separate the plots, some of the enclosures were filled with trees indicating orchards, but the majority of plots were filled with rows of rectangular plant beds reminiscent of those seen in monastic contexts.

Villages and towns naturally expand and the density of occupation increases, and over the centuries redevelopment occurs obscuring evidence for the use of former burgage plots and their gardens. However, archaeological excavations in urban areas have discovered surviving plant material because it had either been charred (from waste disposal) or had become mineralised due to its deposition in a cesspit. At Chester seeds of chamomile, fennel, leek and poppy were uncovered from a former cesspit.[16] At the Deansway site at Worcester a wide range of plant species was discovered. Apple and celery were from mineralised deposits, but the majority were charred remains, they included cereals, grasses and weeds. Some of the following plants could have grown in the garden plots nearby or were brought to the site from elsewhere: opium poppy, flax, vetch, broad bean, pea, blackberry, raspberry, strawberry, sloe, bullace, apple, pear, hazel, fig, buttercup, greater celandine, fumatory, mustard, radish, sweet violet, campion, chickweed, fat hen, mallow, holly, gorse, clover, hawthorn, hemlock, pimpernel, henbane, mint, plantain, elder, ragwort, mayweed, corn marigold, cornflower.[17] The finding of sweet violet (*viola odorata*), a popular medieval plant, was particularly interesting as it is considered a decorative plant for gardens.[18] These give indirect evidence for the presence of gardens in the area.

Names for a garden, orchard and gardeners

The Old Norman-French word *gardin* (mod. French *jardin*) is the root of our own word garden. Another term encountered in this period is the Middle English *erber* mainly used for a small garden area, and this derives from the herber or Herbarium – the herb garden. Wortes (or *wyrt*) was the Old English word for vegetables, and these could be grown in a *leac tun* mentioned above. Interestingly the Anglo Saxon word for a gardener was *leac-ward*, other names were corruptions of Latin, such as: gardinarius, hortolanus and ortolanus, all three are found in documents of the period.

Our word orchard derives from the Old English *ortgeard* meaning an ort yard. The 'ort' section of this word originated from the old Roman name for a garden *hortus*, a word that was still current at that time in monasteries and other Latin speaking households. There was, however, another word used to denote an orchard and this was Latin: *pomarium*, by definition it was an area of fruit trees. But to the French *pomme* is specifically an apple. Some orchards did have only apple trees, such as the 139 ordered for Cuxham manor in Oxfordshire, but other orchards may have been solely stocked with cherries or pear trees.[19] We hear that Henry III had 100 pear trees planted for Rosamund's Bower in 1268.[20] Necham (1157–1217) mentions a new form of pear, the pear of St Règle, which was introduced from France.[21] Another 'new' pear was produced by the Cistercian monks of Wardon, in Bedfordshire, this was ideal for baking and has survived the test of time. Of the varieties of apple grown at that time the Costard and Pearmain were well recorded and are still known today. Apparently in some places an annual rent to be paid in kind was calculated in fruit, such as at Runham in Norfolk where, in 1204, 200 pearmain apples and four firkins of apple-wine (made from pearmains) was duly paid.[22]

According to surviving palace records, transactions indicate that fruit trees and other plants were sourced from nursery gardens, often supplying large numbers such as the 100 cherry trees destined for Westminster Palace in 1277. Three quince trees and two peach trees apparently cost 3 shillings, whereas the purchase of a quart of lily bulbs amounted to 1 shilling.[23] These were sourced by the aptly named William le Gardener. William also appears to have worked on the gardens at the Tower of London where he was given a wage of 3 pence per day (1262–1278), whereas Roger le Herberur working at Westminster Palace received 2¼ pence a day (1268–1286).[24] Grafted trees were also required and some of these were supplied by John le Fruter. There must have been a number of growers to supply the numbers of plants required. The names of other medieval gardeners have survived in the documents relating to royal houses. The work of some is specified, such as John Heydon, the keeper of the King's garden at Windsor who was given 6 pence a day for life in 1390. In contrast women were sometimes employed to weed plant beds and were given up to 2½ pence per day.[25] A number of gardeners (William, John, Edmund, Thomas, Robert and Alan) had been given a simple surname Gardener or Gardyner, and of these one was later known as Mayster Jon Gardener who wrote the *Feate of Gardeninge* a book on horticulture composed before 1350.[26]

The *hortus conclusus* form of garden

The *hortus conclusus*, meaning an enclosed garden, was a particularly attractive feature of medieval courtly life, more often in association with a castle or manor. Wherever possible space was found within the confines of a castle or outer bailey for a small garden enclosure where the ladies of the court could spend time outside and enjoy the fresh air emanating from plants growing there. The enclosure would serve to protect the ladies within from the lewd glances of soldiery. In 1250 Henry III of England requested the creation of a royal *hortus conclusus* garden for his queen, at Woodstock. It was stipulated that the garden (here termed a herbary) should be walled: 'well built and high with a good herbary in which the same Queen may be able to disport herself; and a gate from the herbary next the chapel of Edward our son, into the aforesaid garden.'[27]

It appears that two years later the herbary was turfed, perhaps so that long gowns would not be spoilt by clods of damp earth. The garden would have contained an arbour or seating of some kind that could have provided a pleasant area for the queen to sit and enjoy the verdant setting in the garden. It could be a welcoming quiet secluded place to rest, or entertain her ladies. The arbour or bower could be made of withies, or wood. A trellis fence or a pergola could partition a section within the garden, the framework would allow climbing plants such as vines, roses, eglantine or woodbine to clamber up. Both red and white roses are seen in contemporary illustrations.

FIGURE 144. Details of a *hortus conclusus* enclosed by a lattice fence. The garden's elements are labelled, the fence, fountain and plants: lily, rose and olive tree, Grimani Breviary, *c.*AD 1510.

Depiction of a *hortus conclusus*

One of the earliest illustrations of a medieval *hortus conclusus* is in an illuminated manuscript (of *c.*1400) detailing Marco Polo's travels. The scene in question shows a king and queen playing chess in their castle garden. This is a rather simplistic scene, where the garden is simply a turfed area with a plant filled linear border running alongside a picket fence. A more enlightening illustration is found in the Grimani Breviary, which is of a slightly later date (*c.*1510) but it shows many features that would be found in courtly enclosure gardens. Gardens were fitted into spaces within fortifications, but on occasion, perhaps where space was limited or the soil was poor, gardens were created a short distance away on more fertile ground. The scene in the Grimani Breviary shows one of these; the castle, where the owner lived, is shown on the top of a hill. It would have been a pleasant journey down from the castle to spend an afternoon in the garden below. The garden was created on good fertile land, and a well (marked *aquarum*) highlights the main water source for the garden plants. All the features are labelled, and in the foreground the light wooden lattice fence carries those illuminating words: *Ortus Conclusus*. Here the 'H' of hortus is omitted, but the meaning is the same. Within the '*Ortus Conclusus*' two plants were distinguished above others and are named, the rose and the lily, both highly valued for their rich scent. One tree outside the enclosed garden was identified as *olive speciosa*, it was obviously a prized specimen, but olives do not normally grow in northerly climes. Within the garden there is a decorative fountain marked *Fons Ortorum*; it is of a type fashionable at that time where two or four streams of water trickle down into a shallow quatrelobe basin below.

Hidden Christian messages were often sought from objects and one poet, Guillaume de Machaut in the *Laye de la Fonteinne* (*c.*1350), suggested that the medieval fountain could epitomize the Trinity. He saw that fountains comprised three parts, of a whole. These were: the 'spout' the source of the water, and the 'stream' the water flowing down, and finally the 'bowl' which received the water. These 'three parts' can be seen in the fountain illustrated in the Grimani Breviary and many other fountains of this period.

Archaeological discovery of a *hortus conclusus*

At Whittington Castle in Shropshire, a ditched garden enclosure was created near the outer bailey, creating a private area surrounded by a moat, dating to *c.*1315–1336. Documents mentioned a garden here with fruits, herbage and a dovecote, and after geophysical surveys of the area a 5 m high viewing mound was found to be in alignment with the garden. The mound would have appeared to be an island partly surrounded by the moated ditches of the garden.[28] This mound is believed to be one of the earliest surviving of its kind, however we hear that a mound was built in 1302 and a tower 'in the bower yard' by Henry de Bray a courtier to Edward I at Harlestone in Northamptonshire.[29] Clearly this was intended as a pleasure garden. Henry had built a new grange and garden in 1292, and called it the 'New Yerde', there was also a walled herber or *hortus conclusus*, fishponds and a dovecote.[30] Apparently in 1297 to make the herb garden and build its walls cost 62 shillings and 4 pence, compared to the 46 shillings and 8 pence for constructing a 'dove-house in the corner of the herb garden' a few years later in 1303.[31]

A special detached garden was created at Kenilworth in Warwickshire by Henry V (in 1414–1417). For security the garden (called The Pleasance) was surrounded by two moats, effectively making it like an island at the edge of the Great Pool. The garden could only be approached by boat across this great expanse of water. The Pleasance covered an area of 2½ acres (*c*.1 ha). References mention a banqueting room on this site, and seven gardeners working in the pleasance and six on the '*aleyes*', the paths lined with trees.[32] The Pleasance would have been a wonderful secure place to relax in, and somewhere slightly exotic in which to take the air. The moated garden at Kenilworth was not an isolated case; there was a precedent. A Herbarium, again with double moats (and in this case a bridge) was made for Abbot Godfrey of Crowland in 1302 at Peterborough. It was a comparable size, two acres (0.8 ha), and apparently it cost the princely sum of £25. The moat would have been stocked with fish.

Medieval stew ponds

A 'stew' was basically a pond for keeping fish, it derived from the Old French word *estui* (meaning to shut up). Royal and manorial estates, as well as monastic complexes, and villages, also had one or more stew ponds that could provide yet another source of food, especially in winter months. Also, fish were needed on a regular basis for meals on Fridays and on days of fasting, so the river fish stocked in these ponds would make a change from salted sea fish. The earthworks and dam are often all that survives of the ponds, but on occasion archaeologists do discover the remains of fish. An example is at Bredwardine in Herefordshire, where scales of perch were found in the silt accumulation at the bottom of the pool.[33] More species are documented as stock in medieval ponds, and there is an interesting case which provides ample evidence. A felon from Solihull was tried at Warwick courts in 1361 for stealing 40 pike, 40 bream, 40 tench, 100 perch, 100 roach and 200 eels.[34] The pond must have been a large well stocked one! A survey of fishponds in Warwickshire has shown that ponds were created at numerous sites and at times multiple stew ponds were created, such as at the granges at Bockendon and Cryfield. Bockendon had four fish ponds and Cryfield had three, the lowest dam of the latter was apparently *c*.1.5 m high.[35] One of a series of rare surviving medieval frescoes in the Pope's Palace at Avignon (1343) depicts a stew pond. The frescoes illustrate the popular themes of hunting and fishing on an estate, and each of these lively scenes have several members of the household staff taking part. The wall featuring the fishpond shows a rectangular shaped pool edged in white stone. Two men carry nets while another throws bait to attract the fish towards them. In general such stew ponds were much larger than this example; but owing to limited space on the wall it had to be painted on a reduced scale, it is still likely to be representative of larger fishponds seen elsewhere.

Depictions of medieval garden features

Many medieval paintings, and miniatures in manuscripts, depict Biblical topics and traditionally the first miniature painting in a religious Genesis Book would feature the Tree of Jesse which would be shown in the form of a tree, or vine-tree, emerging from the reclining figure of Jesse. The tree's branches sport vignettes of Christ's ancestors and family. Another theme often featured is the Biblical Garden of Eden and Paradise, which are often depicted as a walled *hortus conclusus*; the central image being of Adam and Eve standing on either side of the tree of life/knowledge. On occasion flowers at its base give the impression of Paradise.

Many medieval paintings from the Low Countries were made to celebrate the Madonna and Child, and interestingly the artist often set them in a room with a garden scene in the background. In the Flemish painting by the Master of Blicks and St Gudule (1470) the room had a columned opening leading directly onto the *hortus conclusus* which is clearly enclosed by a crenelated wall. This garden with its rectangular plant beds was evidently within a castle. During the 14th–15th centuries the emergent class of burgers also started to develop their own pleasure gardens.

Paintings and illuminations from manuscripts depict other features that could be seen in a *hortus conclusus*. You would perhaps find a pergola, as seen in the walled garden of a manor or dower house in the *Très Riches Heures* manuscript, which featured in the illumination for the month of April. Along the rear of the garden and along the sidewall there was a long continuous pergola. In this season the trellis is bare, but in a few months' time the trellis would form a shady vine covered tunnel for promenades. What is also visible is the way that some medieval lawns were subdivided into a checkerboard-like design, where squares of green lawn alternated with square earth filled plant beds. Some squares contained fruit trees, and as this scene is representative of April the trees are shown in full blossom.

A pergola/arbour is beautifully depicted in a painting of the Madonna, by Lucas Cranach, who places her on a seat under its shade, the arch of the pergola provides a fitting frame to highlight this holy figure. The trelliswork supports a fruitful grapevine, with large luscious bunches of grapes hanging down. This painting is so well executed that the details of the arbour's construction is plain to see. The wooden spars have all been carefully tied together with withies rather than nails. This painting, like many others of this period, shows that for pergolas

FIGURE 145. Detail showing a walled *hortus conclusus* of a manor or dower house, containing a tunnel pergola and a checkerboard layout in the garden. Squares of turf alternate with plant beds. As this page represents the month of April trees are shown in full blossom, *Très Riches Heures* manuscript, *c*.AD 1411–1416.

and tall trellises people favoured a design with squared apertures (unlike the diamond pattern favoured during the Roman period). However, it seems that a diamond pattern was still preferable for decorative low lattice fences. For a more utilitarian barrier withies were interwoven to make a wattle fence.

Many medieval gardens would have been furnished with a wooden bench or an occasional chair sited within the garden, but in this period a turfed seat was quite popular, and these were permanent fixtures in the garden. The painting by Cranach (mentioned above) showed that in some cases the earth filled seat could be held in place with wooden boards. Or alternatively the soil and turf was retained by a brick wall, as seen in a Flemish painting (attributed to the School of Dieric Bouts) where the Madonna is seated on one. This turf seat was U shaped, making it reminiscent of the three-sided outdoor dining couches of Roman times. Turf seats were narrow and were intended for sitting upon, rather than reclining, but they still enabled several people to sit and converse together. In this case the *hortus conclusus* was created between a manor house and its surrounding moat. In the painting by the Master of Blicks and St Gudule a columned entrance of the manor opened onto the gardens. The garden was split into two sections, the secluded seating area with the Madonna was in the foreground, a little gate shut off this private area. The rest of the garden contained raised brick edged plant beds. A peacock stands on one of the outer garden walls giving an exotic touch, and was probably a prize possession of that household. The peacock was a symbol of incorruptibility in art and its inclusion here may also have been as a reference to the Virgin.

In the miniature from the *Roman de Renaud de Montauban* the garden is shown as a place where you could dally in courtly love. But in this case Maugis and La belle Oriande are seated on the lawn with their backs leaning against the U shaped brick-edged turf seat. On the right is an ornamental fountain, and their faithful pet dog lies down on the grass but remains alert; dogs were always symbolic of fidelity. As in the previous painting the lattice fenced *hortus conclusus* was created in the outer bailey of the castle, as were many discovered by archaeological means (such as at Whittington mentioned previously). Two decorative pottery containers have been placed onto the turf seat. In one we see a carefully clipped tree, the other is full of red carnations supported by a network of twigs. The carnations were obviously placed there so that their scent would more easily be appreciated.

Several illuminations in manuscripts show carnations, and sweet scented stocks, in a container of some kind be it pottery, earthenware, metal, or a wicker basket. Both species are seen in border designs of the Bedford *Hours*, notably on folio 227v. Both carnation and stocks were highly valued for their strong scent and as we have seen above, they were often brought close to seating areas in a medieval garden, where the blooms scent, and beauty, could be appreciated more closely. Carnations had recently been introduced into northern Europe and there would have been a cachet in owning these valuable plants therefore the patron could well have requested their inclusion in the manuscript painting.

FIGURE 146. Maugis and La belle Oriande in a scene of courtly love in a garden, seated on the grass leaning against a turf seat. Two ceramic pots with carefully staked carnations and a dwarf clipped tree have been placed on the seat so that they can be better admired, *Roman de Renaud de Montauban*. Ms 5072f.71v The Garden of Love, from the Renaud de Montauban Cycle (vellum), Liedet, Loyset (fl. 1448–78)/ Biblioteque de l'Arsenal, Paris, France/Giraudon/ The Bridgeman Art Library.

Other plants, and bushes, were staked and trained to grow through a supporting frame, as shown in several 15th century well illustrated versions of the horticultural book *Liber ruralium commodorum*, written by Crescenzi *c.*1304–1309. One method was to use a cartwheel-like frame that allowed blooms to remain upright. A frame was also used to attach shoots of bushes so that they would grow into the desired shape. When clipping bushes and selected small trees the medieval topiarist favoured forming three tiers of greenery.

Depictions of medieval gardeners and tools

Manuscripts are a mine of information because many also contain little drawings in the margins or border. Sometimes agri/horticultural workers are depicted in scenes in the *bas de page* (foot of the page); a good example is in an 11th century manuscript in the British Library[36] where men labour with much vigour. On the left one raises his arms so that he has more force when wielding his mattock to break the ground. The next man applies his foot to a spade, another sows seed, while the next rakes the soil over the cast seed. These illustrate all the stages of preparing the ground for vegetables or other crops.

Gardeners are on occasion included in tapestries, and an example is the 12th-

FIGURE 147. Violets
growing in the *bas
de page* scene, with a
rinceaux border around
a miniature depicting
the Madonna and Child
seated on a turf seat in
their Paradise garden, in
front of a tunnel pergola
of roses, French Book
of Hours (© British
Library Board. All Rights
Reserved. Add. MS 31835
f.27), *c.*AD 1430.

century Romanesque tapestry in Gerona Cathedral (Spain) depicting scenes of
the creation accompanied with a calendar of the agricultural year. To illustrate
the month of April (*Aprilis*) a serf guides his pair of mules to plough a field/
hortus plot, with a tree in the background. Another square represents the main
activity of the season of Autumn, so here a vine dresser raises his pruning
hook to pluck a bunch of ripe grapes from the twisting vine. The style of this
particular scene is curiously reminiscent of those in late antique mosaics.

Most of the gardeners within miniature paintings show workmen, either
bending down to plant seedlings, or digging the plant beds. Often the spades
they use appear to have a cross handle, and some have a metal spade shoe, as in
the stained glass window in Canterbury Cathedral that depicts Adam toiling in
the garden after his fall from Eden. There were also wooden iron shod spades
that had the blade off set to one side. Women also toiled in gardens and one is
shown using her spade in a Dutch miniature of *c.*1475. In the Breviary of Mayer
Van den Berg of Antwerp, gardeners are working even through winter months.
Men are digging or mending the pergola, while a maid is weeding, or she may be

planting something, because there are two flower pots placed on top of the wall ready to be planted. The owners keep an eye on the work being done.

In Jacopo della Pergola's copy of Pliny the Elder's *Natural History* (of *c.*1460, now in the Victoria and Albert Museum, London) numerous initial letters within the manuscript incorporated little garden scenes, several of these feature gardeners at work. Within the loop of a letter P we can see a gardener with his foot on an iron-shod wooden spade ready to dig a planting hole for a new vine tree, in the background there was a pergola covered with vines. An illuminated initial H showed a worker up a tree wielding a tree pruning hook, and an initial M depicted a rustic vegetable garden enclosed by a wattle fence. Within this space a gardener secures the ripening gourds upon a trellis. His wife takes home a basket full of gourds, balanced on her head. She also carries a ewer, and we can presume that she has just given her husband some refreshment in his toil.[37]

A special kind of plant watering pot, a ceramic finger pot, is shown in a French tapestry (in Paris). A beautifully attired lady shows how such watering devices were used. She holds a water filled pot over the plant (in this case a carnation) and is shown lifting her thumb away from the top of the pot. This action lets in air through the hole at the top and allows the water inside to trickle out gently through the numerous small holes in the base of the pot. It

FIGURE 148 *(left)*. A cartwheel frame used to support plants in a garden with raised beds. A gardener works in the fenced section nearby, 15th century (after Huxley 1978, 87).

FIGURE 149 *(right)*. Lady holding a finger pot to water choice plants, in this case carnations, French tapestry *c.*AD 1400.

is a simple but effective method to give a gentle cascade rather than a torrent onto choice plants. Fragments from watering pots discovered at London have shown that there were at least two forms.[38]

Inventories of garden equipment are rare but one has survived for 1389 at Abingdon Abbey, Oxfordshire.[39] It lists the items you would expect such as three spades and two iron forks, two rakes, three shovels, two pairs of shears, two sickles, a scythe, two sieves and a seed-basket. There are also items such as four ladders, perhaps to collect fruit and nuts from trees. The mallet, trowel, axe, saw and three augers are usually thought of as carpentry tools but many medieval gardens had raised plant beds and seats that were often edged in wood.

One of the greatest introductions for gardeners in this period was the wooden wheelbarrow. They were noticed *c*.1170,[40] and later appear in manuscript paintings. In the Huth *Book of Hours* (folio 110, *c*.1480) peasants are shown transporting a large wicker plant pot of red carnations on a sledge-like wheelbarrow.

The flowery mead and *mille fleurs* tapestries

The ground of orchards, and pleasance, were often grassed over so that the household and guests could make use of the space in fine weather. These areas were often covered with wildflowers and were generally referred to as a flowery mead. People could picnic outside sitting on the grass and children play around. It makes a good venue for reading *en plein-air* or for playing music. Groups could gather there for the retelling of stories, a scenario envisioned in Boccaccio's *Decameron*. Many illustrations show flowers growing in the grass and this was considered normal, unlike our modern weed-free lawns. Turf was tended by hand, not machine, and only the noxious weeds would have been eradicated, for flowers were looked upon as jewels in the grass.[41] A superb example of a flowery mead appears in the Rhenish painting known as the *Garden of Paradise* (1410–1420). The flowers in the mead are all so well defined that it is possible to make out the ones considered as species left to colonise the lawn. There were: campion, columbine, cowslip, daisy, dame's violet, forget-me-not, lily of the valley, lychnis, periwinkle, snowdrop, strawberry and violet. As on turf seats, texts mention the inclusion of camomile, pennyroyal, daisies and violets so that the bruised aromatic foliage would perfume the air. Off centre in this painting there is a crown grafted tree, and on the left a decorative dwarf cherry tree with two twisted stems. The larger flowering plants depicted are a red peony beside the grafted tree; then roses, balm, lilies, blue irises and hollyhocks planted against the garden's walls.

There was a fashion for tapestries depicting scenes with a bejewelled sward, or flower filled lawns, and of these there are two sets of *mille fleurs* tapestries made in Brussels that are outstanding. In each of the tapestries the thousand flowers (*mille fleurs*) overwhelm the viewer, so many are present. A series of seven tapestries (*c*.1500) known as the *Unicorn Hunt* series are now in the Cloister Museum, New York. One of these features the unicorn coming to drink/purify the waters issuing from a large ornamental garden fountain, while hunters gather in the

bushes around. The final scene shows the unicorn in captivity inside a circular wooden barrier fence, the foreground and background is thickly covered with flowers. Over 70 different species have been identified of plants that were carefully woven into the landscape scenes of these tapestries.[42] The flowers included: yellow adonis, bistort, bluebell, campion, white carnation, clary, clover, columbine, cornflower, cowslip, cuckoopint, daffodil, daisy, dame's violet, dandelion, elecampane, eyebright, feverfew, flax, forget-me-not, iris, lady's mantle, Madonna lily, marguerite, marigold, mint, mugwort, orchid, pansy, periwinkle, pimpernel, pinks, plantain, primrose, rose (red and white), rue, sage, sorrel, stock-gillyflower, thistle, violet, wallflower, yellow flag. There were also blackberries, strawberries and a range of trees such as: apple, apricot, ash, beech, birch, cherry, elm, hawthorn, hazel, holly, lime, medlar, oak, orange, peach, plum, pomegranate, strawberry tree and walnut.

The six tapestries of the *Lady and the Unicorn* series (*c*.1480) are now in the Cluny Museum, Paris. These tapestries have a theme depicting the five senses: sight, hearing, smell, touch and taste. The sixth tapestry labelled *Mon Seul Desir* (my only desire) is dominated by a central lavish garden pavilion/tent. Each of these tapestries features a lady, with a unicorn and lion as heraldic beasts, but also small animals such as rabbits, a lamb and dogs cavorting in the flowery mead. Some of the elements within the tapestries have an allegorical significance, because the lion is representative of courage and strength in men, and the unicorn symbolises the goodness and purity of a pious woman. Five of the tapestries depict four large trees: a pine, mulberry, orange and holm oak. The trees conveyed a

FIGURE 150. A Rhenish painting depicting *The Garden of Paradise*. Mary reads a book while Christ plays below, all on a marvellous flowery mead. Against the wall we see hollyhocks, blue flag iris, dame's violet (sweet rocket), sweet marjoram and roses, plants favoured throughout the Middle Ages. Numerous birds (*aves* in Latin) sing their praises to the Virgin, and serve to remind us of the *Ave Maria* sung or recited in churches, *c*.1415 (tempera on panel) Master of Oberrheinischer (15th century). Stadeisches Kunstinstitut, Frankfurt-am-Main, Germany. The Bridgeman Art Library.

FIGURE 151. Manuscript border filled with realistic flowers that frame a scene of the Annunciation. Flowers include: white rose, borage, speedwell, daisy, red carnation, forget-me-not, sorrel, sweet scented stocks and dame's violet, *Hastings Hours* Add. 54782, f.73v: *c.*1475–83 (vellum), Flemish School (15th century), British Library, London/© British Library Board. All rights reserved/The Bridgeman Art Library.

message of fertility and regeneration. The orange tree, the pomegranate and the mulberry were seen as emblems of fertility, while the oak (holm oak) and its northern equivalent the holly became symbols of regeneration.

A medieval regeneration myth associated with the oak and holly

The oak has always been revered; it was long used as a symbol of strength, and in the Roman era it was associated with Jupiter; it was also known in Celtic rituals. The holly was also important because it was evergreen, and in winter months it became the counterpart to the oak. There is even a traditional Christmas carol that reflected the important role holly and ivy played at that time of the year: 'Of all the trees that are in the wood, the holly bears the crown.' In the Mediterranean the holm oak (also known as the holly oak) is an evergreen species, and this is where the myths originated of the Oak and Holly Kings. For it was originally the holm/holly oak that was referred to, but in northern regions, *i.e.* Britain, the true holly took over this role. This seasonal contrast developed into a myth with the holly being the symbol of the waning year and the oak's successor when the leaves fall from the oak. So in places where seasonal regeneration myths still held sway, the oak and holly were turned into two mythical divine kings who every year had to engage in battle to ensure the fertility and fruitfulness of the ground. In effect every midsummer and midwinter one king had to be sacrificed.[43] At midsummer the Holly king would do battle with the oak king and would slay the poor old weakened Oak king, but at midwinter the new Oak king would fight back and regain his true place. This does appear to be a medieval counterpart to the earlier ancient regeneration myths such as Osiris in Egypt, and Adonis, Ceres and Persephone of the Graeco-Roman world.

Plants depicted in medieval manuscripts

Early medieval plant depiction was often quite schematic, but around 1300 a more realistic rendition of specimens was made, and the plants are often beautifully portrayed. Flowers and foliage would emanate from a bar surrounding text on one or more sides of a page. They appear in full border designs, decorated initials, roundels, vignettes, in the bas de page scenes (at the bottom of the page), and on occasion within a miniature painting itself. Coloured flower heads were added to rinceaux borders.

On the folio pages f120 and f19 of the Bedford *Hours* (c.1423) there are centrally placed studies of particularly well admired plants: in the former we see the statuesque spikes of a blue iris, and in the latter the lovely nodding sweet scented blue flowers of violet – *viola odorata*. Both of these are shown growing as a clump with a pheasant reaching through its flower stems in its search for insects to eat. Even vegetables are sometimes depicted, as in the Salisbury Breviary which has a super flowering gourd tree laden with fruit growing around the vignettes of the bas de page. The plant's small yellow flowers fill the space between the short columns of text on this folio (Fig. 150).

In the 1470s there was a fashion to portray greater realism and sometimes a deep flower filled border was painted around miniatures. Flemish illuminators excelled at this, and their manuscripts show a delight in the naturalistic rendition of flowers, with seed heads and leaves shown beside the flower itself. Insects alight on petals or crawl nearby and painted shadows created depth so that these trompe l'oeil images become like real flowers scattered across the page. Two of the most beautiful manuscripts using this style are the Hastings and Huth *Hours*.

The most frequently seen flowers in manuscript borders are here listed in colour groups.[44]

Blue: speedwell, borage, forget-me-not, iris, violet, cornflower, columbine and heartsease.
Pink: stocks, campion, cranesbill, carnation and thistle.
Red: rose and carnation.
White: lily, rose, carnation, stocks, violet and daisy.
Tricoloured: viola/heartsease.

All of the above named flowers are familiar, often being much loved examples, and are distinctive enough to be easily recognised. Their colourful presence brightens the whole work, and they serve to remind the viewer of the extent of God's bounteous creation.

Medieval plants with a special meaning

The first of these are the Marian flowers. In scenes of the Virgin Mary's Annunciation a garden is often hinted at in the background. On most occasions, as in the Salisbury Breviary, a white lily is included in the picture; sometimes it is growing in a pot, or is in the garden, but in this case the lily was placed in a white jug which had been placed between the Virgin Mary and Archangel Gabriel. The pure white lily (which would be *Lilium candidum*) is often associated with Mary, and is alternatively called the Madonna Lily, it became a symbol of her purity. The lily's scent was much admired and therefore was often planted in medieval gardens. Other Marian flowers are: lily of the valley which is another plant that reflected the purity of the Virgin; the violet became a symbol of Mary's humility because their flower heads nod downwards as a sign of respect. Purple iris represented her royal lineage from King David. Roses were the most favoured of all the flowers, for their wonderful scent and the beauty of their blooms, they were also symbolically linked to the Virgin Mary, and were representative of her motherhood, they reflected her love and pure beauty. Roses were also associated with the rosary, for the string of beads were likened to a chaplet (or a garden) full of roses. Each 'rose' or bead was used to count the *aves* in praise to the Virgin Mary.

Some plants were associated with certain families, and the inclusion of certain blooms in art makes a quiet but direct reference to that family. The white rose was used as an emblem of Eleanor of Provence, and her son Edward I adopted it as well, while the red rose was used as a badge of his brother Edmund. The two colours later became associated with the two factions in the War of the Roses: the House of York with the white rose and the House of Lancaster with a red rose. Several pages of the Bedford *Hours* include an illustration of red and white roses; in one they are intertwined together to form a wreath of alternating red and white blooms. Here the two coloured roses are representative of the Duke of Bedford who belonged to the House of Lancaster and the white rose was used for his Burgundian wife. In this case the white rose was linked to purity and therefore was suitable for a bride.

The white rose of olde England was *Rosa alba*, and the red was the apothecary rose, or *Rosa gallica*. The white rose associated with Scotland is the Burnet rose.

A versicolour rose, a sport of *Rosa Gallica*, called Rosa Mundi is thought by some to be a medieval plant as it was named after the tragic Fair Rosamund, a beautiful maiden much loved by King Henry II, however, this 'new' plant was first referred to in the 17th century. A special garden was created for Rosamund, and Higden (a monk from Chester) wrote the following about her (*c*.1350):

> She was the fayre daughter of Walter, Lord Clifford, concubine of Henry II, and poisoned by Queen Eleanor, AD 1177. Henry made for her a house of wonderful working, so that no man or woman might come to her. This house was named Labyrithinus, and was wrought like unto a knot in a garden called a maze. But the queen came to her by a clue of thredde, and so dealt with her that she lived not long after.

This text indicates that the design of mazes and knot gardens actually pre-dates the Tudor period which is usually attributed with their conception. The owner of Coughton Court in Warwickshire is descended from Fair Rosamund and has created a wonderfully scented rose garden in the form of a labyrinth, and at its centre is 'Rosamund's bower' surrounded by hedges of Rosa Mundi, with an archway covered with the white Burnet rose.

The flag iris was the basis of the *fleur de lys* motif of French rulers, and therefore the inclusion of these flowers in a French manuscript would be in deference to them. A broom plant was an emblem of the Plantagenet family, and we can detect in this name how it arose from the Latin *planta genista* (*Genista* being the botanical name of the greenweed/broom family). Broom flowers are shown in f.65 of the Bedford *Hours*. The yellow blooms, narrow leaves and distinctive seed pods are well observed.

Traditional plant lore can be used to indicate why certain medieval garden worthy plants were picked for inclusion on a particular page in a manuscript or painting. For instance, the two names of the columbine flower, also known as *Aquilegia vulgaris*, were derived from the Latin for a dove (*columba*) and an eagle (*aquila*). Because the spurs of the columbine flowers were seen to resemble a bird's wings, it therefore came to symbolise the Holy Spirit or Holy Ghost.[45] Another oft used flower in manuscripts was borage which was a useful herb that could dispel melancholy and was therefore thought to promote courage. Daisy buds were a popular motif used as early as 1320 and feature in the Luttrell Psalter. Daisies were the symbol of innocence and could be used as a measure of one's love by recalling the old saying 'he loves me, he loves me not ...' Strawberry plants appear to be a popular motif in manuscript border designs; their leaves, stems and distinctive bright red fruit are shown but rarely their flowers. These delicious fruits were also dedicated to the Virgin Mary, and were seen as a symbol of perfection and righteousness, but paradoxically they also represented sensuality and earthly desire. The trifoliate leaves of the strawberry also meant that it could symbolise The Holy Trinity. The strawberry therefore had a dual function, one being a religious connection the other secular because the decorative motif used for ducal coronets comprised eight strawberry leaves.

The list of garden plants for the medieval period accompanying this chapter has three columns to reflect the nature of evidence for each plant identified:

Literature, Herbals and Archaeology. In the first category are plants mentioned in documentary sources as well as literature. The plants listed in the column devoted to archaeology were compiled with the inclusion of information from a database at York focusing on botanical remains from Roman and medieval sites in Britain discovered by archaeology.[46]

Gardens in medieval literature

Alexander Necham (1157–1217) of St Alban's wrote the *De Naturis Rerum* that contains a vivid description of what should be grown within a '*nobilis ortus*'.[47] He saw that gardens should be for pleasure as well as for utilitarian purposes. In his eyes, a courtly garden consisted of an orchard of fruit and nut trees. In those days an orchard was not exclusively devoted to fruit trees, and Necham shows there should also be an area arrayed with roses, lilies, violets, poppies, narcissus and sun flower (the latter would be Elecampane). His work reflects ideas current abroad at that time, but some species such as the citron and pomegranate are species that would not be able to grow without protection in England. He did, however, include named varieties of fruit trees that were considered select for that period, this included the St Règle pear (previously mentioned).

An arbour features in a poignant poem that was written by James I of Scotland about the gardens at Windsor Castle where he was a prisoner for 9 years (1413–1424). It is a brief description but nevertheless it is a vivid recollection of the garden with its shady arbours where he first saw his future wife, Jane Beaufort.

> Now was there made, fast by the Tower wall,
> A garden fair; and in the corners set
> An arbour green, with wandis long and small
> Railed about and so with trees set
> Was all the place, and hawthorn hedges knet
> That lyf was none walking there forebye
> That might there within scarce any one espy.
> So thick the boughes and the leaves green
> Beshaded all the alleys that were there,
> And mids of every arbour might be seen
> The sharpe greene sweet Juniper
> Growing so fair with branches here and there.[48]

King René d'Anjou wrote a book on *The Mortification of Vain Pleasure*, part of the action/punishment takes place in a walled garden. In this unusual work Man's heart is nailed to the Cross, and afterwards is returned, chastened!

In *Love's Game of Chess* which was created for the French King Francis I (*c*.1500) we see another symbolic but more ornamental garden. In an illustration to accompany the text the master leads his pupil up to a rather grand castellated *hortus conclusus*, here defined as a 'Garden of Nature'. Dame Nature herself is waiting at the gate, holding a large key, to open the door. The pupil is shown three different ways of living represented by having to make a choice between a lady in the form of *amus* (representative of fleshly love), or *pallas* (wisdom), or *Juno*

FIGURE 152. Detail of a castellated *hortus conclusus* in the late 15th century manuscript *Love's Game of Chess*. The garden has numerous flowers in a border running alongside the castellated walls, and a chessboard layout of turf beds in the middle. The garden represents Nature and the young man must choose one of three ways of living represented by *Amus, Pallas* or *Juno* (respectively love, wisdom or virtuous conduct).

(who symbolises virtuous conduct). This seems to be a medieval version of the Classical myth of Paris having to choose between three goddesses: Juno, Athene and Venus (Juno – the Queen of the gods, Athene who was wise, and Venus the goddess of love and fertility). The garden itself has lots of flowers alongside the walls, and square turf beds that are reminiscent of a chess board. This was intentional in this story, and perhaps this interpretation accounts for a chequered turf design seen elsewhere.

The *Roman de la Rose* (the story of the Rose) as its name suggests, has a large part of the narrative taking place within a garden. This early French poem has over 20,000 lines, and is an elaborate allegory on the Art of Love, and has many Classical allusions. The romance was begun by Guillaume de Loris in 1237 and 40 years later was continued by Jean de Meun. In the story, a young man called Désiré (the lover) is approached by Dame Idleness (we need to interpret her as a personification of Human Nature). She leads him to the Palace/castle of Pleasure, which was a wondrous garden where he meets a group of young people making merry, dancing and singing. Each member of this group are also personifications of various aspects of human nature: Love, Sweet-looks, Riches, Jollity, Courtesy, Liberality, and Youth. They lead Désiré into the garden, where he sees Narcissus by the fountain. He then comes upon a bed of roses (the rose being the symbol of love) he singles out one, and promptly falls in love with this beautiful bloom. He attempts to pluck this beautiful rose, but an arrow is loosed from Cupid's bow and Désiré falls to the ground. He is found lying unconscious, and is carried far away from his beloved flower. On awakening he decides he must go and search once more for this beautiful bloom. Welcome accompanies him; but three facets of nature, Danger, Shame-face and Slander try to hinder his progress. Reason advises him to abandon the pursuit, but he carries on. Only Pity and Liberality help him in his quest for the rose. Venus allows him to lightly kiss the rose, but at the last minute Slander and Jealousy, capture Welcome and Désiré and lock him up in a strong castle, where he mourns over his sad fate. This tale is full of joy and sadness, which we all have at some part of our lives.

Several illustrations accompany the text of the *Roman de la Rose*. In one version woodcuts were used, one of these is shown here, it may be simplistic but is still able to convey the dramatic moment when Désiré spies the beautiful rose. The garden around him is basically just a gateway and a rustic interwoven hurdle fence. Arrow-like marks serve to indicate turf within the enclosed garden. Chaucer's translation (1340–1400), captures the essence of this delightful tale, and this extract reveals just how lovestruck the young man was after he found his rose:

FIGURE 153. Woodcut from the *Roman de la Rose* depicting that special moment when Désiré spies his beautiful rose, *c*.AD 1480.

In thylke myrrour sawe I thro,
Amonge a thousande thynges mo,
A roser* charged ful of rosis,
That with an hedge aboute enclos is.
Tho had I suche luste and enuye,
That for Parys ne for Pauye
Nolde I haue lefte to gone and se
There greatest heape of roses be.
When I was with this rage hente,
That caught hath many a man and shente,
Towarde the roser gan I go;
And whan I was not ferre therfro,
The sauour of the roses swote
Me smote right to the herte rote,
As I had al enbaumed [be].

And if I ne had endouted me
To haue ben hated or assayled,
My thankes, wol I not haue fayled
To pull a rose of al that route
To bere in myn honed aboute,
And smellen to it where I went;
But euer I dredde me to repent,…
I loue wel suche roses rede;
For brode roses, and open also,

Ben passed in a day or two;
But knoppes** wyl [al] fresshe be
Two dayes at leest, or els thre.
The knoppes greatly liked me,
For fayrer may there no man se.
Whoso might haue one of all,
It ought him ben ful lefe withal.
Might I [a] garlonde of hem geten,
For no richesse I wolde it leten.
      Amonges the knoppes I chese one
So fayre, that of the remenaunt no[n]e
No preyse I halfe so wel as it…
The swote smell spronge so wyde
That it dyed al the place aboute–[49]
(*roser = a rose garden; ** knoppes = flower buds)

Medieval Middle English is difficult to read today, but it aptly conveys the spirit of the age. A more readable translation of the section that describes the garden has been put in an appendix at the end of this chapter. This text shows all the features that could be seen in large noble gardens and gives a superb example of medieval thought about gardens.

The Harley Manuscript (British Library MS 4425) presents a series of wonderful illuminations to accompany their version of the *Roman de la Rose*. One painting shows Désiré finding the dancers in an enclosed orchard. In another cupid stands under a rose bower ready to loosen his arrow as Désiré stands with hand crossed on his heart smitten with the rose he has just found. The finest illustration is on folio 12v which shows Bel Acueil (Welcome) and Désiré (who is dressed in blue) approaching the garden, which is represented as a beautiful *hortus conclusus*. Two forms of medieval garden are depicted here. The one on the right has raised rectangular and square plant beds plus a turf seat, which is separated from a more ornamental garden by a lattice fence and gateway. After entering the herber Désiré looks to the left, over the fence and spies the merry makers sitting on a flowery mead around an elaborate fountain. The fountain had numerous water-spouts that were fashioned as lion's masks, another survival from Classical times. The water poured gently down into a pool at the base of the fountain and a rill took away the excess channelling it out through the small portcullis at the bottom of the crenelated wall.

Another form of medieval garden is one likened to the Virgin Mary and called a 'Mary Garden', an example can be seen in a manuscript from Paris. In Church Literature the Virgin Mary was often likened to a *Hortus Conclusus*, hence she was often depicted in the middle of one (usually one filled with roses). This link was originally inspired by the Old Testament *Song of Songs* written by King Solomon. The *Song of Songs* was also known as the *Canticles*, so the Mary Garden is also known as the Garden of Canticles. As we know, the *Song of Songs* is a love poem where the garden symbolised the loved one, a passage reads: 'She is my garden enclosed, my sister, my wife.' ('sister' being an old form meaning a good friend/comrade). In the 4th century we have St Jerome and St Ambrose linking garden imagery with the Virgin Mary, and by the 12th century the Virgin's intact womb was quoted as being like 'a garden enclosed, a sealed fountain.' She was also 'a fountain of gardens, a well of living waters,' which was a metaphor for her fecundity in producing Our Lord. This Marian garden was seen to be protected and pure, yet also fecund, and these were the aims of a medieval *Hortus Conclusus*. This would give a plausible explanation why we see so many garden scenes with fountains within enclosed gardens of this period.

Gardens of the medieval period were made in monastic establishments, there were physic gardens to provide medicinal herbs for apothecaries, peasants had their leek beds and vegetable plots surrounded by a rustic wattle fence. Nobles and gentry created both utilitarian and pleasure gardens, and where possible found space for a *hortus conclusus* and a flowery mead. The ideal elements of a medieval garden are expertly summed up in the following passages from *How to make a Pleasure Garden*, written by Albertus Magnus *c.*1260:

> There are, however, some places of no great utility or fruitfulness but designed for pleasure … these are what are called pleasure gardens. They are in fact mainly designed for the delight of two senses, viz, sight and smell … [He describes how to prepare a turfed area, then how it should be planted with:] every sweet-smelling herb such as rue, and sage and basil, and likewise all sorts of flowers, as the violet, columbine, lily, rose, iris and the like. So that between these herbs and the turf, at the edge of the lawn set square, let there be a higher bench of turf flowering and lovely; and somewhere in the middle provide seats so that men may sit down there to take their repose pleasurably when their senses need refreshment. Upon the lawn too, against the heat of the sun, trees should be planted or vines trained, so that the lawn may have a delightful and cooling shade, sheltered by their leaves… let them be sweet trees, with perfumed flowers and agreeable shade, like grapevines, pears, apples, pomegranates, sweet bay trees, cypresses and such like … If possible a clear fountain of water in a stone basin should be in the midst, for its purity gives much pleasure … It is then delight rather than fruit that is looked for in the pleasure garden.[50]

Garden Plants of the Medieval Period

Common name	Botanical name	Literature	Herbals	Archaeology
Agrimony	*Agrimonia eupatoria*	x	x	
Alexanders	*Smyrnium olusatrum*		x	x
Almond	*Prunus communis*	x	x	x
Anise	*Pimpinella anisum*		x	
Apple	*Malus domestica*	x	x	x
Archangel	*Lamium album*		x	
Artichoke	*Cynara scolymus*		x	
Ash	*Fraxinus excelsior*		x	
Asparagus	*Asparagus officinalis*		x	
Avens	*Geum urbanum*		x	
Balm	*Melissa officinalis*	x	x	
Barberry	*Berberis vulgaris*		x	
Basil	*Ocimum basilicum*	x	x	
Bay	*Laurus nobilis*	x	x	
Bean (Broad)	*Vicia faba*	x	x	x
Bean (Kidney)	*Vigna cylindrica*		x	
Beech	*Fagus sylvatica*		x	
Beet	*Beta vulgaris*	x	x	x
Betony	*Betonica officinalis*	x	x	
Borage	*Borago officinalis*	x	x	x
Box	*Buxus sempervirens*		x	
Bugle	*Ajuga reptans*		x	
Bugloss	*Anchusa officinalis*	x	x	
Bullace	*Prunus insititia*		x	x
Butcher's broom	*Ruscus aculeatus*		x	
Cabbage/ Colewort/Kale	*Brassica oleracea*	x	x	x
Calamint	*Calamintha nepeta*	x	x	
Caraway	*Carum carvi*		x	
Carrot	*Dracus carota*	x	x	x
Catmint	*Nepeta cataria*		x	x
Celandine, Greater	*Chelidonium majus*	x	x	x
Celery; Smallage	*Apium graveolens*	x	x	x
Chamomile	*Anthemis nobilis*	x	x	x
Cherry	*Prunus cerasus*	x	x	x
Chervil	*Anthriscus cerefolium*	x	x	
Chestnut	*Castanea sativa*	x	x	
Chicory	*Cichorium intybus*	x	x	
Chives	*Allium schoenoprasum*		x	
Clary	*Salvia sclarea; S. pratensis*	x	x	
Clover/Trefoil	*Trifolium alexandrinum*	x	x	x
Columbine	*Aquilegia vulgaris*	x	x	x
Comfrey	*Symphytum officinale*		x	
Coriander	*Coriandrum sativum*	x	x	x
Costmary	*Chrysanthemum balsamita*	x	x	

Common name	Botanical name	Literature	Herbals	Archaeology
Cowslip	*Primula veris*		x	x
Cress	*Lepidium sativum*	x	x	
Crocus (Saffron)	*Crocus sativus*	x	x	
Cucumber	*Cucumis sativus*	x	x	
Cumin	*Cuminum cyminum*	x	x	
Cypress	*Cupressus sempervirens*		x	
Daisy	*Bellis perennis*	x	x	
Dianthus/Pink	*Dianthus* spp.	x	x	
Dill	*Anethum graveolens*	x	x	x
Dittander	*Ledidium latifolium*		x	
Dragon arum	*Dracunculus vulgaris*	x	x	
Elecampane	*Inula helenium*	x	x	
Endive	*Cichorium endivia*		x	
Fennel	*Foeniculum vulgare*	x	x	x
Fenugreek	*Trigonella foenum-graecum*	x	x	
Feverfew	*Chrysanthemum parthenium*		x	
Fig	*Ficus carica*	x	x	
Fumitory	*Fumaria officinalis*	x	x	x
Garlic	*Allium sativum*	x	x	
Germander	*Teucrium chamaedrys*	x	x	
Gooseberry	*Ribes uva-crispa*	x	x	x
Gourd	*Lagenaria vulgaris*	x	x	
Grape Vine	*Vitis vinifera*	x	x	x
Hartstongue Fern	*Phyllitis scolopendrium*		x	
Hawthorn	*Crataegus monogyna*	x	x	x
Hazelnut	*Corylus avellana*	x	x	x
Hellebore	*Helleborus niger*	x	x	
Henbane	*Hyoscyamus niger*		x	x
Holly	*Ilex aquilfolium*	x	x	x
Hollyhock	*Althaea (Alcea) rosea*		x	
Horehound	*Marrubium vulgare*	x	x	x
Houndstongue	*Cynoglossum offivinale*		x	
Houseleek	*Aeonium arboreum*		x	
Hyssop	*Hyssopus officinalis*	x	x	
Iris	*Iris* spp.	x	x	
Ivy	*Hedera helix*	x	x	
Juniper	*Juniperus communis*	x	x	
Lavender	*Lavandula* spp. (inc. *L. stoechas*)	x	x	
Leek	*Allium porrum*	x	x	x
Lettuce	*Lactuca sativa*	x	x	
Lily	*Lilium candidum*	x	x	
Lovage	*Levisticum officinale*	x	x	
Mallow (garden, shrub, tree, mashmallow)	*Malva neglecta, Hibiscus syriacus, Lavatera arborea, Althaea officinalis*	x	x	x
Mandrake	*Mandragora officinarum*	x	x	
Maple	*Acer* spp.		x	

Common name	Botanical name	Literature	Herbals	Archaeology
Marigold	*Calendula officinalis*	x	x	x
Marjoram	*Origanum vulgare*	x	x	
Marjoram (Sweet)	*Origanum majorana*		x	
Medlar	*Mespilus germanica*	x	x	x
Melon	*Cucumis melo*		x	
Mint	*Mentha* spp.	x	x	x
Mulberry (Black)	*Morus nigra*	x	x	x
Mullein	*Verbascum thapsus*		x	
Mustard	*Sinapis alba*	x	x	x
Narcissus/daffodil	*Narcissus* spp.	x	x	
Oak	*Quercus robur*	x	x	
Onion	*Allium cepa*	x	x	x
Orach	*Atriplex hortensis*		x	x
Oregano	*Origanum vulgare*		x	
Parsley	*Petroselinum crispum*	x	x	
Parsnip	*Pastinaca schekakul*	x	x	x
Pea	*Pisum sativum*	x	x	x
Peach	*Prunus persica*	x	x	x
Pear	*Pyrus communis*	x	x	x
Pellitory	*Parietaria diffusa*	x	x	
Pennyroyal	*Mentha pulegium*	x	x	
Peony	*Paeonia* spp.	x	x	
Periwinkle	*Vinca pervinca, V.minor*		x	
Pimpernel	*Anagallis arvensis*	x	x	x
Pine	*Pinus sylvestris*		x	
Plantain	*Plantago* spp.		x	x
Plum	*Prunus domestica*	x	x	x
Pomegranate	*Punica granatum*		x	
Poplar (black & white)	*Populus nigra, P.alba*		x	
Poppy	*Papaver somniferum, P.rosea*	x	x	x
Primrose	*Primula vulgaris*		x	
Purslane	*Portulaca oleracea*		x	
Quince	*Cydonia oblonga*	x	x	
Radish	*Raphanus sativus*	x	x	x
Reed	*phragmites*		x	
Rocket	*Eruca sativa*		x	
Rose	*Rosa* spp.	x	x	x
Rosemary	*Rosmarinus officinalis*	x	x	
Rue	*Ruta graveolens*	x	x	
Sage	*Salvia officinalis*	x	x	
St John's Wort	*Hypericum perforatum*		x	
Savory	*Satureia* spp.	x	x	x
Scabious	*Knautia arvensis*		x	
Service tree	*Sorbus domestica*	x	x	
Shallot	*Allium ascalonicum*	x	x	
Southernwood	*Artemisia abrotanum*	x	x	

Common name	Botanical name	Literature	Herbals	Archaeology
Spinach	*Spinacia oleracea*	x	x	
Squill	*Urginea maritima*		x	
Strawberry	*Fragaria vesca*	x	x	x
Tansy	*Chrysanthemum vulgare*		x	
Thyme	*Thymus* spp.		x	
Turnip	*Brassica rapa*		x	x
Valerian	*Valeriana officinalis*		x	
Vervain	*Verbena officinalis*		x	x
Vetch	*Vicia sativa*	x	x	x
Violet	*Viola odorata*	x	x	x
Wallflower	*Cheiranthus cheiri*	x	x	
Walnut	*Juglans regia*	x	x	x
Watercress	*Rorippa nasturtium-aquaticum*		x	
Waterlily	*Nymphaea alba*		x	
Willow	*Salix* spp.		x	
Woad	*Isatis tinctoria*		x	
Woodbine/honeysuckle	*Lonicera periclymenum*	x	x	
Wood sage	*Teucrium scorodonia*		x	
Wood sorrel	*Oxalis acetosella*		x	
Wormwood	*Artemisia absinthium*	x	x	
Yarrow	*Achillea millefolium*		x	
Yew	*Taxus baccata*		x	

APPENDIX

Le Roman de la Rose (Romance of the Rose)

by Guillaume de Loris, 13th century, trans. F. S. Ellis, London, 1900
[*The section describing the garden*]

I noted that from side to side
The garden was nigh broad as wide,
And every angle duly squared.
The careful planter had not us spared
To set of every kind of tree
That beareth fruit some two or three,
Or more perchance, except some few
Of evil sort. Among them grew
Pomegranates filled with seeds and thick
Of skin, most wholesome for the sick;
Strange nut trees, which in season bore
Rich fragrant nutmegs, good for store,
And nowise cursed with nauseous taste,
But savouring well. Near by were placed
Almonds and gillyflower cloves,
Brought hither from hot land's far groves,

Dates, figs, and liquorice which deals
Contentment while misease it heals,
And wholesome aniseed's sweet spice,
And much-prized grains of paradise,
Nor must rare cinnamon be forgot,
Nor zedoary, which I wot
At end of great repasts man eat
In hope 'twill bring digestion meet.
Moreover in this garden rare
Grew many a tree familiar,
As cherry, pear and knotted quince,
'Neath which a tender tooth will wince,
brown medlars, plums both black and white,
Apples and chestnuts bright;
Sorb-apples, barberries, fruit of lote
And many more of lesser note.

And all around this pleasant close
Holly, and laurel, and holm arose
With yew and hornbeam, fit I trow
For flitting shaft, and speeding bow;
The cypress sad, and pines that sigh
To soft south breezes mournfully,
Beech, loved of squirrels, olive dark,
And graceful birch with silvery bark;
The shimmering aspen, maple tall,
And lofty ash that topped the wall,
The limber hazel, oak trees hoar, …
… … such skilful art
Had planned the trees that each apart
Six fathoms stood, yet like a net
The interlacing branches met,
Through which no scorching rays could pass
To sear the sward, and thus the grass
Kept ever tender, fresh and green,
Beneath their cool and friendly screen.
Roebuck and deer strayed up and down
The mead, and troops of squirrels brown
The tree-boles scoured, while conies grey
Shot merrily in jocund play
Around their burrows on the fresh
And fragrant greensward, void of mesh.
Within the glades sprang fountains clear:
No frog or newt e'er came anear
Their waters, but 'neath cooling shade
They gently soured. Mirth had made
Therefore small channelled brooks to fling
Their waves with pleasant murmuring
In tiny tides. Bright green and lush,
Around these sparkling streams, did push
The sweetest grass. There might one lie
Beside one's love, luxuriously
As though 'twere bed of down. The earth,
Made pregnant by the streams, gave birth

To thymy herbage and gay flowers,
And when drear winter frowns and lowers
In spots less genial, ever here
Things bud and burgeon through the year.
The violet, sweet of scent and hue,
The periwinkle's star of blue,
The golden kingcups burnished bright,
Mingled with pink-rimmed daisies white,
And varied flowers, blue, gold, and red,
The alleys, lawns and groves o'erspread,
As they by Nature's craft had been
Enamelled deftly on the green.
And all around where'er I went
Fresh blooms cast forth odorous scent.
Small need there is to fabulate
More fully of the fair estate
Of this most comely garden, lest
It weary your patience; nought expressed
Could all the glorious beauty be
Of this most wonderous place by me.

[*The section describing the fountain*]
… Without the door
Of paradise the blest, I ween,
No sight more beauteous may be seen
Than this bright well. The gushing source
Springs ever fresh and sweet. Its course
It takes through runnels twain, full deep,
And broadly trenched; it knows no sleep
By day or night, for ne'er 'tis dried
By wasting drought of summer tide,
Nor hath stern winter's iron hand
The power to make its waters stand
Immovable, but out the ground
Its babble calls, the whole year round
Close, tender herbage, which doth push
Unceasingly, strong, thick, and lush.

Notes

1. Harvey 1981, 27.
2. The 1873 edition of the Colchester Palladius has useful side notes in a readable English style. A new translation of Palladius's *Opus Agriculturae* was translated by J. G. Fitch in 2013.
3. *Etymologies* XVII, ix, 88, trans. S. A. Barney *et al.*, Cambridge, 2006.
4. Mentioned by the 1st century AD geographer Pomponius Mela (2,124).
5. *Etymologies* XVII, x, 6, trans. S. A.Barney *et al.*, Cambridge, 2006.
6. Walafrid Strabo, *Hortulus*, cited by Rohde, E. S. *The Story of the Garden*, London, 1989, 30.
7. Steane 1985, 264.
8. Creighton 2009, 174.
9. Luxford, J. M. 'The Charterhouse of St Anne, Coventry,' *Coventry*, 2011, 244.
10. Soden, I, *Coventry, the Hidden History*, Stroud, 2005, 94.
11. Dickson, 1994, 66; Robinson, M. 'Plant and invertebrate remains from the Priory Drains,' in *Further Excavations on the Second Site of the Dominican Priory, Oxford*, *Oxoniensia* 50, 1985, 196–201.
12. As at Chester and Coventry: Carrington, P. *Chester*, Chester, 1994, 77; Charles, F. W. B. 'Timber-framed houses in Spon Street, Coventry,' *Birmingham and Warwickshire Archaeological Society Transactions* 89, 1979, 95.
13. Miller E. and Hatcher, J. *Medieval England, Towns, Commerce and Crafts*, London, 1995, 262.
14. Steane 1985, 214.
15. Landsberg 1995, 46–47.
16. Dickson 1994, 64.
17. Moffett, L. C. 'Botanical remains from Worcester Deansway,' Ancient Monuments Laboratory Report 123/91, Portsmouth, 1991, 24–28.
18. Moffett, L. C. 'Botanical remains from Worcester Deansway,' Ancient Monuments Laboratory Report 123/91, Portsmouth, 1991, 11.
19. Landsberg 1995, 17.
20. Landsberg 1995, 17.
21. Turner 1848, 297ff; Rohde, E. S. *The Story of the Garden*, London, 1989, 43.
22. Harvey 1981, 54. Costard apples and varieties of pears such as the Martin, St Regele, Pesse-pucelle and Caillou are mentioned in a list of prices in 1292 (Harvey 1981, 82).
23. Harvey 1981, 82.
24. Harvey 1981, 82.
25. Harvey 1981, 115.
26. Harvey 1981, 115; appendix 1, Some royal gardeners, 155–158.
27. Liberate Roll, 34 Hen III.m6; Rohde, E. S. *The Story of the Garden*, London, 1989, 39.
28. Guest, G. 'An early moated garden is unearthed at Whittington Castle,' *The Times* 25/1/2003; Creighton, O. H. 2009, *Designs upon the Land: Elite Landscapes of the Middle Ages*, Woodbridge, 68–69.
29. Estate Book of Henry de Bray, fig. 11.
30. Estate Book of Henry de Bray, fig. 11; Steane 1985, 213–214.
31. Estate Book of Henry de Bray, fig. 11.
32. Harvey 1981, 106.
33. Steane 1985, 172.
34. Information from Leighton Bishop, cited by Aston, M. *Medieval Fish, Fisheries and Fishponds in England*, Oxford, 1988, 431.
35. Aston, M. *Medieval Fish, Fisheries and Fishponds in England*, Oxford, 1988, 423–425.

36. Cotton MS. Julius A.VI, f4. The illumination was for the month of March.
37. The illuminated initials concerned are respectively on p. 33 top, p. 33 bottom, p. 29 in Whalley, J. I. *Pliny the Elder Historia Naturalis*, London, 1982.
38. Steane 1985, 215.
39. Harvey 1981, 114.
40. Steane 1985, 215.
41. In the dry summer of 2014 my own lawn was turned into a stunning flowery mead when heartsease and violets self seeded across the stunted grass.
42. Williamson 1986, 232–239 provides an annotated drawing with a list of all the plants depicted in each of the seven tapestries.
43. Williamson 1986, 64.
44. Fisher (2004, 61–62) lists 140 different plant species that feature in medieval manuscripts.
45. Fisher 2004, 33.
46. Dickson 1994, 60–61.
47. Turner 1848, 297ff.
48. Adapted from de Gex 1995, 27.
49. Written (in French) by Guillaume de Lorris, translated by Chaucer into Middle English (lines 1649–1775).
50. Harvey 1981, 6.

CHAPTER TEN

Conclusions

Throughout the periods examined it has been possible to identify elements that could reasonably be described as a garden. These could be said to be different to the general practise of agriculture where the sole motive is the maximum production of food. There was a desire to produce something which in modern terms could be described as an amenity, which would give pleasure to the people who used it. This amenity/garden took many forms, from extensive parkland to the enclosed space within a dwelling or even the informal planting of small patches of ground with decorative plants.

One source of information comes from the field of archaeology. Archaeologists have long given up the simple search for art treasures, and in recent years have been prepared to examine areas that would once have been left blank because they contained no visible structures. Today archaeologists can use geophysical surveys to reveal evidence for garden areas and find evidence for cultivation. New scientific techniques such as pollen and soil analysis make it possible to give accurate identification of plant genera and species. Although the plant may not have grown exactly where the pollen was found we can be sure that it was grown nearby. For large gardens aerial photography can identify changes in ground levels that can mark out boundaries and sunken garden features (such as former fish pools). The new science of LIDAR, that uses laser imaging to identify ground contours over large areas to a surprisingly detailed scale, may well give us a great deal of new data in future years. A new area of research has been to examine anew ancient pottery. For instance, until recently we valued Minoan pottery for the information that we could deduce from their use of flower and plant motifs painted on their ceramic vessels, but now we can analyse traces left behind on the pot's inner surface to identify the original contents and vegative remains. Science is not static and we can hope for unexpected new techniques in the future.

Surviving ancient literature (where it exists) is the ideal source for factual information on ancient gardens. The most prolific sources are probably from the Roman and medieval periods. The art of gardening was recognised as a worthy pursuit, and various Romans mention how their gardens gave them inspiration for either poetry or prose (Ovid and Pliny the Younger).[1] Even an emperor was known to enjoy his gardens, such as Hadrian at Tivoli, and Emperor Diocletian once declared that he enjoyed his retirement growing

FIGURE 155. Garden fresco, House of the Marine Venus, Pompeii.

vegetables!² However, this may just have been a facetious way of saying he would have no further involvement in state affairs. The Roman writers in particular, on occasion, described their gardens or those of a friend and the details are enlightening for aspects of garden art. The agricultural manuals deal mainly with farming practice but indirectly illuminate some aspects of horticulture and gardening techniques. It is noticeable that Romans of high social standing wrote on these matters, in the same way that some 18th-century English aristocrats had a similar interest in land improvement. Byzantine, Islamic and medieval writers continued to produce agricultural manuals that incorporated elements of horticulture. Numerous Classical texts were re-discovered and examined in the late medieval and early Renaissance era and these gave inspiration for many Classical inspired gardens of the Renaissance and later periods.

FIGURE 156. Fresco detail with garden plants, House of the Golden Bracelet, Pompeii.

Many earlier cultures compiled a herbal, for medicinal use and to enable practitioners to identify plants correctly before use. Medicinal texts have been found belonging to the Egyptians and Assyrians. There are even hints from references to medicinal plants in the Linear B tablets that indicates that the peoples of the Greek Bronze Age may have had knowledge that was passed down, but sadly not in a form that has survived. In the Islamic world there was a continuing interest in the work of Dioscorides, and the Greek tradition of Herbal Books. In Spain several noted Islamic gardeners wrote books on botany and a herbal. Medieval writers also provided plant lists and herbals, all of these were useful for identifying plants current to each period.

Religion played an important role in people's lives in the past, and many cultures had a deity, or several, that had a responsibility for ensuring the fertility of plants as well as of animals and humans. There was a need for people to approach a god that could be petitioned to act on their behalf. Myths were woven about the lives and roles of the various gods and goddesses, and perhaps the best known are those of the Greeks and Romans, but we find that later a number of Christian saints appear to partly take over this role. The saints become someone who might intercede for you to God, and this helps to satisfy a basic age-old need, whether it was for help to combat a plague of insects or for an increase in the productivity of fruit and vegetables.

Many cultures had myths about the interactions between deities and plants, and again the Greeks more than others excelled at this. But we also find that other cultures wove a myth, or poem, based on the merits of certain trees/plants.

The first one concerned the palm and the tamarisk of Mesopotamia that vied with each other, then there as the laurel and the olive of Greek literature, and later the oak and the holly played their part in the medieval period.

Some elements of gardening have passed down through the ages, partly because similar problems produce similar solutions. For instance, many garden tools have changed little because their basic design still works. Similarly, a water feature was a regular and favoured component of a garden wherever water was available in sufficient quantity. Provision of water varied from an aqueduct to supply the king's private garden in Assyria, to a Roman town house with a small fountain pool where the aqueduct supplied the whole town and was chargeable. In the latter the water supply might let the fountain operate only part of the time, but this would still make a special notable feature in the garden.

Gardens evolve over time, and in some cases the countries concerned absorbed influence from outside, whether from diplomatic means or as a result of military expeditions abroad. For instance the finding and transplanting of newly discovered garden worthy plants. Another facet of cross cultural influences can be detected in the Greek translation of the Achaemenid Persian term for an enclosed garden, which then became a *paradeisos*, this was in turn translated into Latin and was the basis of our word paradise. The meaning had fundamentally changed so that the old hunting parks then became a peaceful kingdom in which the lion and lamb could lie down together. Some cultures did liken gardens to a paradise, a form of heaven on earth (Early Christian, Byzantine, Islamic and medieval). Eden was another Biblical theme used for comparative purposes. In a similar way the Greeks, Romans and Byzantines referred to the ever-fruitful Classical Homeric Gardens of Alkinoös, often claiming that theirs were better. Elements of continuity can be found in the groves of Greece translated into named themed garden areas on large country estates in Italy (e.g. Cicero's 'Academy'). Further examples of continuity are the peristyles of Rome that influenced the form of monastic cloister gardens. It also appears that Roman and Byzantine gardens influenced Islamic gardens and they in turn influenced garden designs of the Mughal court. Travellers to and from the Timurid Persian court may have brought ideas from distant lands (such as China and India) to the west, and contributed to the early introduction of more unusual/exotic plant species, but Chinese and Indian gardens are out of the scope of this current book.

One of the most famous gardens of antiquity is the Hanging Gardens of Babylon, one of the Seven great Wonders of the Ancient World. No-one has copied the model that was set so long ago, or none to our knowledge have survived. But, their place alongside the Pyramids and the Colossus of Rhodes, perhaps reinforced the idea that a garden could be a 'wonder'. It promoted the idea that a garden was a proper interest for royalty and powerful individuals, and gardens came to be seen as a status symbol. To many the possession of a garden was another status indicator, and owners could vie with their neighbours on the expanse and expense in creating such a marvel, whether this was in Assyria, Babylon, Persia, Rome or in medieval Britain. Gardens whatever their size are an expression of their owners, then as now, and there is always a tendency to personalise the space, therefore few are slavish copies.

Gardeners are shown at work in the stone reliefs and frescoes of Egypt, the mosaics of Rome, the manuscripts of Persia and in medieval art. Whether the gardeners are depicted watering the garden laboriously using water-pots on a shoulder-yoke or a shaduf (as in Egypt and Mesopotamia), planting out, pruning or digging, their toil is recorded. The fact that their humble work was also commented on, and that their occupation was specified apart from being just labourers shows a recognition of their particular work. In the Roman period there were even specific titles for each specialism in the garden (*arboritor*, *olitor*, *topiarius*). Several Roman tombstones recorded the personal names of individual gardeners, such as Lucrio and Florus *topiarii* working in Campania.[3] The skills of *topiarii*, especially their topiary work, was much admired and commented upon. Individuals in the various societies became head gardeners, and some were noted for their creative designs, such as Mirak-I-Sayyid Ghiyas the Persian from Herat. However, many garden designers remain anonymous for their work is often attributed to their ruler or the owner of the garden. This book has tried to shed light on the gardeners' hard work to let their achievements shine through and live on.

One of the benefits to present society is the early introduction and dissemination of plants, and this commenced from the Egyptian period onwards. As mentioned there were times when the ruler, or his general, led expeditions to foreign lands with the intention to seize or quell cities and expand territory. One of the indirect consequences of this was that different trees and plants were noted en route and examples were 'captured' and transported back to the victors homeland. Not all specimens would have survived, but of those that did some notable plant species became established on new soils. The vine and pomegranate are among the early plants introduced to Egypt, and later the 'Botanical Garden' room at Karnak depicted plant trophies on its walls. We hear that fruit trees were transported from Anatolia to Mesopotamia by the Assyrians. The Roman general Lucullus returned from Pontus (on the Black Sea coast of Turkey) with the sweet cherry which was previously unknown to Rome. Roman individuals actively sought new or better plant species, of fruit trees, and even of roses to extend their flowering season. Garden worthy specimens were acclimatised and then introduced to places throughout the Roman Empire. Islamic rulers introduced numerous plants to gardens in southern Spain, one of these being the orange. When dialogue commenced between Islamic Spain and its Christian neighbours an exchange of ideas were possible and there are instances when horticultural practises, and new plant species were brought into the medieval world. Several further plant introductions were made during the medieval period, such as the hollyhock. This was called *Holyoc* or the Rose of Spain, which perhaps indicates the region where it was previously known (Pays d'Oc or northern Spain) for it is believed to have been introduced by Queen Eleanor of Castile in 1255.[4] The process of plant introductions continues even today.

The plant lists that accompany each chapter of this book will aid the identification of plants known during any particular epoch. The lists might also help people when contemplating making a period garden of their own, or for their community. Several reconstructions of gardens have been made for the public and these enable the viewer to visualise the setting in person.

Reconstructions of period gardens

Egyptian

There is a small Egyptian area at Biddulph Grange, near Stoke-on-Trent in Staffordshire, but this is really a showcase of Egyptian architecture with an Egyptian style doorway flanked by a pair of sphinx and tiered hedges, there are no pools or flowers in this area. There are ancient Egyptian plants in the Botanic Gardens in Cairo, and on the Botanical Island near Aswan.

Mesopotamia and the Near East

Three Bible Gardens have been created at Elgin and Golspie in Scotland, and Garstang in Lancashire. All three contain plants mentioned in the Bible within a modern setting.

Greek

The Greek garden temple at Clumber Park, Nottinghamshire, and the Classical inspired temple at Stourhead Gardens, Wiltshire, are situated in landscape settings that evoke the groves of Greece. In the Agora excavations area at Athens the grove of trees around the Temple of Hephaestus have been replanted in the original ancient Greek plant pits. In the Diomedes Botanic Garden in Athens (to the left of the main gate) there is an area devoted to Greek plants mentioned by Theophrastus and other ancient Greek writers.

Roman

Apart from Pompeii in Italy, there are several Roman-style gardens in the UK and elsewhere in the former provinces of Roman Empire.[5] At Fishbourne Roman Palace, near Chichester, in West Sussex, the large garden with architecturally inspired topiary has been recreated from archaeological evidence found on site. There is a small museum dedicated to Roman gardening, and nearby there are several display beds with plants of the period.

Part of the Roman Museum at Caerleon in Wales has a Roman-style garden with period plants and an al fresco dining area. At South Shields, on Hadrian's Wall, there is a Roman-style garden with herbs and box hedges.

Chester Zoo's Millennium project saw the creation of a Roman-style garden area containing a decorative garden with ornamental pools, statuary, pergolas and period ornamental plants, plus a section with herbs and vegetables.

Islamic

The Prince of Wales garden at Highgrove, Gloucestershire, contains an Islamic-style garden based on a design from a Persian carpet. This garden was created for the Chelsea Flower Show and subsequently was re-laid at Highgrove.

The Islamic gardens of Granada, and especially the Patio Acequia, have provided the inspiration for the Alhambra Speciality Garden created in Roundhay Park in Leeds. It contains areas with an elongated pool, fountains, pavilion, and some period plants in a formal setting with elegant cypress trees and hedges.

Medieval

A medieval style garden was designed by Sylvia Landsberg to reflect the three herbers that were created for Henry III and his Queen Eleanor in the castle at Winchester *c*.1235. The recreated garden was made next to the Great Hall. The royal herber was provided with a tunnel pergola, a *hortus conclusus* with a turf seat and an elegant fountain.

A garden was made at Tretower Court in Powys, Wales, designed by Elizabeth Whittle for Cadw. In the 15th century this was the home of Sir Roger Vaughan. The garden is split into two halves. One section is enclosed by latticework fences and contains a gothic fountain as a centrepiece, this is surrounded by borders of lavender and other herbs. A pergola covered with white Burnet roses runs along two sides of this garden. The second half is a *hortus conclusus*, or Mary Garden, with an arched entrance facing a turf seat. The whole is ringed by a hedge of red *Rosa gallica* and *Rosa mundi* roses. The scent from the roses all around you as you sit there is wonderful.

FIGURE 157. Recreated medieval garden at Tretower Court, Wales.

At Prebendal Manor House, near Peterborough the recreated medieval gardens extends to 5 acres (*c*.2 ha). It was designed by Michael Brown. He aimed to give an idea of what you might expect to find in a garden of a wealthy establishment of the late 14th century. There is a medieval dovecote on site and, next to the old tithe barn, a gardener's hut with replica tools such as a wooden spade with an iron shoe, and watering pots (a thumb watering pot, see Fig. 142). One section of the garden recreates the raised plant beds seen in physic gardens, a second area is enclosed by a lattice fence making a *hortus conclusus*, full of herbs and with a central fountain. A third part is laid out as a flowery mead with a rose pergola to one side, and a fourth features a secluded bower with turf seats. There are fishponds, orchards and beds that demonstrate medieval methods of growing vegetables and other plants of the period. Of the period plants grown at Prebendal there are exotic ones such as mandrake and a dragon plant (*Dracunculus vulgaris*) a member of the Arum family.

Notes

1. Ovid *Trista*, I, 11, 37. trans. A. L. Wheeler, London, 1986; Pliny, *Epistles* IX, 36, 3. trans. B. Radice, London, 1969.
2. *Epitome de Caesaribus*, 39, 5–6. www.thelatinlibrary.com/victor.caes2.html
3. CIL.X.1, 1744; CIL 9945; c.f. Farrar 1998, 161.
4. Harvey, 1981, 127–130.
5. See Farrar 1998, 200–203; more are included in the Farrar 2011 edition, History Press.

Select Bibliography

General

Blamey, M. and Grey-Wilson, C. (1993) *Mediterranean Wild Flowers*. London.

Budge, E. A. Wallis. (1978) *Herb-Doctors and Physicians in the Ancient World*. Chicago.

Carroll, M. (2003) *Earthly Paradises*. London.

Carroll-Spillecke, M. (ed.) (1992) *Der Garten von der Antike bis zum Mittelalter*. Mainz.

di Pasquale, G. and Paolucci, F. (eds) (2007) *Il giardino antico da Babilonia a Roma*. Livorno.

Gothein, M. L. (1966) *A History of Garden Art* I, trans. L. Archer-Hind. New York.

Hobhouse, P. (1997) *Plants in Garden History*. London.

Houdret, J. (2002) *Practical Herb Garden*. London.

Huxley, A. *An Illustrated History of Gardening*, London, 1978.

Hyams, E. (1971) *A History of Gardens and Gardening*. London.

Shoemaker, C. A. (2001) *Encyclopedia of Gardens, History and Design*, 3 vols. Chicago and London.

Singer, C. (1929) The Herbal in Antiquity and its transmission to later Ages. *Journal of Hellenistic Studies* 47, 1–52

Archaeology

Brown, A. E. (1991) *Garden Archaeology*. York, 1991.

Ciaraldi, M. (2007) *People and Plants in Ancient Pompeii, a New Approach to Urbanism from the Microscope Room*. London.

Currie, C. (2005) *Garden Archaeology, a handbook*. York.

Dickson, C. (1994) Macroscopic fossils of garden plants from British Roman and medieval deposits. In Moe, D. (ed.) *Garden History: garden plants, species, forms and varieties from Pompeii to 1800*. Journal of the European Study Group on Physical, Chemical, Mathematical and Biological Techniques applied to Archaeology (PACT) 42, 47–72.

Dimbleby, G. (1978) *Plants and Archaeology*. London.

Evans, J. G. (1981) *An Introduction to Environmental Archaeology*. London.

Gleason, K. L. (1994) *The Archaeology of Garden and Field*. Philadelphia.

Jashemski, W. F. and Meyer, F. G. (eds) (2002) *The Natural History of Pompeii*. Cambridge.

Liljenslotpe, P. and Klynne, A. (1999) 'The Prima Porta Garden Archaeological Project…'. In Docter, R. F. and Moorman, E. M. (eds) *Proceedings of the XVth International Congress of Classical Archaeology, Amsterdam, July 12–17, 1998*, Amsterdam, 234–236 and figs 91–92.

Taylor, C. (1983) *The Archaeology of Gardens*. Aylesbury.

Chapter 1. Egyptian

Bellinger, J. (2008) *Ancient Egyptian Gardens*. Sheffield.

Bigelow, M. H. (2000) Ancient Egyptian gardens. *Ostracon* 2(1), 7–11

Brewer, D. J. *et al.* (1994) *Domestic Plants and Animals, The Egyptian Origins*. Warminster.

Daines, A. (2008) Egyptian Gardens. *Studia Antiqua* 6(1), 15–25.

El-Maenshawy, S. (2012) Aspects of the office of Temple Gardener in ancient Egypt. A reconsideration of the recently published stela TN.20.3.25.3. *Discussions in Egyptology* 65, 53–66.

Frazer, J. G. *Adonis Attis Osiris*, Vol II. New York, 1963.

Gothein, M. L. (1966) *A History of Garden Art*, I, trans. L. Archer-Hind. New York.

Hepper, F. N. (1990) *Pharaoh's Flowers, the Botanical Treasures of Tutankhamun*. London.

Manniche, L. (1999) *An Ancient Egyptian Herbal*. London.

Stevens, C. J. and Clapham, A. J. (2014) Botanical insights into the life of an ancient Egyptian village. In Stevens, C. J. *et al.* (eds) *Archaeology of African Plant Use*. London, 61, 151–164.

Wilkinson, A. (1994) Symbolism and design in ancient

Egyptian gardens. *Garden History* 22(1), 1–17.

Wilkinson, A. (1998) *The Garden in Ancient Egypt*. London.

Chapter 2. Mesopotamia and the Near East

Dalley, S. (1993) Ancient Mesopotamian Gardens…. *Garden History* 21, 1–13.

Finkel, I. L. (1989) The Hanging Gardens of Babylon. In Clayotn, P. and Price, M. (eds) *The Seven Wonders of the World*. London, 38–58.

Hepper, F. N. (1987) *Planting a Bible Garden*. London.

James, W. (1984) *Gardening with Biblical Plants*. Chicago.

Langgut, D. *et al.* (2013) Fossil pollen reveals the secrets of the Royal Persian Garden at Ramat Rahel, Jerusalem. *Palynology* 37(1), 115–129.

Leach, M. (1982) On the origins of kitchen gardening in the ancient Near East. *Garden History* 10(1), 1–16.

Olmstead, A. T. (1948) *History of the Persian Empire*. Chicago.

Oppenheim, A. L. (1965) On Royal gardens in Mesopotamia. *Journal of Near Eastern Studies* 24(4), 328–333.

Stronach, D. (1978) *Pasargadae: A Report on the Excavations Conducted by the British Institute of Persian Studies from 1961 to 1963*. Oxford.

Stronach, D. (1990) The Garden as a political statement: some case studies from the Near East in the first millennium BC. *Bulletin of the Asia Institute* 4, 171–180.

Stronach, D. (1994) Parterres and stone watercourses at Pasargadae: notes on the Achaemenid contribution to garden design. *Journal of Garden History* 14(1), 3–12.

Thompson, R. C. (1924) *The Assyrian Herbal*, London.

Watson, W. G. E. (2004) A botanical snapshot of Ugarit. Trees, fruit, plants and herbs in the cuneiform texts. *Aula Orientalis* 22, 107–155.

Wiseman, D. J. (1983) Mesopotamian gardens. *Anatolian Studies* 33, 137–144.

Zohary, M. (1982) *Plants of the Bible*. Cambridge.

Chapter 3. Greek Bronze Age

Baumann, H. (1993) *Greek Wild Flowers and Plant Lore in ancient Greece*. London.

Evans, A. J. (1901) Mycenaean Tree and Pillar Cult and its Mediterranean Relations. *Journal of Hellenistic Studies* 21, 99–204.

Morgan, L. (1988) *The Miniature Wall Paintings of Thera*. Cambridge.

Morgan, L. (ed.) (2005) *Aegean Wall Painting*. London.

Raven, J. E. (2000) *Plants and Plant Lore in Ancient Greece*. Oxford.

Schäfer, J. (1992) Garten in der bronzezeitlichen ägäischen Kultur? Rituelle Bildsprache und bildliches Konzapt der Realität. In Carroll-Spillecke, M. (ed.) *Der Garten Von Der antike Bis Zum Mittelalter*, Mainz am Rhein, 101–140.

Shaw, M. C. (1993) The Aegean garden. *American Journal of Archaeology* 97, 661–685.

Tzedakis, Y. and Martlew, H. (eds) (2002) *Minoans and Mycenaeans, Flavours of their Time*. Athens.

4. Greek gardens and groves

Bauman, H. (1993) *Greek Wild Flowers and Plant Lore in Ancient Greece*, trans. W. Stern. London.

Bedal, L.-A. (2003) *The Petra Pool-Complex, A Hellenistic Paradeisos in the Nabataean Capital*. New Jersey.

Bernard, P. (1994) An Ancient Greek city in Central Asia', *Ancient Cities*. Scientific American, 66–75.

Carroll-Spillecke, M. (ed.) (1989) *ΚΗΠΟΣ Der antike Griechische Garten*. Munich.

Carroll-Spillecke, M. (1992) The gardens of Greece from Homeric to Roman times. *Journal of Garden History* 12(2), 84–101.

Detienne, M. (1994) *The Gardens of Adonis*. Trans. J. Lloyd. Princeton.

Evyasaf, R.-S. (2010) Gardens at a crossroads: The influence of Persian and Egyptian gardens on the Hellenistic Royal gardens of Judea. *Bollettino di Archeologia On Line*, vol. speciale D/D9/5, 27–37.

Gleason, K. L. (1988) Garden excavations at the Herodian Winter Palace in Jericho, 1985–7. *Anglo-Israel Archaeological Society*, 21–39.

Nielsen, I. (1994) *Hellenistic Palaces*. Aarhus.

Raven, J. E. (2000) *Plants and Plant Lore in Ancient Greece*. Oxford.

Thompson, D. B. (1963) *Garden Lore in Ancient Athens*. Princeton.

Vatin, C. (1974) 'Jardins et Vergers Grecs'. *Mélanges Helléniques offerts À Georges Daux*, 345–357. Paris.

Chapter 5. Etruscan

Barker, G. and Rasmussen, T. (2000) *The Etruscans*. Oxford.

Haynes, S. (2000) *Etruscan Civilization*. London.

MacIntosh Turfa, J. (ed.) (2013) *The Etruscan World*. London.

Chapter 6. Roman

Bergmann, B. (2008) Staging the supernatural: interior gardens of Pompeian houses. In Mattusch, C. C. *et al. Pompeii and the Roman Villa*. Washington, 53–69; See also the associated *Courtyards and Gardens Catalogue*, 170–203.

Bowe, P. (2004) *Gardens of the Roman World*, London.

Ciaraldi, M. (2007) *People and Plants in Ancient Pompeii, a New Approach to Urbanism from the Microscope Room*. London.

Ciarallo, A. (2000) *Gardens of Pompeii*, trans. L. Touchette. Rome.

Ciarallo, A. (1993) The garden of 'Cassa Dei Casti Amanti' (Pompeii, Italy). *Garden History* 21, 110–116.

Cima, M. and Rocca, E. (eds) (1998) *Horti Romani*. Rome.

Conticello, B. and Romano, F. (eds) (1992) *Domus-Viridaria Horti Picti*. Naples.

Daubeny, C. (1865) *Essay on the Trees and Shrubs of the Ancients*. Oxford.

Dickson, C. (1994) Macroscopic fossils of garden plants from British Roman and medieval deposits. In *Garden History: Garden Plants, Species, Forms and Varieties from Pompeii to 1800*. Journal of the European Study Group on Physical, Chemical, Mathematical and Biological Techniques applied to Archaeology (PACT), 47–72.

di Pasquale, G. and Paolucci, F. (eds) (2007) *Il giardino antico da Babilonia a Roma*. Livorno.

Du Prey de la Ruffinière, P. (1994) *The Villas of Pliny from Antiquity to Posterity*. Chicago.

Farrar, L. (1996) *Gardens of Italy and the Western Provinces of the Roman Empire, from the 4th Century BC to the 4th Century AD*. Oxford.

Farrar, L. (1998) *Ancient Roman Gardens*. Stroud.

Farrar, L. (2001a) The pergola in ancient Rome. In Edwards, P. and Swift, K. (eds) *Pergolas, Arbours and Arches*. London, 12–19.

Farrar, L. (2001b) Roman gardens. In Shoemaker, C. A. (ed.) *Encyclopedia of Gardens: History and Design* 3. London, 1127–1132.

Grimal, P. (1943 [1969]) *Les Jardins Romains*. Paris, 2nd edn.

Jashemski, W. F. (1979 & 1993) *The Gardens of Pompeii*, 2 vols. New Rochelle.

Jashemski, W. F. (1995) Roman gardens in Tunisia: preliminary excavations in the House of Bacchus and Ariadne and in the East Temple at Thuburbo Maius. *American Journal of Archaeology* 99, 559–576.

Jashemski, W. F. and Ricotti, S. P. R. (1992) Preliminary excavations in the gardens of Hadrian's Villa: the Canopus Area and the Piazza D'Oro. *American Journal of Archaeology* 96, 579–597.

Lawson, J. (1950) The Roman garden. *Greece and Rome* 19(57), 97–105.

Lloyd, R. B. (1982) Three monumental gardens on the Marble Plan. *American Journal of Archaeology* 86, 91–100.

Macdonald, W. L. and Pinto, J. (1995) *Hadrian's Villa and its Legacy*. Yale, New Haven and London.

MacDougall, E. B. (ed.) (1987) *Ancient Roman Villa Gardens*. Dumbarton Oaks.

MacDougall, E. B. and Jashemski, W. F. (eds) (1981) *Ancient Roman Gardens*. Dumbarton Oaks.

Massari, G. (ed.) (2001) *Il parco Archeologico-Botanico delle Terme Taurine*. Civitavecchia.

Settis, S. (2002) *Le Pareti Ingannevoli, La Villa di Livia e la pittura di giardino*. Milan.

Tomei, M. A. (1992) Nota sui giardini antichi del Palatino. *Mélanges de l'Ecole française de Rome, Antiquité* 104, 917–951.

Villedieu, F. (ed.) (2001) *Il Giardino dei Cesari*. Rome.

Von Stackelberg, K. (2009) *The Roman Garden*. London.

Chapter 7. Byzantine

Littlewood, A. R. (1979) Romantic paradises: The role of the garden in Byzantine romance. *Byzantine and Modern Greek Studies* 5, 95–114.

Littlewood, A. R. (1992) Gardens of Byzantium. *Journal of Garden History* 12, 126–153.

Littlewood, A. R. (2013) Gardens of the Byzantine World. In Bodin, H. and Hedlund, R. (eds) *Byzantine Gardens and Beyond*. Uppsala, 30–113.

Littlewood, A. R., Maguire, H. and Wolschke-Bulmahn, J. (eds) (2002) *Byzantine Garden Culture*. Dumbarton Oaks.

Maguire, H. (2000) Gardens and parks in Constantinople. *Dumbarton Oaks Papers* 54, 251–264.

Maguire, J. (1990) A description of the Aretai Palace and its garden. *Journal of Garden History* 10(4), 209–213.

Mango, C. (1972) *The Art of the Byzantine Empire 312–1453*. New Jersey.

Chapter 8. Islamic

Conan, M. (ed.) (2007) *Middle East Garden Traditions: Unity and Diversity*. Dumbarton Oaks.

Conan, M. and Kress, W. J. (2007) *Botanical Progress,*

Horticultural Innovations and Cultural Changes. Dumbarton Oaks.

Harvey, J. H. (1992) Garden plants of Moorish Spain: a fresh look. *Garden History* 20(1), 71–82.

Hobhouse, P. (2003) *Gardens of Persia.* London.

Moynihan, E. B. (1980) *Paradise as a Garden, in Persia and Mughal India.* London.

Petruccioli, A. (ed.) (1997) *Gardens in the Time of the Great Muslim Empires.* New York.

Ruggles, D. F. (2000) *Gardens, Landscape, and Vision in the Palaces of Islamic Spain.* Pennsylvania.

Ruggles, D. F. (2008) *Islamic Gardens and Landscapes.* Pennsylvania.

Ruggles, D. F. and Taboroff, J. (2014) Gardens and landscaping. *Oxford Islamic Studies Online*, no. 264.

Titley, N. M. (1979) *Plants and Gardens in Persian, Mughal and Turkish Art.* London.

Wilber, D. N. (1979) *Persian Gardens and Garden Pavilions.* Dumbarton Oaks.

De Gex, J. (1995) *A Medieval Flower Garden.* London.

Fisher, C. (2004) *Flowers in Medieval Manuscripts.* London.

Harvey, J. (1981) *Mediaeval Gardens.* London.

Innes, M. and Perry, C. (2002) *Medieval Flowers.* London.

Jennings, A. (2004) *Medieval Gardens.* London.

Landsberg, S. (1995) *The Medieval Garden.* London.

Steane, J. (1985) *The Archaeology of Medieval England and Wales.* London.

Sutherland, R. (1967) *The Romaunt of the Rose....* Oxford.

Turner, T. H. (1848) Observations on the state of horticulture in England in early times, chiefly previous to the fifteenth century. *Archaeological Journal* 5, 295–311.

Wilkins, E. (1969) *The Rose-Garden Game.* London.

Williamson, J. (1986) *The Oak King, The Holly King, and the Unicorn.* New York.

Chapter 9. Medieval

Collins, M. (2000) *Medieval Herbals.* London.

Creighton, O. H. (2013) *Designs Upon the Land, Elite Landscapes of the Middle Ages.* Woodbridge.

Chapter 10. Conclusions

Farrar, L. (1998) *Ancient Roman Gardens.* Stroud.

Harvey, J. (1981) *Mediaeval Gardens.* London.